DATE DUE

Encyclopedia of
MULTICULTURALISM

Encyclopedia of

MULTICULTURALISM

Volume 1

A. Philip Randolph Institute – Business and corporate enterprise

Editor

SUSAN AUERBACH

Marshall Cavendish
New York • London • Toronto

Published By
Marshall Cavendish Corporation
2415 Jerusalem Avenue
P.O. Box 587
North Bellmore, New York 11710
United States of America

∞ The paper in these volumes conforms to the American National Standard for Permanence of Paper for Printed Library Materials, Z39.48-1984.

Library of Congress Cataloging-in-Publication Data

Encyclopedia of multiculturalism / editor, Susan Auerbach.
   p. cm.
  Includes bibliographical references (p. 1767) and index.
  Contents: v. 1. A. Philip Randolph Institute–Business and corporate enterprise; v. 2. Mother Cabrini–Estonian Americans; v. 3. Ethnic and minority group names–Inner city; v. 4. Daniel Ken Inouye–Mythology, American Indian; v. 5. Names and name changes–Six Nations; v. 6. Slavery–Zoot-suit riots.
  ISBN 1-85435-670-4 (set : alk. paper). — ISBN 1-85435-671-2 (v. 1 : alk. paper)
  1. Pluralism (Social sciences)—United States—Encyclopedias. 2. Multiculturalism—United States—Encyclopedias. 3. Ethnology—United States—Encyclopedias. 4. United States—Ethnic relations—Encyclopedias. 5. United States—Race relations—Encyclopedias.
I. Auerbach, Susan, 1956-
E184.A1E58   1993
306.4′46′0973—dc20

93-23405
CIP
AC

First Printing

PRINTED IN THE UNITED STATES OF AMERICA

Publisher's Note

Multiculturalism has always been a fact of American life. Even before the arrival of the first European explorers, native Indian peoples were diverse in their languages, beliefs, and ways of life. Later, the importation of African slaves, Asian laborers, and Mexican migrants brought further variety to a European-dominated society. By the peak years of European immigration in the early 1900's, some theorists believed that the nation's many peoples, brought together in a single "melting pot," would lose their differences and gain a new national identity. Others favored "cultural pluralism" in which people would preserve their cultural identities while participating in mainstream American society. Over the course of the twentieth century, American views on diversity were transformed by events from the Holocaust during World War II to the Civil Rights and women's movements in the 1960's to the sharp rise in Asian and Latin American immigration after 1965. By the mid-1980's, "multiculturalism" had become the term for the recognition and celebration of American cultural diversity.

Multiculturalism became a new perspective from which to view American history and society, with profound implications for education and public policy. Its boundaries broadened beyond racial, ethnic, and religious groups to include women and others, such as people with disabilities and homosexuals, who had previously been marginalized. Some advocates took up multiculturalism as a cause, stressing the inclusion and empowerment of diverse groups in public life in opposition to Eurocentrism. This stance sparked a debate in the academic community that pitted the "pluralists," who defend a common culture, against the "particularists" or "inclusionists," who defend group interests and demand change to redress past exclusion.

By the mid-2000's, most Americans will be of non-European origin. In some parts of the country, the former white majority has already become a minority. These changing demographics and a greater awareness of multiculturalism have created new expectations for American citizens. Whatever their personal identity, they need to be informed of and sensitive to an array of multicultural issues. Educators are rising to the challenge, revising textbooks and curricula and ensuring the increased participation of women and people of color in higher education. Programs in ethnic, women's, and gay and lesbian studies have become standard on many college campuses. Whole periods of American history have been interpreted to document the experiences of previously neglected groups. Recent studies on race, ethnicity, and intergroup relations have been infused with an insider's perspective by a new generation of scholars. Yet problems persist regarding sources on multiculturalism. They are often too widely scattered or too specialized for the young adult or general reader; moreover, general surveys most often focus on a single group or treat each group separately.

The *Encyclopedia of Multiculturalism* brings together many multicultural topics, and it features scholarship that cannot be found elsewhere in a single source. Its six volumes examine American history and society through the experience of diverse groups whose concerns and contributions have often been overlooked. In addition to portraits of particular groups, it explores intergroup relations and the multicultural implications of seminal events, from the Pueblo Revolt of 1680 to the Los Angeles riots of 1992. Prejudice, discrimination, the struggle for equality, and the challenge of assimilation are emphasized throughout as major themes in the multicultural American experience. Areas covered, as indicated in the comprehensive Subject List in volume 6, include American History; Arts, Entertainment, and Media; Canada; Civil Rights, Discrimination, and Social Movements; Cultural Pluralism, Assimilation, and Intergroup Relations; Culture and Community; Education; Employment, Business, Labor, and the Economy; Ethnic Groups and Ethnicity; Family Life; Gender and Sexism; Health, Science, and Technology; Immigrants and Immigration; Politics, Government, Law, and the Military; Race and Racism; Religious Groups and Religion; Social Conditions, Protest, and Reform; Sports; Professions; and Urban, Rural, and Regional Life. The set's focus on issues that both unite and divide diverse Americans encourages readers to compare, assess, and appreciate multiple perspectives.

True to its name, the *Encyclopedia of Multiculturalism* attempts to be as inclusive as possible. Its most extensive coverage is devoted to the large "minority groups" in the United States that have suffered discrimination and exclusion—African Americans, American Indians, Asian/Pacific Americans, Latinos, and women. The history, politics, culture, and socioeconomic status of these groups are treated in a number of articles that consider the group's experience collectively. Additional information is provided in articles that identify particular events and give brief biographical sketches of selected individuals who have made distinctive contributions. The set takes a broad view of diversity by also covering Jewish Americans and other major religious groups, European national groups, the Canadian population, and contemporary marginalized groups such as older Americans. The sum total of the 1438 entries is a portrait of society that genuinely "looks like America."

Among the controversial issues involved in the study of multiculturalism is the question of appropriate language. The editors of the set have made strong efforts to avoid racist, sexist, or otherwise biased language. For example, the neutral abbreviation B.C.E. (before the common era) is used for ancient dates rather than the more conventional B.C. (before Christ). Decisions about group names were based on the emerging consensus among scholars and within the group itself. Thus, for example, the set uses "American Indian," as preferred by most scholars and by Indians themselves, rather than the term "Native American." Likewise, African American, Latino, and Asian American are used. For specific immigrant groups "American" has been added (as in "Cuban Americans") to differentiate people living in the United States from those in their country of origin. Acceptable group names are constantly in flux, reflecting both changing group identity and social roles. Similarly, the terms "ethnic," "racial," "cultural," and "minority" to describe groups tend to be used interchangeably and inconsistently, suggesting the evolving nature of these concepts. For insight on these issues, readers are directed to entries such as "Ethnic and minority group names," "Race," "Ethnicity," "Assimilation," and "Multiculturalism."

The six volumes of the encyclopedia are arranged alphabetically, using by-word not by-letter alphabetization rules. They contain entries on people, places, concepts, events, laws, and organizations that have shaped multiculturalism in the United States. Entries range from brief hundred-word identifications of key terms and individuals to overview essays of five thousand words that place topics in a broad, interpretive context. Medium-length articles of five hundred to two thousand words offer substantial introductions to a variety of topics, from wars and social movements to cultural developments and professions. Two types of cross-references that appear throughout the encyclopedia allow information to be found easily: Within each article, terms in small capital letters indicate that a separate article exists on the topic; in addition, a number of cross-references have been included as article headings—if readers look up "Protest organizations," for example, a boldfaced heading refers them to "Activist and protest organizations." To promote further study, all entries of five hundred words or more conclude with a narrative bibliography.

Volume 6 features additional research aids that expand upon the material in the entries, covering both the United States and Canada. A unique Time Line highlights essential events in American multiculturalism from 43,000 B.C.E. to 1993. A resource list gives the addresses of prominent national civil rights, advocacy, and educational organizations, as well as selected government agencies, museums, and independent research centers. Visual sources for both fictional and documentary treatments of multicultural themes may be found in the Filmography, which is arranged according to population group. There follows a Bibliography that brings together the most important recent multicultural studies, organized cross-culturally by subject. In an extensive Subject List, all of the encyclopedia's entries are listed under both population and subject categories to assist students in finding relevant information in their area of interest. A comprehensive index which includes extensive cross-references helps further with the location of specific events, people, places, and organizations mentioned in the text.

The contributors to this encyclopedia, who are listed in volume 1, represent a variety of academic and cultural backgrounds as well as multiple approaches to multiculturalism. They met the challenge of presenting clear, objective information in areas that are often poorly documented or fraught with controversy. Several consultants strove to create an inclusive, well-balanced list of entries, while numerous editors worked diligently to polish and illustrate the text. The efforts of all are greatly appreciated.

Editor
Susan Auerbach

Editorial Consultants

Duane Champagne
American Indian Studies Center, UCLA

Laurie Olsen
California Tomorrow

Mary MacGregor-Villarreal
UCLA Folklore and Mythology Program

Ronald B. Querry
Author

Contributors

Julie LaMay Abner
California State University, San Bernardino

Richard Adler
University of Michigan, Dearborn

Ira R. Allen
Independent Scholar

Tiina Allik
Loyola University—New Orleans

Cherri N. Allison
Independent Scholar

Marilyn Dargis Ambrose
California State University, Chico

Addell Austin Anderson
Wayne State University

Gary Anderson
Wayne State University

Kenneth Anderson
Oakwood College

Sharon K. Araji
University of Alaska, Anchorage

Robert A. Armour
Board of Higher Education and Ministry, The United Methodist Church

Eric Arnesen
University of Illinois at Chicago

Bryan Aubrey
Maharishi International University

Charles Avinger
Washtenaw Community College

James A. Baer
Northern Virginia Community College

Jim Baird
University of North Texas

JoAnn Balingit
Independent Scholar

Carl L. Bankston III
Louisiana State University

Carole A. Barrett
University of Mary

Charolette R. Bell
California State University, San Marcos

Stephen Benz
Barry University

S. Carol Berg
College of St. Benedict

James M. Bergquist
Villanova University

Cynthia A. Bily
Siena Heights College

Julia B. Boken
State University of New York College at Oneonta

Michael R. Bradley
Motlow College

John Braeman
University of Nebraska—Lincoln

Gerhard Brand
Independent Scholar

Cynthia Breslin
Independent Scholar

Silvester J. Brito
University of Wyoming

John A. Britton
Francis Marion University

William S. Brockington, Jr.
Historical Perspectives

Norbert Brockman
St. Mary's University

Daniel A. Brown
California State University, Fullerton

Kendall W. Brown
Brigham Young University

Polly Buckingham
Independent Scholar

Larry Burt
Southwest Missouri State University

Malcolm B. Campbell
Bowling Green State University

Byron Cannon
University of Utah

Sharon Carson
University of North Dakota

Donald E. Cellini
Adrian College

Rudolfo Chávez Chávez
New Mexico State University

Karen Har Yen Chow
University of California, Santa Barbara

Daniel L. S. Christopher
Loyola Marymount University

Rodney D. Coates
Miami University

Donna Corlett
University of Portland

John M. Craig
Slippery Rock University

Stephen Cresswell
West Virginia Wesleyan College

Frank Day
Clemson University

Richard A. Dello Buono
Rosary College

Hien Duc Do
San Jose State University

Betty A. Dobratz
Iowa State University

Sharon DuPree
Pratt Institute

Craig M. Eckert
Eastern Illinois University

Clyde Ellis
University of North Carolina at Greensboro

Alan M. Fisher
California State University, Dominguez Hills

Bonita Freeman-Witthoft
West Chester University

Scott A. Frisch
Claremont Graduate School

R. M. Frumkin
Salem-Teikyo University

Carla Funk
Florida State University

Jean Gandesbery
University of California, Santa Barbara

Daniel J. Gelo
University of Texas at San Antonio

K. Fred Gillum
Colby College

Barbara Glass
Wright State University

Stephen D. Glazier
University of Nebraska at Kearney

Edward Gobetz
Kent State University

Douglas Gomery
University of Maryland

Joanne L. Goodwin
University of Nevada, Las Vegas

Nancy McCampbell Grace
The College of Wooster

Roy Neil Graves
University of Tennessee at Martin

Judith A. Green
Kansas State University

Thomas A. Green, Jr.
Texas A&M University

Susan D. Greenbaum
University of South Florida

Forest L. Grieves
University of Montana

Martin Gruberg
University of Wisconsin, Oshkosh

Ramon S. Guerra
University of Texas—Pan American

Michael Haas
University of Hawaii at Manoa

Fred R. van Hartesveldt
Fort Valley State College

Valerie S. Hartman
Bergen Community College

April L. Haulman
University of Central Oklahoma

Judith Haut
University of California, Los Angeles

Jeremy Hein
University of Wisconsin—Eau Claire

Thomas E. Helm
Western Illinois University

Arthur W. Helweg
Western Michigan University

Mary A. Hendrickson
Wilson College

Diane L. Hendrix
New Mexico State University

Howard M. Hensel
Air War College

Gerald Horne
University of California, Santa Barbara

E. D. Huntley
Appalachian State University

Charles Jackson
Northern Kentucky University

Jacquelyn L. Jackson
Middle Tennessee State University

Helen Jaskoski
California State University, Fullerton

Jeff Johnson
Brevard Community College

Sheila Golburgh Johnson
Independent Scholar

Kenneth A. Johnson
State University of New York College at Oneonta

Thomas F. Johnston
University of Alaska, Fairbanks

Sherrie A. Juras
California State University, San Bernardino

Ricki Ellen Kantrowitz
Westfield State College

K. Paul Kasambira
Bradley University

Richard Keenan
University of Maryland, Eastern Shore

Steven G. Kellman
University of Texas at San Antonio

James Knippling
University of Delaware

Sai Felicia Krishna-Hensel
Auburn University at Montgomery

Yasue Kuwahara
Northern Kentucky University

Philip E. Lampe
Incarnate Word College

Robert W. Langran
Villanova University

Michael M. Laskier
World Sephardic Educational Center

Anne K. LeCroy
East Tennessee State University

Janet Lee
Oregon State University

Susan Lehrer
State University of New York College at New Paltz

Anthony John Lemelle
Purdue University

Gregory A. Levitt
University of New Orleans

Leon Lewis
Appalachian State University

James Livingston
Northern Michigan University

Paul T. Lockman, Jr.
Eastern New Mexico University

Janet Lorenz
Independent Scholar

William C. Lowe
Mount St. Clare College

Jens Lund
University of Washington—Tacoma

David E. McClave
Library of Congress

Martha McCollough
University of Oklahoma

Gary W. McDonogh
Bryn Mawr College

Grace McEntee
Appalachian State University

Richard D. McGhee
Arkansas State University

Joseph McLaren
Hofstra University

Timothy J. McMillan
Humboldt State University

Jim McWilliams
Southern Illinois University—Carbondale

Janet Madden
El Camino College

Mark J. Madigan
University of Vermont

Michael E. Manaton
Independent Scholar

Barry Mann
University of San Diego

Kim Manning
California State University, San Bernardino

William J. Mark
Lassen College

Lavonne Mason
California State University, San Bernardino

Thomas D. Matijasic
Prestonsburg Community College

Nancy Maveety
Tulane University

Howard Meredith
University of Science and Arts of Oklahoma

John G. Messerly
Ursuline College

Vasa D. Mihailovich
University of North Carolina, Chapel Hill

Elizabeth J. Miles
University of California, Los Angeles

Barbara Miliaras
University of Massachusetts at Lowell

Mark Miller
Independent Scholar

Sally M. Miller
University of the Pacific

David J. Minderhout
Bloomsburg University

M. L. Miranda
University of Nevada, Las Vegas

Bruce M. Mitchell
Eastern Washington University

Eric Niderost
Chabot College

Norma Corigliano Noonan
Augsburg College

Kathleen O'Brien
Independent Scholar

Carlos F. Ortega
Sonoma State University

William T. Osborne
Florida International University
Florida Memorial College

Maria A. Pacino
Azusa Pacific University

D. G. Paz
Clemson University

Zena Pearlstone
California State University, Long Beach

David Peck
California State University, Long Beach

Hugh J. Phillips
Albany State College

Lela Phillips
Independent Scholar

Marjorie Podolsky
Pennsylvania State University at Erie, Behrend College

Francis Poole
University of Delaware

Verbie Lovorn Prevost
University of Tennessee at Chattanooga

Victoria Price
Lamar University

Michaela Crawford Reaves
California Lutheran University

Lawrence R. Rodgers
Kansas State University

Wendy Sacket
Independent Scholar

Jean Schroedel
Claremont Graduate School

E. A. Schwartz
California State University, San Marcos

Pamela K. Shaffer
Fort Hays State University

Warren Shaffer
Fort Hays State University

Richard A. K. Shankar
Stonehill College

R. Baird Shuman
Independent Scholar

Rodney Simard
California State University, San Bernardino

John K. Simmons
Western Illinois University

Sarah Slavin
State University of New York College at Buffalo

Genevieve Slomski
Independent Scholar

James M. Smallwood
Oklahoma State University

Christopher E. Smith
University of Akron

Bruce Snyder
Claremont Graduate School

A. J. Sobczak
Independent Scholar

Bes Stark Spangler
Peace College

Gretta Stanger
Tennessee Technological University

James Stanlaw
Illinois State University

David L. Sterling
University of Cincinnati

Peggy Lee Denise Stevenson
Claflin College

Earl L. Stewart
University of California, Santa Barbara

Gary Storhoff
University of Connecticut at Stamford

Kathryn Stout
Northeastern Illinois University

M. F. Stuck
State University of New York College at Oswego

James Sullivan
California State University, Los Angeles

Carl Swidorski
The College of St. Rose

Stephen G. Sylvester
Northern Montana College

Sherri Szeman
Central State University

Robert D. Talbott
University of Northern Iowa

Carol B. Tanksley
University of West Florida

David Teske
Russell C. Davis Planetarium

Maxine S. Theodoulou
The Union Institute

Randal Thompson
U.S. Agency for International Development

Jiu-Hwa Lo Upshur
Eastern Michigan University

Tamara M. Valentine
University of South Carolina at Spartanburg

Hernan Vera
University of Florida

Milton Vickerman
Bloomfield College

Maria Isabel B. Villaseñor
New Mexico State University

Mary E. Virginia
Independent Scholar

Indu Vohra
DePauw University

M. C. Ware
State University of New York College at Cortland

Michael H. Washington, Sr.
Northern Kentucky University

Marcia J. Weiss
Point Park College

Ward Weldon
University of Illinois at Chicago

Lucille Whalen
Glendale Community College

Joyce E. Williams
Texas Woman's University

Tyrone Williams
Xavier University

Michael Witkoski
University of South Carolina— Columbia

Susan Wladaver-Morgan
Western Association of Women Historians

Cindy Hing-Yuk Wong
Wongwoman Productions

Ray G. Wright
University of Houston, Downtown

Clifton K. Yearley
State University of New York at Buffalo

Michael L. Yoder
Northwestern College

Sally B. Young
University of Tennessee at Chattanooga

Laura M. Zaidman
University of South Carolina at Sumter

Phil Zampini
Westfield State College

Min Zhou
Louisiana State University

Contents

Encyclopedia of

MULTICULTURALISM

A

A. Philip Randolph Institute (New York, N.Y.): Branch of the AMERICAN FEDERATION OF LABOR and CONGRESS OF INDUSTRIAL ORGANIZATIONS (AFL-CIO) that promotes cooperation between organized labor and minority workers. RANDOLPH, a leading black civil rights activist and unionist, founded the institute with others in 1964-1965 at the height of the American Civil Rights movement to help secure economic justice for African Americans. The institute set up local affiliates in 1968 and had about two hundred of these in thirty-seven states by 1990. The organization supports union activity and works for civil rights, job training, safety and health, and voter registration. Its headquarters are in New York City.

Aaron, Hank [Louis Henry] (b. Feb. 5, 1934, Mobile, Ala.): Professional African American baseball player. A powerful right-handed batter and outfielder,

Founder of the institute that bears his name, A. Philip Randolph is presented with the 1967 Eugene V. Debs Award in the Field of Labor. (AP/Wide World Photos)

Aaron started on all-black teams but spent most of his major league career with the Braves in Milwaukee (1954-1965) and Atlanta (1966-1974). In 1974 he broke Babe Ruth's career record of 714 home runs. He was traded to the Milwaukee Brewers and played for them in 1975 and 1976. By the end of his playing career, Aaron had hit 755 home runs. Overall, he held eighteen major league records. In 1982 he was elected to the Baseball Hall of Fame. As an Atlanta Braves executive, a position he took in 1976, Aaron has also supported charities and education.

AARP. *See* **American Association of Retired Persons (AARP)**

Abdul-Jabbar, Kareem (Ferdinand Lewis "Lew" Alcindor, Jr.; b. Apr. 16, 1947, New York, N.Y.): Professional African American basketball player. Over seven feet tall and a top scorer and rebounder, Lew Alcindor was a New York City high school star. At the University of California, Los Angeles (UCLA) from 1965 to 1969, he averaged 26.4 points per game, was twice named the country's best college player, and led his team to three National Collegiate Athletic Association (NCAA) championships. His professional career, which began with a $1.4 million contract, was with the Milwaukee Bucks (1969-1975) and the Los Angeles Lakers (beginning in 1975). The *Sports Illustrated* Sportsman of the Year (1985) and an all-time leading National Basketball Association (NBA) scorer, Abdul-Jabbar has also acted in films and on television, and he co-authored an autobiography, *Giant Steps* (1984).

Abiko, Kyutaro (1865-1936): Japanese American publisher, activist, and entrepreneur. Coming to the United States in 1885, Abiko settled in the San Francisco Bay area and the San Joaquin Valley of California, where in 1899 he founded *Nichibei Shimbun*, a newspaper for Japanese Americans. In 1902, he cofounded the Japanese American Industrial Corporation, which contracted immigrant labor. He encouraged Japanese Americans to settle permanently in the United States and to acquire land. In 1906, he created the Yamato Colony, a model Japanese farming community that thrived well into the next decade.

Abolitionist Movement: Organized efforts to end the institution of slavery in the United States. The crusade began during the first administration of Andrew Jackson (1829) with a declaration of war against slavery and

ended nearly thirty-five years later when Abraham Lincoln signed the EMANCIPATION PROCLAMATION in 1863. This movement witnessed a continuing moral assault on southern institutions, bitter encounters with northern resistance, intense clashes with mob rule, major engagements against both political parties, and, finally, an insurrection within the abolitionist camp itself. From beginning to end, abolitionism was a militant movement.

Early Objectives. The first strategic objective in the abolitionist cause was the annihilation of the AMERICAN COLONIZATION SOCIETY. Organized in 1816, the society aimed for the complete removal of African Americans from the United States. Some southern planters supported the society in the hope that exporting freed slaves would strengthen the institution of slavery, while northern philanthropists endorsed colo-

Lakers center Abdul-Jabbar shoots one of his famous sky hooks in a 1984 game against the Utah Jazz. (AP/Wide World Photos)

nization in the equally futile expectation that it would purify American democracy by ridding the country of slaves. On one crucial issue, however, both northern and southern colonizationists agreed: African Americans were seen as inherently inferior to European Americans and had no place in a democratic society.

It was precisely this sweeping assumption of inferiority that the pioneer abolitionists rejected. They maintained that slavery was a sin and a crime, a sin because it denied to the African American the status of a human being, a crime because it violated the natural rights to life, liberty, and the pursuit of happiness guaranteed in the DECLARATION OF INDEPENDENCE. These two beliefs—in the spiritual equality and the political equality of all Americans—served as the chief moral weapons in the attack on slavery.

The American Anti-Slavery Society. The American Anti-Slavery Society, organized in 1833, functioned chiefly as a clearinghouse for a vast propaganda campaign. They advertised their indictments in their own press, organized societies, wrote pamphlets, compiled statistics, and circulated petitions pressing for abolition.

The years immediately following the organization of the American Anti-Slavery Society witnessed a period of intense abolitionist energy. Thousands of petitions with hundreds of thousands of signatures swept Congress. A dozen state auxiliaries and numerous abolitionist newspapers sprang up in the North. Women were very active in the movement, and many black activists, such as Frederick DOUGLASS, worked in coalition with white abolitionists. By 1836, the crusade against slavery had succeeded in turning the tide of American politics.

Political Struggle. Such an outburst of moral indignation against a deeply rooted institution, however, was bound to provoke intense reaction. Northerners and Southerners alike countered the abolitionist attack by resorting to political suppression. Congress found a way of terminating the deluge of antislavery petitions; the Postmaster General helped southern states close the mails to abolitionist literature. State legislatures in both the North and the South considered "gag" laws restricting the activities of the opponents of slavery. Mobs incited by local demagogues disrupted antislavery meetings, destroyed abolitionist property, and threatened the lives of movement leaders.

The abolitionists responded to these repressive tactics with a firm and effective defense of civil liberties. The alliance between abolition and CIVIL RIGHTS,

Rochester, N.Y., honored abolitionist Frederick Douglass by erecting a statue. (The Associated Publishers, Inc.)

struck early in the fight against slavery, survived until the CIVIL WAR.

Strong public resistance to any discussion of the slavery question and the recognition that moral coercion had reached an impasse produced a crisis and division in the abolitionist movement itself. One branch of abolitionists, led by James C. Birney, Joshua Leavitt, and Myron Holley, turned to politics. Their road led toward the Liberty Party and the Free Soil movement, and eventually to the confused antislavery politics of the mid-nineteenth century Republican Party. The political abolitionists hoped to use compromise and concession to win elections. They were willing to accept the role of a political minority and exploit party politics on behalf of the enslaved population.

A smaller but more militant group of abolitionists, led by William Lloyd Garrison and Wendell Phillips, took another and—so they believed—loftier route to emancipation. They demanded that abolitionists have "no union" with slaveholders. They refused to seek office, vote for antislavery candidates, or in any way support the political abolitionists, whom they denounced as traitors to the cause.

Height of the Antislavery Enterprise. Although abolitionist organization had been eclipsed by the time of the Mexican-American War (1846-1848), the antislavery enterprise continued to flourish. Agitators increased their attack on the slave system, and reformers intensified their efforts to improve the lot of the freed slaves in the North.

When the Compromise of 1850 linked the territorial question and the fugitive slave issue together, a ten-year sectional struggle ensued, eventually ending with the firing on Fort Sumter. Though few Americans were prepared to accept all the abolitionists' premises, northern convictions that slavery needed to be abolished intensified. The abolitionists had done part of their job well.

tions of the triumph of slavery until, in one desperate act, John Brown tried to reverse the balance of power with a rebellion at HARPERS FERRY, WEST VIRGINIA.

When the Confederate batteries stopped firing on Fort Sumter, few abolitionists doubted that their battle against slavery was coming to an end. Yet none of them had expected their crusade to end in bloodshed. They, as well as the nation, had to accept responsibility not only for a moral struggle but also for the eventuality of a total war. When Lincoln signed the EMANCIPATION PROCLAMATION on January 1, 1863, abolitionists concluded that the divine will that had seemingly directed their crusade had finally triumphed.

Abolitionist Movement Time Line

1775	Society for Relief of Free Negroes Unlawfully Held in Bondage established in Philadelphia
1777-1804	Northern states abolish slavery
1807	United States outlaws slave trade
1816	American Colonization Society established to return freed slaves to Africa
1820	First regular abolitionist journal begins publication
1821	Missouri Compromise admits Missouri as slave state and Maine as free state
1827	140 American antislavery groups active
1829	William Lloyd Garrison founds *Liberator*
1831	Nat Turner's rebellion leaves sixty white people dead
1833	Slavery advocates wreck abolitionist printing office. Elijah P. Lovejoy killed
1844	Arrest of Charles Torrey, founder of the Underground Railroad
1850	Compromise of 1850 determines basis for free- slave-state status, includes Fugitive Slave Act
1852	Publication of *Uncle Tom's Cabin* by Harriet Beecher Stowe
1857	Dred Scott Case permits slavery in U.S. territories
1859	Abolitionist John Brown leads raid on U.S. arsenal at Harper's Ferry
1863	Emancipation Proclamation frees slaves in South
1865	Thirteenth Amendment abolishes slavery in United States

Source: Adapted from Bruce Wetterau's *The New York Public Library's Book of Chronologies.* New York: Prentice Hall Press, 1990.

The Compromise of 1850 set in motion a sequence of events in the mid-1800's that proved irreversible. THE FUGITIVE SLAVE ACT was countered throughout the North with state personal-liberty laws. A series of daring slave rescues dramatized the futility of attempting to enforce a law which the moral sense of one-half of the nation would not support. The Kansas-Nebraska Act and the doctrine of "squatter sovereignty" sparked a race for control of the new territories culminating in violence and fraud. The Dred Scott decision appeared to be the fulfillment of dire abolitionist predic-

SUGGESTED READINGS. The best bibliography on the abolitionist movement that is easily available is Louis Filler's *The Crusade Against Slavery, 1830-1860* (1960). For the nonspecialist, a valuable collection of essays is *The Antislavery Vanguard: New Essays on the Abolitionists* (1965), edited by Martin Duberman. The reader who wishes to trace the thinking of the abolitionist leader William Lloyd Garrison can consult John L. Thomas' excellent *The Liberator: William Lloyd Garrison, a Biography* (1963), which points out connections between Garrison's beliefs and his intellectual milieu. Another excellent work by Thomas is *Slavery Attacked: The Abolitionist Crusade* (1965), a collection of essays written by members of the movement. For an overview of the role of African Americans in the abolitionist movement, see Vincent Harding's *There Is a River: The Black Struggle for Freedom (2d ed., 1993)* and Benjamin Quarles's *Black Abolitionists (1969).—Genevieve Slomski*

Abortion: When the United States Supreme Court expanded women's right to an abortion in *ROE v. WADE* (1973) and the companion case of Doe v. Bolton (1973), it brought a firestorm of controversy that had not yet abated in the early 1990's. Most feminist groups lauded the decisions for opening up opportunities for women to

restrictive state and federal laws. Access to abortions has also been limited by subsequent court and legislative decisions, and by a short supply of American physicians and clinics willing to perform abortions. It is widely believed that these restrictions have had a more severe impact on poor and minority women.

In the first few years after abortion became more available, the incidence increased sharply. Between 1973 and 1983, for example, the number of abortions doubled. Since the mid-1980's, the number of abortions performed has leveled off at about 1.5 million abortions per year, according to the Alan Guttmacher Institute.

Historical Background. In early American history, abortion was an accepted practice prior to the point

These women are protesting to keep abortion safe and legal. (Sally Ann Rogers)

control their own destinies and worked to ensure the permanence of legal abortion. Meanwhile, abortion opponents led an effective political campaign against legalized abortion, resulting in the passage of numerous

of "quickening," when fetal movement was perceptible to the mother. By the mid-1960's, however, all fifty states had adopted restrictive abortion laws. In most states, abortions were available only when the mother's life was at stake. Affluent women traveled abroad to obtain legal abortions, while women of modest means sought illegal, sometimes unsafe, abortions. While precise figures on numbers of illegal abortions performed are not available, some sources claim that illegal abortions were common. In the 1960's, hundreds of women each year are believed to have died from complications resulting from abortions.

By the late 1960's, the women's movement successfully brought pressure on some states to liberalize abortion laws. This made it possible for women who could afford it to seek abortions by traveling to states that permitted them. Texas, where the case of Roe v. Wade arose, was one of those states that permitted abortions only when the mother's life was at stake.

In the landmark case Roe v. Wade, the Supreme Court declared unconstitutional state laws that restricted abortions to instances where they were needed in order to save the life of the mother. The Court ruled that a woman's "right to privacy" extends to abortion choice. It is said that the government's "compelling state interest" to regulate abortion procedure begins at the end of the first three months (first trimester) of pregnancy, at which point states may regulate abortion in the interest of maternal health and safety, for example, by specifying who is qualified to perform abortions, the licensing of such persons, or the kinds of facilities in which abortion may be performed. The Court ruled that the state's interest in regulation increases over the length of the pregnancy. At the point of viability of the fetus, approximately the third trimester (last three months) of pregnancy, the state

may control or even prohibit abortion in order to preserve the life of a "viable" fetus, that is, one that could survive outside of the womb.

The Abortion Debate. The decision in *Roe v. Wade* gave rise to an ongoing public debate on fundamental issues of when life begins, the meaning of "humanity," and the place of traditional family values in modern society. In this debate, "pro-life" forces have pitted themselves against "pro-choice" forces.

The "pro-life" movement holds that life begins at conception. Its advocates point to the "human" characteristics of a fetus, such as its ability to feel pain and respond to stimuli. In the documentary film *Silent Scream*, produced by the pro-life movement, a fetus is shown seemingly recoiling in pain as the procedure is performed and opens its mouth in a "silent scream" as it is sucked from the mother's body. They oppose the implication in *Roe v. Wade* that life begins at birth,

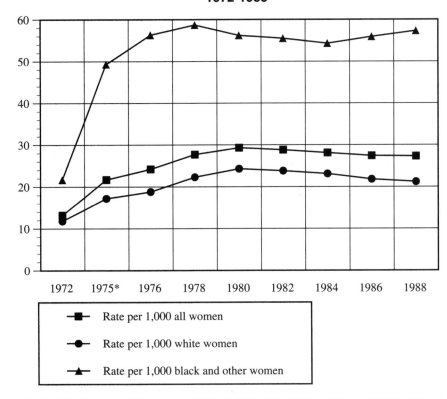

Growth in Abortions since *Roe v. Wade* (1973): 1972-1988

- Rate per 1,000 all women
- Rate per 1,000 white women
- Rate per 1,000 black and other women

Source: Data are from *Statistical Abstract of the United States, 1992*. Table 100. Washington, D.C.: U.S. Government Printing Office, 1992.
*No data are available for 1974.

or at the point of viability, when the fetus can live outside of the mother's body.

The "pro-life" movement views *Roe v. Wade* as disregarding the fundamental rights of the "unborn child." Support for the "civil rights" of the fetus is provided by such groups as the U.S. Catholic Conference, evangelical Christians, the National Right to Life Committee, and others. In addition to traditional lobbying techniques and political tactics, the pro-life movement has adopted strategies of the Civil Rights movement, such as nonviolent demonstrations and picketing of abortion clinics. Operation Rescue, one antiabortion group, has staged major demonstrations in Buffalo, New York, and Wichita, Kansas, to publicize their cause.

For some groups, such as the former Moral Majority, the abortion decision pointed up the decline of family values and an erosion of moral standards. They feared that the ability of women to obtain abortions "on demand" would encourage sexual promiscuity and devalue women's role as mother with the traditional family structure.

The antiabortion movement has achieved substantial political success through traditional political participation. For example, the national platforms of the REPUBLICAN PARTY between 1980 and 1992 staunchly opposed abortion rights. The opposition of Presidents Ronald Reagan and George Bush to *Roe v. Wade* affected appointments of federal judges, including Supreme Court justices.

The "pro-choice" movement is also a potent political force. Groups such as the National Abortions Rights Action League (NARAL), the NATIONAL ORGANIZATION FOR WOMEN (NOW), and PLANNED PARENTHOOD FEDERATION OF AMERICA have worked to uphold *Roe v. Wade* in the courts as well as through the political process. Support for *Roe v. Wade* by women's groups reflects a belief that women's self-determination requires the right to control reproduction. For example, they point out that unwed pregnant teenagers required to carry a fetus to term have limited economic opportunities. About one-half the teenagers who become pregnant seek abortions. Of those who do not, 95 percent keep their babies. Eighty percent of pregnant teenagers drop out of school and a majority of these never complete their education. In addition, the pro-choice coalition argues that many pro-life supporters have a punitive attitude toward women, even failing to acknowledge that some women do not choose to engage in the sexual activity that led to their

pregnancies, as in the instances of rape or incest.

Public opinion polls on abortion show that many Americans believe that abortion is morally wrong but accept the right of an individual to decide for herself whether or not to seek an abortion. Public attitudes demonstrate the success of the pro-choice movement in shaping Americans' views about abortion. These attitudes suggest an emerging "middle ground" position in which many Americans dichotomize their personal views from choices they are willing to provide to others.

Legal Decisions After Roe v. Wade. Subsequent decisions of the Supreme Court have modified and clarified *ROE V. WADE*, upholding the basic abortion right, while allowing a variety of regulations on it by state and federal government. In *Casey v. Planned Parenthood of Southeastern Pennsylvania* (1992), the Supreme Court made it easier for states to regulate abortion by rejecting the trimester scheme underpinning *Roe v. Wade* and by adopting a less strict standard for review of abortion laws, thereby giving states more authority to regulate abortion.

In early cases following *Roe v. Wade,* the Court clarified which kinds of abortion regulations would be permissible. In *Planned Parenthood v. Danforth* (1976), the Court rejected a requirement for the consent of a woman's spouse before allowing an abortion. While acknowledging the strong interest of the spouse, the Court held that it is fundamentally the woman's right to decide whether to have an abortion since she is most directly affected by the pregnancy. Spousal notification was also rejected by the Court in *Casey v. Planned Parenthood.* The justices reasoned that spousal notification poses a substantial obstacle to abortion, particularly for women who suffer from physical abuse at the hands of their husbands.

The Court upheld parental consent and notification for minors seeking abortions, providing that a separate judicial approval route is also available. In *Planned Parenthood v. Ashcroft* (1983), the Court approved parental consent laws for unmarried minors. Judges could consent to the abortion in lieu of parents if the minor was declared mature enough to decide independently, or if a judge ruled that the abortion was in the minor's best interest.

Public opinion polls have indicated strong public support for parental notification. Some pro-choice groups, however, oppose parental consent and notification as being unduly burdensome to a minor who may be intimidated by a judge or physically abused by her parents as a consequence of the pregnancy. A public campaign has been waged by the parents of Becky Bell against parental notification regulations. Bell died from an unsafe, illegal abortion apparently performed because she did not want to disappoint her parents by informing them that she was pregnant and seeking an abortion.

An antiabortion activist who believes that God is the ultimate judge. (Sally Ann Rogers)

The Supreme Court initially rejected provisions designed to discourage women from seeking abortions, such as "informed consent" and waiting requirements. In *Casey v. Planned Parenthood* in 1992, however, the Court upheld a Pennsylvania "informed consent" regulation that required a talk by a doctor about the characteristics of the fetus at the patient's stage of pregnancy and information about abortion alternatives. The requirement of a twenty-four-hour waiting period between the initial consultation with the phy-

sician and the abortion was also upheld.

Impact of Abortion Regulations. While the Court did not view the "informed consent" and waiting period provisions as an "undue burden," poor, rural, less informed and less well-educated women may be disproportionately affected by such regulations. For example, costs of abortions may rise since counseling under the Pennsylvania law must be done by physicians, rather than by nurses, as was frequent in the past. The waiting period also increases costs since working women need to take two days rather than one day off from work. In addition, women in rural areas must often travel long distances to receive abortions since they are not always available locally. In Pennsylvania, several metropolitan areas do not have abortion providers. Thus motels, transportation, and child care must often be factored into the costs of an abortion. Informed consent and waiting period regulations are inconvenient for middle-class women, but may be a far more severe constraint on indigent women. For example, when the poor, rural state of Mississippi adopted informed consent and waiting period provisions, some clinics reportedly experienced precipitous drops in numbers of women seeking abortions. Women seeking abortions in Mississippi and elsewhere in the early 1990's also reported an emotional barrier to abortion resulting from the tactics of abortion protesters who stand outside clinics shouting at women patients as they arrive to seek an abortion. Car license plate numbers of young women patients were used to obtain their addresses so that their parents could be notified by the protesters that their daughters were seeking abortions.

The Availability Barrier. Beyond legal regulations, another important barrier to women seeking abortions is the insufficient availability of clinics and physicians who will perform abortions. Twenty-five percent of all U.S. abortions occur in five major urban areas. In the Midwest and South in particular, there are few clinics, mostly concentrated in cities. In North Dakota, for example, there is only one clinic, located in Fargo.

Many American hospitals no longer perform abortions except to save the life of the woman. For example, abortion providers in Pennsylvania dropped from 147 in 1978 to 90 in 1992, according to the Alan Guttmacher Institute. Fewer physicians are receiving training in abortion techniques. In 1992, only 12 percent of residency programs required obstetrician/gynecologist specialists to learn first trimester abortion procedures, and only 7 percent gave instruction in late-pregnancy abortions, while in 1985, almost 25 percent of residency programs required both types of training. Less than one-third of all American obstetricians and gynecologists perform abortions, reportedly because of low fees for such work as well as fear of harassment by abortion opponents.

The Funding Barrier. In *Webster v. Reproductive Health Services* (1989), the Supreme Court upheld a ban on the use of public employees and facilities for nontherapeutic (medically unnecessary) abortions. This decision is one example in a line of decisions that have allowed states and Congress to deny use of public funds for abortions. Congress passed the Hyde Amendment in 1976 forbidding the use of federal funds to reimburse costs of abortion for poor Medicaid patients with a few narrow exceptions, such as when the mother's life is at stake. In *Harris v. McRae* (1980) the Court upheld the Hyde Amendment against a claim that it violated the U.S. CONSTITUTION's First Amendment Establishment of Religion clause by imposing a moral, religious viewpoint. In *Maher v. Roe* (1977), the Court ruled that states accepting Medicaid funds need not pay for abortions for indigent women seeking elective abortions. States may make policies that provide incentives for childbirth rather than abortions according to the Court.

Some of the justices who dissented in the *Maher v. Roe* decision felt that the Court had shown a "distressing insensitivity" to the plight of impoverished, pregnant women. The justices argued that poor women might have no choice but to carry their pregnancies to term if they lack money to pay for the abortion procedure. The dissenters wrote, "Disparity in funding by the state clearly operates to coerce indigent pregnant women to bear children they would not otherwise choose to have . . . This coercion can only operate upon the poor, who are uniquely the victims of this form of financial pressure."

While legislative decisions to deny public funding for elective abortions and judicial ratification of these decisions may place a larger burden on poor women, some statistics show that approximately 94 percent of women eligible for Medicaid funding before 1976 were still able to obtain alternative forms of funding for abortions.

Impact on Racial Minorities. The African American community has not strongly embraced the pro-choice cause. While some African American leaders, such as Faye Wattleton, president of Planned Parenthood Federation of America, and national political leader Jesse JACKSON have taken strong pro-choice positions, many African Americans view the pro-choice movement as dominated by white middle-class women. In addition, some African Americans believe that economic issues are more vital than abortion rights to the well-being of black Americans.

Abortion, nevertheless, is an issue that touches the lives of many African American women. Black women are estimated to have 25 percent of all abortions in the United States while constituting about 6 percent of the population. A few African Americans view abortion as genocidal to minority populations, and condemn what they feel are societal pressures on poor minority women to have abortions.

Because of conservative cultural and Catholic religious traditions, many Latinos oppose abortion. The birthrate among Latino teenagers is estimated to have undergone the fastest growth rate of any American racial or ethnic group. Opposition by powerful Roman Catholic leaders to abortion may explain the reluctance of many Latinos to consider the option of abortion.

American Indians residing on RESERVATIONS have less access to abortions than many Americans because health care facilities there are federally funded and, therefore, do not provide elective abortions.

The RU-486 Controversy. Abortion is an issue that continues to divide Americans on moral grounds. The availability of a pill called RU-486 which could provide an alternative method of abortion through chemical means may change the nature of the abortion debate. Widespread availability of such a pill could make the abortion decision a private one, reduce costs, and increase access to the abortion process. In the early 1990's, the pill had been tested in some countries but was not available to American women. When, or if, RU-486 is permitted in the United States, many of the issues of availability and access will be vastly transformed or eliminated.

SUGGESTED READINGS. Essays on various aspects of the abortion debate are available in *Abortion: Understanding Differences* (1984), edited by Sidney and Daniel Callahan. Leslie Goldstein's *The Constitutional Rights of Women: Cases in Law and Social Change* (1988) includes many of the Supreme Court's abortion decisions. The cultural basis for different opinions on the abortion issue are discussed in Kristin Luker's *Abortion and the Politics of Motherhood* (1984). Gerald Rosenberg writes about the impact of the Supreme Court's abortion decision on society in *The Hollow*

Hope: Can Courts Bring About Social Change? (1991). Distinguished philosopher Ronald Dworkin presents his own insights on the abortion issue in *Life's Dominion: An Argument About Abortion, Euthanasia, and Individual Freedom* (1993).—*Mary Hendrickson*

Abzug, Bella (Bella Savitzky; b. July 24, 1920, New York, N.Y.): Lawyer, politician, and leading civil and

academic activity. Schools, colleges, and universities have been both the testing ground for new attitudes toward diversity and a battleground for the many conflicts that multiculturalism has sparked in contemporary society.

History and Demographics. The first step toward greater multicultural inclusiveness at colleges and universities has been to increase the numbers of cultures

Women's rights advocate Abzug (center) flanked by her friends (from left) Dr. Ruth Westheimer, Marlo Thomas, and Gloria Steinem. (AP/Wide World Photos)

women's rights advocate. Abzug practiced law in New York between 1944 and 1970 and served as chair of the NATIONAL WOMEN'S POLITICAL CAUCUS (1961-1970). In 1971 she won a seat in the U.S. House of Representatives, where she was a strong advocate of welfare rights. In 1976 she lost a race against Daniel Patrick Moynihan for a Senate seat. Abzug is a member of the NATIONAL ORGANIZATION FOR WOMEN (NOW), the AMERICAN CIVIL LIBERTIES UNION, and Americans for Democratic Action. She has written a regular column for *Ms.* MAGAZINE since 1979.

Academics: Much of the movement toward MULTICULTURALISM in the United States has been the result of

represented on their campuses. Prior to the 1960's, the American system of higher education was largely segregated and controlled by white males. Although significant institutions enrolled students of all races and employed some minority faculty, the majority of American students and faculty were associated with same-race institutions. In 1960, 95 percent of students in American colleges and universities were white, and 96 percent of their faculty were white.

THE CIVIL RIGHTS ACT of 1964 outlawed discrimination in all institutions, including those devoted to HIGHER EDUCATION. President Lyndon Johnson supplemented this legislation with Executive Order 11246, which required these institutions to take "AF-

FIRMATIVE ACTION" to employ substantial numbers of minorities and women. Since their inception, these actions have directly influenced college and university admissions and hiring practices. Institutions set up offices for affirmative action, which are charged—among other duties—with overseeing the compliance of searches for faculty and key staff with federal legislation. Searches for new faculty and administrators have become national in their scope, and search committees routinely advertise their openings in national

African American professor Angela Davis won notoriety for her radical political views. Increasing numbers of women and minority academics have helped make academic curricula more inclusive of multicultural issues. (Library of Congress)

publications, including those most likely to be read by minorities and women. Records are kept to document the fairness of the search. Nevertheless, despite federal regulations, only 36 percent of the colleges responding to a 1991 survey reported having an active program to attract underrepresented groups to their faculty.

By 1990, there were more than 500,000 faculty members and 137,561 administrators and managers in American colleges and universities. It was calculated that 88.5 percent of faculty members and 87.3 percent of administrators and managers were white. (African Americans were represented with 4.5 percent faculty and 8.6 percent administrative positions.) Thus, while it is evident that there has been some increase in the numbers of minorities hired since the civil rights legislation of the 1960's, progress has been slow. All minority groups except Asians remain underrepresented in the academy when compared with their percentage of the general U.S. population. It is interesting to note, however, that the percentage of African Americans in the administration and management staff is nearly twice the percentage of African Americans on the faculty. The story with gender is much the same. In 1990, women made up 51 percent of the U.S. population, yet they held only about 30 percent of faculty positions.

Generally speaking, minorities and women tend to hold lower ranks and make less money on average in the academy than white males, although these figures are improving as institutions attempt to reach some parity.

Despite the underrepresentation, the number of minorities and women on college and university faculties has increased. In fairness, it should be observed that their presence alone does not explain the growth of multiculturalism on campuses; white males have often been the leaders of the movement, and many have joined in the changes.

Academics and the Multicultural Curriculum. There is scholarly disagreement about the meaning and purpose of multiculturalism in the academic program. Nevertheless, the key question seems to be whether students are exposed to cultures other than their own in meaningful ways. Faculty debate the numerous ways of achieving this goal, but the goal itself has achieved some measure of acceptance.

Enhanced multicultural elements in the curricula are valued components of a student's learning, regardless of one's perspective on the purpose of education. Scholars Edmund W. Gordon and Mait Bhattacharyya hold that the primary purpose of education is to nurture the development of intelligence and that multicultural readings and experiences will assist students with critical analyses, interpretations, and understandings that are the signs of intelligence. Others argue that the purpose of education is to change the systems that have disenfranchised and disempowered people. James Banks, for example, proposes "multiple acculturation," which will, in turn, promote "cross-cultural competency." John U. Ogbu holds that multicultural-ism will help minority students develop a sense of pride in their own culture, while promoting cultural understanding in all students. Within these various theories, there is a sense that multiculturalism has a place at the center of higher education.

In a 1991 survey, Arthur Levine and Jeanette Cureton reported the following findings concerning the presence of MULTICULTURAL EDUCATION in colleges and universities in the United States: About one-third of institutions have some sort of multicultural requirement in their general education component as well as ethnic- and gender-based courses, centers, or institutes such as WOMEN'S STUDIES centers. More than half have multicultural components of their majors and have multicultural advising programs. The survey also showed that four-year institutions are ahead of two-year colleges in the development of multiculturalism, that research universities are more active than smaller institutions, and that public institutions lead their private counterparts in this regard. Results also varied widely by geographic regions.

The movement toward a multicultural curriculum has led to serious debate over the canon—the body of material that is essential to any quality education. This debate has been most public in the controversy over what should be included in courses in literature. Since time available for a course is finite, only a limited amount of material can be included. If instructors are going to introduce new multicultural subject matter, such as a poem by a hitherto little-known woman poet or a play by a Latino writer, they will have to leave out something that previously was considered worthy of study—most likely something written by a white male. The critical question here is to decide by what standards a writer is included or excluded. For example, traditional standards place Nathaniel Hawthorne and Herman Melville in the highest pantheon of writers, but new paradigms for judgment elevate American Indian writer Leslie Marmon Silko and Japanese writer Shūsako Endō into the most respected category. These examples are from literature, but the issue of canon inclusivity applies to all areas and has become one of the most crucial decisions for academics.

Gordon and Bhattacharyya see canons of all disci-plines as living documents that, rather than protecting traditional bodies of knowledge, enhance learning and the intellect. To this end, they propose criteria by which the integrity of any canon might be judged. It should, for example, reflect the comprehensiveness of

knowledge, demonstrate the capacity for change, be-come accessible to a broad range of audiences, and acknowledge the relationship between prior knowl-edge and the demands of new knowledge.

Predictably, any movement that replaces familiar and respected works with little-known or untested works will cause controversy. Conservatives resist the

After a twenty-year career as a book editor, novelist Toni Morrison accepted a professorship at SUNY-Albany in 1984 and received a faculty appointment at Princeton University in 1989. (AP/Wide World Photos)

loss of tradition, specifically the loss of the symbols and icons of Western civilization. The multicultural movement in the academy has its backlash, a counter-movement that protests what its proponents see as the loss of standards. The voices of the backlash in the late 1980's and 1990's included Allan Bloom, E. D. Hirsch, William Bennett, Lynne V. Cheney, and others.

Faculty Issues. The multicultural movement forces faculty to redefine their qualifications of what is nec-essary to become members of the academy and to per-form its main functions. The question of qualifications falls into two categories: qualifications for member-ship on the faculty and qualifications to teach particu-lar subject matter.

Any new subject matter (for example, science in the mid-1800's, sociology in the later 1800's, American literature at the turn of the century, AFRICAN AMERICAN STUDIES in the 1970's, and women's studies in the 1980's) takes time to become established in the academy. Membership on a faculty is conferred by those who already hold that membership. When a new candidate presents new and innovative qualifications, the old line faculty may resist. For example, if a new candidate for tenure in ASIAN AMERICAN STUDIES has published in journals that are unfamiliar to members of the review committee, he or she is likely to have to convince the committee of the quality of published research. Faculty who work in emerging multicultural fields must demonstrate that their teaching and scholarship are equivalent in quality to professional activities in established disciplines.

The second issue of qualifications deals with the right to teach particular courses. It is argued by some that only those who have experienced minority status at first hand should be allowed to teach certain courses. According to this view, only an African American knows what it is like to be African American, and therefore, only an African American should teach courses that explore the African American experience. The intricacies of AMERICAN INDIAN RELIGION AND MYTHOLOGY are best understood by active members of their tribes; therefore they should be the ones who analyze the meanings of a GHOST DANCE or explain the importance of the coyote archetype. Similarly, proponents of this position contend that only women can properly teach works by and about women and that only Latinos can properly teach the Latino experience. On the other hand, others argue that no contemporary historian was at the Battle of the Little Bighorn or lived with the poor in Czarist Russia, yet scholars are supposed to be able to put aside personal biases and examine experiences that are not their own. As this argument goes, a sensitive white male should be able to teach the poetry of Emily Dickinson or analyze the paintings of Diego Rivera. This controversy continues.

One key issue for faculty is faculty development. If older faculty want to become part of the multicultural movement, they must be given the opportunity to retrain themselves. Institutions must provide time for reading and research into new subjects and new ways of looking at old ones if multicultural perspectives are to take root in the academy. Forty percent of U.S. colleges and universities report that they have

faculty development programs specifically designed to improve multicultural activities on the part of faculty; another 22 percent report that they include multicultural activities as part of their general faculty development.

Institutional Issues. The multicultural movement within higher education forces the colleges and universities to confront some serious issues dealing with faculty and student representation. The acknowledged need for minority and women faculty causes some institutions to modify their expectations for a new faculty member. They may now, for example, eagerly recruit a person with a degree from a less well-known university. Although the concept of quotas raises concern in the mind of any administrator, many institutions reserve certain positions for which they hope to recruit minority or women faculty.

The influx of minorities and women onto faculties and into student bodies has given rise to previously unreported incidents of harassment. In order to make public their stand on such matters, most institutions have approved written policies concerning sexual and racial discrimination as well as SEXUAL HARASSMENT. These documents typically state that harassment of any sort will not be tolerated and that those found guilty of such behavior will be subject to censure and removal. These policies have generated controversy for their effects on free speech on campus, and are often associated with the "POLITICAL CORRECTNESS" movement.

Multiculturalism has called for a new flexibility on the part of institutions. They must find faculty positions that can be shifted to cover new academic areas, and they must find money to fund new multicultural endeavors. In times of tight budgets, the only way this can be accomplished is for administrators to take money and positions from established programs and shift them to meet new demands.

Some progress has been made since the 1960's in making the world of academics more multiculturally inclusive, yet much remains to be done. Full realization of the potential held by multiculturalism to improve and revitalize the academy will take leadership from top administrators, commitment on the part of the institutions (including their boards), and dedication and flexibility from faculty.

SUGGESTED READINGS. The debate over multiculturalism has produced a large, diverse, and steadily growing body of books and articles. One influential voice is that of African American scholar Henry Louis

Gates, Jr., whose book *Loose Canons: Notes on the Culture Wars* (1992) gathers essays for a general audience. Dinesh D'Souza's *Illiberal Education: The Poli-*

various issues of *Higher Education and National Affairs,* the semimonthly publication of the American Council on Education.—*Robert A. Armour*

The diversification of academic faculty and curricula help to ensure that these 1993 graduates will be prepared to face the real world. (James L. Shaffer)

tics of Race and Sex on Campus (1991) is a widely cited conservative contribution to the debate. In *Culture of Complaint* (1993), art critic and historian Robert Hughes, a native of Australia long resident in the United States, finds fault both with many of the advocates of multiculturalism and with their conservative critics. Numerous articles on multiculturalism in the academy can be found in *The Chronicle of Higher Education.* For statistical data, consult the *Almanac* published by the *Chronicle* each summer. The entire issue of *Change* for January/February, 1992, was devoted to the topic, and there is an especially insightful article by Frank F. Wong, entitled "Diversity and Community: Right Objectives and Wrong Arguments," in *Change* for July/August, 1991. See also

Academies—female: Institutions that educated the daughters of wealthy European American families between the late eighteenth and nineteenth centuries. Instead of stressing academic attainments, these institutions emphasized "ornamentals"—accomplishments such as musical performance, amateur sketching, a smattering of languages to indicate "culture," a graceful posture or "carriage," domestic skills such as needlework, and social skills such as the appropriate behavior for entertaining guests. The acquisition of such "ornamentals" was supposed to enhance girls' chances of marrying well.

By 1820, the nature of female academies began to change. Such institutions of advanced study known as female "seminaries" were then being widely established in New England; between 1830 and 1860, similar schools appeared in the Northeast, Midwest, and Southeast. An outgrowth of the ambitions and aspirations of an increasingly prosperous middle class, the spread of female academies was seen as an indication of a rise in the status of women, since women were recognized as the chief influence within the home.

Often, female academies were run by ministers, although some were headed by influential female educators, such as Catharine BEECHER (Hartford Academy) and Mary LYON (Mount Holyoke Seminary). Although many academies came to believe in the importance of some academic instruction for young women, the academies generally stressed the tempering of such academic knowledge with a sense of education appropriate for the middle-class "female sphere." Thus, female academies embodied the belief that middle-class women inhabited a domestic world quite separate from the public world of men, and that the place and function of women were determined by the circumstances of female biology. Along with religious instruction, moral philosophy and domestic science figured heavily in the curricula of such institutions; thus, the administrators of the academies contended that this sort of advanced education for females would enable young women to be better housekeepers and mothers. Their education would also be socially useful, enhancing the function of women as moral influences on society. In particular, one significant and socially useful byproduct of female advanced education was considered the preparation of young women as teachers of children, a calling for which women were believed to be naturally designated.

The educational program of the academies emphasized religious piety to such an extent that the academies produced hundreds of female missionaries. The seminaries also graduated large numbers of women who did, indeed, take up the work of education both in other female seminaries as well as in the "common schools," thus bringing many of the elements of middle-class white female education to the nation's schoolchildren.

SUGGESTED READINGS. The first volume of Thomas A. Woody's *A History of Women's Education in the United States* (1929) remains the classic work on the subject of female education, including the academies, in the U.S. *The Educated Woman in America* (1965), edited by Barbara M. Cross, also contains useful information on the nature and structure of academies as does Barbara Solomon's *In the Company of Educated Women: A History of Women and Higher Education in America* (1985).

Academies—military. *See* **Military Academies**

Acadians in the U.S.: "Acadia," a Micmac Indian word meaning "plenty," was the original name of present-day Nova Scotia. The Acadians were FRENCH colonists who settled there in the seventeenth and eighteenth centuries, some eventually moving to the East and Gulf coasts of the United States, especially Louisiana.

Colonization and Expulsion. Samuel de Champlain and Sieur de Monts, with their band of French pioneers, founded the Acadian settlement at Port Royal on the banks of the Annapolis Basin in 1605. Shortly after the arrival of the Europeans, life for the indigenous Micmac people changed dramatically. Large numbers died from exposure to European diseases as well as from territorial clashes. Despite several attacks by English colonists from the south, the Acadian settlers managed to survive, and their communities spread along the length of the Annapolis Valley. They erected dikes to reclaim marshland from the sea, and their farms prospered.

In 1713 Nova Scotia as well as the rest of Acadia was ceded to England under the Treaty of Utrecht. The Acadian farmers remained on their land, content to maintain an uneasy neutrality toward their new masters. By the 1740's, however, England and France had once again drifted toward war, and the presence of French settlers in the colonies troubled the British governors in Halifax. In 1755 Governor Lawrence issued expulsion orders for all Acadians living in present-day Nova Scotia, Prince Edward Island, and New Brunswick. In Nova Scotia, British soldiers assembled the Acadian settlers at Fort Edward and placed them on ships bound for British colonies to the south.

The more than six thousand expelled Acadians dispersed throughout Massachusetts, Pennsylvania, North Carolina, Virginia, Maryland, Georgia, and Louisiana. The Louisiana settlement took root as an isolated pocket of French culture, with the largest French-speaking minority in the United States. These people later became known as "Cajuns," a frontier American corruption of the word "Acadians."

Many Acadians returned to Nova Scotia in 1763, after the Seven Years' War. The majority of the eighty thousand Acadians living in Nova Scotia today are the direct descendants of these returning REFUGEES. The returning Acadians were granted lands in less desirable areas than the lush farmland they had once occupied. Close family ties helped to preserve the Acadian culture and language, and they continued to live and work independently of the English villages.

The Cajun Flight to Louisiana. The original Acadian flight to Louisiana began with Salvador and Jean Diogène Mouton, uncle and nephew, who arrived in the St. Jacques de Cabanocey area in 1754. According to legend, they walked along the Great Lakes to the upper reaches of the Mississippi River; then they walked and rafted the rest of the way down to Louisiana. This was a relatively well-known path through the center of the continent by 1754.

In 1764 Louisiana was ceded to Spain. Though Spain did not take charge of the colony until two years later, the refugees once again found themselves under a foreign flag with a foreign government; five more years of unrest ensued before the Cajuns were reassured that they had landed in Louisiana to stay. By the end of the 1700's, some four thousand Acadians had taken refuge in Louisiana; at the time they comprised two-thirds of all Acadians.

The United States bought the Louisiana Territory in 1803. In 1815, the Battle of New Orleans compelled all classes of Louisiana society to join forces to keep the English invaders at bay. The Acadians' full capitulation to the new American masters did not occur until after the CIVIL WAR, when Louisiana devised its first all-English constitution. The key to understanding this phenomenon of cultural resistance for half a century after the LOUISIANA PURCHASE and beyond lies in the adaptations the Cajuns learned to make to their new homeland. Wheat did not grow well in Louisiana, but the Indians taught the Cajuns to plant corn. As families multiplied and subdivided their farms, and as churches moved in, followed by stores and schools, village clusters formed at eight-to-ten-mile intervals along the bayous. These bayous continued to play a historic role in transportation and communication in the region.

The Cajun refuge in Louisiana lay even farther away from the original Acadia than Acadia had been from France. Yet trouble still arose from the English-speaking PURITANS of the English-speaking Atlantic seacoast, who continued their influx into the region. The Louisiana Purchase in 1803 and statehood in 1812 swept the Acadian coast into irreversible change, and by 1853 the Cajuns found themselves scattered and dispersed again throughout southern Louisiana in a "second expulsion" that is often neglected by historians.

Cajun Cowboys. From the bountiful soil of their first settlements on the Mississippi River's Acadian coast (extending from the Mississippi River southeast toward New Orleans), the Cajun refugees were driven by the Americans farther into Louisiana's wilderness, into the Atchafalaya Basin to the new frontier of the prairie.

The cattle industry of the West that is the basis of the Anglo American diet and the source of romantic memories of the nineteenth century was originally an Acadian enterprise. The modern American cattle industry started on the Cajun prairie almost a full century before the Anglo Americans even began their emigrations to Texas. Louisiana's cattle industry dates back at least to 1739, the date the first cattle brand was recorded in the state's French "brand book." The brand book continued to be the legal register for Louisiana cattle until 1954.

Cultural Contributions of the Cajuns. Paul Octave Hébert, Louisiana's second Cajun governor (from 1853 to 1856), was a direct descendant of both Louis Gaston Hébert, a member of the original 1604 expedition that founded Acadia, and Paul Gaston Hébert, who burned his house in Annapolis Royal shortly before the expulsion, when he refused to take the English oath. Paul Octave Hébert was a major force behind the state's antebellum golden age, and the founder of both the state's first public library and an educational institution that eventually became Louisiana State University.

It was on Louisiana's Acadian coast in the years following the first expulsion that the French government allowed the Cajun people to regroup and rebuild the New World Acadia. By the time Hébert ascended to power, predominantly French-speaking Louisiana, with its Creole capital at New Orleans, had grown to be the wealthiest region in North America.

Crafts and Cooking. Weaving is the principal and most accomplished craft of the Cajuns. Aside from music and the rich Cajun language, weaving is the oldest, and least modified, surviving folk tradition of the culture. Creating a whole cloth from tattered strands of homemade yarns, weaving "straw" hats from palmetto (dwarf palm) leaves, or weaving a split-oak basket or chair from oak saplings, Cajuns have long seen imaginative possibilities in their surroundings. Among the most precious of their botanical materials is a yellowish-brown cotton the Cajuns call *coton jaune*.

Cajuns are renowned for their cooking, especially

dishes such as gumbo, a spicy stew made of seafood or meat with vegetables. The word "gumbo" is said to be derived from the African word "guingombo," meaning okra—the particular seedpod vegetable that is added to most gumbos for taste and thickening.

Chowders are common in the maritime areas of Canada inhabited by Louisiana's Acadian relatives, but the meal-in-a-pot idea is the only similarity between the two cuisines. The Canadian *fricou* features potatoes, meat, and dumplings which may be seasoned with a bunch of summer savory inserted top-down into the boiling stew. Louisiana's Cajun gumbo, on the other hand, has a unique taste not only because of its African and African American influences but also because of its SPANISH and CHOCTAW Indian contributions.

Crawfish are another Cajun delicacy. Cajun folklore asserts that the crawfish is descended from lobsters that followed the exiles from Maritime Canada to Louisiana. The yellow crawfish fat is the secret of dishes such as crawfish bisque and crawfish *étouffée* (smothered).

Music. The Acadian music in Canada before and after the expulsion had featured the violin; this instrument continued to be popular in Louisiana until the GERMAN immigrants of the Midwest introduced the button accordion when they began remigrating south to the Cajun prairies in the railroad/rice boom years of the 1880's. In present-day Louisiana, the accordion dominates, blended with a country and western element of electric guitars and Nashville sound. Dancing, in one form or another, has always accompanied Acadian music, and is still an integral part of all Cajun music, especially waltzes and two-steps.

Cajun musicians born after WORLD WAR II of instrumental and melodic combinations still rooted in old forms. This "progressive Cajun" sound, a sensation at the 1975 New Orleans Jazz Festival, started each tune in the traditional Cajun idiom before drifting into a mixture of JAZZ, ROCK, COUNTRY AND WESTERN, and bluegrass-style variations. Another strain of Cajun-influenced music is called zydeco—a corruption of *les haricots ne sont pas sal*, meaning "beans aren't salty." Zydeco is black Cajun music, blending French influence with RHYTHM AND BLUES and ROCK AND ROLL, popularized principally by Clifton Chenier and other African American musicians.

Mardi Gras. In the pre-Christian era, Mardi Gras marked the last day of the previous year's calendar. It was treated as one last splurge celebrating the bounty of the past followed by a period of reduced consumption until the ground gave forth sustenance again. When Catholicism spread over western Europe, the church turned this pagan celebration into pre-Lenten Carnival. In Cajun country, the seasonal transition has evolved into a community ritual of festive song, dance, and processions in which everyone participates and rejoices. Cajun Mardi Gras, like Cajun traditions in cooking and music, has experienced a revival since the 1970's and continues to fascinate non-Cajuns as well.

SUGGESTED READINGS. For a particularly lyrical account of life on the Cajun prairie, see Lauren C. Post's *Cajun Sketches from the Prairies of Southwest Louisiana* (1962). William Faulkner Rushton's *The Cajuns: From Acadia to Louisiana* (1979) is an accurate and balanced popular account of a distinctive American people. *The Founding of New Acadia* (1987) by Carl A. Brasseaux looks beyond long-standing mythology to provide a critical account of early Acadian culture in Louisiana and the reasons for its survival. An anthology entitled *The Cajuns: Essays on Their History and Culture* (1978), edited by Glenn R. Conrad, presents insightful and varied viewpoints on their cultural contributions.—*Genevieve Slomski*

Acculturation: Cultural change that occurs when members of a minority group adopt characteristics of the dominant culture (they "become acculturated"). The term "acculturation" is sometimes used interchangeably with "ASSIMILATION," but technically the former is only one dimension of the latter. Examples of acculturation are Asian Indian women abandoning saris for dresses, Vietnamese American teenagers preferring American fast food to traditional ethnic dishes, or Mexican Americans celebrating THANKSGIVING. One may be acculturated without being fully socially, economically, or politically assimilated into American life.

ACLU. *See* **American Civil Liberties Union**

Acquired immune deficiency syndrome epidemic (AIDS epidemic): The spread of AIDS, which was first seen in the United States in 1981, has had a strong impact on American culture. It has affected different groups to varying degrees. The gay community has been particularly hard hit by the disease. The community responded to the challenge in the mid-1980's with a campaign to educate its members about how AIDS is spread; many gay people changed their patterns of sexual activity from high-risk to low-risk behavior. The disease has also had a strong impact among heterosexuals belonging to lower socioeconomic groups in large cities. This has occurred largely because of the disproportionately high number of intravenous (IV) drug users among lower socioeconomic urban populations, particularly African Americans and Latinos.

Although the earliest AIDS cases involved gay men, women were increasingly infected with the disease as the 1980's progressed. By 1992, about 10 percent of people with AIDS in the United States were women. AIDS results in a breakdown of the body's immune system, which leaves the body susceptible to a large number of infections from normally harmless microorganisms.

would be associated with chronic diseases such as cancer, degenerative disease, or cardiovascular problems. The appearance of AIDS proved just how vulnerable people really are to new infectious agents in spite of medical advances.

In the United States, the Centers for Disease Control (CDC) in Atlanta, Georgia, serve as a public-health research center and information clearinghouse. State and local health departments are required to file reports with the agency pertaining to any unusual outbreaks of illness. In June of 1981, the CDC received a report from LOS ANGELES that described the appearance of five cases of a rare protozoan pneumonia in the previous eight months. The disease, *Pneumocystis carinii* pneumonia, or PCP, was considered an oppor-

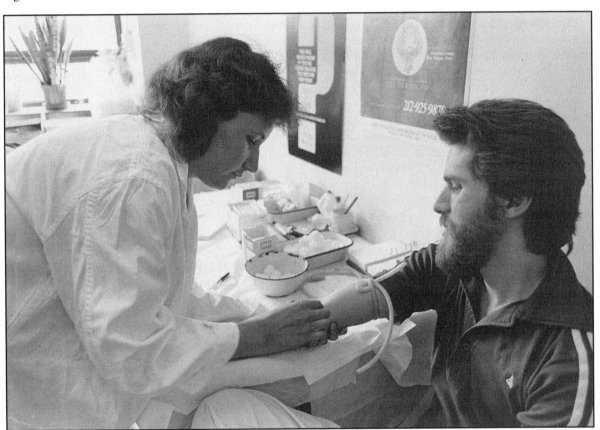

A Puerto Rican man being tested for AIDS. (Hazel Hankin)

Historical Background. During the 1970's, both health care workers and the general public thought that large-scale epidemics of infectious disease in the Western world had largely become a thing of the past. With the exception perhaps of periodic flu epidemics, it was believed that the major threats to public health

tunistic disease (that is, a disease that is serious only if the body's immune system is already weakened). Outbreaks were so uncommon (only two cases had been reported in the previous fifteen years) that the drug for treating the illness was only available from the CDC. What made the outbreak even more unusual

Adult AIDS Cases Reported through June, 1992

Total cases reported: 226,281

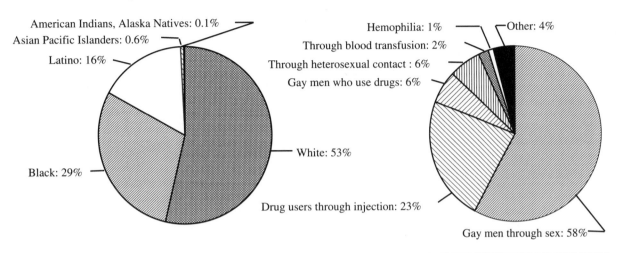

By Race/Ethnicity

American Indians, Alaska Natives: 0.1%
Asian Pacific Islanders: 0.6%
Latino: 16%
Black: 29%
White: 53%

By Type of Exposure

Hemophilia: 1%   Other: 4%
Through blood transfusion: 2%
Through heterosexual contact : 6%
Gay men who use drugs: 6%
Drug users through injection: 23%
Gay men through sex: 58%

Source: Data are from Carol Foster, ed., *Minorities: A Changing Role in America.* Table 5.23. Wylie, Tex.: Information Plus, 1992.

was that all the cases were found among young homosexual men.

Throughout 1981, an increasing number of unusual illnesses was seen within the male homosexual communities of NEW YORK and CALIFORNIA. Among them was another rare opportunistic disease, Kaposi's sarcoma, a form of cancer. In 1982, these unusual illnesses were grouped together in a new disease classification: acquired immune deficiency syndrome, or AIDS. The big question concerned the underlying cause of the outbreaks. Since the patients had common features of age, residence, and sexual orientation, scientists believed that the outbreaks had a similar underlying cause. Most researchers began to suspect that the cause was likely to be an infectious agent. Epidemiological studies performed in 1982 supported this contention.

In 1982 and 1983, it became clear that the disease could spread by means other than sexual contact; cases in people who had received blood transfusions and then cases involving intravenous (IV) drug abusers became known. The disease was also found among heterosexuals (IV drug users) as well as homosexuals. The AIDS virus was isolated in 1983 by two separate research teams, one headed by Robert Gallo in the United States and the other by Luc Montagnier in

France. The virus was eventually designated the human immunodeficiency virus, or HIV; two strains of it, HIV-I and HIV-2, were identified. The identification of the virus paved the way for a blood test that could diagnose the presence of HIV.

Epidemiology. With rare exceptions, transmission of HIV occurs only through specific routes: sexual contact; the sharing or improper use of needles, as in IV drug abuse; or movement across the placenta from an infected mother to her offspring. The disease is not spread through casual social contact such as shaking hands, kissing, or coughing, nor is there any evidence of a single case being spread by insects such as mosquitos or ticks.

AIDS made its first inroads in the United States within the mainly white male homosexual and bisexual populations of the larger cities. From 1981, when AIDS was first reported, until 1990, some 63 percent of the patients were homosexual or bisexual men with no history of drug abuse. About 19 percent of patients were heterosexual men and women who acquired the disease through IV drug abuse, and roughly 3 percent were people who acquired the disease through contaminated blood (nearly all were infected prior to blood screening in 1985).

The gay male population most at risk during the

Many resources that could be used positively to fight AIDS have instead been wasted in a campaign to attack gays; these activists voice opinions on the issue. (AP/Wide World Photos)

early years of the epidemic was predominantly middle class and educated. When it became clear the disease could be sexually transmitted, gay men responded by reducing their number of sexual partners and by instituting safer sexual practices. As a result, the rate at which gay men were becoming infected was significantly reduced. For example, in 1991, the proportion of homosexual and bisexual men among newly reported cases had dropped by 10 percent to 53 percent of AIDS cases, while IV drug users rose to 30 percent.

The most obvious change has been in the numbers of infected individuals. In 1988, it was projected that within four years, approximately 400,000 persons would be diagnosed with AIDS. In fact, the numbers through 1992 were 20 percent below that projection.

The racial and ethnic breakdown of AIDS cases reflects the movement of the disease into the inner city. AFRICAN AMERICANS, approximately 12 percent of the U.S. population, have accounted for some 26 percent of cases among adults and nearly 55 percent of pediatric cases (children younger than thirteen); LATINOS, 7 percent of the U.S. population, have accounted for 14 percent of adult cases and 23 percent of pediatric cases. These numbers reflect the impact of drug abuse on these populations. The result has been an increase in heterosexual transmission from infected partners and a rise in infection of the fetus from infected women during pregnancy. Approximately one in ten persons with AIDS is a woman.

The situation is particularly tragic in that most of these women are in their childbearing years. Most of these women acquired the infection through IV drug abuse (51 percent through 1990) or through sexual contact with an IV drug abuser (21 percent). Consequently, several thousand children (approximately thirty-one hundred through 1990) have been reported as being HIV positive, with the vast majority becoming infected in utero. Three-fourths of the women and children diagnosed with AIDS are either black or Latino. Minorities are expected to account for an even larger proportion of the cases as the epidemic progresses. For this reason, a number of AIDS education and treatment programs have targeted minority communities.

Aids and Gay Community Activism. With the possible exception of hemophiliacs, no single community in the United States has been as affected by AIDS as gay men. Of the 250,000 persons diagnosed with AIDS at the end of 1992, approximately 60 percent were homosexual males. Arguably slow to react at first, gay men, lesbians, and concerned others coalesced by the mid-1980's into a mixture of activist and protest organizations, ranging from the radical AIDS Coalition to Unleash Power (ACT-UP) to the more traditional National Gay Task Force.

It was these groups, not all of whose members were gay, that first emphasized education and social pressure as means of slowing the spread of the disease. For example, gay organizations were the first to promote "safe sex" practices and to urge an end to promiscuity in response to the epidemic. Though such practices could not eliminate all danger of exposure to the AIDS virus, the slowing of the epidemic in the gay community by the late 1980's could be traced in part to changes in gay sexual practices as a result of these campaigns. Efforts such as the NAMES project, which made an enormous memorial quilt for AIDS victims, also drew widespread public sympathy to the cause.

The gay community, long hidden among the American population, has emerged as an increasingly strong political power in the age of AIDS. By the 1990's, government funding for AIDS research and education exceeded that for any other infectious disease, in no small part because of gay political lobbying. Legally, persons who are HIV-positive are now protected under the Americans with Disabilities Act of 1990. The more radical gay groups believe that still more political action is necessary to prevent further tragedy as a result of the epidemic. AIDS is not a "gay disease." The gay community, however, has been drawn together by its concern over the disease and has been a leading force in trying to limit the damage associated with the epidemic.

SUGGESTED READINGS. A scientific account of the AIDS epidemic is found in *The Science of AIDS* (1989), a collection of readings from *Scientific American* magazine. An outstanding and vivid account of the early years of the epidemic is given in Randy Shilts's *And the Band Played On* (1987). Social and public health issues, including the impact of AIDS on American culture, are described in *The AIDS Reader* (1991), edited by Nancy McKenzie, and in *The AIDS Epidemic: Private Rights and the Public Interest* (1989), edited by Padraig O'Malley. For vivid description of the devastating effects of AIDS on the life of a young boy, see Ryan White's autobiography, *Ryan White: My Own Story* (1991).—*Richard Adler*

Activism in the 1960's—student: Protests seeking fundamental social and political changes on campus and in the broader society. American efforts were paralleled by similar movements in Western Europe during a decade of general social upheaval. Though the activists did not win all that they demanded, they revolutionized the political atmosphere on campus, helped other social change movements, and contributed to the growth of a youth counterculture.

tated for radical social and political reforms in the 1960's collectively became known as the "New Left" to distinguish them from an older generation of socialists. Among the many activist groups, local and national, the most widely influential was Students for a Democratic Society (SDS). In 1962, the SDS drafted its "Port Huron statement" criticizing U.S. government

Protesters confront officers of the Chicago Police Department during the 1968 Democratic National Convention. (Library of Congress)

Although the anti-VIETNAM WAR protest movement has come to symbolize the activism of the 1960's, the antiwar movement was part of a broader spectrum of student activism. Student activism was, in many respects, an outgrowth of the participation by young people in the CIVIL RIGHTS movement, particularly the FREEDOM RIDES and the 1963 BIRMINGHAM DEMONSTRATIONS. It eventually encompassed or inspired the WOMEN'S LIBERATION MOVEMENT, many ethnic movements, including the BLACK POWER MOVEMENT, and the GAY AND LESBIAN MOVEMENT.

American protesters, including students, who agi-

policies; in 1965, the group began to direct its efforts specifically against the Vietnam War. It was on the campus of University of California, Berkeley, in 1964, however, that student activism, in the form of the free speech movement, first received widespread national attention. The free speech movement was born to express students' resentment at the university's policies against student involvement in political demonstrations on campus.

Many Berkeley students who had worked hard to enter the prestigious institution were dismayed to discover that many courses were taught by graduate students in gigantic sections; the famous scholars from whom they had expected to learn were busy in their studies or laboratories, turning out the research through which the university had gained its reputation. Much of the research led to weaponry and other support for the Vietnam War, which became the larger target of the students' attack and which affected young people personally through the military draft. Student activism became a critique of all the flaws of modern American society, including POVERTY and RACISM, as the mostly white Berkeley students realized that their privilege and the position of the university had been obtained at the expense of other ethnic groups, particularly AFRICAN AMERICANS. Demanding immediate redress of their grievances, Berkeley students brought the school to a standstill with a student strike and occupation of the administration building.

The Berkeley pattern of confrontation, with its occupation of buildings and demands for social justice as well as a more relevant curriculum, was adopted by students at many other schools. Students for a Democratic Society became a unifying element, with chapters and a common agenda at several institutions. By 1968, activism had spread to Columbia, Harvard, and more than two hundred other college campuses, as well as high schools. Student activists won a number of concessions from college administrations, such as the establishment of ethnic studies and affirmative action programs.

According to news broadcasts, however, most American students maintained traditional values and did not join the protests.

The impact of student activism was felt far beyond college campuses. A generation gap developed as older Americans could not understand why young people for whom their parents had sacrificed were not content with the EDUCATION and the world they were offered. Anger directed at student activists escalated until, in 1970, four students were killed by Ohio National Guardsmen at Kent State University and two more students were killed at predominantly black Jackson State in Mississippi. The increasing violence, coupled with the winding down of the Vietnam War, brought a decline in student activism by the mid-1970's.

SUGGESTED READINGS. A good history and analysis of the Berkeley protests is *The Berkeley Student Revolt* (1965), edited by Seymour Martin Lipset and Sheldon S. Wolin. The Columbia student revolt is documented in *Up Against the Ivy Wall* (1968) by Jerry L. Avorn.

James Simon Kunen presents a personal view of the Columbia revolt in *The Strawberry Statement: Notes of a College Revolutionary* (1969). Another history of the conflict is *1968: A Student Generation in Revolt* (1988), edited by Ronald Fraser et al.

Activist and protest organizations: Groups formed to promote social change. Dissatisfaction with existing social, economic, or political conditions is the principal impetus for the development of these organizations. Sharing a common aim of effecting social change, they exhibit a broad range of specific goals. On one end of the continuum are social action organizations seeking relatively minor changes in either public policy or laws governing single issues. At the other end are protest organizations whose aims embody a revolutionary vision for the total reformulation of society.

Goals and Strategies for Change. Corresponding to their intended goals, protest organizations employ a variety of activities designed to produce change. Engaging in fundraising, congressional lobbying, and lawsuits to influence specific legal reforms contrasts with the development of community-based service organizations or alternative, countercultural communities. In revolutionary groups, tactical measures can even include mobilization for armed action to support military strategies of protest. These three approaches can be seen, for example, in the varied approaches to civil rights of the NATIONAL ASSOCIATION FOR THE ADVANCEMENT OF COLORED PEOPLE (NAACP), STUDENT NONVIOLENT COORDINATING COMMITTEE (SNCC), and the BLACK PANTHER PARTY.

Members of protest groups must also decide what style and form of organizational structures they will create. Some, such as the NATIONAL ORGANIZATION FOR WOMEN (NOW), follow more traditional patterns of hierarchically ordered power arrangements. In this case, decisions flow from the top leadership positions down through the rank and file. More progressive action groups, such as those in the WOMEN'S LIBERATION MOVEMENT, develop alternative organizational structures designed to foster more democratic decision making processes. Similarly, extremely militant protest groups may assume the organizational styles characteristic of highly developed military units. Under hierarchical structures, charismatic leaders can play very important roles in recruiting new members and negotiating with official government representatives.

Organizations in pursuit of social change tend to form around issues of perceived social inequalities or injustices. Understanding the social significance of these organizations, therefore, requires an examination of the complex relationship between the government and various competing interest groups. The U.S. government, through law and official agency practices, protects the privilege enjoyed by some groups at the expense of others. These elite privileges persist even though they directly contradict American democratic ideals and have been the target of a long history of reform movements. For example, racial discrimination is maintained precisely because some groups benefit from these arrangements. When communities with a history of discrimination organize to effect social change, they struggle to influence the government in ways that will result in greater equality of opportunity and therefore greater access to social resources, such as money, status, and political power.

Dynamics of Action and Political Organization Development. Some protest organizations, impatient with the slow speed and limits of reform movement efforts,

come to believe that more militant programs are necessary to achieve change. The more favorably the government responds to a group's demands for reform, the less likely it is that a group will adopt more radical strategies. The government's willingness to incorporate the proposed changes into existing laws and policies, in turn, is shaped by the intensity of political and economic pressures upon it to maintain existing social relations.

In periods of economic crises in which there are increasing numbers of unemployed people, for example, the U.S. government has not been open to reforms that would increase the participation of people of color in the labor market. In contrast, during periods of economic expansion, when more laborers are needed, demands for equality in education, hiring, and promotion are more likely to be accepted by the courts and implemented through the official policies of various governmental agencies.

Like all organizations, social action groups develop

Chinese Americans use political clout to preserve their Chinatown. (Frances M. Roberts)

Young Americans march on Washington, D.C., in 1984 to encourage an end to U.S. intervention in Central America. (Hazel Hankin)

logistical plans for protest based upon an assessment of their available resources. Certain resources are critical for waging a successful battle for social change. Basic material assets such as money, volunteer and paid labor, office space, and equipment for operations become the basis for gaining control over more fundamental resources such as public opinion. Protest organizations may mount education and media campaigns to mobilize public opinion. These can be costly ventures, but they are effective and necessary steps toward securing changes in law and social policy.

Of key importance, however, is one resource available only to the government: the control over use of the police, courts, and law to discredit protest organizations by labeling them "common criminals." An example of this in the 1970's was the COINTELPRO (Counter Intelligence Program) campaign of the Federal Bureau of Investigation (FBI), which involved a systematic and illegal effort to harass, persecute, imprison, and even assassinate some members of civil rights, nationalist, feminist, and militant antiwar groups. In many cases, the government succeeded in "criminalizing" these organizations, making their

members appear to be involved in murder, robbery, conspiracy, or gunrunning for purely personal gain. In this way, the government can discredit social change movements and direct public attention away from the political motivations and goals underlying organized protest.

Struggles for social change are dynamic and ongoing processes that reflect enduring social inequalities and particular historical conditions. These dynamics help shape the nature and character of social action organizations as they develop in accord with the resources available to them. Two specific case studies can illustrate these points.

Case Study: Freedom Now! The Freedom Now! Campaign for Amnesty and Human Rights for Political Prisoners (FN) in the 1980's formed a nationwide collective of representatives from African American and "New Afrikan" groups, the Puerto Rican independence movement, the AMERICAN INDIAN RIGHTS MOVEMENT, and anti-imperialist and peace organizations to organize support for their incarcerated members. The goals were, first, to keep alive the memory of these various struggles that were under threat from government agencies. Second, FN hoped to show, amidst the renewed crises of the 1980's, that these movements and others continued to work for social change. Finally, the campaign aimed to stop the violations of human rights that they believed were imposed on imprisoned members of these organizations.

In the first stage of the Freedom Now! campaign, organizers gave top priority to educating the public about the existence and harsh treatment of these prisoners. Public speaking tours and local mobilizing efforts grew into a national organizing conference and culminated with a highly publicized "tribunal" in

these independent organizations improved their ability to bring their respective cases to the public.

Officially, the U.S. government denies that it incarcerates persons for their political beliefs and actions. It relies instead on "criminalizing" protest group members as a means of quelling political dissent. The FN organization challenged this governmental strategy, seeking to portray their members' actions as legitimate political expressions of principled activities. By mobilizing public opinion on their behalf, FN kept the focus on the nature of the problems being faced by oppressed communities.

Everyone has a cause—this woman has taken to the streets to help resolve a controversy over fishing rights in Madison, Wis. (James L. Shaffer)

which the U.S. government was "put on trial" for its "crimes." The campaign reflected the coalition-building efforts of several distinct social protest organizations. By cooperatively sharing their resources,

The Sanctuary Movement. In a similar manner, the SANCTUARY MOVEMENT of the 1980's was a coalition of small, independent protest groups that amassed their resources to form an international network. This movement developed in response to the U.S. government's unwillingness to accept as REFUGEES the flood of Salvadoran and Guatemalan nationals fleeing violent political upheavals in their homelands, and in protest of gross inconsistencies in the official application of immigration laws.

Unlike earlier migrations of mostly Mexican citizens who came across the U.S. border seeking better economic opportunities, the Salvadoran and Guatemalan nationals who arrived in the 1980's were seeking asylum as political refugees. They recounted horrific stories of threats, torture, and kidnappings sponsored by their governments and some rebel groups.

Believing that the U.S. government would be open to providing refuge, some border area residents began to help the Salvadorans and Guatemalans pursue all available legal avenues for addressing their needs. These citizens were increasingly confronted, however, with hostility on the part of agents of the U.S. BORDER PATROL and the IMMIGRATION AND NATURALIZATION SERVICE (INS). This led sanctuary supporters to study the special circumstances underlying the migration, particularly the historic relationship between the United States and the Salvadoran and Guatemalan governments.

From a careful reading of the REFUGEE ACT OF 1980 and of United Nations documents, sanctuary movement workers concluded that these Salvadorans and Guatemalans clearly qualified for asylum in the United States. Supporting evidence was collected from documented testimonies of torture and rape, evidence of gunshot wounds and electrical shocks, and stories of people being "disappeared" (kidnapped) by government troops. This evidence helped shift public opinion on the issue, but not the official U.S. position.

At the same time that Central Americans were streaming across the Mexican border, U.S. immigration policy was put to the test by the sudden arrival of tens of thousands of Cuban and Haitian "BOAT PEOPLE." Both groups were attempting to secure political refugee status and to be allowed, therefore, to remain in the United States. Highly inconsistent U.S. government responses revealed fundamental contradictions in official immigration policies. As in previous applications of U.S. immigration law, those seeking refuge from nations with "friendly governments" (Haiti) were overwhelmingly denied legal entry, despite ample evidence of human rights violations. On the other hand, "open door" policies were applied to those seeking asylum from nations whose relations with the United States were less friendly, or even hostile, such as Cubans.

Confronted with antagonistic government agents, and believing that offering sanctuary was the correct moral and legal response, protestors began to explore alternative routes for providing aid. Some sanctuary groups adopted the use of extralegal tactics while advancing to the stage of a full-blown social movement. Among these tactics were the development of a new "underground railroad" to shelter undocumented refugees who were at risk of being deported if captured. Additionally, sanctuary workers presented a direct challenge to U.S. immigration law by actually entering Mexico to assist refugees crossing into the United States. The government's response was to charge prominent members of the movement with having violated laws against aiding and abetting illegal migration. Although the trial was of international concern, only minor reforms in asylum application acceptance rates resulted.

The success or failure of organized efforts to produce social change through protest can be assessed in various ways. The case of Freedom Now! represents an innovative strategy for coordinating the efforts and resources of struggling protest organizations. Social action groups must choose protest strategies that take into account the dilemma posed by the legal limits of acceptable practices. The case of the sanctuary movement exemplifies this dynamic process in which protest organizations unfold. As long as social inequities persist in American society, there is no doubt that social protest groups will continue to emerge and develop.

SUGGESTED READINGS. For a general discussion of action and protest organizations, see *Collective Behavior and Social Movements* (1993), edited by Russell L. Curtis and Benigno E. Aguirre. William Gamson's *The Strategy of Social Protest* (2d ed., 1990) provides a comprehensive analysis of social action groups existing between 1800 and 1945. For a first-hand account of the sanctuary movement, see *Sanctuary: The New Underground Railroad* (1986) by Renny Golden and Michael McConnell. An extensive investigation of the COINTELPRO program is available in *Agents of Repression* (1988) by Ward Churchill and Jim Vander Wall.—*Kathryn Stout*

Addams, Jane (Sept. 6, 1860, Cedarville, Ill.—May 21, 1935, Chicago, Ill.): Leader of American settlement house movement, peace advocate, and social reformer.

In 1889 Addams established Hull House in the heart of Chicago's immigrant community. It consisted of more than forty clubs, a day nursery, and a girls' boarding house. Addams believed that peace could be achieved through internationalism; Hull House welcomed immigrants while most of the city remained inaccessible to them. She was the first woman president of the National Conference of Charities and Correction, the first president of the Women's International League for Peace and Freedom (WILPF), and one of the founders of the American Civil Liberties Union.

This portrait of Jane Addams can be seen in Washington, D.C.'s National Portrait Gallery. (The National Portrait Gallery)

Admissions quotas. *See* **Quotas—admissions**

Adoption: Ideally, adoption matches the needs of three groups: birth parents, who relinquish their parental rights toward their children; adoptive parents, who desire to bring up children; and children themselves, who need families to love and rear them. Tensions in the wider society, however, whether related to marital status, class, disability, or race, sometimes become apparent in adoption, when social prejudices and inequities literally come home.

Imbalances Between Birth Parents and Adoptive Parents. A woman's choice to relinquish her child may not be completely free. Lack of money, the stigma of unwed motherhood, or relative youth may force this decision. Adoptive parents tend to be older, better educated, and more economically secure, all of which may imply an element of economic coercion on the birth parents. This problem becomes manifest in "gray-market" adoptions, whereby a child is exchanged, directly or indirectly, for money. Birth fathers sometimes lose their parental rights because they are not told about the pregnancy or birth. Open adoptions, which became increasingly popular in the 1980's, retain these troubling aspects but treat birth parents, especially mothers, more respectfully. Nevertheless, relinquishing a child remains an extremely difficult and painful choice.

At the same time, adoption may represent the only way in which infertile people or those suffering from genetic conditions (such as Tay-Sachs disease) or other medical problems can become parents at all. Simply because of a medical condition, adoptive parents must meet a standard never required of birth parents. They must prove their financial security, mental and emotional stability, and social responsibility with documentation from employers, banks, clergy, physicians, social workers, and law enforcement agencies (fingerprint checks). Once they receive a child, a caseworker evaluates their family interaction several times before the adoption is finalized. Child welfare agencies demand all this "in the best interests of the child." Nevertheless, custody law usually favors birth parents, except in cases of extreme abuse or negligence.

Transracial Adoptions. When white or Anglo families adopt children of another race, other issues arise. Most authorities consider it optimal for children to be adopted by families of their own race or ethnicity, both to enable them to grow up knowing and honoring their heritage and to learn the skills necessary to survive in a racist society. Experts disagree about whether transracial adoption is preferable to foster care or other impermanent arrangements, which are sometimes the only alternatives.

The question has different implications for particular groups. African Americans have long faced overt discrimination in American society, as well as high rates of poverty and single-parent homes. Historically, there have been too few African American families to adopt African American children, although this may reflect inadequate recruitment rather than a real lack of interested families. If the main goal of adoption is providing young children with loving families, then the parents' race is irrelevant. If the aim is the children's long-term social and emotional well-being, however, race may be extremely relevant. No matter how loving their families, the argument goes, African American children will always face racial discrimination in the wider society. Parents who have not expe-

Adoptions by Type: 1960-1986

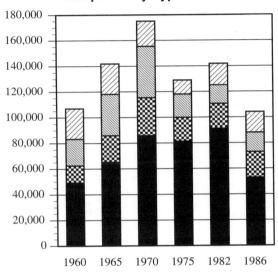

Source: Data are from *Statistical Abstract of the United States, 1992.* Table 599. Washington, D.C.: U.S. Government Printing Office, 1992.

rienced blatant discrimination may not be able to teach children the skills needed to cope with it. Children may be confused between their treatment at home and in the wider community. They may also have trouble forging an African American identity within a white family. Because success, measured in the children's self-esteem and social adjustment, is constantly disputed, adoption agencies and state policies have discouraged, though usually not prohibited, such transracial adoptions.

American Indians have somewhat different con-

cerns, centering as much on the larger Indian community as on the adjustment of individual children. The U.S. government and white society have spent generations trying to erase American Indian culture and have managed to eliminate, assimilate, or marginalize most Indians. In the face of enormous pressure to abandon traditional ways, some Indians are striving to perpetuate their tribal cultures. When an Indian child is adopted by non-Indian parents, the whole tribal community loses one more chance to extend its culture into the future. As tribal membership declines, the culture gradually disappears. Therefore, there are strong cultural norms within this community against allowing adoptions by non-Indians. In addition, Congress passed the Indian Child Welfare Act in 1978, whereby tribes may block the adoption of Indian children by non-Indians, even to the extent of revoking existing adoptions; the law still permits adoptions by those deemed "culturally Indian."

Most children of Latino or Asian origin who are adopted by Anglo or white families were born outside the United States. Thus, these are simultaneously transracial and transnational adoptions. While agencies continue to prefer placing children in families of the same ethnicity, the growing numbers of Latino and Asian American transracial families will tend to encourage more flexibility for these groups.

Transnational Adoptions. The first large-scale U.S. movement for transnational adoption occurred after the KOREAN WAR when the Holt family sought to adopt eight mixed-race war orphans who faced privation and ostracism in Korea. This required an act of Congress to accomplish, and the attendant publicity stimulated hundreds of American families to adopt Korean children as well. "Operation Baby Lift" in 1975, after the VIETNAM WAR, was a similar effort on a much larger scale. Questions began to surface about American motives, however. By the mid-1970's, the availability of legal ABORTIONS and BIRTH CONTROL pills had reduced the number of "adoptable" white infants. Moreover, some of the children involved in transnational adoptions were neither mixed-race AMERASIANS subject to ostracism in Vietnam nor orphans. Critics questioned whether bringing Vietnamese children to the United States served the interests of the children or of American families.

Transnational adoptions continued and, indeed, accelerated into the early 1990's. This trend reflects several factors. On the one hand, there are higher rates of infertility as American couples continue to postpone

A working mother arrives home and is greeted by her son, husband, and adopted Korean daughter. (Cleo Freelance Photo)

MARRIAGE and parenthood, the growing social acceptability of single parenthood, and the consequent shortage of adoptable American infants. On the other hand, countries in Asia, Latin America, and Eastern Europe, which are coping with massive changes caused by URBANIZATION, industrialization, and economic development (as well as severe political instability), find themselves unable to provide even minimal services for many of their children. In Asia, for example, Korea, Thailand, the Philippines, and India have allowed children to be adopted in the United States, Canada, and Western Europe because they cannot be cared for adequately in their homelands. The People's Republic of China began transnational adoptions in the 1990's to deal with an unanticipated consequence of its policy of allowing only one child per family—the widespread abandonment of infant girls. Mexico, Colombia, El Salvador, and Brazil are the more prominent Latin American nations that allow transnational adoptions. In their eagerness to provide homes for their children, these countries often welcome single-parent adoptions, especially of sibling groups. Typically, when a country's economy has improved sufficiently to provide for its children, the country has cut back on transnational adoptions, especially those involving healthy infants who do not need expensive medical care; this has occurred in Korea, for example.

Race is still a factor in transnational adoptions. In the 1970's, for example, families were quickly found for the Vietnamese Baby Lift children, while African American children remained harder to place. The American response to the Vietnamese children hints at racial stereotyping, whereby Asians are seen as easily assimilable model immigrants or as somehow less racially different from whites than other ethnic groups; to a degree, this has also been the case with Latin American children. An even more striking example occurred after the overthrow of Communist regimes in Eastern Europe in 1989 and the collapse of the Soviet Union in 1991. Americans rushed to Eastern Europe, scouring orphanages, hospitals, and villages for adoptable white infants. The problem became so severe that the government of Romania suspended all transnational adoptions until procedures could be set up to ensure that children were not being bought and sold. Significantly, the number of transnational adoptions from Africa remains negligible, despite the desperate economic problems there; in part, however, this reflects the policy of various African nations.

Balancing the Rights of Adults and the Needs of Children. Adoption, like marriage, is at once a strong emotional tie and a legal arrangement that transforms unrelated individuals into a family. Both arrangements seek to balance the rights and needs of the participating parties. When rights and needs conflict, legal action is often necessary to resolve the problem. Several movements have developed since the 1970's to redefine the institution of adoption and the laws regulating it.

Formerly, adoption involved a degree of secrecy to safeguard the relationship between children and adopting families and to protect the privacy of birth parents. Once an adoption was finalized, the court records were sealed and a new birth certificate was issued. Even when the child became an adult, the records remained closed, making it difficult for adoptees and birth parents to find one another. Legally, this policy treated adult adoptees like children who could not be trusted with vital information about themselves. Hence, a movement has developed among adult adoptees and birth parents to force states to open adoption records. Similarly, the open adoption movement allows adoptive and birth parents to deal with one another directly and encourages continuing contact among all the parties.

New issues have arisen as social conditions have changed. For example, the practice of surrogate motherhood, which usually involves having a birth father's wife adopt her husband's child by another woman, raises complicated questions of custody. As the stigma of unwed motherhood has faded, some birth parents have organized to assert their rights and even, in rare cases, to undo some existing adoptions. Adoptive parents find this trend extremely threatening, since it implies that they are not their children's families but merely temporary caregivers. In conflicts between adoptive and birth parents, the ones who suffer most are often the children, who need to form permanent attachments in stable environments. Indeed, some insist that children's needs are also rights; thus, in the early 1990's, a child successfully sued to terminate the parental rights of his birth mother and to be adopted by his foster family.

While adoptive and birth parents vie for custody of some children, "special needs" children often have difficulty in finding a parent at all. This group includes children with physical or mental disabilities, those who have experienced physical or emotional trauma in their birth or foster families, those with incurable diseases (such as human immunodeficiency virus or

HIV), and those born addicted to drugs or afflicted with fetal alcohol syndrome (FAS) as a result of their birth mothers' substance abuse during pregnancy. Older children (over age four), those of mixed racial backgrounds, and sibling groups who wish to remain together are also considered hard to place. Most states and many adoption agencies have programs to encourage and facilitate the placement of these children into permanent homes. Such programs simultaneously meet the needs of another group—unmarried individuals who are otherwise unable to have children. Agencies prefer to place children in stable two-parent families whenever possible, which in effect discriminates against the unmarried. Single men have a harder time adopting than do single women, while LESBIANS and gay men have traditionally faced the most severe discrimination of all. These policies are slowly changing, state by state, and unmarried persons who meet the other criteria, understand the difficulties of single parenthood, and are willing to accept the challenge of a special needs child often make excellent parents. In these and other familial arrangements, children's need for loving, permanent homes must remain paramount.

SUGGESTED READINGS. Christine Adamec and William L. Pierce's *The Encyclopedia of Adoption* (1991)

presents the main issues and an extensive bibliography. Rita J. Simon and Howard Altstein's *Transracial Adoptees and Their Families* (1987), William Feigelman and Arnold R. Silverman's *Chosen Children* (1983), and Owen Gill and Barbara Jackson's *Adoption and Race* (1983) offer sociological analyses of the debate about transracial/transnational adoption, with special emphasis on African American children. Paul Sachdev's collection of essays, *Adoption: Current Issues and Trends* (1984), discusses the full spectrum of adoption-related issues.—*Susan Wladaver-Morgan*

Advertising: The advertising industry's relationship to various racial and ethnic groups, as well as to women, changed significantly in the late twentieth century. A number of factors were important in these changes; among them was the increasing (and belated) realization that non-Caucasian Americans represent a large and growing consumer base. Another impetus for change has been the slowly increasing importance of people other than white males within the advertising industry itself. By the early 1990's, for example, two large firms had hired women presidents.

Corporate Responses to American Diversity. The

A California billboard warns a large Spanish-speaking population of the dangers of second-hand smoke. (Valerie Marie)

advertising industry responded to its awareness of the buying power of various ethnic groups in a number of ways. Beginning in the 1960's (partly in response to the criticism of all-white advertising that grew out of the CIVIL RIGHTS movement), it began to include images of nonwhites in campaigns designed for the general American population. When a group of people was shown in a television commercial, for example, one of the group was often an AFRICAN AMERICAN or member of another minority. The other, more sophisticated, response lay in the industry's development of marketing strategies that specifically targeted a certain group.

Neither of these approaches was without controversy and criticism. The simple addition of one or two nonwhite faces to a group of people in a television or print ad soon brought charges of "tokenism"—the inclusion of a person of color as a visible but shallow attempt to demonstrate a commitment to civil rights. The "token Negro" was an image that was often criticized by civil rights leaders and other activists in the 1960's. The targeting of specific ethnic groups brought harsh condemnation in a few well-publicized incidents in which advertising companies cynically developed and marketed harmful or potentially harmful products (brands of cigarettes or malt liquor) to a particular group, such as inner-city African Americans, deemed to be especially receptive to certain exploitive marketing strategies.

Beginning in the mid-1970's, American corporations began to use special advertising campaigns and promotional packages, designed by their general marketing agencies, to reach minority consumers. This approach was intended simply to reach a greater consumer base. In the 1980's, with the emergence of MULTICULTURALISM and an emphasis on "POLITICAL CORRECTNESS," this process changed dramatically. Major corporations, including United Airlines, Campbell Soup, Citibank, and McDonald's, developed a variety of products and services that are culturally specific yet have broad appeal.

By the 1990's, advertisements included a broad spectrum of American groups as well as a variety of styles of portraying nonwhite Americans. Major corporations had taken note of the huge ethnic markets and expanded their television, radio, and print advertising campaigns to include minorities in much the same way that they had developed marketing strategies to address the spending habits of teenagers and senior citizens. In spite of controversies, advertising

had come a long way since the days when ads were created with a strictly white audience in mind. Gone were the days when such offensive racial or ethnic STEREOTYPES as the "Frito bandito" cartoon character were considered acceptable.

Impact on the African American Community. African Americans spend $280 to $300 billion annually on consumer products, including clothes, music, and automobiles. Studies have indicated that they have a preference for top-of-the-line merchandise and a high willingness to try new products. These statistics have not gone unnoticed by the advertising industry, which has defined its initiatives to strengthen its economic base among African Americans as imperative in a highly competitive field. The awakening sense of African American pride and identity in the United States since the 1960's has produced a desire for products that acknowledge and affirm cultural identity.

K mart, the second-largest retailer in the United States, hired black-oriented Burrell Advertising to coordinate a major marketing campaign focusing on selling products in African American periodicals and through radio advertising on stations with large African American listener bases. Toys "R" Us, the largest toy retailer in the United States, hired the Mingo Group to lead its campaign to court African American consumers.

Impact on the Asian American Community. Studies indicate that ASIAN AMERICANS have become the fastest growing minority group in the United States, increasing from a half million in 1970 to six million in 1990. This sizable market has not been overlooked by big business. On the West Coast, where a large number of Asian Americans live, marketing campaigns are considered ineffective unless built on an understanding of Asian consumer habits. Marketing executives recognize that many Asian immigrants are young adults who will soon enter their prime earning and spending years.

One research project, conducted by a New York advertising firm in conjunction with St. Johns University Institute, studied the buying habits of Asian Americans in an attempt to develop foreign-language advertising. A marketing survey designed for consumers of Chinese, Filipino, Asian Indian, Japanese, and Korean descent was circulated in a number of ethnic newspapers. The survey found important differences among the various nationalities; for example, the Chinese chewed the most gum, and Asian Indians preferred pizza restaurants to hamburger chains, perhaps because of their high rate of vegetarianism. The research indicated that Asian Americans spoke English more frequently at work than at home, validating the need to design language-specific programming for television and radio advertising.

Impact on the Latino Community. The LATINO COMMUNITY has received increasing attention from major corporations and advertising agencies, who recognize the viability of this large group's buying power. With more than twenty million Latino residents in the United States, ad agencies have sought to identify the distinct buying habits of this population. They have found that Latinos favor brand-name products and tend to shop together as a family unit. Marketing campaigns have been built around these findings in an attempt to capitalize on the patterns of consumer behavior within the Latino community. This family-oriented advertising has generally been considered more acceptable by Latinos than that which targets buyers with potentially harmful products, such as alcohol and tobacco, through billboards.

Some companies commit millions of dollars each year to advertising on Spanish-language television and radio networks, newspapers, and magazines. Mendoza, Dillon and Associates, the largest Latino advertising agency in the United States, is a multimillion dollar business. The economic impact of Latinos has modified their image in the media and has helped in the effort to reduce the amount of negative target advertising of alcohol and tobacco products to Latinos.

Impact on Women. About half of all people employed in the advertising industry are females; however, women have traditionally been relegated to lower-level positions in buying, research, and production. With the growth of women's general economic rights and power in American society, however, women are increasingly being placed in management roles. These promotions have led to changes in how women are depicted in ad campaigns.

Ads have traditionally depicted women as sex objects and "bimbos." Indeed, the presence of a beautiful woman has been considered essential to selling everything from liquor to cars. Since the 1970's, proponents of feminism have objected to such ads on the grounds that they debase women and promote sexist stereotypes. *Ms.* MAGAZINE, for example, began to refuse ads that it found offensive to women and eventually banned all advertising. Gradually, the advertising industry responded to women's concern by trying to reduce stereotyping.

By the 1990's, ads were focusing more on life from a female perspective. This was partly because women had gained some creative control as executives in advertising agencies. Two of the nation's top firms, DDB Needham (Chicago) and Oglivy & Mather (New York), hired female presidents, opening the door to greater leadership opportunities for women. Account management has usually been viewed as the training ground for advertising executives on the road to key managerial and decision-making positions, positions routinely held by men. An influx of female account managers is expected to bring about a more humane treatment of advertising subjects and to reduce the use of traditional stereotypes as well as unrealistic images such as the "superwoman."

Los Angeles' Chinatown attracts a large population of Chinese American consumers. (Valerie Marie)

Criticisms of Ethnic Advertising. The movement toward ethnic inclusiveness in the advertising industry, hailed by many, has also had staunch opponents. Most of the opposition has come in response to marketing tactics that appear to threaten the health of consumers. In 1990, R. J. Reynolds, the tobacco division of

RJR Nabisco, attempted to market "Uptown" cigarettes primarily to minorities. The product, packaged in a black and gold box, was marketed with the slogan, "The Place, The Taste," designed to provide a sense of having arrived. Angry protesters rallied against the release of the cigarette. The tremendous outcry caused Reynolds to withdraw the $10 million campaign.

In 1992, the Marin Institute, an advertising watchdog group advocating accurate and appropriate marketing, campaigned against the sale of St. Ides malt liquor, which was being marketed to minority youth by a Portland, Oregon, brewery. The group claimed that the product was being promoted as one that would increase sexual ability and that the ads featured gang symbolism. These and other promotions have been decried as exploitive, the result of manufacturers and advertisers who pay little attention to the health concerns of ethnic groups.

SUGGESTED READINGS. Among the books that contain information about advertising targeted at ethnic groups are *Ethnic Minority Media: An International Perspective* (1992), edited by Stephen Harold Riggens; *Black Economics: Solutions for Economic and Community Empowerment* (1992) by Jawanza Kunjufu; and *Latinos in a Changing U.S. Economy: Comparative Perspectives on Growing Inequality* (1993), edited by Rebecca Morales and Frank Bonilla. Specialized topics are examined in articles in advertising, business, and other journals. Examples include Robert Mayberry's "Targeting Blacks in Cigarette Billboard Advertising: Results from Down South," in *Health Values* 17 (Jan. 1, 1993), p. 28, and Joseph G. Albonetti's "Major Influences on Consumer Goods Marketers' Decision to Target to U.S. Hispanics," in *Journal of Advertising Research* 29 (Feb. 1, 1989), p. 9.—*Kenneth Anderson*

Affirmative action: Public and private programs in business, EDUCATION, and government that are designed to redress the effects of historical discrimination against minority groups and promote greater minority hiring or admissions. In some cases, affirmative action simply means that an employer or a college will mount aggressive recruitment drives to find qualified minorities to fill vacant positions. Promotion programs may also be set up to give preferential treatment to members of victimized groups in order to redress past inequities. At the extreme end of the scale, affirmative action involves the setting of quotas—a certain percentage of jobs or college places to be filled by minorities only.

Origins. The term affirmative action was first used by President John F. Kennedy in 1961, when he called for more equality of opportunity among the races in jobs provided by federal contractors. Contractors were told to set hiring goals for minority workers that would result in a work force that represented the ethnic diversity of the American population.

Affirmative action received a boost under the landmark CIVIL RIGHTS ACT OF 1964, which prohibited discrimination on the basis of race, color, or national origin in federally financed programs and by firms with twenty-five or more employees. The act, however, was couched in terms that favored equality of opportunity; it said nothing about equality of results.

The scope of affirmative action was vastly extended under the administration of President Richard Nixon, from 1969 to 1973. Programs were established to encourage employers to set goals, timetables, and preferences for minority hiring. The concept of affirmative action was upheld by a series of court cases in the late 1960's and early 1970's. For example, a Supreme Court decision invalidated intelligence tests and other criteria used in hiring because these tended, because of inherent biases in the tests, to discriminate against minorities.

Affirmative action policies showed quick results: Between 1974 and 1980, black male employment grew 17 percent among federal contractors. A particularly striking example was in public employment in Alabama, formerly a bastion of SEGREGATION. In 1972 a state judge ruled that the Alabama Department of Public Safety, which employed almost no blacks, had to impose a racially based quota, under which it would be required to hire one black trooper for each new white hired, until blacks made up 25 percent of the force. By 1985, Alabama had the most integrated state police force in the United States. Similar progress was made elsewhere. The police force in Washington, D.C., went from being 20 percent black in 1967 to 67 percent black in 1991, a figure which is much closer to the actual percentage of African Americans who live in the city. In the private sector, a 1990 survey found that all 202 companies surveyed had affirmative action programs. To take only one dramatic example: In 1962, International Business Machines (IBM) had only 750 black employees. In 1980, the figure was 16,546.

In spite of these gains, the pace of affirmative action slowed for the most part during the 1980's. The first and second administrations of Ronald Reagan, from 1981 to 1989, did little to promote the policy. Admini-

Active recruitment and hiring of minority candidates has helped to integrate the work force at all levels. (James L. Shaffer)

stration officials preferred instead to refer to a "color-blind" society in which everyone had an equal opportunity to succeed, regardless of race, so that no one should be given special preferences.

Supreme Court Rulings. In 1988-1989 this conservative view found its way into several U.S. Supreme Court rulings that limited affirmative action. In *Richmond v. J. A. Croson Co.* (1989), for example, the court ruled as unconstitutional a policy in which the city of Richmond, Virginia, set aside 30 percent of its public works contracts for minority-owned firms. In 1989, more than thirty-six states and two hundred local governments had similar programs. The Court ruled that the Richmond policy violated the constitutional rights of white contractors to equal protection under the law, but it stopped short of invalidating all government-sponsored affirmative action programs.

Other Supreme Court rulings made it more difficult for minority workers to bring lawsuits against employees alleging bias. These cases included *Patterson v. McLean Credit Union* (1989) and *Jett v. Dallas Independent School District* (1989). In the first of these, the Court ruled that minorities could not sue private parties for discrimination under the old Civil Rights Act of 1866. This act had been used successfully to challenge employment discrimination in the 1960's and 1970's. In the second case, the same ruling was applied to the suing of state or local governments for racial discrimination. Such rulings reflected the shift to the right that had taken place as a result of the three Court appointees (Justices Sandra Day O'Connor, Antonin Scalia, and Anthony Kennedy) made by President Reagan.

Affirmative Action in Education. Affirmative action has been aggressively applied in the sphere of education. Colleges and universities have developed different admission standards for different ethnic groups in order to create a more representative diversity among students and faculty. The results have been mixed. College enrollment of African Americans has increased from only 15.5 percent of the black population in 1970 to 23.5 percent in 1989. Yet the college dropout rate is high for African Americans. At the University of California at Berkeley, for example, only one in three black students graduates. Among Latino students, the figure is less than one in two. The number of African American students who pursue graduate study has declined. In 1988, of 13,158 American Ph.D.s awarded in the sciences, only 275 went to African Americans. This represents a much lower percentage than in 1977.

The constitutionality of affirmative action policies in education was challenged in 1978 in REGENTS OF THE UNIVERSITY OF CALIFORNIA V. BAKKE, the renowned "Bakke case." This Supreme Court case was brought by a white student, Allan Bakke, whose application for admission to the University of California School of Medicine was rejected. Bakke charged that his application was rejected because of a university policy of allocating places to fulfill minority quotas. The high Court ruled in 1978 that ADMISSION QUOTAS were prohibited under the Civil Rights Act of 1964, but that the act did not bar the university from using race as a factor in admissions.

Growing Controversy. When affirmative action programs were first introduced in the 1960's, there was fairly widespread agreement among Americans of all racial groups that such programs were necessary. Through the CIVIL RIGHTS MOVEMENT, most whites had become acutely aware that centuries of oppression had to be countered by active, government-sponsored programs that enhanced training and employment opportunities for African Americans. During the 1980's, however, affirmative action became increasingly controversial. There was a white backlash which exacerbated rather than alleviated racial tensions. Many whites complained of "reverse discrimination," in which a qualified white applicant would be automatically rejected, based on his or her race, for a vacant job that fell under a quota earmarked for African Americans or other minorities. In many cases, whites suspected that minorities were being hired over white applicants even when the whites had superior qualifications for the job.

Although hundreds of thousands of minority group members have benefited from affirmative action programs, leading to the emergence of an authentic African American and Latino middle class, many minority leaders in the 1990's have begun to rethink their traditional support for such programs. Some civil rights leaders claim that affirmative action programs are aimed at the better-educated, middle-class minorities and therefore do not help those who need it most: poor blacks, Latinos, and others living in the inner cities. These leaders claim that too much of the contemporary civil rights effort has focused on enabling qualified African Americans to move up the corporate ladder and break through the "GLASS CEILING" of hidden RACISM that often bars their promotions to high-level management positions.

Many successful African Americans are also increasingly concerned that their achievements are being undermined rather than enhanced by affirmative action. If they are hired or promoted to a responsible job, they have to live with the perception by whites that they got the job only because they are black. No matter how hard successful blacks work, or how well they perform, they feel stigmatized and not fully accepted in their own right.

Affirmative action hiring has opened doors to many qualified women of color. (Dick Young, Unicorn Stock Photos)

This point of view found expression in at least two important books by African American scholars. In The Content of Our Character (1990), San Jose State University professor Shelby Steele argued that affirmative action undermines black self-confidence. He pointed out that African Americans who attend predominantly white schools are five times more likely to drop out as whites. Steele claimed that what is needed is not preferential treatment but a greater emphasis on education and self-reliance from within the African American community, which will help to free it from dependency on the dominant white culture. Stephen L. Carter, as a professor of law at Yale University who benefited from affirmative action to become one of the youngest tenured professors in the country's history, in Reflections of an Affirmative Action Baby (1991), noted that the "extra degree of scrutiny that attaches to those who are suspected of having benefitted from racial preference" was burdensome.

Most civil rights leaders, however, continue to believe that black conservatives such as Steele and Carter underestimate the extent of white resistance to black progress (and that of other minorities). They point out that past racism has left minorities with a significant disadvantage when trying to compete with whites. While opponents of affirmative action claim that the playing field is now open to all, and therefore no one needs to be given preferential treatment, supporters of affirmative action say this ignores the fact that whites have been given a three-hundred-year advantage over people of color.

Affirmative action was a leading issue when Judge Clarence THOMAS, who is African American, was nominated to the U.S. Supreme Court in 1991. The conservative Thomas had spoken out against affirmative action policies. Thomas' critics, who included many civil rights leaders, were quick to point out that Thomas himself had been admitted to Yale Law School in 1971 under an affirmative action program that was designed to increase minority enrollment to 10 percent of the entering class. Critics also said that Thomas' nomination to the Supreme Court was a result of affirmative action on the part of President George Bush, who, it was argued, had invented a Supreme Court "quota" in replacing Justice Thurgood MARSHALL, the Court's first black judge, with Thomas. Bush denied this, saying that Thomas was simply the best man for the job.

Whatever the controversies surrounding affirmative action, such programs are not likely to be abandoned quickly. Most responsible leaders agree that American society must continue to make a special effort to absorb minority groups into the mainstream, or else face the disaffection and alienation of a significant percentage of the population. Economic analysts point out that changing American demographics (by the year 2000, women, minorities, and recent immigrants will make up a majority of the work force) and the need for highly trained employees who can succeed in an increasingly competitive global economy make affirmative action not only morally desirable but also economically necessary.

SUGGESTED READINGS. Affirmative Action, edited by Donald Altschiller (1991), is a useful collection of previously published articles covering topics such as the legal dimensions of affirmative action, its role in education, white reaction, and the prospects for affirmative action in the twenty-first century. Frederick R. Lynch's *Invisible Victims: White Males and the Crisis of Affirmative Action* (1989) discusses white reaction and its dangers. Stephanie L. Witt's *The Pursuit of Race and Gender Equity in American Academe* (1990) is a detailed study of the effects of affirmative action in education. The complexities and shifts in Supreme Court attitudes to affirmative action are traced in Bernard Schwartz's *Behind Bakke: Affirmative Action and the Supreme Court* (1988).—Bryan Aubrey

Afghan Americans: The modern country of Afghanistan sits between Iran and Pakistan, just below the former Soviet Union. About 60 percent of the Afghan people are descendants of the native Pushtun, or Pathan, tribes. Yet Afghanistan has a heterogeneous population. This reflects the waves of central Asian invaders that crossed and conquered the country on their way to attack India or Iran. Islamic Arabs brought their RELIGION when they invaded Afghanistan in the eighth and ninth centuries. As a consequence, almost all Afghans are MUSLIMS.

In ancient times the area that became Afghanistan was known as Ariana and as Bactria. In the Middle Ages it was called Khorasan. In the nineteenth century, this land acted as a buffer between the Russians in central Asia and the British, who controlled India. In the 1880's, the territory united under one government and for the first time officially adopted the name "Afghanistan."

The Afghan people maintain passionate tribal, religious, and family loyalties that outweigh their allegiance to the state. Tribal rivalry has always played a divisive role in Afghan politics. In the 1980's, the Soviet Union used military force to back a Marxist regime there. When the Russians withdrew their troops at the end of the decade, the Communist government soon fell. The lack of a strong central government plunged the country into a ferocious civil war.

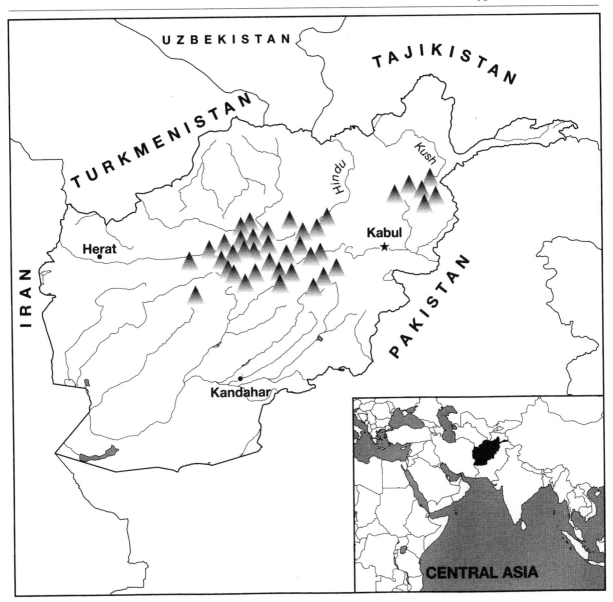

AFGHANISTAN

Although exact records were not kept then, the first Afghans probably came to the United States in the 1930's and 1940's. Immigration has been sporadic since that time, with a marked increase after 1978 because of the fighting there.

In 1980, there were about twenty-five hundred Afghans in the United States. Many were students who remained in the country after their visas expired. Almost all Afghan Americans belong to the elite class of their native country. They are highly educated and often teach at colleges and universities in the United States.

Many Afghan Americans settled near WASHINGTON, D.C., or in LOS ANGELES and NEW YORK. They are educated professionals who are drawn to big cities by employment opportunities. A number of them have opened Afghan restaurants, introducing Americans to their cuisine. Afghan Americans generally retain their Muslim faith in their adopted country. They give their children Islamic or Afghan names to maintain cultural ties to their homeland. They have been active in humanitarian relief efforts and political organizations to bring peace to their homeland.

AFL. *See* **American Federation of Labor (AFL)**

African American–American Indian relations: African Americans and American Indians share a historical bond in that they were the first two groups to experience racial oppression and exploitation at the hands of Europeans in the New World. In both North and South America, European colonists—primarily the Spanish and, later, the English—needed sources of cheap labor to do the mining and harvesting upon which their colonial economies depended. Initially the Europeans believed that American Indians represented a ready-made labor force, but this idea proved unworkable. The colonists found African slaves, on the other hand, well-suited to their work requirements.

Another bond between the two groups is that their cultural traditions have more in common with each other than with those of European Americans. Blacks and Indians traditionally shared what could be called a "group view" of social purpose: The group was viewed as the heart of life. This idea was very different from the individualistic social philosophy of the European PURITANS. Children and elderly people were esteemed, and the spirits of ancestors were cherished. RELIGION was not separated from daily life but was considered a part of all life. There existed a rigid set of rituals for accomplishing social goals. Both African and American Indian social systems were based on economic cooperation rather than competition.

In the eighteenth and nineteenth centuries, the DOMINANT CULTURE of the United States used many stereotypical images to continue its subordination of African Americans and to justify the institution of SLAVERY. Many of these representations were also applied to American Indians (similar images were also used against Asians, Latinos, and certain white ethnic groups, such as IRISH and ITALIAN AMERICANS). These stereotypes portrayed minority groups as being lazy, unclean, promiscuous, heathen, and childlike. In sociological terms, these cultural representations both "pushed" African Americans who were escaping or rebelling against slavery and "pulled" American Indians to accept them in their villages. Eventually, small colonies developed in which fugitive slaves (MAROONS) established settlements, frequently with Indians.

The maroon colonies were organized to maintain family, agriculture, and defense. A minority of them engaged in raids on rich Europeans. Most of the maroon colonies developed some cultural constancy within which American Indians and African Americans shared methods of planting, irrigating, and harvesting crops. African patterns became prominent in the maroon settlements in terms of agriculture, architecture, defense, and culture. INTERMARRIAGE was common, and a new ethnic group, "black Indians," evolved.

The British introduced slavery to the American Indians in the mid-1700's. The FIVE CIVILIZED TRIBES of the Southeast included the CHEROKEES, Chickasaws, CHOCTAWS, Creeks, and Seminoles; all except the Seminoles practiced slavery. Their practice of slavery was distinctive, however, in that slave children were "free" and slaves were allowed to marry into the tribe. Indian slaves were generally treated with respect.

In the twentieth century, African Americans and American Indians have been brought into close proximity as Indians have moved into urban areas where African Americans live. Between 1877 and 1966, American Indians were dispossessed of 60 percent of their land base, primarily through the General Allotment Act (DAWES ACT), which forcibly divided reservation holdings into individual parcels. Increasingly, American Indians moved into inner-city GHETTOS, living among poor African Americans; by 1970, only 39 percent of the American Indians lived on RESERVATIONS.

Although the two groups share a common bond of centuries of oppression by the United States' dominant white culture, there are differences. Indians did not suffer the chains of slavery, for example, but they were displaced from their land and saw their numbers decimated by disease. In the 1960's, the activism of the CIVIL RIGHTS MOVEMENT impressed young American Indians and led to the formation of groups such as the activist AMERICAN INDIAN MOVEMENT (AIM) that used protests and confrontation to bring attention to injustices.

Since then, American Indians and African Americans have sometimes united in support of particular causes. During 1991 and 1992, for example, American Indian groups across the United States held protests as the year-long celebration of the five-hundredth anniversary of Christopher COLUMBUS' 1492 voyage to the Americas began. In many cities they were joined by African Americans, PUERTO RICANS, MEXICAN AMERICANS, and other groups denouncing the human rights violations in their collective experiences.

SUGGESTED READINGS. William Loren Katz's *Black*

Indians (1986) and Rodolfo Acuña's *Occupied America* (1981) present introductory histories of the relationship between American Indians and African Americans. Additional information can be found in Steve Talbot's *Roots of Oppression* (1981) and Ronald Takaki's *Iron Cases: Race and Culture in Nineteenth Century America* (1979).

African American colleges. *See* **Colleges—African American**

African American Evangelical and Pentecostal congregations. *See* **Evangelical and Pentecostal congregations—African American**

African American–Jewish American relations: Until about the mid-1960's, relations were generally friendly between African Americans and American Jews. Both groups had a history of oppression and persecution as minority groups, and both found common ground in working to eliminate PREJUDICE and DISCRIMINATION in American society through the CIVIL RIGHTS MOVEMENT. They had some common enemies, such as RESTRICTIVE COVENANTS that forced them to live in certain neighborhoods and the KU KLUX KLAN, which targeted both groups for harassment and violence. They also shared (and continue to share) basically liberal political views and strong support of the DEMOCRATIC PARTY. After the turbulent 1960's, however, the circumstances and interests of the two groups began to diverge as the movement for black liberation became more militant, ZIONISM became an issue, and intergroup violence erupted in NEW YORK CITY.

The problems underlying the conflict stem from a variety of sources. Both African Americans and Jews feel deep frustration with the social and economic oppression they have experienced. There is a lack of cultural and religious understanding about one another in

Nation of Islam leader Louis Farrakhan (speaking) has incited tension between African Americans and Jews by making openly anti-Semitic remarks. (AP/Wide World Photos)

spite of their shared minority status, whether the issue is THE HOLOCAUST or BLACK NATIONALISM. Tension and competition arise between oppressed people when there are limited or decreasing resources; in particular, Jews were ambivalent about aspects of AFFIRMATIVE ACTION that would tend to exclude them from certain jobs while helping blacks. Differences over Israel and over certain American political races have also divided the two groups in a war of words.

From Cooperation to Conflict. The bond between blacks and Jews in the United States dates back to the early 1900's, when the NATIONAL ASSOCIATION FOR THE ADVANCEMENT OF COLORED PEOPLE (NAACP) was formed. American Jews generously supported its efforts and the Spingarn brothers each served as its president, founding the prestigious SPINGARN MEDAL for blacks who made significant achievements. In the 1950's and 1960's, Jews joined the Civil Rights movement in great numbers and contributed much of the money to sustain it. Jews and blacks walked hand-in-hand during protest marches, and two Jews (Andrew Goodman and Michael Schwerner) were among the three civil rights workers murdered by the Klan in Philadelphia, Mississippi, in 1964. Martin Luther KING, JR., had many close contacts in the Jewish community, with whom he expressed solidarity.

The rise of the BLACK POWER MOVEMENT in the late 1960's led to a call for all-black leadership of the civil rights struggle and a tendency to push out Jewish activists. Black Muslim leader MALCOLM X made a number of ANTI-SEMITIC remarks and spread the notion of Jews as exploiters of those living in the black GHETTO, since Jews were often owners of small businesses and rental properties there. Many African Americans resented what they saw as the growing success and prominence of Jews in certain fields while people of color were still economically oppressed. Meanwhile, some Jews felt threatened by government affirmative action policies in EDUCATION and EMPLOYMENT, since as a very small minority (about 2 percent of the American population), they had nothing to gain by quotas and in some areas (such as university employment) had much to lose. Nevertheless, in many cities, blacks and Jews maintained powerful political coalitions, such as the one that helped elect Tom BRADLEY as the first African American mayor of LOS ANGELES.

The conflict escalated into a war of rhetoric in the late 1970's and early 1980's. Some militant black leaders joined Third World countries in efforts to discredit Zionism, calling it a form of RACISM. This stung many American Jews, who believed that Zionism had been their own national liberation movement and who were strong supporters of Israel. African Americans further criticized Israel's treatment of Palestinians as well as its extensive trade with racist South Africa. Among those to meet with Palestinian leader Yasir Arafat was African American presidential primary candidate Jesse JACKSON. His casual reference to New York City as "hymietown" (a play on a common ethnic slur) in 1984 alienated Jewish voters, as did his close affiliation with Louis FARRAKHAN, head of the NATION OF ISLAM.

Relations between Jews and the Black Muslims had long been strained. Nation of Islam doctrine mixed the teachings of Islam and the tenets of black nationalism with a strong racial slant against Jews and whites in general. Farrakhan, who made vicious anti-Semitic remarks (such as calling JUDAISM a "gutter religion"), enjoyed a huge following in African American communities. Whenever Farrakhan was invited to speak in a public place, there was controversy and black-Jewish relations worsened. Yet Jackson and many influential African Americans defended the Nation of Islam for its success in promoting discipline, self-sufficiency, and black enterprise in poor, INNER-CITY areas.

Violence in New York. New York City, where large numbers of African Americans and Jews live, became a flash point for black-Jewish conflict. The stage was set in 1968, when a mostly Jewish teachers' union clashed with black neighborhood councils who demanded greater control over their schools. Later, tension was evident on the streets of parts of Brooklyn, where growing numbers of ultra-Orthodox Hasidic Jews were moving into or near predominantly black neighborhoods.

Tension between the two groups simmered in the Crown Heights neighborhood until it erupted in the worst anti-Semitic riot in American history in 1991. Crown Heights was home to large numbers of African American and Caribbean people and a visible concentration of Hasidic Jews, who are recognized by their traditional black coats and hats. The area is literally a community divided by a six-lane highway. In spite of each group's history of persecution and oppression, this highway symbolically reflects the psychological and emotional chasm between them. The conflict that evolved has been described as "a clash of two disparate worlds sharing the same streets, each viewing itself as the victim," or more succinctly as a "victim's competition." It could also be described as America's black-Jewish conflict in microcosm.

Resentment in Crown Heights was mutual. African Americans were angry at the Jews for allegedly buying up property in the black section of the community, not repairing it, and holding on to it for future profit. In addition, blacks had long felt that the Hasidic community used its political clout to win a disproportionate share of community services and preferential treatment (such as police escorts for their religious leader, the Lubavitcher Rebbe, and closure of part of the highway on the Sabbath and other religious holidays). While blacks accuse the Hasidic Jews of ignoring their presence and needs, the Jews feel that black violence has made the area unsafe. Each group knows little about the beliefs and lifestyles of the other, although some individuals reportedly have friendly neighborly contact.

Violence between the groups was not new; in 1986, for example, three members of a Hasidic patrol were found guilty of beating a black teenager with a bat, hammer, and hose. In 1987, a Jewish man's face was slashed by a black and in 1989, another Jew who later died was beaten unconscious by a group of black teens.

August 19, 1991, was a hot evening in this neighborhood plagued with the problems common to an urban ghetto, and the streets were filled with African American youth. The problem began with an automobile accident involving the last car in a police-escorted motorcade transporting the eighty-nine-year-old Lubavitcher Rebbe to his weekly visit to his wife's grave. The car ran a red light, swerved onto the curb, killed a seven-year-old African American child, and injured another child. Rumor spread that the ambulance responding to the call was Hasidic-run and that its personnel tended to the Hasidic driver while ignoring the black children. Police later defended the driver's actions, stating that officers were attempting to remove the driver from the angry crowd that had gathered and that city paramedics were en route to treat the youngsters.

For three nights following this incident, angry mobs torched cars, looted stores, and set buildings on fire. Even Mayor DAVID DINKINS, an African American who called for order, was hit and booed by the demonstrators. The community finally quieted down after 1,500 riot-clad police were called to duty, 163 people were arrested, 66 civilians and 173 police were in-

jured, and 28 police cars were smashed. In the course of the riot, a twenty-nine-year-old rabbinical scholar from Australia, Yankel Rosenbaum, was surrounded by a mob of angry blacks and stabbed to death.

Both groups saw the other as the perpetrator of the violence that resulted. African Americans questioned what they saw as the indifference of the Hasidic community toward the death of a child, which they felt could have been avoided. The Jews felt that they were victimized when the alleged murderer of Rosenbaum was acquitted and protested vigorously. They turned their resentment toward the black mayor, whom they felt condoned the violence perpetrated by the black residents of Crown Heights. Dinkins was deeply hurt by the accusations because of his long record of support for Jewish American causes and for Israel, as well as his previous ability to win the Jewish vote.

Efforts to heal the Crown Heights community included a gathering of twelve hundred people at the Apollo Theater, where a documentary was shown on the black soldiers who liberated Jews from Nazi concentration camps during World War II. Jesse Jackson spoke at the rally and urged both blacks and Jews to remember that they are bound by historical links. Other groups met both formally and informally to heal the rift, which had spread to blacks and Jews elsewhere in the city who identified with the anger of each group. One hopeful sign was a band of Hasidic musicians who performed RAP MUSIC with a message of peace at local black high schools, and who won praise from some local black musicians.

Efforts at Dialogue. Since the 1980's, African American and Jewish American leaders have come together for dialogue on the black-Jewish conflict at both the national and the local levels. For example, rabbis and black ministers have encouraged their congregations to attend each other's services so as to better understand each other. In 1991, Samuel DuBois Cook, president of Dillard University in New Orleans, Louisiana, sponsored the second annual conference on black-Jewish relations. Cook is a protégé of Benjamin Mays, former president of Morehouse College, who mentored Martin Luther King, Jr. Cook established the National Center for Black-Jewish Relations at his university to serve as a clearinghouse for information on the topic and to offer relevant courses. Farrakhan has not been allowed to speak at Dillard since Cook feels that it would deeply offend some people, mainly Jews. Some critics have questioned his reasons for trying to improve the relations of African Americans and Jews, stating that it is a ploy to attract Jewish money to Dillard—a charge that Cook denies.

The issues for blacks and Jews are different, yet both derive from the challenges of multiculturalism. Unfortunately, a legacy of mistrust and resentment has come to replace that of cooperation and friendship between two groups that have long shared the pain of bigotry and oppression.

African American–Korean American relations: Most studies on this topic have found relations between these two groups to be relatively amicable. The serious conflicts have emerged in big cities such as NEW YORK and LOS ANGELES, where new immigrant, middle-class Koreans have established small businesses in predominantly poor black GHETTOS. In such neighborhoods, the Korean owners of mom-and-pop grocery stores are a

Korean Americans meet with African American leader Jesse Jackson to discuss racial relations after the 1992 Los Angeles riots. (Steve Young)

SUGGESTED READINGS. For more information, see *Broken Alliance: The Turbulent Times Between Blacks and Jews in America* (1988) by Jonathan Kaufman. Hillel Levine and Lawrence Hamilton's *The Death of a Jewish American Community: A Tragedy of Good Intentions* (1992) presents a profile of relations in one Boston community. William M. Phillips, Jr.'s *An Illustrious Alliance: The African American and Jewish American Communities* (1991) presents useful historical background.—*Charolette R. Bell*

strikingly visible minority both for their economic success and their sometimes tragic social failures. It appears that there are at least three causal factors at work in the Korean-black conflicts: differences in social class (status), differences in cultural values and behaviors, and mutual hostility based on feelings of relative deprivation vis-a-vis white society.

Like other Asians, KOREAN AMERICANS tend to be more formal and conservative in dress and manner than the more informal, casually or poorly dressed ghetto residents. Since most of these Koreans are new immigrants with a poor command of American English and even less of BLACK ENGLISH, there is often poor communication leading to gross misunderstandings between Koreans and African Americans. In Korea, avoiding direct eye contact is considered a sign of politeness, whereas such behavior is often perceived as unfriendly, hostile, and even racist by African Americans. Many blacks mistakenly believe that the Koreans are able to start their own businesses because they get special financial support from the U.S. government and from banks. Most Korean American businesses, however, are established with the help of Korean mutual aid societies that offer credit and loans; many Koreans actually resent white institutions for denying them loans that would have allowed them to set up shop in middle-class neighborhoods. Under these circumstances, Korean Americans and African Americans each become the surrogate SCAPEGOAT for frustrations caused in large part by the PREJUDICE and DISCRIMINATION of the white majority.

Various tensions led to the vandalism and burglary of Korean American businesses beginning in the 1980's. A Korean store owner struck back in the tragic killing of Latasha Harlins, an African American teenager, in Los Angeles on March 16, 1991, by Soon Ja Du, co-owner of a small Korean grocery and liquor store. The store had been held up three times and burglarized forty other times in two years. After arguing with Harlins over her allegedly stealing a $1.79 bottle of orange juice, Du shot her in the head. Following Harlins' death, African Americans in Los Angeles boycotted Korean stores, several Korean stores were burned, and twelve Koreans were killed in robberies. During the LOS ANGELES RIOTS of 1992, hundreds of Korean stores were burned or looted.

To prevent future tragedies, blacks and Koreans in Los Angeles formed the Black-Korean Alliance. In face-to-face meetings, members encouraged dialogue, cooperation, and learning about each other's cultures, while Korean merchants began to hire neighborhood blacks to work in their stores.

SUGGESTED READINGS. The best general source on the nature of subcultures and minorities in American culture is Norman Yetman's *Majority and Minority* (1991). Excellent pieces specifically devoted to the clash between Korean businesspersons and African Americans are Chris Herlinger's "Culture Clash," in *Scholastic Update* 124 (March 20, 1992), pp. 16-18, and Earl Ofari Hutchinson's "Fighting the Wrong Enemy," in *The Nation*, November 4, 1991, pp. 554-556.

African American population—diversity within: Although African Americans have often been presented as members of a monolithic community, they are in fact members of a community teeming with diversity. This diversity can be seen in the racial and socioeconomic backgrounds of African Americans, as well as their cultural interests, religious beliefs, and political opinions.

Racial Diversity. Experts have estimated that four out of five African Americans have at least one white ancestor and that at least one out of five white Americans have at least one black ancestor. Historically, whites, blacks, and American Indians have engaged in racial mixing since early colonial times. Some unions between blacks and whites were the result of labor conditions on plantations and farms where white indentured servants worked and lived with black slaves. Though intermarriage was discouraged by custom and later by statute, a large community of free blacks emerged during the colonial period as a result of intermarriage between slaves and indentured servants. During the era of slavery, some black women were subjected to rape and others were kept as concubines by white masters; mixed-blood offspring of these unions were known as mulattoes. In antebellum Louisiana, where slave women from Africa and the Caribbean intermarried with or were kept as concubines by French Creole planters, terms such as quadroon and octoroon were used to describe mixed-blood Creoles based on the perceived degree of their black ancestry. Some American Indian tribes, such as the CHEROKEES and Chickasaws, owned black slaves with whom they intermarried or had illicit relationships. The Seminoles, a group of Indians who had fled to Spanish-controlled Florida after being forced from their traditional lands by English settlers, provided a safe haven for slave runaways; intermarriage between the two peoples led to the development of Black Seminoles.

In more recent times, there have been mixtures between those of African descent and various Asian populations. In the wake of conflicts in Korea and Vietnam, African American soldiers who were posted in these areas brought Asian women home as war brides. AMERASIAN children born of unions between black soldiers and Vietnamese women were allowed to immigrate to the United States under provisions of the Amerasian Homecoming Act of 1987. African Americans of mixed racial heritage have begun to demand that the U.S. BUREAU OF THE CENSUS and other official bodies designate a category that recognizes and accurately reflects the reality of their mixed heritage.

Regional and Cultural Diversity. Estimates from the 1990 census show that the African American population stands at somewhat more than 35 million. Although they live in all regions of the United States, African Americans are found in concentrated numbers in the South and in the large cities of the Northeast and Midwest. More than half of all African Americans reside in the eleven southern states that once formed the Confederacy. In contrast to this overwhelmingly rural concentration, the largest black urban population is found in the state of New York, with a total population of more than 2 million and the largest urban concentration found in NEW YORK CITY.

It should be noted that what makes the black population of New York City unique is that a substantial portion of this community is composed of immigrants hailing from Jamaica, Trinidad, Barbados, and other Caribbean islands. Famous AFRICAN AMERICANS OF WEST INDIAN DESCENT include Academy Award-winning actor Sidney POITIER (born to Bahamian immigrants), General Colin POWELL (born to Jamaican immigrants), former Congresswoman Shirley CHISHOLM (born in Barbados), and civil rights activist Stokeley CARMICHAEL (born in Trinidad). Some scholars have suggested that West Indian immigrants have developed a different collective psychology than that of American-born blacks. Although sharing a common history with American-born blacks—African ancestry, a slave past, and the post-emancipation experience of racism and segregation—West Indian blacks are perhaps more akin to other immigrant populations who have come to the United States with a clear determination to achieve social and economic success for themselves and their children. This strong desire for upward mobility has sometimes outweighed the ties of racial solidarity and has led to conflict between West Indians and other blacks, particularly in New York City.

Economic Diversity. African Americans represent a variety of economic backgrounds. Although there are growing numbers of black entrepreneurs and wealthy black celebrities from the sports and entertainment fields, the African American population is overwhelmingly composed of working-class wage earners. African Americans are overrepresented in trade unions with respect to their percentage of the overall American population. During the CIVIL RIGHTS MOVEMENT

of the 1960's, these trade unions played a pivotal role in organizing black workers and in mobilizing support for their demands for improved working conditions and opportunities. Indeed, from that period through the early 1990's, more blacks were union members than were members of civil rights organizations. As a result of their concentration in industrial jobs such as auto manufacturing, African Americans have been hard hit by the decline of manufacturing industries during the 1980's and 1990's in the Midwest. A significant percentage of the black membership of the United Auto Workers, the United Rubber Workers, and the United Steelworkers has left these unions because they have been unable to find other jobs in these industries.

Similarly, African Americans have been overrepresented in public sector employment, particularly in civil service employers such as the U.S. Postal Service. While they have been largely absent and thus have wielded relatively little influence in the private sector—where power depends on one's status as a shareholder, an executive, or a member of the board of directors—African Americans have wielded increased influence in the public sector, where their voting power has influenced the electoral process. The reforms instituted by the VOTING RIGHTS ACT OF 1965 provided the foundation for the rise of black mayors in large cities and the increase in the number of black legislators—trends that simultaneously led to an increase in the appointment and hiring of black public sector employees, including firefighters, police officers, and sanitation workers. With the attack on big government launched during the Reagan and Bush administrations, many public sector jobs filled by black employees have disappeared. This trend, like the decline in manufacturing jobs, has had a disproportionately negative effect on the African American community.

The implementation of AFFIRMATIVE ACTION programs in the public sector also accelerated the hiring of African Americans in the private sector. Affirmative action regulations mandated that a fixed percentage of government contracts be awarded to minority-owned businesses. These provisions encouraged the expansion of a black entrepreneurial class—a class that had developed in the post-CIVIL WAR era in such professions as banking, insurance, undertaking, and publishing. This black business class continues to prosper, as seen in the success of John H. Johnson's Johnson Publishing, which produces the popular mass-circulation

A recent African immigrant to the United States hugs her grandchildren. (Aneal Vohra, Unicorn Stock Photos)

magazines *Ebony* and *Jet*, and Pierre Sutton's Inner City Broadcasting, which owns and operates a number of radio stations across the nation as well as television and cable television franchises. Affirmative action has also increased the number of African Americans who have entered the professions, particularly law, medicine, and academia.

Historically, African Americans have played a significant role in the fields of entertainment and sports. As incomes in these areas of employment have increased, many black celebrities have used this income as capital to be invested in various business concerns. Among the top hundred businesses of 1991 as named by *Black Enterprise* magazine, The Bing Group and Superb Manufacturing, Inc., were owned by former Detroit Pistons star Dave Bing; Orchem, Inc., and Orpack-Stone Corporation were owned by former Milwaukee Bucks star Oscar Robertson; and Crest Computer Supply was owned by Football Hall of Famer Gale Sayers. Mel Farr, a former football star with the Detroit Lions, is one of the leading black employers in DETROIT.

Religious Diversity. African Americans have diverse religious backgrounds. While overwhelming numbers of African Americans are affiliated with PROTESTANT churches, particularly black BAPTIST and METHODIST congregations, there are significant regional variations; for example, Louisiana has a significant percentage of black CATHOLICS. Some African Americans have joined PENTECOSTAL and Holiness sects, while others have left the Protestant faith in favor of the separatist teachings of the NATION OF ISLAM. As part of an ongoing trend of religious pluralism, many African Americans have become adherents of Islam, Judaism, and BUDDHISM; others have subscribed to indigenous African religions or have become adherents of syncretic religions such as SANTERÍA, whose roots are in Africa but whose traditions draw upon a mix of New World traditions.

Political and Ideological Diversity. African Americans' political beliefs reflect the wide spectrum of ideologies found in the United States. While the liberal political beliefs of many African Americans place them within the left portion of the spectrum, there is a growing contingent of black conservative thinkers. The views of those such as U.S. Supreme Court Justice Clarence THOMAS reflect this conservative movement within the black community. While liberals favor the political message espoused by Jesse Jackson, conservatives are likely to side with the vision of community self-sufficiency espoused by Robert L. Woodson, founder of the National Center for Neighborhood Enterprise. African American voters still overwhelmingly support the liberal ideology of the DEMOCRATIC PARTY, as reflected in the political affiliation of the forty-member congressional Black Caucus, of whom only one—Gary Franks of Connecticut—is a Republican.

Although there are some trends within the African American community that reflect a certain degree of solidarity—their location on the political spectrum, for example—it would be a mistake to overlook the burgeoning evidence of diversity among its members. Migration trends, for example, have brought more African Americans to the western United States at the same time that many upwardly mobile black urban residents have chosen to move to the suburbs. Affirmative action probably will continue to increase the economic diversity within the African American community. Black religious, political, and social organizations will continue to provide alternative forums for addressing the various needs of African Americans. Diversity will no doubt continue to be a hallmark of the African American experience.

SUGGESTED READINGS. Works that explore issues of racial diversity within the African American community include Virginia R. Domínguez's *White by Definition* (1986), Joel Williamson's *New People: Miscegenation and Mulattoes in the United States* (1980), and Kathy Russell, Midge Wilson, and Ron Hall's *The Color Complex: The Last Taboo Among African-Americans* (1993). On the issues of affirmative action, the law, and related matters, see Gerald Horne's *Reversing Discrimination: The Case for Affirmative Action* (1992). On the impact of changes in the U.S. economy on African Americans, see Barry Bluestone and Irving Bluestone's *Negotiating the Future: A Labor Perspective on American Business* (1992).—*Gerald Horne*

African American studies programs: Academic units that integrate the systematic study and interpretation of the black experience in the United States, as well as the collective experiences of people of Africa and of African descent, into the curricula of institutions of HIGHER EDUCATION. Variously labeled Afro-American, pan-African, Africana, and black studies programs, they consist of four interrelated components: curriculum, cultural/community programming, research, and evaluation. Black studies programs have made a major impact on American higher education, precipitating the emergence of other ethnic studies programs as well as WOMEN'S STUDIES and GAY AND LESBIAN STUDIES programs, while reforming the traditional Eurocentric curricula.

In general, the purpose of black studies programs is to reform American EDUCATION radically so that it is historically accurate and equally reflective of the integral historical, social, and cultural role of blacks in American and world civilizations. Although the objectives for individual black studies programs vary, most aim to counteract myths, STEREOTYPES, and distortions about the history and social roles of Africa and its descendants in the world; revise the perceptual foundations of traditional academic disciplines so that the African American experience has educational parity with other ethnic experiences; engage in ongoing collection, research, and dissemination of scholarly information and increase the number of graduate programs in order to develop a cadre of trained scholars in the field; encourage the use of diverse theoretical approaches rather than a single theory, model, or methodology to address the unique nature of the black experience; and develop social policies to meet the challenges that African Americans face within the multicultural context of American society.

Historical Foundations. The ideological foundations for African American studies programs were laid in the late nineteenth and early twentieth centuries as distinguished black scholars W. E. B. DU BOIS and Carter G. WOODSON fought for the inclusion of the systematic study of black social and cultural studies into American institutions of higher education. These pioneers made unprecedented contributions by creating an African American intellectual history and tradition. Added impetus for the institutionalization of black studies was provided between the HARLEM RENAISSANCE in the 1920's and the end of WORLD WAR II. During this period, black and white scholars such as Robert Parks, St. Clair Drake, Langston HUGHES, Melville J. Herskovitz, Alain Locke, Thomas Woofter, and William Stanley Braithwaite created a professional critical coterie and brought an interdisciplinary consciousness to the field. It was not until the late 1960's, however, that black studies programs became a formal academic discipline.

Aided by the broader social and political struggles of the CIVIL RIGHTS MOVEMENT, BLACK POWER MOVEMENT, and student activism, the demands for the integration of African American studies in American

Black scholar Carter G. Woodson laid the ideological foundations for African American studies programs. (The Associated Publishers, Inc.)

education began in the 1960's. They intensified after the assassinations of MALCOLM X in 1966 and Martin Luther KING, JR., in 1968. Black students on predominately white college campuses protested the historical, systematic exclusion of minorities from higher education as well as the omission and distortion of the African American experience in the traditional academic curriculum.

In 1966 the first black studies program and department was established at San Francisco State College (SFSC). By 1969 Harvard, Yale, and Columbia universities had programs, giving the movement greater legitimacy. Black studies programs were officially established on campuses throughout the nation. Their apparent success inspired other ethnic and minority groups, including Chicanos, Asian Americans, AMERICAN INDIANS, and European American ethnic groups, as well as women, to join the educational reform movement and to demand the inception of ETHNIC STUDIES programs.

African American studies programs went through three major phases of development. The institutionalization of the programs was the first, experimental phase in the late 1960's and early 1970's. Varied programmatic approaches were conceived to meet the demands of African American students and to suppress campus unrest. In response to the pressures of the times, programs were set up with little regard for aca-

sues of definition, objectives, finances, staffing, curriculum, and theoretical coherence. By the 1980's, the interdisciplinary model had been established and widely used in undergraduate teaching, and graduate

Integrating black studies into academic curricula better informs all students of the African American heritage and teaches black students to feel pride in their roots. (James L. Shaffer)

demic, budgetary, or staffing consequences. Many programs failed because of the lack of a sound foundation. The academic formulation phase was a time of retrenchment as the programs searched for credibility within academe. Programmatic concerns included is-

programs had been instituted. The third phase of development is characterized by an intellectual renaissance movement. New paradigms, theories, and methodologies for African American studies programs are debated in relation to the integration of the programs within ethnic and multicultural studies programs.

Organization. Four organizational patterns characterize most black studies programs. First, the undergraduate interdisciplinary program consists of a director or coordinator and qualified faculty members who hold joint appointments in the programs and existing departments of their academic specializations. Incorporating a core curriculum of traditional disciplines, such as history, art, political science, English, and sociology, these programs synthesize the African American experience into the total academic curricula from multidisciplinary perspectives. This type of program offers undergraduate students concentrations as majors and minors. The second type of degree-granting program is the black studies department. A competitive academic unit within one of the colleges of the university, the department has responsibility for hiring faculty and designing the structure and curriculum of the program under the administration of the department chair. Third, the model of the black studies college, such as Malcolm X College and the Third College of the University of California at San Diego, is distinguished by its commitment to the development of a total African American consciousness and collective identity to counteract the influence of white Western European culture in academe. Fourth, there are two alternative organizational patterns that exist for the inclusion of African American studies in the university curriculum: institutions that offer courses without formal organized programs, and centers or institutes, such as the Center for Afro-American Studies at the University of California, Los Angeles (UCLA), and the Africana research center at Cornell University.

Theories and Methodologies. Several different theories and ideologies shape the models chosen for African American studies programs and guide their research. These include BLACK NATIONALISM, AFROCENTRISM, PAN-AFRICANISM, Marxism, COLONIALISM, and critical theory. Black nationalism, which gained popularity in the early twentieth century, emphasizes the separation of races and the overthrow of the dominant political and social institutions for the liberation of African Americans. Afrocentrism is an interdisciplinary theory that advocates an African-centered worldview to free the study, research, and peoples of Africa from Eurocentric scholarship and control. Pan-Africanism stresses a link between the politics, protest, and oppression of all peoples of African descent and strives to unify this political alliance for their liberation.

Methodological approaches, like the theoretical constructs, are still highly debated as scholars challenge the divergent concepts and standards of Afrocentrism and Eurocentrism as they are used to study black people and their experiences. According to African American scholars, this discord arises from the uniqueness of black culture and the inappropriateness of applying Eurocentric cultural standards to that culture. Thus, a growing number of new approaches inform the field, such as positivist and critical methodologies.

Problems and Potential. African American studies programs continue to cope with campus politics and such necessities for survival as curriculum building and retention of students. Competition for black scholars, funding problems, and struggles to achieve and maintain academic legitimacy plague most programs. The MULTICULTURALISM and ethnic studies movements further complicate the status of many black studies programs as administrators debate the role, curricula, and diverse approaches such studies should have within a multicultural context. Since their inception, African American studies programs have been challenged to provide self-definition and theoretical and methodological coherence. Another major challenge is to design and integrate black studies programs into the public school curricula and into the general studies programs of colleges and universities throughout the nation. In the 1990's, program faculties still saw a pressing need to broaden the perceptual foundations of traditional academic disciplines to eradicate RACISM and correct misinterpretations of the African American experience.

The establishment of the first doctoral program in African American studies at Temple University; the creation of endowed chairs in research centers, institutes, and on some college campuses; and the availability of grants to support research in the field are evidence of the stability of some established black studies programs. Scholars are engaging in ongoing critical research and inquiry to provide the scholarly foundations necessary for the permanence of African American studies as an academic discipline.

SUGGESTED READINGS. Two comprehensive introductions to African American studies as an academic discipline are *Introduction to Black Studies* (1982) by Maulana Karenga and *Introduction to Afro-American Studies* (1986) by Abdul Alkalimat. For an introduction to interdisciplinary theoretical, ideological, and methodological issues, *Black Studies* (1990), edited by

Talmadge Anderson, provides additional resources. Several professors analyze the future directions of black studies programs in a number of articles in *Black Scholar* 22, no. 3 (1991). In *Journal of Negro Education* 53, no. 3 (1984), a special issue on black studies programs, Carlos Brossard's "Classifying Black Studies Programs," pp. 278-295, and Alan Colón's "Critical Issues in Black Studies: A Selective Analysis," pp. 268-277, are useful.—*Jacquelyn L. Jackson*

African American women: Overcoming tremendous odds, African American women have managed to make remarkable contributions to African American culture and to American culture in general. They have faced both RACISM and SEXISM, and have therefore had to overcome a double burden of oppression. Often constrained by how others have interpreted their race and gender, they nevertheless have been powerful allies of both males of color and feminists in struggles for a more equitable society. There are also many differences within the huge classi-

Although African American women are gaining more access to professional careers, their earnings are still far less than those of their white counterparts. (James L. Shaffer)

fication "African American women" with regard to CLASS, EDUCATION, origins, color, and opportunity. Although there have been many highly visible individual triumphs and achievements, these must be viewed within the context of the limitations placed on a large number of African American women as both black and female, including the stark reality of the poverty in which too many must live.

Early History. African women first arrived in the United States as slaves at the beginning of colonial American society. Women worked alongside men in fields and workshops, but they also filled household roles. Under the institution of slavery, they were valued by white owners for their breeding capacity, yet they were expected to care for their owners' children, even before their own. At the same time, they were viewed as sexual objects that white plantation dwellers could use at will.

Within the slave community, some women gained power through their practical knowledge, skills in medicine and midwifery, religious expertise, and leadership in covert activities. It should also be remembered that there were free women of color in Creole Louisiana as well as in other cities in both the North and South, and they sustained their own domestic and social lives.

Even during two centuries of slavery, some women, both free and enslaved, gained renown or notoriety. In 1773, Phillis WHEATLEY, a poet, became the first African American author to have work published. Maria Stewart gained fame as a Boston orator in the 1830's despite public opposition because of her race, gender, and politics. The work of nineteenth century abolitionist and feminist Sojourner TRUTH was aided by others who indicted women's conditions under SLAVERY. Harriet Jacobs detailed such conditions in her autobiographical *Incidents in the Life of a Slave Girl* (1861), and Harriet Wilson described them in *Our Nig* (1859), the first African American novel. Harriet TUBMAN led slaves to freedom on the UNDERGROUND RAILROAD. Other women took on new roles within institutions such as churches. Jarena Lee preached in the AFRICAN METHODIST EPISCOPAL (AME) CHURCH, while Elizabeth Lange from Santo Domingo and Henriette Delille of New Orleans founded black orders of CATHOLIC nuns.

After the Civil War. During the CIVIL WAR, African American women became caregivers, nurses, and organizers. After emancipation, these women explored new opportunities that epitomized regional and class differences in the African American experience. Women of the black upper and middle classes became teachers and leaders, as chronicled by Frances E. W. Harper in *Iola Leroy* (1892). Women's clubs and sororities became vital community organizations; among leaders of the club movement were Mary Church TERRELL and Margaret Murray Washington, wife and coworker of Booker T. WASHINGTON. Ida Bell WELLS manifested a fiery independent spirit as a journalist and activist in the crusade against LYNCHING.

At the same time, black women advanced in medicine and nursing, education, missionary work, and social reform. Rebecca Lee Crumpler became the first black woman doctor in 1864, while C. E. (Charlotte) Ray was admitted to the Washington, D.C., bar in 1872. By the beginning of the twentieth century, some four thousand African American women had been graduated from colleges and normal schools.

Yet the majority of black women in the RECONSTRUCTION-era South continued to work on small farms or as SHARECROPPERS, laborers, and domestics, echoing their roles under slavery. Their status deteriorated with subsequent repressive measures against blacks which characterized the growth of JIM CROW legislation. African American women in the North, too, entered domestic service, but many lost these positions to European immigrants until the latter, not limited by the racism that suppressed African Americans, were able to find jobs in expanding industries. Lynching, although overwhelmingly directed against black males, also claimed the lives of at least two dozen African American women between 1882 and 1927.

Early Twentieth Century. Twentieth century migrations, particularly the GREAT MIGRATION to northern cities, opened new areas for African American women. In the arts, writers such as Zora Neale HURSTON, Jessie Fauset, and Nella Larsen established dynamic reputations during the HARLEM RENAISSANCE. Their fiction evoked dilemmas of interracial relations and broken or abusive families as well as complex, heroic figures such as Hurston's Janie Crawford in *Their Eyes Were Watching God* (1937). Augusta Savage gained renown as a sculptor, while Shirley Graham composed the opera *Tom-Toms* (1932). Perhaps no area indicated the possibilities of racial and cultural crossover in celebrities and audiences so much as music. By the 1920's, Gertrude "Ma" Rainey, Bessie Smith, and Josephine BAKER gained fame which later would be augmented in many musical fields by

Marian ANDERSON, Mahalia Jackson, Billie HOLIDAY, Lena HORNE, Sarah Vaughan, and scores of contemporary talents.

Black women also challenged male-dominated public arenas. Madam C. J. WALKER became a millionaire through her beauty care products, a fortune which she and her daughter A'Lelia devoted to politics and artistic patronage. Mary McLeod BETHUNE founded Daytona Educational and Industrial Institute (later Bethune-Cookman College) in Florida in 1904. Her power grew during her terms as president of the National Association of Colored Women and the NATIONAL COUNCIL OF NEGRO WOMEN. In 1936, she became director of the Negro division of the National Youth Administration and a keystone in Franklin D. Roosevelt's "black cabinet." In 1938, Pennsylvanian Crystal Bird Fauset was the first black woman elected to a state legislature. Meanwhile, by the 1930's, two-thirds of black elementary and high school teachers were women, although few became principals.

The GREAT DEPRESSION was hard on African American women and their families, most of whom still lived in the rural South. NEW DEAL agencies found intense rural poverty and calculated neglect in segregated schools, underfunded health care, and decaying housing in black areas. Competing for jobs with black men as well as whites, African American women servants and workers throughout the nation faced unemployment and underemployment in their struggles to survive.

After World War II. The emergence of the CIVIL RIGHTS MOVEMENT after WORLD WAR II opened new vistas and new ambiguities. Rosa PARKS, for example, whose refusal to surrender her seat on a segregated bus sparked the MONTGOMERY BUS BOYCOTT, was often portrayed as a victim rather than as the educated, committed pioneer and NAACP worker she was. Women such as Ella Baker, of the SOUTHERN CHRISTIAN LEADERSHIP CONFERENCE (SCLC) and STUDENT NONVIOLENT COORDINATING COMMITTEE (SNCC), and Fannie Lou HAMER, founder of the Mississippi Freedom Democratic Party, organized and fought in many civil rights struggles.

The Civil Rights movement of the 1960's began an era during which fundamental changes occurred regarding INTEGRATION and a redefinition of the limits for Americans of all races and backgrounds. African American women began to enter previously all-white southern universities; among them was Charlayne Hunter-Gault, who became a well-known television

journalist. In 1968, Shirley CHISHOLM, the daughter of residents of Barbados, became the first black woman elected to the U.S. House of Representatives; from there, she campaigned for the presidency in 1972. Patricia Roberts Harris broke barriers as ambassador to Luxembourg and as a cabinet member in the Carter Administration. In politics, however, women's gains lagged behind those of African American men. Although Carol Moseley BRAUN of Illinois became the nation's first black female senator in 1992, as of the early 1990's there were no black female governors and few metropolitan mayors apart from Sharon Pratt Kelly, who was elected mayor of Washington, D. C., in 1990. Similarly, African American women hold judiciary positions but have gained no nominations to the Supreme Court. Their power also has grown in the armed forces: Hazel Johnson became the first black female Army general in 1979, followed by Sherian Cadoria in 1985. Nearly half the women who fought in Operation Desert Storm in 1991 were black.

Since the 1950's, black women have appeared increasingly in the white-dominated mass media. Few, however, have gained power as producers, directors, investors, or even primary heroines. After the 1939 Academy Award for best supporting actress was awarded to Hattie McDaniel for her stereotypically "Mammy" role in *Gone with the Wind*, the next Academy Award to go to a black woman—again for a supporting role—came in 1990 for Whoopi Goldberg for her performance in *Ghost*. In the 1980's, Oprah WINFREY gained clout within television through her talk show conglomerate, while filmmaker Julie Dash wrote, produced, and directed *Daughters of the Dust* (1991) amid the gradually increasing roles for women behind the camera. In music, black women have become stars in genres ranging from GOSPEL and SOUL to opera.

In literature, Ann Petry, Pulitzer-Prize winner Gwendolyn BROOKS, Alice Childress, and Lorraine HANSBERRY were forerunners of a powerful black women's literary renaissance that includes Toni Morrison, June Jordan, Tony Cade Bambara, Alice WALKER, Ntozake SHANGE, and Gloria Naylor. Their audiences cross racial and gender lines; Walker and Morrison received Pulitzer Prizes, in 1982 and 1988, respectively. Poet and Pulitzer winner Rita Dove in 1993 became poet laureate of the United States. She was the second woman, the first black, and the youngest person to be so honored. Poet Audre Lorde, speaking and writing from a black LESBIAN viewpoint,

Carol Moseley Braun of Illinois became the United States' first black woman senator in 1992. (AP/Wide World Photos)

was a voice both for the acceptance of diversity and for reform.

African American women have made remarkable achievements in sports, although they have rarely received the recognition or financial rewards that males have. Well into the twentieth century, women's sports organizations were SEGREGATED; black women were, however, allowed to join American OLYMPIC teams beginning in 1932. They subsequently achieved victories in track and field and basketball, from Nell Jackson and Wilma Rudolph to medalists Florence Joyner and Jackie Joyner-Kersee. Tennis star Althea GIBSON integrated the U.S. Open in 1950 and won singles titles in Wimbledon in 1957 and 1958.

In education, African American women hold striking power but nevertheless continue to encounter limitations. By the 1940's, proportionately more African American women attended college than either black males or white females (although few entered the sciences). While black women increased on college faculties, only Willa Player at Bennett College and Johnetta Cole at Spelman College became presidents of black institutions. Yolanda Moses earned a breakthrough appointment as president of New York's City College in 1993. Similarly, in RELIGION, black women have been mainstays of congregations without necessarily holding official church office. In 1988, however, Barbara Harris became the U.S. EPISCOPAL church's first female bishop. Other African American women have assumed pulpits in EVANGELICAL and Holiness churches and have led missionary organizations and assemblies of Catholic sisters.

The African American women who have become well known for their achievements tell only a part of the African American woman's story. Many must face the everyday struggles of underemployment and poverty and encounter racism in their daily lives. Many are the heads of single-parent households; in 1990, 51 percent of African American families were single-parent families headed by a woman. Although African American women are gaining more access to professional careers, their earnings are still far less than their white male counterparts.

There is great diversity within the community of

African American women, reflecting many economic levels and philosophies. They have faced both racial discrimination and the "GLASS CEILING" that women of all ethnicities face as they try to advance in the American corporate structure. They have sometimes found their priorities divided between seeking their civil rights as African Americans and, as women, demanding equality with men. The many perspectives of black women within the United States' multicultural society are as complex as that society itself, and they reflect memories of oppression, ongoing struggles, and hope for exciting achievements in the future.

SUGGESTED READINGS. A tremendous number of sources are available on this topic. Among some of the most valuable and accessible are *Black Women in America: An Historical Encyclopedia* (2 vols., 1993), edited by Darlene Clark Hine, *Notable Black American Women* (1992), edited by Jessie C. Smith, *When and Where I Enter* (1984) by Paula Giddings, *All the Women Are White, All the Blacks Are Men, but Some of Us Are Brave* (1982), edited by Gloria T. Hull, Patricia Bell-Scott, and Barbara Smith, and *Labor of Love, Labor of Sorrow: Black Women, Work, and Family from Slavery to the Present* (1985) by Jacqueline Jones.—*Gary McDonogh*

African American women—matriarchy debate: Many contemporary African American children are reared primarily or solely by a female, be she mother, grandmother, aunt, sister, or other female relative. This is by no means a universal situation; there are many African American nuclear families with two parents in the home. Nevertheless, in 1990, more than 60 percent of African American families were single-parent families, the vast majority of them headed by a woman. It has also been noted that even in some homes in which

The American black woman often plays a dominant role in the family. (AP/Wide World Photos)

a man is present, his role in rearing the children is a limited one, and the true authority figure is a woman. These situations reflect a historical pattern of black women's family roles in the United States.

A number of elements have combined to produce this pattern, and historians and sociologists are still debating the relative importance of various factors. Among the greatest contributors to the problems confronting African American families have been the institution of SLAVERY and ongoing white RACISM. Re-

unit. A "matriarch" can be defined as a woman who is the head of a family (particularly an extended family) or is the leader of a larger entity, even a country. The implication is that a matriarch has a position of power. The portrayal of the African American woman as matriarch is defended by some and rejected by others. Most scholars agree, however, that regardless of whether the American black woman can be considered a bona fide matriarch, she does often play a dominant role in the family.

The perpetuation of the concept of the black matriarch, it has been argued, has damaged relationships between black men and women. (Robert Fried)

lated causes include the twentieth century migration from rural to urban areas and the resulting ghettoization and "CULTURE OF POVERTY." Some scholars have argued that the strong family roles of African American women may date back to women's traditional roles in African societies.

The Black Matriarch: Myth or Reality? The concept of the African American matriarch has emerged from the reality that many African American women have had to assume the authoritative role within the family

The label "matriarch" angers and offends many FEMINIST critics, Barbara Smith, Gloria Hull, and Bell Hooks among them. Hooks reasons that the term "matriarch" as applied by white sociologists is misleading because it leads many people to identify as a matriarch any woman present in a home in which no man resides. Hooks and others believe that the matriarch theory is a cruel myth; they note that the African American woman possesses very little political or economic power, living in a society in which the decisions that determine how she lives are made by others—white and/or black men.

The theory of the black matriarch was brought to national awareness by the MOYNIHAN REPORT in 1965. The report, which was highly controversial, stated the findings of a group commissioned by President Lyndon Johnson to describe the problems impeding African Americans' progress toward equality with whites. It said that the central problem was the breakdown of the black family, leading to a matriarchal system that caused young black men to "flounder and fail" because of a lack of strong father figures or other role models. These findings outraged many in the black community, especially men. According to Patricia Bell Scott, black men view the black matriarch theory as an attempt to victimize and ostracize them by stating that they cannot take care of their families. The perpetuation of the concept of the black matriarch, it has been argued, has severely damaged relationships between black men and black women.

Some African American critics, however, align themselves in a limited sense with the theory of the black matriarch. Merle Hodge contends that the Caribbean and black America on the whole have produced the new black matriarch—the strong female figure who is responsible for the survival of the black race. Robert Staples notes that had black women been passive creatures content to observe their menfolk make history, "then the travail of the past four centuries might have found the black race just as extinct as the dinosaur." Yet Staples insists that the black female often finds herself in the position of matriarch because there is a shortage of eligible black men to marry. Too many African American males have been removed from circulation by wars or incarceration, or have died young because of the effects of impoverished living conditions.

Whatever one's view of the black matriarch theory, the fact is that in many families the black woman is either the dominant figure or is the sole provider or breadwinner. As a result, she has had to take on characteristics usually ascribed to men. Her sometimes independent, upwardly mobile, and resilient attitude has caused much friction with black men, some of whom feel that she has deliberately usurped their position.

Anthropologist Melville Herskovitz reasons that the African American woman retained the position of authority in the household from her African heritage. In traditional polygamous unions in West Africa, the husband/father lives in separate dwellings from his

wives and children. Each wife lives in her own separate quarters with her children, and the wives take turns cooking for and sleeping with their husband. This arrangement automatically establishes the woman as the apparent head of her own household. Yet in traditional Africa, the man was the *de facto* head not of one household but of many; his success was often measured by the number of wives he could support. Some critics take a middle ground in proposing that the preponderance of the matriarchal black family is the result of a synthesis of an AFRICAN CULTURAL SURVIVAL with the realities of slavery.

Slavery and Its Effects. Some believe that the image of the black matriarch was born of the black female's role under slavery. Because she was made to work side by side with black men in the fields, she was viewed as masculine rather than feminine. According to Bell Hooks, white men attempted to dehumanize the female African American slave in order to explain her ability to perform tasks that were culturally defined as "man's work"; they characterized her not as a real woman but as a male subhuman creature. Angela Davis suggests that white men viewed black slave women as beasts in order to justify their mistreatment and sexual abuse.

Male African American slaves were not allowed to participate in the upbringing of their children. Nor were they in a position to defend, protect, provide for, or act as head of their families because, in a very real sense, there were no families. A male slave seldom lived in a family unit with his wife and children; he might not even know his children. Under slavery, his manhood was defined by his brawn and reproductive skills. Merle Hodge relates this experience to the fact that some contemporary African American men do not take responsibility for the children they father.

In the plantation establishment, slave owners ensured that the woman's role was more important than that of her husband. She was in charge of the cabin, and all rations were issued to her. She made the decisions, and if the family received any special favors it was generally through her efforts. Slavery, therefore, forcibly prepared the black woman for the role of family provider, whereas it had an emasculating effect on black men.

A large number of contemporary African American males have overcome the limited family role assigned them during slavery. They are strong heads of households, upwardly mobile family providers, and successful and dedicated fathers. Yet many other African

American men are deeply disillusioned because they believe they cannot succeed in a society in which racism still persists and that perpetuates favoritism of and reliance on the African American female.

SUGGESTED READINGS. For further information on this subject, see Angela Davis' "Reflections on the Black Woman's Role in the Community of Slaves," in *The Black Scholar* 3 (December, 1971), pp. 2-15; Carole Anne Douglas' "Impressions and Confessions: Racism and Sexism," in *Off Our Backs* 9 (November 9, 1979), p. 16; and Melville J. Herskovitz's *The Myth of the Negro Past* (1958). Additional works that discuss black women include Patricia Bell Scott's "Debunking Sapphire: Toward a Nonracist and Nonsexist Social Science," in *All the Women Are White, All the Blacks Are Men, but Some of Us Are Brave* (1982), edited by Gloria T. Hull, Patricia Bell Scott, and Barbara Smith; Robert Staples' "The Myth of the Black Matriarchy," in *The Black Scholar* 1 (January-February, 1970), pp. 8-16; and Jacqueline Jones's *Labor of Love, Labor of Sorrow: Black Women, Work, and the Family from Slavery to the Present* (1985).—*Peggy L. D. Stevenson*

African Americans—early history and cultural contributions: In *They Came Before Columbus* (1976), Ivan Van Sertima argued that there is evidence for an African presence in the Western Hemisphere well before 1492. There were also Africans accompanying Christopher COLUMBUS and other explorers. The African presence in the Americas today, however, descends overwhelmingly from the slave population that was imported to the New World as a source of labor for plantations controlled by Europeans.

The Origins and Extent of Slavery. Most of the Africans imported to North America as slaves hailed from West Africa in the region stretching from present-day Guinea through Nigeria to Angola. There was also an East African slave trade that lasted longer than the Atlantic slave trade and led to a larger depopulation of the continent. In addition, particularly in the southern states of Florida, Alabama, and Louisiana, a number of the slaves arrived by way of the Caribbean, although they originated in Africa. After SLAVERY's end, there was substantial immigration of blacks from the Caribbean, with these immigrants adding to the African American population.

Slavery existed throughout the thirteen colonies that came to form the nucleus of the United States of America. Slavery also existed in parts of the North American continent outside the colonies, such as Texas and other parts of the West before these regions entered the union. The greatest concentration of slaves from 1619 forward, however, was centered in the area that comprises present-day Virginia and the Carolinas.

A historical controversy concerns the status of those early Africans, especially the first group of twenty to arrive in Jamestown in 1619. Though there was African slavery on American shores in the 1600's, apparently there was some fluidity in the status of imported Africans; they may actually have been more akin to INDENTURED SERVANTS than chattel slaves. In the mid-1600's, the Maryland Assembly legislated that indentured servitude for blacks would be for life, thus setting a precedent. BACON'S REBELLION in 1676 in Virginia is seen as a turning point in the evolution of those who came to be called African Americans. Some scholars argue that this uprising of landless whites and blacks caused colonial elites to assuage their demands by moving west to seize Indian land, turn it over to the poorer whites, and stock this land with African slaves. This led, in turn, to an ossification of the inferior status of Africans and their subsequent dispersal into the interior of the nation.

Although African slavery was centered in the South, it was far from unknown in the North. NEW YORK CITY, for example, as late as the early 1800's, had a sizable African slave population. Urban slavery was prevalent throughout the history of this institution. Often urban slaves were "hired out" by their masters; this practice allowed the slaves a modicum of autonomy in a manner that their rural counterparts did not enjoy. In other words, these slaves sometimes lived apart from their masters in cities working in a manner akin to wage workers, although they were "owned." American slavery, however, came to be most typically associated with plantations focused on production of cash crops such as cotton, tobacco, rice, and sugar, which were produced mostly in the South.

Africans from West Africa played a crucial role in the development of agricultural techniques leading to an increase in rice production in South Carolina. This could be traced to their origins in regions of Africa where production of rice was prevalent. Improvements in AGRICULTURE are only one of the many ways that Africans helped to shape the economy and culture of the United States. African slaves were also involved in household production, industrial production, mining, construction, skilled crafts such as blacksmithing and tailoring—indeed, all forms of labor.

Plantation slaves, pictured here in 1862, played a crucial role in the development of agricultural techniques and helped to shape the economy and culture of the United States. (Library of Congress)

African slaves were active from the early days in sustaining their culture and helping to shape American cultural forms. Again, their African origins played a role in this process. For example, drumming and the use of string instruments similar to the banjo and guitar were staple features of African cultural life, and these AFRICAN CULTURAL SURVIVALS were adapted to

"free" states into the Union would erode their political power and possibly put the entire institution of slavery in jeopardy. It has been argued that the need for further slave territory was partly responsible for the United States' decision to fight the MEXICAN AMERICAN WAR, which brought Texas into the Union as a slave state. Concomitantly, the addition of new slave states led to

African American politicians began to organize after the Civil War, holding meetings such as the 1876 Colored National Convention in Nashville, Tenn., pictured here. (The Associated Publishers, Inc.)

form the basis of the developing "American" culture. Likewise, Africans brought to American shores a number of words that linguists believe were incorporated into what has come to be called "American English." The first independent black churches were established in the South in the latter half of the 1700's, forming the foundation of what would later become a crucial institution for the black community.

Political Conflict over Slavery. Political leaders from the South were constantly searching for new territory where slavery could be introduced. One reason was that slavery in the South was part of an antiquated system of agricultural production that eventually led to the exhausting of the soil. Another was that slave-owners came to fear that the introduction of new

the dispersal of African Americans across the nation.

Slavery was a major issue at the Constitutional Convention in 1787. Slaves were counted as three-fifths of a person for purposes of apportioning members of the House of Representatives. The political power of the slave states is reflected in the disproportionate number of Virginians who served as president before the CIVIL WAR. The very location of the nation's capital in WASHINGTON, D.C., rather than a northern city such as New York or PHILADELPHIA (both of which had served as the capital at one time), represents a compromise between the northern and southern states. The new capital shared a border with the slave state of Virginia. The friction sparked by the existence of African slavery was a defining factor in the early history of the United States long before the Civil War.

Just as the interests of the slaveowners led to the appropriation of more territory for slavery and the dispersal of Africans across a broad swath of the nation, the actions of slaves themselves had a decided impact on the trajectory of slavery. The slave revolution in Haiti at the beginning of the nineteenth century forced France to liquidate part of its colonial empire in North America, which led to the sale of the Louisiana Territory to the United States in 1803. This revolution also caused apprehension in American slaveowning circles, prompting many people to reassess the viability of the institution and bringing about a growth in abolitionist sentiment.

Slave rebellions were common in the United States and the Caribbean from the early years of the institution. Rebellions ranged from sabotage of production, to arson directed at mansions, to poisoning of masters, to organized uprisings. MAROONS, or runaway slaves

who fled into swamps and other inaccessible regions, often staged raids and fomented rebellions from their hideouts. Maroon communities also served as a hospitable environment for the preservation of African cultural forms and practices.

More slave uprisings took place in the Caribbean than in the United States because in nations such as Jamaica, there was a ratio of nine slaves to every one nonslave, whereas in the United States the latter generally outnumbered the former. South Carolina, which had a slave majority in the period before the American Revolution, was the exception to the rule.

In addition to slave rebellions, opposition from European Americans served to help restrain slavery. This opposition arose in part from humanitarian concerns and in part from the fact that a number of whites believed that the existence of chattel labor dragged down the wages and working conditions of "free white" labor. The slave bloc in Congress tended to

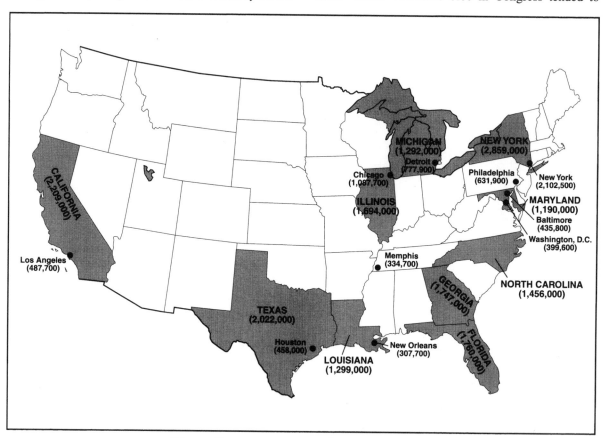

TEN STATES AND CITIES WITH LARGEST AFRICAN AMERICAN POPULATIONS

Source: Bureau of the Census, 1991, in *Minorities: A Changing Role in America*, 1992.

weaken the political strength of nonslave areas in the Northeast and Midwest, which also helped to bolster antislavery sentiment for sheer political reasons. The growth of the ABOLITIONIST MOVEMENT in the early 1800's began to hinder the spread of slavery and the dispersal of Africans across the nation.

Antislavery sentiment also was a barrier to the spread of the slave trade itself. The U.S. CONSTITUTION mandated that this trade should be halted by 1808. An illegal slave trade continued, however, until the abolition of slavery in the 1860's. Yet, the population that is now termed African American is predominantly a product of a community that had been formed by the early part of the nineteenth century. This makes African Americans—like American Indians—a people with some of the deepest roots in the United States.

The fight against slavery brought a number of brilliant African American leaders to national prominence. Frederick DOUGLASS, born a slave in 1817, became a powerful abolitionist editor, orator, and symbol of the intellectual potential of an oppressed race. Women such as Harriet TUBMAN and Sojourner TRUTH were courageous leaders in the UNDERGROUND RAILROAD for escaped slaves as well as eloquent speakers for abolition and the plight of their people. Even before the EMANCIPATION PROCLAMATION, blacks in the North were active as religious leaders, educators, and inventors, among other professions.

Reconstruction. The Reconstruction era (1865-1877) brought tremendous changes to African Americans, particularly in the South. The community was in upheaval at the war's end, in search of work and lost relations. The federal FREEDMEN'S BUREAU set up schools, hospitals, and labor contracts to assist the former slaves, but African Americans also took responsibility for their own welfare through MUTUAL AID SOCIETIES and political conventions. There was a boom in the establishment of AFRICAN AMERICAN COLLEGES, which would become an essential training ground for full participation in American society. For the first time the MARRIAGES of former slaves became legal.

The new political opportunities of the period were profound in spite of the efforts by southern states to curtail the freedom of black people through BLACK CODES and other means. African Americans won citizenship, "equal protection under the law," and the vote (for males) with the THIRTEENTH, FOURTEENTH, and FIFTEENTH AMENDMENTS, reinforced by early CIVIL RIGHTS LEGISLATION. The Fourteenth Amendment, in particular, would ultimately transform the legal and political landscape of the nation by applying the concept of equal protection to women, other ethnic minorities, and all those who suffered DISCRIMINATION. Once enfranchised, African Americans won fourteen seats in the U.S. Congress, controlled the South Carolina legislature, and served in numerous state and local offices in all the other former states of the CONFEDERACY. In the process they wrote new constitutions that helped to democratize the South.

Significantly, the KU KLUX KLAN was formed in 1865 in horrified response to the gains made by African Americans. Race RIOTS—which were not new in American life—erupted at flashpoints of black success or numerical power. Eventually, when federal troops and supervisors were withdrawn from the South in 1877, the southern states moved to reassert their power, and many of the gains made by blacks were swiftly lost.

Both before and after emancipation, African Americans managed to make significant contributions to American cultural life. An essential aspect of this contribution has been in music, as in the development of the BLUES, a form of lyrical music that grew out of the difficult experiences of blacks, toward the end of the nineteenth century. Other influential black musical forms range from SPIRITUALS to JAZZ. Closely aligned with musical contributions has been the development of various popular dance forms that have come to be exported to the world as a quintessentially American product.

The Jim Crow Period. After a brief hiatus, the African American community was faced once again with daunting legal barriers. The late decades of the nineteenth century imposed a policy of official SEGREGATION on African Americans through JIM CROW LAWS in the South, where the vast majority of blacks still lived. For example, southern states imposed LITERACY TESTS and poll taxes that effectively deprived poor, uneducated blacks of the right to vote. In 1896, the U.S. Supreme Court gave sweeping sanction to SEGREGATION in the case of *Plessy v. Ferguson*, which authorized the "separate but equal" policy. Some blacks sought a better life in the West in the Exodus of 1879, but met with hostility from both American Indians and white settlers.

In spite of these restrictions, African Americans continued to organize and educate themselves to play a greater role in determining their fate. Networks for advocacy developed, such as the Colored Farmers Alliance in 1886, the National Association of Colored Women in 1896, and the NATIONAL NEGRO BUSINESS LEAGUE in 1900. During the 1880's, Booker T. WASH-

OF COLORED PEOPLE (1909), demanding greater equality for African Americans. His agenda outlined the concerns that would preoccupy the black community well into the twentieth century.

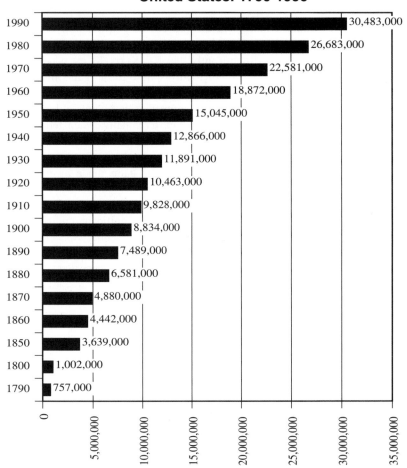

Growth in the African American Population of the United States: 1790-1990

Year	Population
1990	30,483,000
1980	26,683,000
1970	22,581,000
1960	18,872,000
1950	15,045,000
1940	12,866,000
1930	11,891,000
1920	10,463,000
1910	9,828,000
1900	8,834,000
1890	7,489,000
1880	6,581,000
1870	4,880,000
1860	4,442,000
1850	3,639,000
1800	1,002,000
1790	757,000

Source: Data are from *Statistical Abstract of the United States, 1992.* Table 14. Washington, D.C.: U.S. Government Printing Office, 1992.

Ironically, the Jim Crow laws and segregation that followed the abolition of slavery provided an atmosphere for the growth and solidifying of an African American community. Black clubs sprang up to aid in the development of black music. The beginnings of the black press and black athletic teams, such as baseball franchises, provided opportunities to blacks who faced barriers to participation in mainstream American society. In the 1890's, gifted individuals ranging from black jockeys to black poet Paul Laurence Dunbar won acclaim. Meanwhile, both urban and rural churches continued to be the social, cultural, and educational backbone of African American life, encouraging leadership.

Thus, before the advent of the twentieth century, Africans came to reside in all parts of the United States. Their presence was essential to the development of the nation and indelibly marked the direction and emphases of American law and politics. Black cultural contributions were and are profound, particularly in the area of music, dance, and sports.

SUGGESTED READINGS. For an analysis of the African presence in the Americas before 1492, see Ivan Van Sertima's *They Came Before Columbus* (1976, repr. 1989). On the issue of early colonial slavery, see Edmund S. Morgan's *American Slavery, American Freedom: The Ordeal of Colonial Virginia* (1975). On the question of slavery and its opponents, see Merton L.

INGTON promoted vocational education, self-discipline, and accommodation to white society at TUS-KEGEE INSTITUTE, where he was president. His philosophy influenced both existing black colleges and the many more that were established as a result of the Second Morill Act in 1890. W. E. B. DU BOIS made black intellectual history when he earned a Ph.D. at Harvard University in 1895. He went on to become one of the leaders of the NIAGARA MOVEMENT (1905) and the National Association for the ADVANCEMENT

Dillon's *Slavery Attacked: Southern Slaves and Their Allies, 1619-1865* (1990). On the situation in the United States after slavery, see Edward L. Ayers' *The Promise of the New South: Life After Reconstruction* (1992). Alton Hornsby, Jr.'s, *Chronology of African-American History* (1991) is also useful.—*Gerald Horne*

African Americans and Creole Culture. *See* **Creole culture and African Americans**

African Americans of Latin American or Caribbean descent: Descendants of enslaved or free individuals formerly living in Latin American countries and Caribbean islands possessed by Spain. As a result of the institution of SLAVERY, the ancestors of many African Americans from Latin America absorbed aspects of Spanish or Portuguese culture while lacing them with strong African overtones. Because of their places of origin and the fact that some speak Spanish, these African Americans are often grouped under the category "LATINO."

From the latter part of the fifteenth century to the end of the sixteenth century, some parts of Latin America and most areas of the Caribbean were colonies of Spain and Portugal. Africans were shipped to these places in abundance to work on plantations established to produce items such as sugar, which was one of the leading profit-making crops of early settlers. In Latin America and the Caribbean, the institution of slavery was so harsh that many Africans died within a seven-year period; "fresh" Africans had to be shipped to replace the deceased. By the time slavery was abolished in the Caribbean and Latin America in the mid- to late 1800's, Brazil alone had received more than three times as many enslaved Africans as had the United States.

Like most other migrant and immigrant groups, many African Americans from Latin America came to the United States for better opportunities following economic problems in their own countries. This was the case, for example, with the large wave of PUERTO RICANS, both black and white, who left the island for the mainland from 1945 to 1955, settling in NEW YORK, WASHINGTON, D.C., and MIAMI. Some Spanish-speaking blacks also fled devastating political situations such as the effects of the Cuban Revolution (1959), especially in the MARIEL BOAT LIFT of 1980.

A number of these communities in the United States exhibit strong AFRICAN CULTURAL SURVIVALS, especially when compared with the traditions of African Americans whose ancestors were enslaved in the United States. The Yoruba people of West Africa were the first Africans to arrive in Cuba and northeastern Brazil, and many of their cultural practices were adapted by later arrivals from elsewhere in Africa. Those practices included West African RELIGION, which was the cultural practice least affected by contact with Europeans and by the institution of slavery. Africans were essentially allowed to practice what was thought by Europeans to be ROMAN CATHOLICISM but what in reality was a masked version of their own African religion. The Catholic image of the Virgin Mary, for example, was associated with Yemenja, the Yoruba goddess of the waters and of purity. Known

A Caribbean emigrant who now lives in south Florida. (Michael L. Kimble)

as SANTERÍA, this folk religion has been transplanted to the United States mainly by Afro-Cuban and Afro-Brazilian immigrants, many of whom are fine musicians. For a variety of reasons, including general American distrust of Africanisms, Santería and other survivals are kept hidden.

African Americans from Latin America not only carry strong cultural clues to African American history but also add their own Creole elements to American culture overall. Living in a multicultural society of many socially stratified cultures, they are faced with the decision of whether to identify with the broader African American or Latino community beyond their national groups.

African and the Caribbean: The Legacies of a Link (1979), and Leslie B. Rout's *The African Experience in Spanish America, 1502 to the Present Day* (1976).

African Americans of West Indian descent: Descendants of enslaved or freed individuals from the West Indies, who first immigrated to the United States as early as 1725. Significant numbers began arriving around the beginning of the nineteenth century. In 1924 the National

African Americans of West Indian descent march in a New York City parade. (Richard B. Levine)

SUGGESTED READINGS. *Hispanics in the United States: A New Social Agenda* (1985), edited by Pastora San Juan Cafferty and William C. McCready, contains information on black Americans with Latin American and Caribbean ancestry, as does *Africanisms in American Culture* (1990), edited by Joseph E. Holloway. Historical background can be found in Graham W. Irwin's *Africans Abroad: A Documentary History of the Black Diaspora in Asia, Latin America, and the Caribbean During the Age of Slavery* (1977), Margaret E. Crahan and Franklin W. Knight's edited volume

Origins Act, which favored Europeans, all but stopped the continuous flow of West Indians to the United States. Not until the removal of national quotas in the IMMIGRATION AND NATIONALITY ACT OF 1965 did West Indians resume immigration in large numbers.

African Americans of West Indian descent can be found in many places throughout the United States, including Florida, PHILADELPHIA, DETROIT, and the NEW YORK CITY area, where they maintain ethnic cuisine, dance, music, speech, and customs that celebrate their multicultural backgrounds. West Indian culture is a fusion of influences from African, East Indian, Carib, Anglo, Spanish, French, Chinese, and Middle Eastern societies. For example, MARDI GRAS parades and the annual LABOR DAY Festival in Brooklyn, New York, are showcases for distinctive West Indian musical creations such as steel drum bands and for brilliantly costumed dancers who perform interpretations of important religious, political, and historical homeland events.

African Americans of West Indian descent formed sustaining social organizations such as ethnic clubs and rotating credit associations to help members adapt to the difficulties of American city life. These credit associations not only allowed undocumented aliens to set up savings accounts for immigration money matters but also offered help in small ways by providing money for everyday living expenses when necessary.

West Indians have made their mark on American society in various ways. Many started and maintained their own businesses, such as the Antillean Realty Company, once one of the biggest companies of its kind in Harlem, New York, which was established by A. A. Austin from Antigua. Well-known West Indians in politics and literature include PAN-AFRICANIST Marcus GARVEY and famed HARLEM RENAISSANCE writer Claude McKay.

There has been tension between American-born African Americans and those of West Indian descent. This tension has been caused by the relative success of the West Indians when compared with African Americans as a whole, which in turn is related to the different historical experiences and worldviews of the two groups. West Indians were also descendants of enslaved Africans, but the institution of SLAVERY was different in the Caribbean. Though slavery was even more brutal there than it was in the United States, slave revolts were more successful in the Caribbean because of the relatively low population of whites. This contributed to black West Indians' sense of group power. Also, enslaved people in the West Indies were given plots of land on which to grow their own food and were allowed to sell any surplus in markets off the plantation, thus gaining generations of simple but effective business experience.

Black West Indians were also able to take advantage of certain opportunities for advancement after emancipation that were not possible for freed American slaves. The absence of a large white working class in the West Indies meant that there was a large job market; freeborn persons of color or freed slaves were not restricted to the most menial occupations, as was generally the case in the United States.

SUGGESTED READINGS. For more information, see *An Anthropological Approach to the Afro-American Past: A Caribbean Perspective* (1976) by Sidney W. Mintz and Richard Price and *Caribbean Contours* (1985) by Sidney W. Mintz and Sally Price. Other valuable sources include *From Africa to the United States and Then . . .* (1969) by Renneth G. Goode, *Essays and Data on American Ethnic Groups* (1978), edited by Thomas Sowell, *This Was Harlem* (1982) by Jervis Anderson, and *Caribbean Festival Arts* (1988) by John W. Nunley and Judith Bettelheim.

African cultural survivals: Aspects of African life, such as customs and beliefs, which were brought to and influenced the New World. In the not too distant past, the subject of African survivals drew little scholarly attention, for it was held that Africa—the "dark continent"—simply had no culture. Over time, however, historians have changed such interpretations and proved that Africa historically had flourishing kingdoms and civilizations. Moreover, they found that many elements of those civilizations made the transition to the Americas and deeply influenced the development of music, dance, religion, and language in African American life and American life in general.

The story of African cultural survivals goes back at least to the day the first slaves arrived in the New World, but it may extend back even further. A theory advanced by some scholars holds that Africans had made contact with the New World by the fourteenth century. Linguistic, archaeological, and anthropological evidence, as well as oral traditions and some written sources, has been cited to support this idea. Evidence suggests, for example, that Abubakari II of Mali sponsored an expedition of hundreds of ships to the New World in the 1300's. There are intriguing correspondences between artifacts and traditions of Africans and those of the original inhabitants of the New World. Huge granite heads and small statues have been found in Mexico that seem to represent Africans, for example, and similarities exist between Egyptian and American Indian mummification techniques. Anthropologists have found many similarities between ancient Mexican and Mandingan civilizations.

When Christopher COLUMBUS reported on his own expeditions in the late fifteenth century, he wrote of Indians' descriptions of black men who traded and had spears tipped with gold. The theory of early African

The Alvin Ailey American Dance Theater has incorporated African tribal rhythms and dress into modern dance choreography.
(Library of Congress)

penetration of the Americas, although it is controversial, offers exciting possibilities for further study and rediscovery of both African and American history.

Slavery. Given the African slave's need to survive, one of the first cultural survivals to appear in the New World after Columbus was the West African knowledge of pastoral AGRICULTURE. Historically, conquerors worldwide had difficulty enslaving nomadic food gatherers, hunters, herdsmen, and fishermen and found trouble enslaving members of strong kingdoms that had centralized governments and efficient armies. Hence, the first slaves taken from West Africa were from sedentary tribes such as the Wolof, Ibibio, Serer, Ibo, and Ewe, whose members were accustomed to agricultural labor. Because the great majority of slaves would be used as field laborers, their agricultural skills and customs proved useful and took root in the New World.

Another African survival, the memory of the institution of SLAVERY as practiced in Africa, probably helped enslaved Africans understand their new situation. This was important in getting over the shock and trauma of being kidnapped by slave hunters, forced to march to barracoons on the coast, branded, and forced to endure the MIDDLE PASSAGE to the New World. Once there, at least the enslaved Africans knew what would be expected of them.

Religion. Many West Africans had been converted to Islam, and their God was Allah; other tribes believed in the concept of a Creator, and some also had a host of lesser gods. The revering of ancestors was common. It was relatively simple for the enslaved Africans to see the similarities between their religion and the new, complex Christianity that confronted them. Many viewed Christianity as a polytheistic religion that worshiped at least three gods. Thus, in a sense, Allah still reigned supreme, but the new name was Jehovah; the new names of the lesser gods were Jesus, the Holy Ghost, and the saints. Over the generations, a majority of African Americans apparently forgot their African deities. Yet the black church has preserved many African traits as seen in religious music, dances, feasts, prayers, festivals, amulets, and funeral dirges.

Music and Dance. Another central part of their culture which enslaved Africans brought with them to the New World was music. They played instruments such as flutes, piccolos, whistles, horns, guitars, banjos, and drums, often homemade. Impromptu variations were characteristic of the music—fast changes in tone, in-

tonation, timbre, and pitch. In work songs, field hollers, and other songs sung in the fields, Africanisms could be heard: group participation, call and response, percussion (stamping feet or clapping hands), rhythmic complexity, and improvisation. Unlike European and Anglo American music, which usually contained one rhythm, African and African American music often contained at least three or more rhythms. One English scholar who examined African music called European music "childishly simple" by comparison.

The father of American BLUES MUSIC, W. C. HANDY, was directly influenced by African music patterns. Around the beginning of the twentieth century, band leader Handy was touring Mississippi, playing in various black clubs. One night, he was "upstaged" by an opening act that featured music patterned after African folk music; the audience so loved the three-man band that Handy decided to copy and refine their style. When later performers added horns and pianos, the result was JAZZ; when other performers added an entire orchestra (minus strings), the result was swing. Eventually these African American-based styles led to ROCK AND ROLL.

Another African survival related to both religion and music is the Negro SPIRITUAL. Though the early spirituals of the Old South used English words, they included several African stylistic elements, particularly strong West African call and response patterns and swinging rhythms. Similar patterns can be found later in GOSPEL music.

Many freed people who left testimony about the slave days demonstrated that they knew their spirituals came from Africa. One woman interviewed in the 1890's mentioned that when she attended church, she would put English words to "some old shout song" that she had heard in Africa before she had been kidnapped and sold. She would sing loud, she said, and the whole church would "take it up" without realizing that they had learned an African song. A few old songs and spirituals actually retained the African words. As late as the 1880's, African-born freed people in New Orleans still sang "Ouende, ouende" ("to go, to continue, to go on") with all African lyrics.

If much modern American music can trace its roots to African antecedents, so, too, can certain dance styles. Whereas imported European dances often involved stiff, stylized movements or formalized patterns, African dance displayed rapid movements to strong rhythms, more leaping, and sinuous movements of the torso. These African traits helped to shape the swing, rock and roll, disco, break dancing, and other popular styles of American dance.

Folklore. A less well-known African cultural survival is the folktale and other forms of FOLKLORE. As a favorite evening's entertainment, Africans would gather to hear tales accompanied by beating drums, singing, dancing, acting, and audience participation. The tales did more than entertain; they also taught values such as religious beliefs; the importance of knowledge; the importance of family and the extended family (clan, tribe). Additionally, the tales tried to explain natural phenomena; retold old legends about creation; recounted the deeds of heroes; and even told of witches and magic.

These children adorn themselves in traditional African garb at an African American Day parade. (Frances M. Roberts)

The actors in these stories, as in much African American folklore, often are animals with human characteristics, such as the ability to reason and to speak. Famous are the Ghanian ananse (spider), the Nigerian tortoise, and the ever-present rabbit. The heroes of the stories—usually boastful, guileful, and mischievous—always find themselves in trouble, perhaps besieged by stronger or faster animals, but they use superior intelligence, cunning, and patience to outwit their foes; thus, good always triumphs over evil. Such stories sustained the morale and group identity of African Americans through SLAVERY and SEGREGATION, and are still enjoyed today. One need only read a few of the African American folktales about "Brer Rabbit," "Brer Bear," and "Brer Fox" to understand the borrowing from the African tales. For example, the African American story of the hare and the "tar-baby" is almost identical to the Ewe tribe's story about "why the hare runs away." Many old slave tales with protagonists that are lions, elephants, and monkeys came from Africa.

Language. There were also linguistic survivals from Africa. Travelers to the American colonies during the eighteenth century, for example, said that they heard a patois spoken in the slave quarters containing both African and English languages. Some of the most rebellious Africans not only refused to accept an English name but also refused to speak English. According to Frederick DOUGLASS, even as late as the nineteenth century, the slaves on many Maryland plantations spoke a mixture of English, "Guinea, and everything else you please." The area of the strongest linguistic survivals was along the Georgia and Carolina coast where the GULLAH dialect (which mixed African and English words) was spoken as late as the mid-twentieth century. As late as the 1940's, Gullah African Americans on the Sea Islands retained literally thousands of West African names, which the Gullah considered secret, not to be known by whites. Many African words were also absorbed into English, among them "banjo," "goober," and "yam."

Just as there are many cultural survivals, there have also been cultural revivals as the African American generations of the twentieth century tried in their turn to re-embrace Africa. Marcus GARVEY's followers, for example, stressed African cultural revival, as did the protest generation of the 1960's. Even in the 1990's, African American youth were seeking a way to retain something of their African heritage in everything from fashion to music to food.

SUGGESTED READINGS. For a thorough study of early African survivals, see Ivan Van Sertima's *They Came Before Columbus* (1976) and a shorter work by Robert L. Harris, Jr., *Teaching Afro-American History* (1985). Further perspective on the subject may be found in Melville J. Herskovitz' *Myth of the Negro Past* (1941), Basil Davidson's *The African Genius* (Boston, 1969),

Roland F. Oliver's *Africa in the Iron Age* (1975), and John Blassingame's *The Slave Community* (1972).— *James M. Smallwood*

African immigration and cultural contributions in the twentieth century: Most black Americans are descendants of Africans brought forcibly to the United States as slaves before the slave trade was outlawed in the early 1800's. African-born Americans are a small and somewhat invisible population. A significant percentage are white (more than 80 percent in the censuses of 1910, 1930, and 1960); they tend to blend in with various European ethnic populations, such as South African Jews who live in JEWISH AMERICAN communities. Many black Africans arrived in the 1970's and 1980's after the opening of U.S. immigration to the countries of the Third World. Some came originally on student visas and stayed to pursue their careers, while others

Ethiopian immigrants attending a church service in Washington, D.C. (L. Gubb/UNHCR)

continue to live alternately in their native country and in the United States, depending on political changes in their homeland.

Throughout the nineteenth century, voluntary immigration from Africa was sparse, generally no more than a few hundred people per decade. From 1900 to 1930, the numbers jumped to several thousand per decade, but this flow was stopped by restrictive IMMIGRATION LEGISLATION and the GREAT DEPRESSION. WORLD WAR II was a turning point in both African history and African voluntary migration to the United States. African colonies began winning their independence from European rule, and nationalist movements gained strength throughout the continent. Stripped of their former political power, some white residents were motivated to leave Africa for the United States or other countries. From 1941 to 1960, more than twenty thousand African immigrants arrived in the United States. THE IMMIGRATION AND NATIONALITY ACT OF 1965 opened the gates to far greater arrivals: 27,000 in the 1960's, 81,000 in the 1970's, and a record 144,000 in the 1980's. (These figures also include Egyptians since 1967.) Some postwar African immigrants have left their homes because of an unfavorable political situation, such as the upper-class and well-educated Ethiopians who fled after a 1974 military coup toppled Emperor Haile Selassie or the white Rhodesians who fled when the country (now Zimbabwe) was turned over to black rule in 1980. Others are simply seeking better educational and professional opportunities, in spite of the barriers that remain in the United States against people of color.

Although their numbers are relatively small in the United States, black Africans such as Nigerians, Kenyans, Ghanians, and others have made their mark in various sectors of American society. Some serve in international government or nonprofit agencies in WASHINGTON, D.C., or NEW YORK, promoting a better understanding of African politics and economics. Some teach African studies or other advanced subjects in American colleges and universities. Many African immigrants are active as volunteers in political and humanitarian campaigns to aid their homeland. Ethiopians have been particularly visible as restauranteurs in various cities, introducing Americans to traditional savory stews that are eaten with large, pancake-like spongy bread. A number of African musicians and dancers have brought their talents to the United States, spurred by the enthusiasm for African traditional and popular music since the 1970's. For example, Du-

misani (Dumi) Maraire, a musician from Zimbabwe, taught music at the University of Washington in Seattle in the mid-1970's, returned to his homeland to do cultural work for the new government, and eventually resettled in Seattle. His work touched hundreds

Dressed in Nigerian clothes, this couple attends a traditional Nigerian wedding in the United States. (James L. Shaffer)

of American music students, brought other African musicians to town, and inspired the formation of several different types of performing ensembles, leaving Seattle with a thriving homegrown African musical scene. African artists such as Maraire have had a profound impact on African Americans seeking to rediscover their cultural roots. The late twentieth century has seen increasing efforts to bring together the African and African American communities in events such as cultural festivals based on the concept of the African diaspora.

African Methodist Episcopal church (AME church): Largest African American Methodist denomination in the United States. It has nineteen Episcopal districts throughout the United States, Canada, Africa, and the Caribbean. The church's Southern California Conference claims at least forty-five churches within the Los Angeles area. The impressive size of the AME church is a reflection of the steadfastness of its early founders. Their intense dedication to the dream of a church of their own, as well as their perseverance in working to achieve that end, was rewarded when the Philadelphia Supreme Court confirmed the church's full independence in 1816.

The church traces its origins to incidents that occurred a few years after the 1784 meeting in Baltimore that unified all Methodist societies that had been established in America by missionaries from Ireland. During the opening prayer on a Sunday morning at Philadelphia's St. George's Methodist Episcopal Church in November of 1787, Richard Allen and a group of other black worshipers left the service after white church members forced them to move from the spots at the altar rail where they were accustomed to pray. Angered by the discrimination they faced, Allen, Absalom Jones, and other black Methodists met together in a group known as the Free African Society, which eventually established and dedicated the Bethel African Methodist Episcopal Church in 1794. Other autonomous black congregations, such as the Colored Methodist Society in Baltimore, separated from white Methodist churches and were the forerunners of a national church. On March 24, 1807, various black Methodists drew up articles of self-government which gave legal control of black-owned church properties to the African Methodist Episcopal church. In the wake of the court ruling confirming its independence, the AME church convened an organizational meeting in which Allen was elected as the church's first bishop and various rules and documents of constitution were adopted.

The AME church continues to hold annual conferences in accordance with practices initiated soon after the church's founding. A large general conference is held every four years to discuss important church issues and to conduct church business, including the election and reassignment of bishops. Church-run schools include Wilberforce University in Ohio, Morris Brown College in Georgia, and Allen University in South Carolina. The AME church also maintains a publishing house, the first such publishing concern owned and operated by African Americans.

SUGGESTED READINGS. For a detailed account of the founder and first bishop of the AME church, Curtis E. Alexander's *Richard Allen: The First Exemplar of African American Education* (1985) offers insight into the personal life and religious struggle of Richard Allen. Daniel A. Payne's autobiography, *Recollections of Seventy Years* (1888, repr. 1968), documents his early life and involvement in the AME church, his election as bishop eleven years after joining the church in 1841, and his life as an educator. Howard D. Gregg's *History of the African Methodist Episcopal Church* (1980) provides an insider's history of the church.

Afrocentrism: Philosophy that encourages African Americans to study African culture to formulate their ideas about art, literature, religion, science, and communication. It challenges the popularly held belief that the Eurocentric view of such intercultural fields is universal. It further holds that the Eurocentric approach to African studies has distorted African history and has conveyed debilitating and distorted images of Africa and the African diaspora. Identification of African Americans with Africa gives them a sense of historical time and place which they cannot get from traditional Eurocentric study. Twentieth century proponents of Afrocentrism include W. E. B. Du Bois, Cheikh Anta Diop, Ivan Van Sertima, Molefi Kete Asante, and Eric Williams.

Agriculture: The U.S. Department of Agriculture defines agriculture very broadly to include crop and livestock farming, related businesses, and agricultural research and invention. Crop and livestock farming includes raising food, flowers, cotton, and even Christmas trees; dairy farming; maintaining orchards; hatching fish; herding cattle; keeping bees; and many other efforts. Related businesses include wholesaling and retailing farm products, processing food, crop dusting, providing banking and support services for farmers, transporting produce, and manufacturing farming equipment. Agricultural research and invention covers occupations in food safety, genetic engineering, soil conservation, food development, and wildlife study.

American Indians. The agriculture of the indigenous Americans has had enormous significance worldwide. Scientists and historians now recognize that the greatest impact of Christopher COLUMBUS' voyage to the New World may have been agricultural. American crops such as potatoes, corn, peanuts, and sweet potatoes were relatively swiftly adopted around the world. They supported population growth and industrialization in Europe, helped curb devastating famine, and stimulated new cuisine in many cultures.

Essential to these agricultural riches was the superbly healthy ecosystem, a product of thousands of years of stewardship, that the Indians bequeathed to European settlers. Indians' spiritual values and profound respect for the land are reflected in Sitting Bull's reference to "this mother of ours, the Earth," and Chief Seattle's comment, "Every part of this soil is sacred in the estimation of my people. Every hillside, every valley, every plain and grove has been hallowed."

Native crops included maize or corn, potatoes, sweet potatoes, tomatoes, manioc, peanuts, pumpkins, cranberries, blueberries, strawberries, pecans, sunflower seeds, wild rice, and maple syrup, as well as many kinds of peppers, beans, and squash. In addition, the Indians used native seasonings and flavorings such as gumbo filé, red peppers, paprika, mints, and wintergreens. In all, American Indians cultivated more than three hundred food crops, many of which had numerous varieties. More than 60 percent of all foods now in cultivation originated with American Indians.

Indian foods profoundly influenced the American diet. The traditional American THANKSGIVING meal, for example—turkey, cornmeal dressing, cranberries, sweet potato casseroles and pies, potatoes, green beans, stewed squash, and pumpkin and pecan pies— is entirely based on indigenous dishes. In addition, baked beans with maple syrup, succotash, hominy, hush puppies, Brunswick Stew, popcorn, corn chips, dried meat sticks and jerky, corn cakes and spoonbreads of many sorts, and many other favorites were first served by American Indians.

American Indians also developed important agricultural technologies. They understood hybridization and practiced plant experimentation for thousands of years before Columbus arrived. They used fertilizer and advanced methods of seed preservation. Indian agricultural techniques included planting corn, beans, and squash together. The tall corn supported the bean and squash vines while shading the more delicate beans from the sun. Squash leaves provided good ground cover, preventing erosion while capturing rain water and effectively keeping out weeds. This technique also reduced plant destruction by insects and other pests. The result was an increase of up to 50 percent in crop yield over other methods.

American Indians developed food preparation methods that increased nutrition. Their techniques for harvesting and processing maple sap have admitted of little improvement. In the American Southwest, they grew and wove cotton and built irrigation systems. Modern American farmers are deeply indebted to Indian agriculture.

Latinos. Among the earliest LATINO contributions to American agriculture was the establishment of the ranching industry. Cattle ranching is essentially Latino, with roots in medieval Iberia (Spain and Portugal). Cowboy skills, roundups, branding, and cattle drives were developed in Europe. The first VAQUEROS, or COWBOYS, in North America rode horses of Spanish ancestry. Texas longhorns descended from swift, lean, resourceful Castilian range cattle which could protect themselves from a variety of predators, travel long distances between water holes, and forage their own food.

By the mid-sixteenth century, central Mexican plains and valleys were dotted with haciendas. By the 1680's, cattle ranches had been established north of the Rio Grande in what is now Texas.

Mexican Indians and mestizos (people of mixed European and Indian heritage) moved steadily northward into the American Southwest from the time of the first ranches through the twentieth century. Initially they were drawn by the ranching industry. After the MEXICAN-AMERICAN WAR, many stayed because the TREATY OF GUADALUPE HIDALGO guaranteed that they could keep their land, language, and culture.

These promises disintegrated as PREJUDICE, unfair legal practices, and Anglo laws stripped Latinos of their land and forced them into the lowest economic stratum. Still, thousands more Latinos came because Mexico's economy was faltering and the lure of American jobs was irresistible. These thousands fueled the farm and MIGRANT LABOR force. In 1890, about 75,000 Latinos were counted in the U.S. census. By 1900, the count was 562,000; by 1920, it was 900,000. Many of these Latinos were agricultural laborers in cotton fields, fruit orchards, and vegetable farms. They picked, processed, packed, and shipped the growing yields made possible by improved agricultural methods, year-round farming, irrigation, and reservoirs. Some who moved north and east remained agribusiness laborers, such as workers in the meat-packing industry in Gary, Indiana.

Most Latino migrant workers were poorly paid, often living in unspeakable conditions. They became part of the American LABOR MOVEMENT, demanding decent treatment. In 1913, Latino workers protested

Hupa Indians oversee a newly planted crop on the reservation. More than 60 percent of all foods now in cultivation originated with American Indians. (Ben Klaffke)

conditions on a hops ranch near Wheatland, California. The riot that followed called the nation's attention to their plight. In the 1920's, California migrant workers formed the Confederation of Unions of Mexican Workers, and in 1928 the group led a historic strike against Imperial Valley melon farmers. The movement was continued by César CHÁVEZ, whose leadership in nonviolent protest paralleled the efforts of Martin Luther KING, JR., on behalf of African Americans.

By the early 1950's, Chávez was organizing California wine-grape pickers. A decade later, he founded the National Farm Workers Association, forerunner of the UNITED FARM WORKERS. In 1965, he led grape pickers on a 300-mile march from Delano, California, to Sacramento, heightening public awareness of the exploitation of migrant workers. Chávez called for repeated boycotts of grapes and lettuce in an effort to force growers to accept the union as collective bargaining agent for migrant workers.

In spite of Chávez' efforts, however, Latino migrant workers still lacked good housing, child care, and schools in the 1990's. Federal money appropriated for their benefit did not always meet their needs, and they often traded a stable life for subsistence. Latino migrant workers are not confined to the American Southwest but follow seasonal jobs in orchards, nurseries, fields, and packing plants across the United States.

Latinos have made an indelible impact on agribusiness through their cuisine. Mexican foods are American favorites, and this marketing reality has significantly affected the planting, processing, and packing of food in the United States.

African Americans. Many enslaved Africans brought ancient agricultural knowledge and skills with them to the United States. Agriculture had begun in Africa in very ancient times. Some African slaves

During the antebellum period, the agricultural economy of the South was based on black slave labor. These slaves are picking cotton. (National Archives)

knew more about plantation crops than their white overseers and owners. In South Carolina, the rice fanner, storage baskets, and mortars surviving from SLAVERY times are examples of African technology.

During the antebellum period, most black Americans were slaves, and the agricultural economy of the South was based on their labor. After the CIVIL WAR, these realities did not change a great deal; African Americans, as sharecroppers and hired laborers, continued to produce a substantial portion of southern crops. By 1910, more than half of all African Americans were still engaged in farming. Nearly 900,000 of them (about 14 percent of all American farmers) were farm operators.

African Americans have also contributed to American agriculture as individual inventors and experimenters. For example, George Washington CARVER is best known for his research at TUSKEGEE INSTITUTE on the peanut, sweet potato, and other foods. Norbert Rillieux revolutionized the production process of sugar by inventing the first practical multiple-effect evaporator. Frederick McKinley Jones invented a mobile refrigeration system, helping make possible the modern food transportation system. Andrew Beard designed improved farm plows; Lloyd Hall discovered ways to cure meat and sterilize food; and Henry Blair invented plows, a corn harvester, and a corn planting machine.

A multitude of other black inventors contributed new designs and improvements to equipment for agribusiness. Among these were George Murray, who patented a cultivator, cotton planter, and six other inventions; Joseph Lee, who invented a dough kneader; and A. P. Ashbourne, who invented processes for treating and refining coconut oil.

Asian Americans. Asian immigrants poured into the United States during the second half of the nineteenth century and the first decades of the twentieth. Many of them went first to Hawaii, where they provided cheap labor for sugar and pineapple plantations. Ultimately, many moved to the mainland. Altogether, nearly a million CHINESE, JAPANESE, KOREANS, FILIPINOS, and ASIAN INDIANS immigrated to Hawaii and the United States during this period.

Vast numbers of these immigrants became agricultural laborers, doing "stoop work" in fields for wages white workers found unacceptable. These Asians frequently became migrant workers, adapting to the seasonal patterns of a variety of crops. Discriminatory hiring limited other work opportunities to menial jobs,

and many Asians preferred to stay in agriculture.

Although the stories of Asian immigrants are complex and are different for each ethnic group, it is generally accurate to say that they tended to escape migrant work by saving money; buying cheap, infertile land; and using labor-intensive methods to make it yield good crops. ALIEN LAND LAWS often prevented Asians from owning land. Nevertheless, through land rental, tenant farming, and other methods, they raised enormous quantities of produce. In 1917, for example, Japanese farmers grew almost 90 percent of California's asparagus, onions, celery, tomatoes, cantaloupes, and berries; more than 70 percent of floral products; 50 percent of seeds; 45 percent of sugar beets; 40 percent of leafy vegetables; and 35 percent of grapes.

A Japanese American farm worker in Nyssa, Oreg., 1942. (Library of Congress)

There were individual successes, as well. George Shima arrived as an impoverished immigrant in 1887 and found a job picking potatoes in the San Joaquin Valley. By 1912, he owned more than 10,000 acres of potatoes worth $.5 million. Koreans Kim Hyung-Soon and Kim Ho became partners in a spectacularly successful nursery and orchard business. Asian Indian Divan Singh developed a 1,600-acre vegetable farm in

Arizona that employed hundreds of workers.

Asians also achieved success in related businesses. About ten thousand Chinese endured brutal conditions to help build the first transcontinental railroad, providing a transportation system that took western fruits and vegetables to customers in the East. Asians formed cooperatives to buy and sell agricultural labor, products, and land. First generation Japanese (ISSEI) farmers created credit-rotating associations (*tanomoshi*) to pool group resources for land purchase. They also set up cooperatives (*kobai kumiai* and *sango kumiai*) to buy bulk foods and market crops. Chinese and Korean efforts (*woi* and *kae*) served similar functions.

Some Asians were agricultural inventors and experimenters. A Chinese farmer in Oregon, Ah Bing, developed the Bing cherry, and a Florida farmer, Lue Gim Gong, created the frost-resistant orange. Joseph Park, a Korean chemical engineer, developed refrigerants for keeping food fresh, and Asian Indian Dalip Singh Saund manufactured a chemical fertilizer. The Kim Brothers Company developed the "Le Grand" or "Sun Grand" fuzzless peach.

Asians have also had a profound impact on American cuisine. "Oriental" foods, in all their variety, have become part of American culture, affecting farming, food processing, and marketing.

SUGGESTED READINGS. The U.S. Department of Agriculture's 1990 yearbook, *Americans in Agriculture: Portraits of Diversity,* provides a comprehensive definition of agriculture along with a series of sketches of contemporary Americans from a variety of cultural groups. Information on agricultural contributions can also be found in standard histories of ethnic groups in the United States. These include Ronald Takaki's *Strangers from a Different Shore: A History of Asian Americans* (1989); H. Brett Melendy's *Asians in America: Filipinos, Koreans, and East Indians* (1977); Sucheng Chan's *Asian Americans: An Interpretive History* (1991); Julie Catalano's *The Mexican Americans* (1988); Lerone Bennett's *Before the Mayflower: A History of Black America* (1982); and Jack Weatherford's *Native Roots: How the Indians Enriched America* (1991). Another important work about multicultural contributions to American farming and diet is *Seeds of Change: A Quincentennial Commemoration* (1991), edited by Herman J. Viola and Carolyn Margolis.—*Barbara Glass*

Ah Moy case. *See* **In Re Ah Moy, on Habeas Corpus**

Ahn, Philip (Mar. 29, 1911, Los Angeles, Calif.—Feb. 28, 1978, Los Angeles, Calif.): Korean American actor. The son of Korean immigrants, Ahn was graduated from the University of Southern California and in 1936 embarked on a film career in *The General Died at Dawn.* Over the next four decades, Ahn appeared in more than fifty films, including *Thank You, Mr. Moto* (1937), *Love*

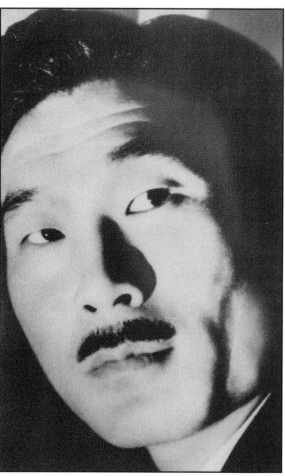

Korean American film actor Philip Ahn. (AP/Wide World Photos)

Is a Many-Splendored Thing (1955), and *The World's Greatest Athlete* (1973). He became known for his portrayal of stereotypically cold, cunning Asian American villains, especially in World War II films. Ahn was familiar to television audiences as the master Kan in the *Kung Fu* series (1972-1975). He was the first Asian American actor to be honored with a star on the "Walk of Fame" by the Hollywood Chamber of Commerce.

AIDS. *See* **Acquired immune deficiency syndrome epidemic**

Ailey, Alvin (Jan. 5, 1931, Rogers, Tex.—Dec.1, 1989, New York, N.Y.): African American modern dancer, choreographer, and artistic director. A former high school athlete, Ailey studied dance while attending various California colleges (1949-1953) and became a dancer and choreographer with the pioneering Lester Horton Dancers (1951-1953). In 1958 he founded his own troupe, the Alvin Ailey American Dance Theater in New York. Tours abroad during the 1960's brought acclaim that was unprecedented for an American company. Critics have called Ailey's unique jazz style "stark," "violent," and "beautiful." His many honors include the United Nations Peace Medal.

Alvin Ailey, founder of the critically acclaimed Alvin Ailey American Dance Theater. (AP/Wide World Photos

Ala Moana incident (1931): Alleged rape of a white woman by five Asian and native Hawaiian men and the legal and illegal repercussions of the allegation. Because of the role of the U.S. military in toppling the Hawaiian monarchy in 1893, many native Hawaiians have long resented the continuing presence of the predominantly *haole* (Caucasian) armed forces on military bases in Hawaii. The Ala Moana incident dramatized the polarization between native or Asian Hawaiians and Anglos.

On September 12, 1931, Thalia Massie, the wife of naval Lieutenant Thomas Hedges Massie, attended an officers' club party at the Ala Moana Inn in Waikiki. Deciding to walk down toward the beach, she encountered persons unknown in a beat-up car. She later claimed they were dark-skinned locals who proceeded to rape her. After the incident, she staggered to the Ala Moana road, where a man saw her and gave her a ride home. Seeing her lips swollen, her face bruised, and her jaw broken, Massie's husband notified the police, who soon rounded up five young local men and placed them in custody. The five (a Chinese Hawaiian, two native Hawaiians, and two Japanese) went on trial. So circumstantial was the evidence of rape on the part of the five that a jury of local residents refused to bring in a verdict in *Hawaii v. Ahakuelo* (1931).

Convinced that justice had not prevailed and angry that the defendants were freed on bail while awaiting a retrial, Grace Fortescue, Thalia Massie's mother, decided to take an extralegal approach. Joe Kahahawai, one of the defendants, was soon abducted, and tortured by Lieutenant Massie and two military officers in the hope that he would confess; in the process, Kahahawai was accidentally shot. When police found the body of the man in Mrs. Fortescue's car, they arrested her, Lieutenant Massie, and the two military officers involved. In *Hawaii v. Massie* (1932), the four conspirators were convicted of manslaughter despite an eloquent defense by their attorney, Clarence Darrow, who had been recruited from the mainland to plead his last case. Judge Charles Davis pronounced a sentence of ten years hard labor at Oahu Prison; however, Territorial Governor Lawrence Judd commuted the sentence to one hour of detention in the governor's chambers under the custody of the high sheriff.

To Asians and Hawaiians, it seemed that Judd had meted out *"haole"* justice." For some, including whites outraged by Judd's cavalier action, a campaign for self-rule (statehood) seemed the best strategy to prevent future Massie cases and further racial polarization. Other *haoles*, however, were insensitive to this change in political climate, believing that special treatment for whites sent a signal to nonwhites that *haoles* alone could hold the Territory of Hawaii together.

SUGGESTED READINGS. The best narrative on the Ala Moana incident and the subsequent Massie case is Theon Wright's *Rape in Paradise* (1966). Masaji

Marumoto presents an excellent analysis of the two court cases in "The Ala Moana Case and the Massie-Fortescue Case, Revisited," *University of Hawaii Law Review* (vol. 5, 1983).

Alamo, Battle of the (1836): Thirteen-day struggle during the Texas war for independence from Mexico at a mission-fortress in San Antonio, Texas. Within the walls of the Alamo, a band of Texans made a heroic resistance against the overwhelming forces of the Mexican army. The Alamo became a symbol of steadfast courage and sacrifice to Anglo Americans.

tured and occupied the fort in December of 1835. The following month, when news arrived of an impending invasion by a strong army under General Santa Anna, Texas General Sam Houston ordered the Alamo abandoned and destroyed. Instead, the garrison chose to defend it.

The commanding officers of the fort were Colonels William Barret Travis and James Bowie. Incapacitated by illness, Bowie relinquished full command to the twenty-six-year-old Travis early in the siege. David Crockett, recently arrived from Tennessee, was also one of the well-known defenders.

Schoolchildren visit the Alamo in 1992. (James L. Shaffer)

Founded in 1718 as the Franciscan mission San Antonio de Valero, the Alamo was converted to a fort and military barracks after 1793. It served as Mexican military headquarters in Texas when the revolution broke out against the rising dictatorship of General Antonio López de Santa Anna. A group of Texans cap-

The tone of the battle was set early. The vanguard of Santa Anna's army entered San Antonio on February 23, 1836, and the general demanded the immediate surrender of the Alamo. Travis answered with a cannon shot, and the next day he dispatched messengers to other parts of Texas carrying appeals for aid. Only thirty-two reinforcements were able to cross enemy lines to reach the besieged Texans on March 1. The new arrivals brought the fighting force within the Alamo to 184 men. Meanwhile Mexican troops continued to arrive, reaching an estimated total of six thousand.

In the dawn of Sunday, March 6, Santa Anna gave the order to attack. Troops bearing ladders and muskets stormed the fort from all four sides. Although the Mexicans suffered grave losses, they eventually overcame the resisters in hand-to-hand combat in the courtyard and surrounding buildings.

The siege ended with the deaths of all 183 defenders. Only about fifteen people, including three Texan civilians, were spared. The bodies of the fallen Texans were burned. The Mexicans suffered about 1,550 casualties; their dead were buried in the cemetery.

The Battle of the Alamo provided fellow Texans with time to rally their defenses. "Remember the Alamo" was the battle cry of Houston's forces when they decisively defeated Santa Anna's army at San Jacinto six weeks later.

SUGGESTED READINGS. For an excellent analysis, see C. D. Huneycutt's *The Alamo: An In-Depth Study of the Battle* (1986). A very readable account of the siege is presented in Virgil E. Baugh's *Rendezvous at the Alamo* (1985). Novelist and poet Robert Penn Warren's account of the battle is given in *Remember the Alamo!* (1958). Another insightful work is Jeff Long's *Duel of Eagles: The Mexican and U.S. Fight for the Alamo* (1990). For a personal narrative of the battle, see José Enrique de la Peña's *With Santa Anna in Texas: a Personal Narrative of the Revolution* (1975).

Alaska Native Claims Settlement Act (1971): Law granting $1 billion and 40 million acres of state land to the Alaskan Federation of Natives in settlement of claims between the government and communities of American Indians, INUITS, and ALEUTS in Alaska. Paving the way for the legislation was increased public awareness of native land claims as a result of the INDIAN RIGHTS MOVEMENT and a pattern of vastly increased compensation payments to Indian tribes by the federal Indian Claims Commission. A victory for native peoples in Alaska, the law was vigorously opposed by non-native mining, energy, hunting, and fishing interests in the state.

Albanian Americans: Albania is a Balkan country that has traditionally been divided into two ethnic groups, the Tosks in the south and the Gegs in the mountainous

ALBANIA

north. The Tosks have traditionally had contact with people in other countries, but the Gegs lived in isolation until WORLD WAR II. The first Albanians to come to the United States in large numbers were Eastern Orthodox Tosk men. They arrived in the first decades of the twentieth century to make money to send back to their families. Many of these men returned to Albania after WORLD WAR I.

After World War II, a different group of Albanians emigrated to the United States. These were Gegs fleeing the Communist government. Most were MUSLIM, but a small number were ROMAN CATHOLIC. The Gegs brought their strict, patriarchal moral codes with them to the United States. Traditional Geg families are ruled by men. They do not like their wives to hold jobs, and they may be reluctant to let their daughters attend school past age thirteen. The Gegs also imported their blood feuds. They had to learn to settle their differences through American law rather than by violence.

Most Albanian immigrants arrived in Boston and spread from there to other parts of New England. Others went to CHICAGO, DETROIT, St. Louis, and the

Bronx in NEW YORK CITY. In the 1970's, Albanian immigrants formed a community in LOS ANGELES.

The more than seventy thousand Albanian Americans in the United States maintain their family and ethnic ties with large communal picnics. There they enjoy songs and dances from their homeland and enjoy delicacies such as roast lamb, olives, feta cheese, and vegetable pies called *lakror*. They keep in touch with the political events in their native land through Albanian-English periodicals. In spite of efforts to teach young Albanian Americans their language, few third- and fourth-generation descendants speak or understand the Albanian language.

SUGGESTED READINGS. This population is poorly documented in general sources except for "Albanians" in the *Harvard Encyclopedia of American Ethnic Groups* (1980), edited by Stephan Thernstrom, and *The Albanian Struggle in the Old World and New* (1939) by the Federal Writers' Project of Massachusetts.

Alcatraz Island, occupation of (1969-1971): Action by a multitribal group of American Indian students from the San Francisco Bay area who seized control of the island from late 1969 until 1971. They claimed that previous agreements between Indians and the U.S. government gave Indians rights to abandoned federal property. From 1934 until 1963, Alcatraz Island was the site of the most infamous federal penitentiary in the United States. A military prison since 1868, the island had originally been part of the tribal land of the Ohlone Indians. When the Federal Bureau of Prisons terminated use of this facility, the group of American Indian students, newly organized as the Indians of All Tribes, occupied the island until they were forcibly evicted in 1971.

Alcoholism and drug abuse: Substance abuse is responsible for great loss of human productivity as well as for much suffering and dysfunction in Americans of every RACE and ETHNICITY. While excessive use of alcohol has long been a social problem, drug abuse only became widespread in the twentieth century. A greater stigma, as well as risk, is attached to drug abuse because many abused drugs are illegal. Alcohol, while widely and legally available, has been increasingly classified as a drug because of its harmful chemical effects, but this "drug" is often considered socially acceptable when used in moderation.

Rates of drug usage vary according to cultural, so-

cial, and psychological conditions in various communities. Some groups attach cultural value to drug use for specific purposes, as with PEYOTE in ceremonies of the NATIVE AMERICAN CHURCH. Times of greater stress, including war, economic depression, or cultural fragmentation, can lead to increased rates of addiction. Substance abuse is also linked to a host of social problems such as HOMELESSNESS, CRIME AND GANGS, the ACQUIRED IMMUNE DEFICIENCY SYNDROME (AIDS) EPIDEMIC, and the crisis in the INNER CITY. Regarding crime, for example, the majority of persons arrested for various crimes in major cities such as CHICAGO, DETROIT, LOS ANGELES, and NEW YORK in 1990 and 1991 tested positive for drug use at the time of arrest, according to the National Institute of Justice. It is important to realize that substance abuse can be both a cause of social problems, as when drug addicts commit robbery to support their habit, and an effect of social problems, as when people turn to drink or drugs to escape from the conditions and hopelessness of POVERTY.

A number of STEREOTYPES prevail about the typical

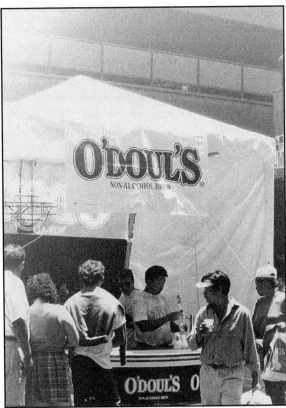

Shoppers sample a nonalcoholic beer and avoid the dangerous side-effects of alcohol. (Valerie Marie)

alcoholic or drug addict, yet experts have found that substance abuse crosses all lines of CLASS, ethnicity, and EDUCATION level. In 1991, for example, the National Institute on Drug Abuse found that more whites (52.7 percent) and LATINOS (47.5 percent) than AFRI-

and thirty-five, except for alcohol and cigarettes, which are also heavily used by those over thirty-five. Children and teenagers are being exposed to a wider range of drugs at increasingly younger ages.

Substance abuse has an enormous impact on HEALTH AND MEDICINE in the United States. For example, intravenous drug users who use contaminated needles are among the high-risk groups for contracting and spreading AIDS. Substance abuse among pregnant women often leads to serious and tragic complications in CHILDBIRTH such as fetal alcohol syndrome, which may impair a child's functioning for years. Detoxification and rehabilitation programs at hospitals are costly and often out of reach financially to the people who need them most. In the 1980's and 1990's, the trend has been toward more preventive, educational programs and community-based or family-centered treatment efforts. Among the more successful approaches to the problem of addiction is the support-group-based twelve-step recovery program which is modeled on a plan devised by the Alcoholics Anonymous organiza-tion founded in 1935.

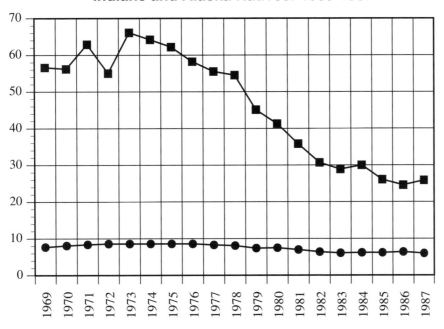

Rates of Death Due to Alcoholism for American Indians and Alaska Natives: 1969-1987

— ■ — Death rate per 100,000 American Indians and Alaska Natives

— ● — Death rate per 100,000 of all Americans

Source: Data are from Carol Foster, ed. *Minorities: A Changing Role in America.* Table 5.17. Wylie, Tex.: Information Plus, 1992.
Note: While the rate for Americans of all races is much lower, the numbers are much greater due to the larger overall population (for example, 15,513 Americans of all races died of alcoholism in 1987 compared to only 288 Indians).

CAN AMERICANS (43.7 percent) were users of alcohol. Whites were also more likely to abuse inhalants, hallucinogens, stimulants, sedatives, tranquilizers, and analgesics, while blacks had a higher rate of marijuana, cocaine, and crack use. Women generally had lower rates of substance abuse (only 44.3 percent were alcohol users as opposed to 58.1 percent of men) but came close to men's rate of use for sedatives, tranquilizers, and analgesics. Most drug use appears concentrated in Americans between the ages of eighteen

Symptoms of Addiction. Substance abuse must be understood within the broader concept of addiction, in which people are compelled to perform a habitual, obsessive behavior such as excessive drinking or drug use.

Some addiction theories see all addictive behaviors as related by common symptoms, although causes and populations involved may differ. Addictions include all drugs and combination of drugs and alcohol as well as behaviors such as gambling, sex, eating, purging, and starving. Many researchers draw a distinction between addictive behavior in which something is given up, such as in anorexia nervosa, in which food is avoided, and addictive disorders in which something is compulsively and destructively sought, such as alcohol. While scientists agree on what constitutes addictive behavior, they cannot state definitively why addiction occurs. There are a number of contending theories and models of addiction that attempt to answer the question of why people become addicted.

Addicted individuals are not in control of their drug use; rather, it is in control of them. The pattern of use of a particular substance is not controlled by rational thought or effective willpower. There is, however, wide variety in the patterns of use. Starting to drink only after work versus drinking all day can both be labeled addiction. In both cases, the drug abuse will continue to excess and the decision to limit use will not prevail. The addicted individuals have incorporated the disorder so thoroughly into their lives that much of their conscious time is spent wrapped in involvement with the addiction.

The addicted individual becomes the source of worry, anxiety, or fear in others. Addictions do not remain anonymous; especially within the family and the workplace there are ample opportunities for others to observe the influence of the addiction. These observers will be concerned about the person's growing dependence and by the influence the substance has on their life and functioning.

Addicted individuals experience many negative consequences as a result of their use of the substance. Despite these effects, however, addicts continue to be involved in the pursuit of their substance. Nonaddicted individuals observing this process are often astounded that addicts do not seek help or stop on their own, especially when the consequences are life-threatening. In many cases, the simple fact is that the addicted individuals are not in control of their lives and are unable to stop, even in the face of death.

Relapse into the compulsive use of a substance is a defining element of substance addiction. Despite extensive use of denial as a psychological defense against seeing their problem, people are in fact aware that they are addicted. Addiction has a physiological element in which the individual's body craves the substance. The physiological addiction can be eliminated by withdrawal from the substance which is often quite physically painful. Addiction also has a psychological element, which many theorists believe will remain for the individual's entire life. It cannot be eliminated, but it can be replaced by healthy behavior. Without help, the addicted individuals may withdraw from the substance physiologically, but their psychological dependence will pull them back into compulsive use.

Tolerance for the substance grows in the addicted individual. When individuals begin drug use, they may require very little of the substance. As their addiction develops, they require more and their systems are able to tolerate more. Cumulative toxic effects do occur, however, with some substances such as alcohol.

Addicted individuals increasingly come to believe that they must use the substance in order to experience a conscious state of well-being or the capacity to cope with life. Eventually they may desire to be under the influence of the substance for their every waking moment. As their self-esteem falls, they replace it within their lives with the false security or induced euphoria provided by a drug. Their value system begins to crumble, and they will tolerate increasing levels of failure within their lives. Sometimes they will attempt to preserve some part of their life, such as work or family relationships, yet these have probably already been damaged by the addiction.

Models of Addiction. A historical view of the addiction process that has been abandoned by modern researchers is the moral model. It is derived from philosophical and religious beliefs that judge addicted individuals as immoral. They are seen as voluntarily choosing to abuse substances in an uncontrolled manner. Under the sway of this perspective, treatment and research was inhibited.

The medical model helped to advance treatment and research by replacing the concept of the immoral person with the concept of the individual suffering from a disease. The disease is seen as a consequence of some physical disorder. This model has led researchers to examine many different systems of bodily functioning such as endocrine gland disorders and brain dysfunction due to structural damage.

Some scientists believe that susceptibility to addiction is inherited. Exactly what genes may be affected and what aspects of human functioning are affected is still a source of scientific debate. Some studies have examined the possibility that a predisposition toward certain emotional states such as depression or anxiety would lead people to medicate themselves with various substances. Other researchers believe that an inherited antisocial or dependent personality may be the cause of addiction. Additional studies have examined

A police officer speaks to elementary school children about the dangers of drug abuse. (James L. Shaffer)

the pattern of sensitivity to certain drugs among families and ethnic groups to see if some people have higher levels of physiological susceptibility to the effects of drugs. The search for biochemical differences in the brain has become a very promising area of research on addiction. There is mounting evidence that people differ widely in their biochemical reactions to various drugs: Such differences may account for the physical causes of addiction.

There are many competing psychological models of addiction. The addictive personality theory searches for predisposing psychological traits such as high levels of anxiety, low self-esteem, difficulty in delaying gratification of needs, low tolerance for frustration, and an inadequate ability to express oneself. Other traits that have been examined include high levels of unmet dependency needs, perfectionism, compulsiveness, and social isolation. There are no consistent findings to support any single trait as being paramount in causing addictions. Most researchers agree that the pattern of psychopathology will vary from addict to addict and from drug to drug.

Classical learning theories of addiction approach the problem from the point of view of behavior reinforcement and habit formation. These short-term pleasures of the drug are so reinforcing that its long-term negative effects do not possess the power to extinguish the addiction. Other learning theories have stressed the importance of the social environment of the individual, such as learned patterns of drug use, motivation, attitudes, and rationalizations that come from one's peer group.

Cultural and anthropological models such as the level of stress examine differences in social conditions among various groups to account for drug use patterns. Studies show that high stress groups have increased drug use during times of high stress and higher drug use than other comparable low stress groups at any time. This approach also researches such variables as the use of drugs or alcohol in religious rituals and ceremonies, the culture's attitude toward drug use, traditional social drinking or drug use patterns, and whether drug use for personal pleasure is treated the same as drug use for ritual or social functions.

None of the models or theories cited above can completely explain why addiction occurs in some individuals and not in others. Increasingly, the research in addictions is attempting to integrate as many of the theories as are compatible. The future of research on substance abuse will stress a biological-psychological-sociological-anthropological integration.

SUGGESTED READINGS. For further information on substance abuse and various ethnic groups, see publications of the U.S. Department of Health and Human Services: *National Household Survey on Drug Abuse* (1992) and the very valuable *Alcohol Use Among U.S. Ethnic Minorities* (1989). Also useful is *Alcoholism and Substance Abuse in Special Populations* (1989), edited by G. W. Lawson and A. W. Lawson.—*Warren Shaffer*

Alcott, Louisa May (Nov. 29, 1832, Philadelphia, Pa.—Mar. 6, 1888, Boston, Mass.): Pioneering woman writer. Alcott published more than 270 works, starting at age sixteen, to help her family through financial difficulties. Her father, Bronson Alcott, introduced her to writers Henry David Thoreau and Ralph Waldo Emer-

Little Women *author, Louisa May Alcott.* (Library of Congress)

son, who became her first teachers. She is best known for her juvenile fiction, notably *Little Women* (1868), *Little Men* (1871), and *Jo's Boys* (1886), which remain popular classics. In 1868 she became the editor of the first American magazine for girls, *Merry's Museum.* Much of her work portrayed the details of domestic middle-class American life. She was also a supporter of black rights and suffrage.

Aleuts in the U.S.: Some scholars have speculated that the native population of the Aleutian Islands off the coast of Alaska arrived there around eight thousand years ago, having crossed the Bering land bridge from Asia and found their way to the Aleutian Islands. They adapted well to the harsh environment. Despite some warfare between villages, the Aleuts faced their greatest challenge with the advent of European expansion.

Contact with the Aleuts was established first by the Russians around 1741. Since then, the Aleut population has declined dramatically for a variety of reasons, with the largest decline occurring in the early period of contact as a result of massacres and the introduction of foreign diseases. Scholars estimate the Aleut population to have stood at 15,000 to 25,000 at the time of contact, while the surviving Aleut population on the islands, Alaska, and elsewhere is estimated at 3,500 at the close of the twentieth century.

Almost all areas of Aleutian life, including religion, were affected by the Russian presence. Fur traders introduced Russian customs and religion, and Russian missionaries arrived at the end of the eighteenth century. The first Russian Orthodox church school was founded by Father Ivan Veniaminov in 1825. Because of the Aleuts' vulnerability to European diseases, the power of the traditional shaman rapidly declined. The church gained popularity among Aleuts through ceremonies that acted as substitutes for native rituals and through church services, which were conducted in both Russian and Aleut. The Russian Orthodox church is still active on the islands and has become an integral part of Aleutian life.

The United States acquired the islands as part of its purchase of Alaska in 1867. During World War II, the Japanese invaded the Aleutians and held many Aleuts captive. In 1943, when American forces regained control, the U.S. government ordered the evacuation of all Aleuts west of Unimak Island. Many evacuees were housed in abandoned canneries under poor conditions. In 1945, those who returned to their homes found their villages damaged and their household possessions, including artifacts, stolen or destroyed. For their personal losses, each Aleut received $35 in compensation. Congress later tried to rectify this with a payment of $12,000 to each survivor.

Traditional Aleutian culture included a wide range of arts and crafts. Various tools and decorative objects were made from wood, grass, bone, ivory, and stone. Kayaks were often elaborately engraved, and Aleut women were famous for their fur sewing. Much of the old art has been abandoned, but basketry has been revived and is taught in some school programs.

One of the great arts of Aleutian culture that has survived is storytelling. The stories are mythic, and many were composed while storytellers tended to daily duties. The Aleutian language is expressive and has been called an observer's language, moving easily from observance to description. As do other societies with rich oral traditions, the Aleuts greatly respect silence, not only in the stories but also as a means to foster privacy and individuality. In 1909, Russian ethnologist Waldemar Jochelson spent nineteen months gathering material from the few remaining Aleut storytellers. The material Jochelson published is incomplete, but it is considered an invaluable source of Aleut culture and lore.

SUGGESTED READINGS. See William S. Laughlin's *Aleuts: Survivors of the Bering Land Bridge* (1980). More facts on the history and social patterns of Aleut culture can be found in *Ethnohistory in Southwestern Alaska and the Southern Yukon, Method and Content* (1970) by Margaret Lantis, Robert E. Ackerman, Catharine McClellan, Joan B. Townsend, and James W. VanStone. For a historical view from land-bridge migration to the present, *Aleuts in Transition* (1976) by Dorothy M. Jones, is excellent. *Aleut Tales and Narratives* (1990), edited by Knut Bergsland and Moses L. Dirks, contains Aleut stories collected by Waldemar Jochelson. Dorothy Jean Ray provides a visual display through photographs along with commentary on Aleut art in *Aleut and Eskimo Art: Tradition and Innovation in South Alaska* (1987).

Ali, Muhammad (Cassius Marcellus Clay, Jr.; b. Jan. 17, 1942, Louisville, Ky.): African American professional boxer. Clay won a national Golden Gloves title and Olympic Gold Medal in 1960 before adopting his Muslim name (1963). As a professional, Ali was a three-time world heavyweight champion, beginning with his defeat of champ Sonny Liston in 1964. Ali's title was revoked in 1967, when he refused to serve in Vietnam. The U.S. Supreme Court vindicated him, and he beat George Foreman to make a comeback in 1974. At his peak, Ali earned more than $6 million a year; he was famous for his witty rhymes and for his claim, "I Am the Greatest." He was named Athlete of the Decade for the 1970's by the Associated Press.

Alianza Hispano-Americana, La: An organization founded in Tucson, Arizona, in 1894 and incorporated in 1907. By 1930 it had spread throughout the western and midwestern states. Originally a *mutualista* (MUTUAL AID SOCIETY) in nature, the alliance promoted acculturation and civic virtues among its members while providing them with sickness and death benefits as well as social activities. After World War II, La Alianza Hispano-Americana became involved in promoting civil liberties, education, and legal justice for MEXICAN AMERICANS. It organized a civil rights department in 1955 and a scholarship program in 1956.

Alien and Sedition Acts (1798): Set of federal laws designed to protect the young United States from what were considered undesirable persons and speech. The policies were directed against specific ethnic groups, particularly the French and Irish. There were four acts designed to control individuals and thought, all passed in 1798: the Naturalization Act, two other acts affecting aliens, and the Act for the Punishment of Certain Crimes (Sedition Act).

During the period of the Alien and Sedition Acts, the United States was in its formative years, the U.S. CONSTITUTION having been written a scant eleven years earlier. The AMERICAN REVOLUTION required that the leadership of the newly independent nation establish its relationship to European powers, African Americans, and American Indians. In 1790 the first United States Congress enacted the Naturalization Law of 1790. During the debates, the members evoked the ideals of

The Alien and Sedition Acts were passed during the presidential administration of John Adams. (Library of Congress)

the republican ideology with its agenda of establishing a "City on a Hill" for the "worthy part of mankind" where only "proper and decent behavior" would be tolerated. The Naturalization Law of 1790 connected

race with the republic while it defined permissible behavior and thought: Citizenship was reserved for whites only, specifically those who displayed the appropriate morals and manners, as tested by a probationary period of two years before citizenship certification.

The Alien and Sedition Acts were a victory for the Federalists over the Republicans (not the Republican Party of today). The Federalist Party was concerned that the Republicans had commitments to foreign powers, particularly to the French. They believed that the citizens of the United States should develop their own native patriotism. The Federalists supported the Alien and Sedition Acts, reasoning that the Republican Party was a "French faction" akin to American "Jacobeans." In passing the acts, the Federalists were able to stamp out the French faction, which included fugitives from the uprising of blacks in the French colony of San Domingo. The acts also restricted Irish immigration, which the Federalists looked upon with disdain.

In 1795 the Federalists succeeded in raising the residency requirement for citizenship from two years to five years. This did not satisfy them, however, and they eventually raised the residency requirement to fourteen years through the Naturalization Act of 1798.

The Federalists were also concerned with the political stories appearing in American publications. At that time common law governed issues of seditious libel, protecting the press from government restraints. The Federalists believed that groundless and malignant lies against the government should not be tolerated and that anyone who published such matter should serve a long term of imprisonment. They reasoned that such punishment was necessary to maintain a peaceful, orderly society.

The Alien Act expired on June 25, 1800. The Federalists attempted the re-enactment of the Sedition Act, but Republican President Thomas Jefferson pardoned all still serving terms for violating the Sedition Act when he took office in 1801.

SUGGESTED READINGS. For more information, see John C. Miller's *Crisis in Freedom: The Alien and Sedition Acts* (1951) and Leon Whipple's *The Story of Civil Liberty in the United States* (1927). Alexander Hamilton, James Madison, and John Jay's *The Federalist Papers* (1787, repr. 1966) provides contemporaneous discussions of the acts. Clinton Rossiter's *Seedtime of the Republic: The Origin of the American Tradition of Political Liberty* (1953) provides insight into the threat to liberty posed by the laws.

Alien land laws: State laws that restricted property ownership by noncitizens in the early 1900's. These laws addressed fears on the part of the DOMINANT CULTURE that noncitizen Asians, particularly the JAPANESE, would legally acquire property in the United States and taint the traditional values of society. The alien land laws were controversial; many people argued that such legislation was inherently racist. Twenty-eight states granted the same property rights to aliens as citizens either through their state constitutions or state codes; only Colorado, Nevada, and New Mexico attempted repeals of the rights constitutionally guaranteed.

Congressional debate on the alien land laws was held in 1921 in a conference chaired by Senator Hiram W. Johnson of CALIFORNIA. The alien land laws were often referred to as the "California question," or the "Japanese question," since at that time most of the Japanese in the United States resided in California. California's problems accommodating its Asian population had reached a climax in the mid-1800's with hysterical ANTI-CHINESE VIOLENCE. White working-class attacks resulted in Chinese being beaten in the streets of San Francisco and driven out of Eureka, Truckee, and other California towns. In 1871, a white mob in Los Angeles killed twenty-one Chinese people and looted the Chinese quarters. Eventually anti-Chinese sentiments spread to other parts of the country, resulting in the CHINESE EXCLUSION ACT of 1882. Anti-Asian racism was the precursor for the alien land laws.

In California on November 2, 1920, land ownership by aliens was limited to those eligible for citizenship.

The United States treaty rights were unaffected by the law, and continued to allow the Japanese in the United States to own houses, factories, warehouses, and premises for residential and commercial use. (In 1922, in *Ozawa v. United States*, the U.S. Supreme Court ruled that Japanese could not become U.S. citizens.) The California law specifically attempted to curtail Asian agricultural activity.

Fourteen states followed the lead of California with specific alien land laws. For example, Illinois law stated that aliens could hold land for six years, by which time if they had not become naturalized, the property must be forfeited. Minnesota limited the amount of property that aliens could own to 90,000 square feet unless the property had been acquired by treaty. Delaware allowed aliens eligible for citizenship to hold or transfer property, but aliens ineligible for citizenship could not acquire property other than by rules prescribed by treaty.

SUGGESTED READINGS. For additional information on the history of alien land laws, see Charles F. Curry's *Alien Land Laws and Alien Rights* (1921). Harry H. L. Kitano's *Japanese Americans* (2d ed, 1976) provides information on Japanese American history and lifestyle that highlights the forms of cultural opposition the Japanese confronted. Ronald Takaki's edited volume *From Different Shores: Perspectives on Race and Culture in America* (1987) and his *Iron Cages: Race and Culture in Nineteenth Century America* (1990) provide insight into the origin of anti-Asian sentiment and its connection to legislation such as the alien land laws.

Alvarez, Luis Walter (June 13, 1911, San Francisco, Calif.—Sept. 1, 1988, Berkeley, Calif.): Latino physicist. Born to parents of Spanish and Irish descent, Alvarez studied physics at the University of Chicago, receiving his doctorate in 1936. He went on to the University of California at Berkeley, where he became a professor in 1945 and remained on the faculty until 1978. In the 1940's, he also worked at the Massachusetts Institute of Technology Radiation Lab, developing a revolutionary Ground Control Approach system for radar airplane tracking, and the Los Alamos, New Mexico, laboratory of the Manhattan Project, where he developed the detonators for setting off the plutonium bomb. An experimental physicist with wide-ranging scientific interests, Alvarez received the 1968 Nobel Prize in Physics for his use of bubble chambers to detect subatomic particles.

Amalgamated Clothing Workers of America: The Amalgamated Clothing Workers of America was founded in 1914 and within twenty years became the most successful of many unions in the clothing industry. Many workers in this industry were immigrants and the ACWA was an important force in their lives. Among the benefits the ACWA provided for its members were banks, insurance programs, and cooperative housing. In 1976, the group merged with the Textile Workers Union of America, forming a new and stronger organization. The Amalgamated Clothing and Textile Workers Union maintains a library and bestows various awards.

Amana Colonies: The Amana community of Iowa derived from a religious sect organized in 1714 in Hesse, Germany, that believed in divine inspiration and direct revelation of God's word. To escape persecution, the German community moved to the United States and established itself in Buffalo, New York, in 1842 as the Ebenezer Society. When expansion of the colony necessitated relocation in 1855, it moved to Iowa. Members of the community adopted *Twenty-four Rules Forming the Basis of Faith* and practiced communal ownership of property until a 1932 reorganization in which that system was replaced with the issue of stock certificates to each member. The colonies consist of several villages located around Amana, Iowa, and are organized as a for-profit cooperative engaged in more than fifty different business activities and farming.

Amerasians: People with one Asian and one American parent, particularly children born to Asian women and American servicemen. After WORLD WAR II and the KOREAN WAR, thousands of Japanese, Korean, and Filipino women who had married American servicemen were permitted to come to the United States. This in turn led to a dramatic increase in the number of Amerasian children born during the 1950's. During the VIETNAM WAR, thousands more Amerasian children were fathered by U.S. soldiers abroad, where they were often the victims of ridicule and discrimination. Special immigration acts for Amerasians in 1982 and 1987 allowed some of these children and certain members of their families to come to the United States and obtain refugee services. This term should not be confused with the more general designation Asian American, which refers to any people living in the United States who have Asian ancestry.

American-Arab Anti-Discrimination Committee (ADC): Organization founded in 1980 to protect the rights and monitor the image of ARAB AMERICANS. By the 1990's, the ADC had some twenty-three thousand members in seventy-five local groups with its headquarters in WASHINGTON, D.C. It works to end racist stereotyping of Arabs in film, television, and other media; to combat racist ADVERTISING; and to promote and defend the Arab American heritage. To achieve this, it sponsors college internships, a speaker's bureau, and various monitoring groups.

American Association of Retired Persons (AARP): This organization, founded in 1958, has an active membership of about thirty-two million persons fifty years of age or older. Members may be either still active in the work force or retired. AARP seeks to improve the quality of life for older people by focusing on four basic areas of concern: health care, their women's initiative, worker equity, and minority affairs. Services to members include group health insurance, travel discounts, *Modern Maturity* magazine, and community programs addressing such issues as crime prevention, defensive driving, tax aid, and retirement planning.

AARP provides numerous services to those over the age of fifty. (Cleo Freelance Photo)

American Association of University Women
(AAUW): Educational advocacy organization for
women and girls. Members must be graduates of accredited colleges. The organization's predecessor, the Association of Collegiate Alumnae, was founded in 1882 by
the first generation of women who graduated from college. In 1921, two regional chapters of that group merged
to create the AAUW. The organization works to improve
conditions for women in higher education by funding
research, providing facilities, and raising funds. Its Educational Foundation supports women's advancement
through fellowships, legislative advocacy, and conferences. The AAUW has also advocated civil rights, pay
equity, and anti-discrimination legislation.

American Civil Liberties Union (ACLU): Organization established in 1920 to maintain the rights of all
individuals as delineated in the BILL OF RIGHTS of the
U.S. CONSTITUTION. The ACLU had 375,000 members
in the 1990's. The organization seeks equality regardless
of race, color, sexual orientation, national origin, political opinion, or religious beliefs through its active programs in litigation, advocacy, and public education. The
ACLU has been controversial in the latter part of the
twentieth century for its support of free speech for
NEO-NAZIS, civil rights for victims of the AIDS EPIDEMIC, reproductive choice for women, and a host of
other issues of concern to multicultural communities.
ACLU liberalism was an issue in the 1988 presidential
campaign.

American Colonization Society: A group founded in
1816 to encourage and finance emigration of approximately six thousand free African Americans to Africa,
resulting in the formation of the Republic of Liberia.
Many African American and white abolitionists denounced the society because it deported freed slaves but
did not attempt to abolish slavery. Further, because it did
not encourage the assimilation of African Americans
into American society, the colonization movement perpetuated the notion of their inferiority. For that reason,
many viewed the society as counterproductive even
though it brought the plight of free African Americans
to the attention of American society.

American Federation of Labor (AFL): Founded in
1886, the AFL was a federation of national and local
unions, state federations, and municipal bodies. It
merged with the CONGRESS OF INDUSTRIAL ORGANIZATIONS (CIO) in 1955. In the early 1990's the AFL-CIO

had fourteen million members. The organization is well
known for two annual awards, the Murray-Green-
Meany Award for distinguished service to the nation and
the George Meany Human Rights Award for worldwide
service in the advancement of human rights and dignity.

*Laborers can benefit from union membership which provides
them greater representation.* (Jim West)

American G.I. Forum (AGIF): Mexican American organization founded in Texas in 1947 by Mexican American veterans led by Dr. Hector Garcia. Modeled after the
AMERICAN LEGION, it became one of the largest Mexican
American organizations. Although basically a Texas
organization, AGIF has more than two hundred chapters
in forty-three states. Its main emphasis is on political
and legal action. In 1960 leaders of the forum helped
organize "Viva Kennedy" clubs. It maintains a full-time
lobbyist in Washington, D.C., and publishes a monthly
bulletin called *The Forumeer*.

Many younger Indians must juggle their dual identities of traditional tribal loyalty and modern American lifestyles. (Elaine S. Querry)

American Indian–African American relations. *See* **African American–American Indian relations**

American Indian architecture and dwellings. *See* **Architecture and dwellings—American Indian**

American Indian arts and crafts. *See* **Arts and crafts—American Indian**

American Indian assimilation: In many ways, ASSIMILATION stands in direct opposition to self-determination, the long-standing aspiration of American Indian peoples. Although assimilationist policies have not effectively brought American Indians into the mainstream of U.S. society, they have contributed to the destruction of American Indian nations as distinct cultural entities.

American Indians never willingly accepted the jurisdiction of U.S. federal authority over their nations. Although the earliest U.S. agreements with Indians were negotiated on the basis of treaty agreements between nations, the U.S. Congress unilaterally suspended all treaty-making in 1871, declaring that no Indian nation or tribe would henceforth be recognized as an independent nation.

A series of laws ensued, all designed to assimilate American Indians into the DOMINANT CULTURE. One of the most important was the General Allotment Act of 1887 (the DAWES ACT), which President Roosevelt declared would "pulverize" tribal masses of Indians, thereby bringing them into the Anglo American mainstream. The act stipulated that lands previously set aside for collective ownership by native peoples would now be divided up and given to individual Indian citizens, who would separately own their land parcels. In 1892, the federal government essentially made it a crime for native peoples to engage in indigenous religious practice, a prohibition which remained in effect until 1921. In 1924, all Indians were declared U.S. citizens. Together, these legal interventions were designed to discourage collective Indian traditions in support of forced assimilation.

The land allotment policy was reversed in the 1930's as the U.S. government responded to massive criticism of the policy. The INDIAN REORGANIZATION ACT OF 1934 (the Wheeler-Howard Act) sought to reconstitute tribal authorities along the lines of a federally approved model that resembled community corporations. In the early 1950's, the government reverted to an assimilationist approach as it enacted a policy of "TERMINATION" of its special relationship with Indian tribes. A federal resolution approved in mid-1953 permitted the government to end its recognition of more than a hundred Indian peoples by the end of the decade, thus alleviating federal responsibility to provide services. By the early 1970's, the rise of American Indian activism forced the Nixon Administration to admit that termination policies had failed.

Despite perennial pronouncements to the contrary, federal authorities have often reverted to de facto policies of assimilation in order to solve the so-called problems posed by the persistence of Native American cultures.

SUGGESTED READINGS. M. Annette Jaimes's edited volume *The State of Native America: Genocide, Colonization, and Resistance* (1992) is an excellent anthology concerning attempts to assimilate American Indians into mainstream society. *Natives and Strangers: Blacks, Indians, and Immigrants in America* (1990) by Leonard Dinnerstein, Roger L. Nichols, and David M. Reimers compares the assimilation of American Indians with that of African Americans and other immigrant populations, an approach also taken by Ronald Takaki's *Iron Cages: Race and Culture in Nineteenth-Century America* (1990). Vine Deloria, Jr.'s, *American Indian Policy in the Twentieth Century* (1985) examines federal law regarding relations between Indians and Anglos, while Hazel W. Hertzberg's *The Search for an American Indian Identity: Modern Pan-Indian Movements* (1971) examines intertribal Indian relations.

American Indian Civil Rights Act of 1968: It introduced the BILL OF RIGHTS into Indian tribal law in 1968. From 1832 to 1953, all Indian tribes were recognized legally as "domestic dependent nations," which meant they were not subject to the laws of the particular states in which they were located. As long as its members were within reservation boundaries, each tribe retained its own legal jurisdiction. The Civil Rights Act for Indians introduced, for the first time, the Bill of Rights into Indian tribal procedure, thereby including the various Indian nations within the overall law of the United States.

American Indian creation myths. *See* **Creation myths—American Indian**

American Indian cultural contributions: The American Indian contribution to American society is so widespread and significant that it is really a contribution to the whole of Western society and culture. From Indian use of precious minerals and knowledge of useful plants to the social and philosophical impact of native systems of government and cultural practices, it can be argued that the Indians of North and South America have contributed far more than they have gained from their Western European conquerors.

In his study *Indian Givers: How the Indians of the Americas Transformed the World* (1988), Jack Weatherford notes how many American Indian contributions remain unheralded, if not totally unknown, because so much of what benefited the European Americans and the American West was seized against the will of the native peoples themselves. The most ob-

American Indians are well known for their finely crafted jewelry made from turquoise, silver, and other precious stones and metals mined from their lands. (Ben Klaffke)

vious case is the mineral resources of silver and gold.

Native Mineral Resources. Minerals controlled by the native population, including vast amounts of gold and silver, began to have serious inflationary effects on Spain soon after Spanish involvement in the New World began in the fifteenth and sixteenth centuries. The influx of large amounts of gold drove prices upward and contributed to the decline of Spanish economic dominance in Europe even as it fueled the zeal of Spanish EXPLORATION. By 1600, the supply of precious metals had increased nearly eightfold due largely to exploitation of Latin lands and had a wavelike inflationary impact as far away as the Ottoman Empire. European financial and industrial development would begin to surpass the Near Eastern societies only with the assistance of New World resources and opportunities for production.

Native Agriculture. Weatherford claims that three-fifths of the crops "now in cultivation" in the world are gifts from the American Indian agricultural tradition. Some of the cottons known to American Indians contributed to refinements in the European textile industry. By making a fine grade of clothing affordable to more than only the aristocratic classes of Europe, New World cotton contributed to a reduced European dependence on wool and therefore on sheep breeding. At one point, the American South produced 80 percent of the world's cotton, making the Mississippi Delta states some of the wealthiest agricultural land in the world. After the Civil War, however, and the northern blockade of southern commerce, the Southern cotton industry never recovered its prewar glory. Thus, cotton first developed by Indians provided a major economic boon.

Even more significant was the related industrial development. The influx of raw materials in such abundance provided an incentive to develop more efficient means of production. This, in turn, created more demand which fueled continued European expansion in the New World at the expense of native groups such as the CHOCTAW, Chickasaw, Creek, and CHEROKEE. Scholars such as Weatherford suggest that the Industrial Revolution itself was at least partly dependent on New World agricultural prowess and knowledge of species previously unknown.

Further basic, yet clearly critical, contributions derived from nature include sisal, for making rope, and rubber. The South American tribes had already developed the technology for producing rubber-coated clothing such as jackets and footwear before the arri-

val of the Europeans. It was not until Charles Goodyear duplicated the native refining process in 1839 that Western society would develop a massive industry for rubberized products. Rubberized raingear and containment packaging also had direct impact on military effectiveness, contributing to continued European conquests. It can also be argued that rubber tires made possible the serious development of the bicycle and automotive industries, further advancing the industrial and technological revolutions that shaped the modern world.

In his studies on sugar, historian Sidney Mintz has pointed out the wide influence of native contributions in sugar cane cultivation and production. The social organization of New World sugar production in the form of plantations introduced the model of a command structure over a large and diverse work force. This model set the tone for the social revolutions of industrial society: a massive reorganization of labor into huge pools of workers dedicated to wage labor and mass production. The roots of this system are partly to be seen in the organized exploitation of native labor in the New World.

The introduction of the potato had a major impact on European society—particularly those parts of northern Europe where predominantly grain agriculture was highly susceptible to weather conditions, making famine frequent and devastating. The durable potato produced more nutrition with less labor, with nearly half the growing time. Potato famine drove most of the immigration from Ireland to the United States in the 1800's. Potatoes were also the staple of the diet of other immigrant groups, such as Russians and Poles. American Indians also contributed peanuts, peppers, tomatoes, pecans, strawberries, maple syrup, avocados, wild rice, sweet potatoes, cranberries, blueberries, chocolate, and vanilla to the foods and cooking still found in the United States.

A related aspect of American Indian awareness of plants and their products is medicine. Indian pharmacological practice was often further developed than Western versions. Native practitioners contributed ipecac, quinine, witch hazel, petroleum jellies, and many narcotics such as coca and its derivatives.

Philosophical Contributions. Indian philosophical and social contributions are also significant, though at times more subtle. The discovery of previously unknown civilizations totally unfamiliar with Western modes of thought and religious reflection seriously battered European assumptions about the limits of reality and the veracity of religious dogmas.

During the Enlightenment in the late 1700's, many Europeans believed that American Indians symbolized "natural" human societies apart from the "corruptions" of modern living. This view provided many skeptical philosophers with the basis for questioning European forms of governance and social organization, particularly those based on the Greek and later Christian

a significant role in public discourse. This trend also sparked much non-Indian interest in Indian spirituality, arts, and folklore, especially for tribes such as the HOPI.

Political Organization. When early European American political theorists began to investigate seriously native social organization, they were influenced by Indian concepts of representative democracy and

The 1968 Civil Rights Act for Indians introduced the U.S. Bill of Rights into Indian tribal procedure. (James L. Shaffer)

ideas of basic human frailty and corruption. They theorized that there is a natural law, a natural tendency toward order and cooperation at least as powerful as the natural tendencies toward chaos or corruption. Philosophers such as Jean Jacques Rousseau posited the Indian as the "noble savage" who was a living and irrefutable example of "natural law."

During the 1970's and 1980's in American society, a somewhat similar phenomenon occurred with another romanticized view of American Indian culture as the model of the environmentally conscious "natural human" who lives in harmony with the earth. Though frequently based on shallow understandings of the RELIGION AND MYTHOLOGY OF AMERICAN INDIANS, such forms of environmentalism have played

equal standing among all citizens. The IROQUOIS LEAGUE was a council composed of representatives of five Indian nations: Mohawk, Onandaga, Seneca, Oneida, and Cayuga. Benjamin Franklin, the colonial American philosopher and diplomat, and Thomas Paine, the radical pamphleteer and popular commentator, both were influenced by their study of the Iroquois League (which became the SIX NATIONS with the addition of the Tuscaroras in 1722) and other tribal formulations. For example, the Indian model appears to have contributed ideas for settling the thorny problem of federal and state relations in governance. Furthermore, council or committee leadership was far more common in native practice than centralized leadership. It was the royalist Europeans who often imposed the concept of "chief" on Indian nations who actually had much more democratic systems than their European conquerors. Some American Indian political formulations were known to German socialist Friedrich Engels, and thus gained their place in the theoretical formulation of Marxism as well.

American Indians and Human Rights. Americans of the late twentieth century are more aware of the importance of indigenous populations than at any other time in world history. This awareness can be partly attributed to the visibility of the American Indian nations in pressing for their rights through mass action and legal activism. American Indians have struggled for educational equality, for full treaty rights to natural resources, for the protection of sacred sites and the return of cultural artifacts. They have also protested the use of tribal land for dumping industrial wastes or strip mining. These actions have frequently influenced other indigenous populations outside American borders. For example, Australian Aboriginal campaigns of the 1980's for social and political reforms drew their inspiration from the AMERICAN INDIAN MOVEMENT (AIM), one of the more radical of the American Indian organizations of the 1970's and 1980's. At the same time, the INDIAN RIGHTS MOVEMENT has made more Americans aware of the legacy of injustices done to native people and the socio-economic problems of contemporary Indians.

American Indian Art. Many of the artistic patterns, styles, and media used by American Indians have become staples of contemporary design. For example, the geometric designs of the NAVAJOS and Hopis and the architectural styles of Hopi mesa dwellings have shaped the so-called "Southwest" fashions in architec-

Many American Indians hold a deep sense of respect for natural resources. (Ben Klaffke)

ture, clothing, and interior design. The flowing lines of beaver, killer-whale, and bear designs in black, red, and natural wood colors drawn from the Northwest Coast peoples can be seen in many non-Indian contexts in that region. The media frequently adopts "Indian symbols" with no thought of their actual context; only certain plains groups had "tipi" mobile dwellings or used feathers, for example, and only the Northwest Indian nations had "totem poles." This "blurring" of symbols, however, shows how far these symbols have come to be associated in the national consciousness with Indianness, American heritage, or regionalism. Contemporary artists, composers, and architects, among others, continue to be inspired by the Indian cultural legacy.

SUGGESTED READINGS. The subject is thoroughly and provocatively dealt with in Jack Weatherford's outstanding studies: *Indian Givers: How the Indians of the Americas Transformed the World* (1988) and *Native Roots: How the Indians Enriched America* (1991). Other works of interest include Bruce E. Johansen's *Forgotten Founders: Benjamin Franklin, the Iroquois, and the Rationale for the American Revolution* (1982); and Sidney W. Mintz's *Sweetness and Power: The Place of Sugar in Modern History* (1985).—*Daniel L. S. Christopher*

American Indian demography: Historical estimates of the American Indian population before European contact vary widely; they range from 900,000 to 18 million. The numbers have significant political consequence for American Indians and discussions of treaty and moral obligations. More reliable statistics suggest that the American Indian population was reduced to less than 250,000 at the close of the nineteenth century. If this is true, then the American Indian population growth registered in the 1990 census is quite dramatic; American Indians accounted for 0.8 percent of the total population of the United States, or 1,878,285. There was a 37 percent increase in this population since 1980, compared with a 6 percent increase for European Americans and a 13.2 percent increase for African Americans. Only a part of this can be attributed to an increasing willingness of Americans to claim their American Indian heritage.

The three greatest causes of American Indian population decline historically were disease, warfare, and GENOCIDE. Some estimates of the impact of smallpox alone, for example, suggest that it decimated half of the native population of the Americas, whereas warfare accounted for between 150,000 and 500,000

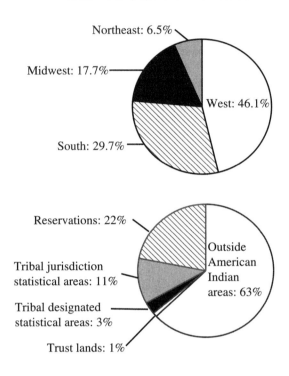

Where American Indians Live: 1990
Total Indian population: 1,878,000

Northeast: 6.5%
Midwest: 17.7%
West: 46.1%
South: 29.7%

Reservations: 22%
Tribal jurisdiction statistical areas: 11%
Tribal designated statistical areas: 3%
Trust lands: 1%
Outside American Indian areas: 63%

Source: Data are from *Statistical Abstract of the United States, 1992.* Table 43. Washington, D.C.: U.S. Government Printing Office, 1992.

deaths, depending on which statistics one uses. In the early 1990's, the greatest threats to American Indian population growth were the effects of ALCOHOLISM and INTERMARRIAGE. American Indians, like JAPANESE AMERICANS, are among the most intermarried of all American ethnic populations.

According to the BUREAU OF INDIAN AFFAIRS, 51 percent of all American Indians (950,000) live on or near federal Indian RESERVATIONS and trust lands. This statistic reveals the importance of mainstream urban existence for modern American Indians, contributing further to social breakdown and loss of cultural identity. Of the 49 percent of Indians living in nonreservation areas, the following major American cities have the largest Indian populations: LOS ANGELES (87,487); Tulsa, Oklahoma (48,196); NEW YORK (46,191); Oklahoma City (45,720); SAN FRANCISCO (40,847); Phoenix, Arizona (38,017); Minneapolis, Minnesota (23,956); and Tucson, Arizona (20,330). The two most populous American Indian tribes, according to the Bu-

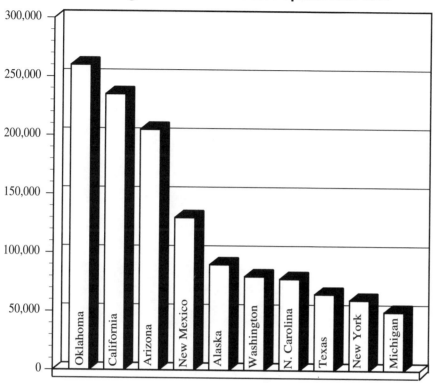

Indian Populations of the Ten States with the Largest American Indian Populations: 1990

Source: From Ronald B. Querry, *Native Americans.* American Voices series. Vero Beach, Fla.: Rourke Corp., 1991.

the twentieth century, Indian RESERVATIONS became known for their sponsorship of bingo games, which were often played by large groups of both Indians and non-Indians.

In 1987, a Supreme Court ruling gave American Indians the legal right to conduct gambling on their reservations, as long as the games (off-track betting, poker, bingo, and many casino games) had been declared legal in the state in which the reservation is located. In 1988, two federal regulations were added to the previous year's ruling: The national commission would allow only milder forms of gambling—such as bingo—and any form of gambling would have to be negotiated between tribal leaders and the United States government. Gambling on reservations has developed

reau of the Census, are the NAVAJO and CHEROKEE nations.

SUGGESTED READINGS. For further details of American Indian demography, see *The Demographics of American Indians: One Percent of the People, Fifty Percent of the Diversity* (1990) by Harold Hodgkinson, with Janice Outtz and Anita M. Obarakpor; Stephen Cornell's *The Return of the Native: American Indian Political Resurgence* (1988), and C. Matthew Snipp's *American Indians: The First of This Land* (1989).

American Indian education. *See* **Education— American Indian**

American Indian gambling: Games involving gambling have long been a part of traditional American Indian culture and social life. Gambling is integral to some forms of AMERICAN INDIAN MUSIC, for example, and an important activity at community gatherings. In

into a $1 billion annual industry.

A controversy developed in 1991, when the federal government raided reservations in several states, including eight in CALIFORNIA, and confiscated all slot machines on the premises. These politically sensitive raids accelerated tension between both parties. In response to the seizures, outraged tribal leaders sought legal action and the government issued a twenty-six-page list of guidelines in order to help interpret the 1988 Indian Gaming Regulatory Act. The government declared that slot machines are legal on reservations only if authorized by the state in which they are used (most states have declared that they will not permit Las Vegas forms of gambling within their borders). Tribal leaders stated that they had been victimized by long delays when they tried to find out, from the newly formed National Indian Gaming Commission, which types of gambling were legal.

Involvement in gambling has made some Indians vulnerable to organized crime. The notorious Mafia mobsters Chris Petti, Samuel Carlisi, and John (No Nose) DiFronzo were arrested in 1992, after a lengthy investigation by the Federal Bureau of Investigation (FBI) and San Diego, California, police officers, on a fifteen-count indictment for trying to persuade members of the Rincon Indian Reservation in San Diego to allow them to skim profits, launder money (reportedly for Colombian cocaine dealers), and conduct other illegal activities.

Interior Secretary Manuel Lujan, speaking in Las Vegas, Nevada, in 1992, surprised his audience by predicting that in ten years every major city in the United States would contain Indian gambling parlors. This speech was given to a group of Nevada gambling casino owners, who historically have had a monopoly on American gambling and continue to deal with the proliferation (and competition) of Indian gambling. Lujan also stated that he had the power to overturn the ruling of any state governor who decided against Indian gambling in her or his state.

In the wake of the 1887 DAWES (General Allotment) ACT, which left American Indians with 1.5 percent of their original, precontact three billion acres of land, gambling, controversial though it may be, ironically has allowed Indians to capitalize on their largely valueless land.

SUGGESTED READINGS. Among the books that include discussions of gambling issues are Rick Hornung's *One Nation Under the Gun: Inside the Mohawk Civil War* (1992) and William R. Eadington's edited volume *Indian Gaming and the Law*. Information can also be found in journal and newspaper articles, such as Gary Sokolow's "The Future of Gambling in Indian Country," in *American Indian Law Review* 15, no. 1 (1990), p. 151, and Josh Getlin's "Against All Odds," in the *Los Angeles Times*, February 21, 1992, p. E5.

American Indian games: Traditional Indian games were basically of two types: games of chance and games of skill or dexterity. Games of chance included gambling games, such as throwing marked stones to see what combination of marks would emerge, and guessing games. In a typical guessing game, a team of players concealed a stick among themselves, requiring other players to guess which opponent held the stick. Games of skill or dexterity included competitive efforts in archery or running as well as a game such as snow snake, in which players slid a spear on ice or snow to see whose spear would go farthest. Wagering on the outcomes of games was common. Games were played by adults and

children of both sexes, though the participants were usually segregated by age and sex.

Perhaps the best-known American Indian game was lacrosse, which is thought to have been invented among the Algonquian peoples of the Northeast. The game spread to many other cultures in the Southeast and Midwest. In lacrosse, teams competed to see which could strike a deerskin ball into an opponent's goal; in the Northeast, players used one stick to strike the ball, while in the Southeast, they used two sticks.

American Indians engage in traditional games and dances that require great skill and dexterity. (Don Franklin)

In lacrosse, teams competed to see which could strike a deerskin ball into an opponent's goal; in the Northeast, players used one stick to strike the ball, while in the Southeast, they used two sticks. Lacrosse was played by men, though a similar game, often called shinny, was played by women. A lacrosse match could last all day, with hundreds of players to a side, and injuries were common.

While Indians played games for their recreational

value, games also served other purposes. Games were often viewed as training exercises to encourage the development of physical prowess or strategic thinking that was useful in other aspects of life, such as hunting or warfare; in the Southeast, for example, games were called "the little brother of war." Games were also integrated into the ceremonial cycle. In the Southeast, for example, lacrosse matches were part of a year-long world renewal cycle. Players made preparations for their participation in a manner identical to the participation in any religious ceremony by avoiding sexual relations for a prescribed period, fasting, and taking emetics as a cleansing ritual.

A number of traditional games, many of them accompanied by singing, are still practiced by contemporary Indians of all ages at social occasions.

SUGGESTED READINGS. General discussions of Indian games may be found in *Native American Heritage* (1976) by Merwyn S. Garbarino; *The Native Americans* (1965) by Robert Spencer, Jesse D. Jennings, et al.; and *Indians of North America* (1962) by Harold E. Driver. For a first-hand nineteenth century account of a game of lacrosse among the CHOCTAWS, see George Catlin's *Letters and Notes on the Manners, Customs, and Conditions of the North American Indians* (1841).

American Indian health and medicine. *See* **Health and medicine—American Indian**

American Indian hobbyist movement. *See* **Indian hobbyist movement**

American Indian hunting and fishing: Traditionally important strategies of subsistence throughout North America and the source of modern conflicts over rights. Prior to European contact, more than half of the residents in North America did not farm, but subsisted on hunting, gathering, and fishing. Indians in nearly all of Canada and Alaska and the middle half of the United States relied heavily on hunting. Fish were the staple source of food along the Northwest Coast, and sea mammal hunting with harpoons was common along the Arctic coast. Bows and arrows as well as thrusting lances were commonly used to dispatch large game. In the Southeast, blow guns were occasionally utilized. In the prairies, Great Plains, Great Basin, and the Southwest, the prey was often induced to move in a prearranged direction through the use of fire or the construction of fences. In the Arctic and subarctic, moose and caribou were driven into the

water where kayak hunters used lances or bows and arrows to dispatch the animals. Pitfalls, deadfalls, snares, and nooses were common throughout native North America. Nets were frequently used to capture rabbits in the West.

American Indian communities maintained a balanced relationship with their prey through supernatural sanctions and religious ceremonies. (Ben Klaffke)

Deceptive hunting techniques, including both visual disguises and auditory decoys, were employed in all areas of North America. Hunters disguised themselves as animals with animal horns, heads, and hides. Camouflaged hunters would stalk their quarry from a downwind direction until close enough to kill their prey. Indians also used sound decoys such as the hitting together of antlers in imitation of fighting bucks and the scraping of a scapula on a tree to sound like a female in heat to attract their prey.

Techniques and technologies associated with fishing were varied. Weirs and traps were the most effective techniques for capturing migrating fish such as salmon and shad. Poison was utilized in California, the Great Basin, and plateau regions; it was effective only in slow-moving streams. Hand, dip, and scoop nets were the most widespread forms of fishing equipment; seine and gill nets were more limited in distribution. Fish

A Hupa Indian oversees business at a salmon hatchery. (Ben Klaffke)

spears were commonly used in clear, shallow water with fire employed to attract fish.

Religion and subsistence were closely related in many hunting and fishing groups. Animals had to be treated with respect in order to ensure their continuation. In the Arctic, for example, the bladder of a sea mammal was returned to the water in order to permit the reincarnation of the animal's soul. Many American Indian communities maintained a balanced relationship with their prey through supernatural sanctions and religious ceremonies.

This balanced relationship was gradually destroyed as white Americans moved onto Indian lands and forced the Indians who lived there to move—first simply westward, then onto specific reservations. In these constricted and frequently alien environments—the reservations could be a thousand miles or more from a tribe's homeland—traditional hunting and fishing practices were no longer as effective. As American industrialization increased in the twentieth century, widespread pollution and the construction of hydroelectric dams further worsened the situation. Moreover, non-Indian commercial fishing interests complained that legal exemptions which had been granted the Indians by treaty inhibited the activities of commercial enterprises. Clashes between white fishermen and Indians occurred. Finally, in the 1960's, tribal groups began demonstrating, protesting that treaties were being broken.

Beginning in 1964, a number of "fish-in" protests were held in the Pacific Northwest by tribes including the Nisqually, Tulalip, and Puyallup. State game wardens had become aggressive, even brutal, in what were essentially attacks on Indian fishermen, and the Indians decided to fight for their rights. In 1966, the U.S. Department of Justice intervened in the legal wrangle and restored treaty rights to several indicted and arrested demonstrators. Many similar struggles have occurred since then, involving tribes throughout the United States, among them Menominees in Wisconsin and Chippewas in northern Minnesota. The issues are complex; they include the binding nature of treaties versus modern fish and game laws as well as the frequency with which the U.S. and state governments have broken treaties. Charges are also made by non-Indian commercial fishermen that special privileges for Indian commercial fishermen give them unfair advantages in what, they claim, should be a modern marketplace that treats everyone the same.

SUGGESTED READINGS. An excellent overview of traditional Indian hunting and fishing techniques can be found in Jon Manchip White's *Everyday Life of the North American Indian* (1979). Other sources of information include *Indians of North America* (2d ed., 1969) by Harold E. Driver; *The North American Indians: A Sourcebook* (1967), edited by Roger C. Owen; and *American Indian Environments: Ecological Issues in Native American History* (1980) by Christopher Vecsey and Robert Venables.

American Indian languages: In 1988, a woman living on an Indian reservation on the Paraguay River in Brazil, died. Along with her died Umutina, her traditional language. In 1993, two other Native Brazilian languages, Macu and Bare, had only one living speaker each.

What is happening in South America (and, to a lesser extent, worldwide) is a duplication of the past two centuries of American Indian linguistic history in the United States. Of more than 2,000 independent tribes from 500 distinct cultural groups before contact with Europeans, at most 500 tribes survive. Of probably about 2,200 languages and dialects in North and South America—more than in all of Europe and Asia at the time—from more than 50 different language groups (compared to two in Europe) in 7 basic language families, fewer than 150 are still spoken in America. Since native cultures were and are based in an oral tradition, language—like culture—is always only one generation away from extinction. Some Indian nations preserved their history through petroglyphs and pictographs but had no written language until SEQUOYAH devised the CHEROKEE syllabary, a system of 85 symbols representing sounds, in 1821.

Before contact, Indians north of Mexico spoke 550 languages and dialects. Just as there was no monolithic Indian culture, there was no single language called "Indian," except in the mistaken view of some European explorers and settlers. American Indian languages were little valued—even held in contempt, often as animal noises—until the first great American anthropologist, Franz Boas, began his insistence on field study and native language acquisition, with a new aesthetic awareness of native cultures in general. His *Handbook of American Indian Languages* (1911, followed by other studies in 1920 and 1929) attempted to establish a conceptual/theoretical foundation for the study and preservation of Indian linguistic systems, identifying fifty-five distinct families. Earlier, J. W. Powell in *Indian Linguistic Families of America North of Mexico* (1891) had discussed fifty-eight different

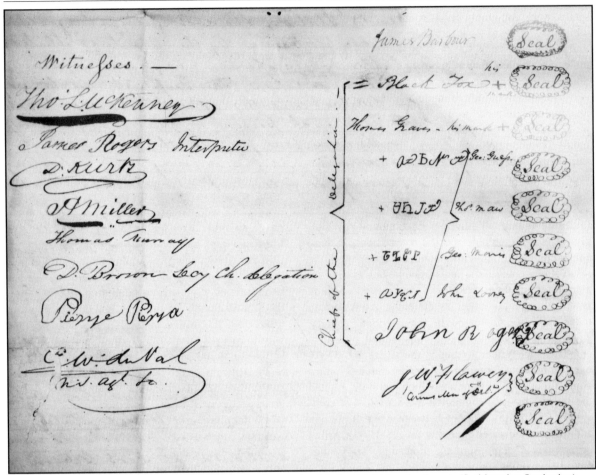

This 1828 treaty was signed by four men in the Sequoyah alphabet (right-hand column). (Smithsonian Institution)

families or "stocks" in some detail, noting the diversity and complexity of native languages, especially such factors as intertribal languages and jargon, gestural features of communication, dialects, and the effects of cultural contact; he also surveyed and appraised scholarship in the area up to that time.

Much disagreement has surfaced in the later twentieth century, and various other linguistic systems have been proposed. Among them is the influential six-division schema of "super-families" espoused by Edward Sapir in the fourteenth edition of *The Encyclopedia Britannica:* Eskimo-Aleut, Algonkin-Wakashan, Nadene, Penutian, Hokan-Siouan, and Azte-Tanoan. Scholars generally agree, however, that American Indian languages have been neglected and are deserving of much more complete and serious study, particularly as they begin to vanish with increasing speed.

If, as many scholars assert, a language is the best key to understanding a society, then Indian ways of thinking and seeing reality are in as much danger as their various linguistic and cultural traditions. Factors such as introduced diseases, assimilationist policies, self-righteous cultural prohibitions, pseudo-military boarding school systems, and SLAVERY have taken heavy tolls on native peoples in all dimensions of their traditional ways of life.

One aspect of American Indian languages, and oral traditions in general, is an essentially different view of the nature of language from that held by non-Indian peoples. Particularly in the European-oriented Western tradition, language is a system of signs and symbols that reflect and represent reality. By contrast, Indians see the individual word in much more essential terms: It does not reflect reality, it actuates it. To say (and frequently even to think) something makes it real, bringing it into existence.

A complex philosophical principle woven into many Indian cultures, the primacy of language has found its most eloquent spokesperson in N. Scott MOMADAY (Kiowa/Cherokee), first American Indian winner of the Pulitzer Prize in 1969 for his novel *House Made of Dawn.* In his widely reprinted essay, "Man Made of Words," Momaday says: "I hope to indicate something about the nature of the relationship between language and experience. It seems to me that in a certain sense we are all made of words; that our most essential being consists in language. It is the element in which we think and dream and act, in which we live our daily lives. There is no way in which we can exist apart from the morality of a verbal dimension." Further, Momaday speaks for many Indians when he asserts: "Generally speaking, man has consummate being in language, and there only. The state of human *being* is an idea, an idea which man has of himself. Only when he is embodied in an idea, and the idea is realized in language, can man take possession of himself."

SUGGESTED READINGS. Momaday's essay can be found in *The Remembered Earth: An Anthology of Contemporary Native American Literature* (1979), edited by Geary Hobson. The best modern study of Indian languages is William Bright's *American Indian Linguistics and Literature* (1984). Many additional insights into Indian languages can be gleaned from *Teachings from the American Earth: Indian Religion and Philosophy* (1975), edited by Dennis Tedlock and Barbara Tedlock. The standard reference work on American Indians is the Smithsonian *Handbook of North American Indians* (1978-   ), under the general editorship of William C. Sturtevant; volume 17, *Languages,* has yet to appear.—*Rodney Simard*

American Indian medicine men, traditional. *See* **Medicine men—traditional American Indian**

American Indian migration legends: Popular myths about the movements of a people which relate to various events in the prehistory and history of many tribes. Even the single legends of individual tribes may combine materials from distinct experiences in the past of the people. For these reasons, it is quite difficult to generalize about the legends. The fact that much of the material was not written down until long after the native peoples had been exposed to European culture makes the situation even more complicated. Native memories have often been adulterated by European elements; the stories that survive are compound rather than pure.

Three types of migration legends stand out. The first

are early and are commonly associated with myths of origin; they deal with a tribe's choice of a particular environment or with its development of a distinct way of life. The second derive from forced migrations into new territory caused by natural disasters or by pressure from competing societies. The third have to do with tribal relocations imposed by outside forces.

A typical example of the first type comes from the Keresan Pueblos of New Mexico. This story begins with a description of the bowels of the earth, which contain four levels called "wombs." Guardian animals bring selected mythical characters to the surface. From here the ancestors of each tribe are brought to their appointed habitats. In the Keresan version, each womb is a world, designated by colors: white, red, blue, and yellow. Iyatiku, the "Mother of Men," builds a fir-tree ladder to the red world, then asks the Woodpecker to peck through to the next. Repeating the process brings them to the last stage, where Badger and Old Man Whirlwind help. Iyatiku orders the first men to head south and gives them the first ear of maize.

Several myths illustrate the second type, based on tribal migrations. The Arikara and Pawnee people originally lived as farmers in what is now Louisiana. Pressure from neighboring tribes forced them up the Missouri Valley and onto the Great Plains in Kansas, which were not suited to their agricultural practices. As a result they became hunters. A number of their tales tell of migrations north and west. Other stories relate the marriage of the tribal hero to both the Maize Mother and the Buffalo-Woman, illustrating the fusion of agricultural and hunting traditions. Similarly, the Sun Dance ritual is primary to both religions; at the time of their relocation, it underwent modifications to make it functional for both planting and hunting.

The best example of the final kind of migration legend centers on the TRAIL OF TEARS, the mass relocation of the INDIANS OF THE SOUTHEAST to Oklahoma. Although this literally affected the CHEROKEE and CHOCTAW tribes around 1835, practically every tribe in the settled states had its own period of forced removal, and the legends about this experience are legion.

SUGGESTED READINGS. The best general collections of migration legends are Pierre Grimal's *Larousse World Mythology* (1965) and Alice Marriott and Carol K. Rachlin's *American Indian Mythology* (1968). The Trail of Tears and related events receive solid objective treatment in William Brandon's *The Last Americans: The Indian in American Culture* (1974).

American Indian Movement (AIM): Militant Indian rights organization founded in 1968 by Dennis Banks and George Mitchell, two Anishinabe (Chippewa) American Indians. Inspired by the BLACK POWER movement, the organizers of AIM put forth the militant slogan "Red Power" in organizing a pan-Indian struggle for self-determination.

In November, 1969, a group of American Indians sympathetic to AIM occupied Alcatraz Island in the San Francisco Bay, demanding that ownership of the island be returned to American Indians for use as a school. The protesters were ordered off the island, but they resisted without electricity or water supplies until mid-1971, when federal marshals raided the island and arrested the occupants.

AIM leader Russell Means, an Oglala SIOUX Indian, became a master at staging protests designed to publicize the AIM cause. In 1973, Means organized a protest at WOUNDED KNEE, South Dakota, the site of an infamous 1890 massacre of Sioux by the U.S. Cavalry. About two hundred AIM members quickly found themselves surrounded by BUREAU OF INDIAN AFFAIRS (BIA) police forces and Indians opposed to AIM. Largely unprepared for a confrontation, the protesters collected firearms from the town's trading post and took up defensive positions. U.S. troops from an army base 300 miles away were summoned, laying siege to Wounded Knee and the armed protestors. Air Force jets made daily reconnaissance flights overhead as tanks were amassed at the outskirts of tiny Wounded Knee.

AIM's offer for a mutual withdrawal of forces was rejected by federal authorities, who instead ordered the protesters to send out all women and children. African American civil rights leader Ralph Abernathy unsuccessfully attempted to negotiate a peaceful resolution to the crisis, later declaring his solidarity with the AIM cause. After two weeks of standoff, federal forces began firing automatic rounds into the village, where about 160 protesters remained. Means voluntarily surrendered to federal authorities as part of a deal to end the siege, but the agreement was subsequently broken by federal forces, who remained stationed until the last holdouts were arrested in the standoff's ninth week.

In following years, AIM's leaders were harassed, arrested, and in some cases killed by federal authorities after being drawn into armed confrontations. In one case, AIM leader Leonard Peltier was present during an armed confrontation in which two federal agents were killed. He was later arrested in Canada and extradited to the United States in 1976, where he was convicted of murder despite tremendous irregularities in the evidence. Peltier's plight drew widespread attention in 1992 when Robert Redford produced and narrated a documentary entitled *Incident at Oglala* that reexamined the evidence presented at Peltier's trial.

By the late 1970's, AIM was nearly extinct. Nevertheless, the organization managed to regroup into several regional offices and in 1992 helped organize protests of the Columbus Quincentenary celebration.

SUGGESTED READINGS. Bruce Johansen and Roberto Maestas *Wasi'chu: The Continuing Indian Wars* (1979) describes the rise of Red Power as does Alvin M. Josephy, Jr.'s *Red Power: The American Indians' Fight for Freedom* (1971). Ward Churchill and Jim Vander Wall's *Agents of Repression* (1988) analyzes federal repression of AIM, as does Jim Messerschmidt's *The Trial of Leonard Peltier* (1983), while Peter Matthiessen's *In the Spirit of Crazy Horse* (1983) chronicles the development of AIM.

American Indian religion and mythology. *See* **Religion and mythology—American Indian**

American Indian reservations. *See* **Reservations, American Indian**

American Indian revitalization movements: Organized efforts by American Indians to create religious systems which allow them to adapt to change. As defined by Anthony F. C. Wallace, revitalization movements generally are triggered by increased stress caused by changes in the natural or cultural environment such as famine or military conquest. To cope with this stress, individuals create new social codes that allow them to make sense of new conditions and adapt accordingly.

American Indian spiritual revitalizations have taken a variety of forms, from militant and separatist to pacifistic and accommodative. A common element in these movements, however, is the projection of cultural confrontation into a spiritual realm. One of the very earliest of these movements, the Montezuma cult, arose among the Pueblo villages of New Mexico in conjunction with the PUEBLO REVOLT OF 1680. This spiritual movement, like later movements such as the GHOST DANCE RELIGION of the late nineteenth century, promised a renewal of the world that would return it to the state which had prevailed prior to the

SUPPORT THE AMERICAN INDIAN MOVEMENT

156 5th AVE RM 618
NYC 255-9570

Too many years
We have kept silent
While our children became orphans
As their Mother earth was taken from them
Today, we must raise our voices,
If need be, we must take up arms.
We are no murderers..., but
We will not commit suicide.

The organizers of AIM worked toward American Indian self-determination. (Library of Congress) arrival of white Europeans. Because they revitalize by reviving or perpetuating elements of a traditional lifestyle, these movements have sometimes been labeled "nativistic."

Although it is possible to find nativistic elements in all American Indian revitalizations, many incline more to syncretism—the combination of native and alien cultural elements. The New Religion introduced by Handsome Lake among the Iroquois in the late eighteenth and early nineteenth centuries is representative. Handsome Lake's "Good Message" urged continuity through belief in the traditional gods and observance of the traditional ceremonies while it also advocated the adoption of elements of alien culture such as western European technology, subsistence farming, and smaller families. More recently, Peyotism, ultimately organized as the NATIVE AMERICAN CHURCH, has served as a focus for spiritual revitalization among American Indians. Originating in the latter half of the nineteenth century, this religion focuses on the ingestion of PEYOTE as a sacrament. While practices of the individual congregations vary, the religion generally incorporates and reinterprets Christian symbolism. For example, the fissures on the top of a peyote button are envisioned as a cross, and Peyote is personified and combined with figures such as Jesus, the Virgin Mary, and God to create a trinity. The rites of the meetings are characteristically patterned on traditional American Indian (particularly Plains) rituals. Underlying the surface diversity of these movements is the fact that all reformulate worldviews to correspond with changes brought on by European contact and provide a means of identification for followers.

SUGGESTED READINGS. Anthony F. C. Wallace 's "Revitalization Movements," in *American Anthropologist* 58 (April, 1956), pp. 264-281, presents a definition of the concept. Wallace and Sheila C. Sheen analyze Handsome Lake's New Religion in *The Death and Rebirth of the Seneca* (1969). J. S. Slotkin combines the perspectives of anthropologist and practicing peyotist to provide insights into the Native American Church and nativism in *The Peyote Religion* (1956). Although focusing on a single movement, Alice Beck Kehoe provides background on other American Indian revitalization movements in *The Ghost Dance: Ethnohistory and Revitalization* (1989).

American Indian rights movement. *See* **Indian rights movement**

American Indian sign language. *See* **Sign language—American Indian**

American Indian studies programs: The scholarly discipline of American Indian studies emerged in the 1960's in the wake of that decade's concerns with CIVIL RIGHTS and MULTICULTURALISM. An amalgamation of existing disciplines, Indian studies replaced history and anthropology as the chief means of knowing and understanding native peoples, who were most frequently treated as traditional, historical abstractions, rather than living, contemporary cultures with unique concerns. Before this period, only three institutions of HIGHER EDUCATION dealing with Indian issues had received any federal financial support: Haskell Institute (later Haskell Indian Junior College) in Kansas, Southwestern Indian Polytechnical Institute in New Mexico, and the Institute of American Indian Arts, also in New Mexico.

The new field of Indian studies, however, was quickly attacked from within and without the academy for lacking what were cited as the four essential criteria for independent intellectual inquiry: a distinct methodology, abstract concepts, a unique area of concern, and scholarly traditions. Despite eloquent rebuttals to these charges, early Indian studies programs were largely intellectually reactionary, attacking existing bodies of knowledge rather than making significant contributions to contemporary understanding and addressing current issues. Then, as now, questions about clientele and mission concerned many colleges and universities. Debate centered on whether such programs should enculturate and prepare Indian students or introduce and sensitize the larger student population to Indian perspectives. Further, the field was divided in views on its role in research, culture, discipline, language, teaching, student support, and service to Indian communities.

Over the next decade, new areas of need and concern were identified. These included investigating the content and methodologies of oral traditions; issues of Indian treaties and contemporary rights; group persistence, especially in the face of historical reassessment; forms of TRIBAL GOVERNMENT and organization; the issue of sovereignty; American Indian epistemology; and contemporary social and cultural problems. Increasingly, university officials came to see that such matters are of concern to a diverse body of students and scholars. Rather than diminishing the core curricula of universities, such lines of inquiry can strengthen an institution in various ways.

Some of the most strikingly successful American Indian studies programs have been at tribally controlled colleges, beginning with the establishment of Navajo Community College in 1968. In 1990, such colleges numbered twenty-four in the United States and three more in Canada with an enrollment of more than twelve thousand students, representing 60 percent of the North American Indian population in higher education.

Financial crises in American education periodically threaten various services and disciplines such as Indian studies, since it is one of the newest, and thus most vulnerable, additions to the curriculum. Support continues to grow, however, with departments becoming increasingly established and respected. Of 107 programs identified in 1984 at two- and four-year institutions, eighteen offered a major, forty a minor, and six graduate study in Indian studies. Information has begun to be shared internationally through respected scholarly journals such as *The Journal of American Indian Education*, *Tribal College: Journal of American Indian Higher Education*, *Studies in American Indian Literatures*, *American Indian Quarterly*, *American Indian Culture and Research Journal*, and several others. Still, various programs stress an ongoing need for more Indian faculty and cite a lack of administrative support and funding, in spite of the growth of the Indian population.

SUGGESTED READINGS. For the history of tribal colleges, see the Carnegie Foundation for the Advancement of Teaching's *Tribal Colleges: Shaping the Future of Native America* (1989) and Wayne J. Stein's *Tribally Controlled Colleges: Making Good Medicine* (1992). Detailed and insightful considerations of American Indian studies are to be found in the journal *American Indian Issues in Higher Education* (1981), issued by the American Indian Studies Center (UCLA), Susan Guyette and Charlotte Heth's *Issues for the Future of American Indian Studies* (1985), and *Tribal Discourse: Proceedings of the Symposium on the Status of American Indians in the California State University* (1993), edited by Rodney Simard.—*Rodney Simard*

American Indian termination and urbanization. *See* **Termination and urbanization—American Indian**

American Indian trade: Archaeological research in North America has shown that American Indians were involved in extensive trade prior to their encounters with Europeans. During the precontact period North America was covered with trade routes and networks of trading relationships connecting every Indian community. Items for trade were effectively moved along these networks. For example, shell beads from the Atlantic, Pacific, and Gulf coasts have been found in a prehistoric village situated on the Missouri River in South Dakota. Exchange of goods occurred not only between communities but also within the community itself. The main mechanisms for such trade were gift giving and ceremonial exchange. Within the village trade was less competitive and generally included more utilitarian objects than intertribal transactions.

Trade between different populations was frequently facilitated by the creation of fictive kin. In this situation, trading partners would adopt each other as relatives. For example, the Mandans situated along the Missouri River tended to adopt fictitious sons in tribes with whom they traded. Trading partnerships were also institutionalized in some regions whereby two individuals from different areas would agree to trade only with each other. On the death of one partner, the relationship would be reestablished with a replacement trade partner from the same group. Systematic INTERMARRIAGE among the families of trading partners strengthened the relationship between these groups.

Among the GREAT PLAINS INDIANS, tribes maintained peace while trading through the use of the calumet ceremony. Prior to engaging in an exchange the participants smoked tobacco in a calumet pipe. Any individual who accepted the pipe was honor-bound to trade in peace.

Since there were numerous AMERICAN INDIAN LANGUAGES, certain mechanisms evolved to facilitate trade across linguistic boundaries. Some Indians were particularly adept at learning foreign languages. It was not unusual for an adult Mandan to speak four languages fluently. Along the Pacific Coast a trade language known as Chinook jargon evolved. In the Great Plains region, INDIAN SIGN LANGUAGE was understood by all. Through the use of this medium of communication, complex messages could be transmitted between different linguistic groups.

Trade became more elaborate with the advent of European American goods. There was an increase in specialized traders and items traded. Trading fairs that had existed prior to contact became larger and more frequent. Certain items, such as horses and firearms,

An Indian woman in Oklahoma practices traditional basket weaving; baskets were always a popular trading item among tribes. (Dale D. Gehman)

changed the balance of power between trading groups. Those groups with access to both horses and guns were able to gain control of trading networks.

SUGGESTED READINGS. Many general sources on traditional American Indian life include discussions of trade, but specialized sources are also available. Among them are Joseph Jablow's *The Cheyenne in Plains Indian Trade Relations: 1795-1840* (1950), Katherine A. Spielmann's *Interdependence in the Prehistoric Southwest: An Ecological Analysis of Plains-Pueblo Interaction* (1991), and *Shell Bead and Ornamental Exchange Networks Between California and the Western Great Basin* (1987). George Catlin's *Illustrations of the Manners, Customs, and Conditions of the North American Indians* (1876) is an eyewitness nineteenth century account.

American Indian urbanization. *See* **Termination and urbanization—American Indian**

American Indian–U.S. government relations: American Indians occupy a unique position in the governmental framework of the United States of America. The U.S. CONSTITUTION recognizes American Indian tribes as domestic, dependent nations. The U.S. Congress has subjected Indians to an entire body of laws applicable to them alone.

The BUREAU OF THE CENSUS uses the term "Native American" to mean ALEUTS, American Indians, INUITS, and more recently, Native Hawaiians and some other PACIFIC ISLANDERS. It counts anyone a Native American who declares himself or herself to be such. To be eligible for federal services, however, a Native American must be a member of a tribe recognized by the federal government. Other restrictions for services are applied by the BUREAU OF INDIAN AFFAIRS (BIA). Most services are restricted to Native Americans living on or near a RESERVATION, which is land a tribe reserved for itself when it relinquished other lands to the United States or land deemed a reservation by executive order or congressional act. Many reservations have non-Indian as well as Indian residents and landowners.

The Bureau of Indian Affairs, within the Department of the Interior, is likewise unique, since it is the only federal agency that governs the lives of one distinct category of people. It controls almost all aspects of reservation life. Its jurisdiction covers land, education, employment, health, welfare, economic and industrial assistance. The bureau supervises only members of federally recognized tribes, however, not all American Indian peoples.

Congress and the Constitution in Indian Affairs. Indians are mentioned in the United States Constitution only twice: "Indians not taxed" are to be excluded from the count determining representation in the House of Representatives, and Congress may regulate "commerce with foreign nations, among the several states, and with the Indian tribes." In addition to the commerce clause, expenditures for the general welfare, decisions on property of the United States, and treaties have also affected Indian legislation. Congressional powers of lesser importance in Indian legislation include the powers to establish post roads, tribunals inferior to the Supreme Court, and a "uniform rule of naturalization."

The broad legislative power of Congress over tribal affairs derives from three of its powers enumerated in the Constitution: the power to declare war, the power to make treaties, and the power to regulate commerce with the Indian tribes. Together, these powers encompass all that is considered necessary for the regulation of the relationships between the United States and the federally recognized tribes.

The U.S. Supreme Court has repeatedly upheld the power of Congress to enact special laws for the protection and benefit of American Indians, even after 1924 when they were granted U.S. citizenship. Citizenship is not incompatible with continued tribal existence or continued guardianship.

Congress' discretion in regulating tribal affairs is unusually broad because there are no constitutional restraints like those which limit congressional power over states and individual citizens. Furthermore, the Constitution does not restrain tribes to the same extent that it limits the power of states and the federal government. In 1938, the Supreme Court declared that "Congress alone has the right to determine the manner in which this country's guardianship over the Indians will be carried out."

American Indian Legal Status. The legal status of tribal Native Americans is considered to be based in law unto themselves. Unlike the members of every other ethnic minority, they constitute distinct political communities, whose complex relationship with the United States is marked by unique distinctions which exist nowhere else in American political life.

The United States has long recognized the American Indian nations, tribes, and villages as separate political entities which possess some degree of sover-

INDIAN LAND FOR SALE

GET A HOME
OF
YOUR OWN

❋

EASY PAYMENTS

PERFECT TITLE
❋

POSSESSION

WITHIN

THIRTY DAYS

FINE LANDS IN THE WEST

IRRIGATED
IRRIGABLE

GRAZING

AGRICULTURAL
DRY FARMING

IN 1910 THE DEPARTMENT OF THE INTERIOR SOLD UNDER SEALED BIDS ALLOTTED INDIAN LAND AS FOLLOWS:

Location.	Acres.	Average Price per Acre.	Location.	Acres.	Average Price per Acre.
Colorado	5,211.21	$7.27	Oklahoma	34,664.00	$19.14
Idaho	17,013.00	24.85	Oregon	1,020.00	15.43
Kansas	1,684.50	33.45	South Dakota	120,445.00	16.53
Montana	11,034.00	9.86	Washington	4,879.00	41.37
Nebraska	5,641.00	36.65	Wisconsin	1,069.00	17.00
North Dakota	22,610.70	9.93	Wyoming	865.00	20.64

FOR THE YEAR 1911 IT IS ESTIMATED THAT 350,000 ACRES WILL BE OFFERED FOR SALE

For information as to the character of the land write for booklet, "INDIAN LANDS FOR SALE," to the Superintendent U. S. Indian School at any one of the following places:

CALIFORNIA: Hoopa.	**MINNESOTA:** Onigum.	**NORTH DAKOTA:** Fort Totten. Fort Yates.	**OKLAHOMA**—Con. Sac and Fox Agency. Shawnee.	**SOUTH DAKOTA:** Cheyenne Agency. Crow Creek.	**WASHINGTON:** Fort Simcoe. Fort Spokane.
COLORADO: Ignacio.	**MONTANA:** Crow Agency.	**OKLAHOMA:** Anadarko.	Wyandotte.	Greenwood.	Tekoa. Tulalip.
IDAHO: Lapwai.	**NEBRASKA:** Macy.	Cantonment. Colony.	**OREGON:** Klamath Agency. Pendleton.	Lower Brule. Pine Ridge.	**WISCONSIN:** Oneida.
KANSAS: Horton. Nadeau.	Santee. Winnebago.	Darlington. Muskogee, SUPT. OF UNION AGENCY Pawnee.	Roseburg. Siletz.	Rosebud. Sisseton.	

WALTER L. FISHER,
Secretary of the Interior.

ROBERT G. VALENTINE,
Commissioner of Indian Affairs.

The U.S. government engaged in a long-term policy of forcing Indians off their homelands and then selling these lands for profit. (Library of Congress) eignty. The U.S. Supreme Court has repeatedly affirmed its time-honored doctrine that the Indian governmental entities—nations, tribes, bands, and villages—are separate, but dependent nations. "Indian Tribes are not states. They have a status higher than states," a federal court declared in *Native American Church v. Navajo Tribal Council* (1959).

The tribes may establish their own courts and penal codes and may levy taxes. No other American ethnic minority has such rights. The tribes may also recognize and support an official religion—a power denied to the states and the federal government. Until 1968, when Congress passed an Indian Bill of Rights as part of the Civil Rights Act, American Indians were generally immune from the protections of the Bill of Rights of the U.S. Constitution. The unique position of the Native Americans is highlighted by the Supreme Court's position that ambiguities in legislation are to be construed in favor of Indians whenever their rights are at stake.

American Indians have a unique legal status because they comprise various nations and tribes which claimed and received the protection of a more powerful nation, the United States. The tribes, however, did not abandon their national character in gaining this protection. Congress' unusual powers over American Indians and the Supreme Court's recognition of their unique place in American law exist not because Indians belong to a different race or ethnic group but because they owe allegiance to the various tribes. The events which led to these decisions of the U.S. government, including treaties and military conquests, have no parallel in the history of non-Indian groups.

The term "Indian" noted within the broader term "Native American," as the United States Constitution, Congress, and Supreme Court have used it, is primarily a political designation rather than a purely racial classification. The relevant constitutional provisions refer not to Indians or Native Americans as a race, but to Indian tribes and "Indians not taxed." In particular, the constitutional provision sanctioning treaties with the Indians, "admits their rank among those powers who are capable of making treaties," according to *Worcester v. Georgia* (1832). Although treaty-making

American Indians have organized protests, such as the "Longest Walk," to ensure that their voice is heard by the U.S. government. (Hazel Hankin)

between the United States and the tribes was generally abandoned by an act of 1871, the treaties previously signed remain in force.

Federal-Tribal Relations. On January 24, 1983, the Reagan Administration issued a policy statement on American Indian policy recognizing and reaffirming the government-to-government relationship between the United States government and the federally recognized Native American nations, tribes, bands, and villages. This policy builds upon the policy of self-determination first announced by President Richard Nixon in 1970. This was reaffirmed by President George Bush on June 14, 1991.

The government-to-government relationship is the result of sovereign and independent tribal governments establishing lasting relationships with the United States through treaties and other agreements. Five hundred and ten Native American political entities, including about two hundred native villages in Alaska, have a continuing relationship with the United States. This is a partnership in which the tribal governments may choose to assume the administration of numerous Federal programs in accord with the INDIAN SELF-DETERMINATION AND EDUCATION ASSISTANCE ACT OF 1975.

An Office of Self-Governance in the U.S. Department of the Interior has the responsibility of working with the tribes to transfer decision-making powers over tribal government functions from the federal government to the tribal governments.

As of 1992, an Office of American Indian Trust was planned to oversee lands and funds held in trust by the United States for the various tribes. This office will ensure that no federal actions will adversely affect or destroy these assets. The United States holds 56.2 million acres of land in trust for various American Indian tribes and individuals, much of it on reservations; however, not all reservation land is held in trust by the federal government.

A number of American Indian tribes and groups in the United States are not federally recognized, although some are recognized by various states. A special program of the Bureau of Indian Affairs works with those seeking federal recognition status. Of 126 petitions for recognition received by the U.S. government since 1978, only eight have been accepted. Twelve other tribes gained federal recognition through legislative action of the Congress.

SUGGESTED READINGS. Felix S. Cohen's *Handbook of Federal Indian Law* (1942, repr. 1971) is an excellent compilation of treaties, U.S. laws, and court decisions regulating American Indian status. Francis Paul Prucha's, *The Great Father: The United States Government and the American Indians* (1984) and Sharon O'Brien's *American Indian Tribal Governments* (1989) focus on U.S. Indian policy and intergovernmental relations. Decision making in tribal, intertribal, and international contexts is the focus of Howard Meredith's *Modern Tribal Government and Politics* (1993).—*Howard Meredith*

American Indian–U.S. government treaties: Documents that formed the basis for official relationships between tribes and the American government from 1787 until 1871, when treaty making was ended. Even before the AMERICAN REVOLUTION, each of the imperial powers in North America engaged to some degree in treaty making, thus establishing precedents that acknowledged government-to-government relations, land cessions, and protection. The process was formalized in the early republic under the U.S. CONSTITUTION. The Commerce Clause in Article I, Section 8, authorized Congress to "regulate commerce with foreign nations, and among the several States, and with the Indian tribes." Though added almost as an afterthought, the clause clearly made Indian affairs a federal matter. Moreover, federal control of the Indian trade and intercourse laws laid the foundation for sweeping plenary powers most often expressed through treaties.

Indian treaties differed in important ways from treaties between truly sovereign states. Though Indian treaties acknowledged tribal entities, going so far in some cases (such as *Worcester v. Georgia,* 1832) as to admit that the CHEROKEES were "a distinct community, occupying its own territory," they also implied a relationship in which tribes were dependent. This was an important component in the treaty-making process. According to Stephen Cornell, treaties "constituted formal recognition of Indian nations as sovereign powers with whom the United States could negotiate an increasingly dependent relationship. . . . Over time they became more and more intrusive, chipping away at the autonomy" of the tribes.

Treaties historically served three purposes. They secured peace; legitimated land cessions; and defined and promoted both "civilization" and ASSIMILATION. A useful model for study is the Treaty of Medicine Lodge Creek, signed in 1867 between the United States and representatives of the Kiowa and CO-MANCHE tribes. Article I called for a cessation of hostilities forever, noting that the "Government of the United States desires peace. . . . The Indians desire peace, and they now pledge their honor to maintain it." Such announcements were typical of all treaties. Article II designated reservation boundaries and in doing so opened the majority of the prereservation do-

ing began to be viewed as an impediment to civilizing Indians. Largely because treaties helped to maintain reservations that segregated Indians from the rest of the country, but also owing to congressional squabbles over authority for Indian affairs, treaty making was abandoned in 1871. Government officials hoped that

Treaty signing by William T. Sherman and the Sioux at Fort Laramie, Wyo., in 1868. (National Archives)

main to white settlement. Article X noted that the tribes would "relinquish all right to occupy permanently the territory outside of their reservation." Articles VI-X contained details of the government's civilizing program such as individual land allotments, education, annuities, clothing, and census taking. By articulating the government's plans for assimilation and absorption, treaties such as this outlined the general goals and assumptions of Indian policy, and they defined what was necessary for tribes to do in order to be treated as worthwhile members of American society.

By the late nineteenth century, however, treaty mak-

this move would accelerate the civilizing process. In the future, legislation, not negotiation, would dominate AMERICAN INDIAN AND U.S. GOVERNMENT RELATIONS.

SUGGESTED READINGS. The standard source for treaty texts is *Indian Affairs: Laws and Treaties* (5 vols., 1904-1941), edited by Charles J. Kappler. Paul Prucha's *The Great Father* (1984) remains indispensable as a guide to policy. Charles F. Wilkinson's *American Indians, Time, and the Law: Native Societies in a Modern Constitutional Society* (1987) is a particularly insightful discussion of the legal issues of treaty making.

American Indian water rights: One of the critical issues in contemporary Indian affairs. As the population of the United States, and particularly of the dry West, expands, competition for scarce water resources pits American Indians against non-Indians in open conflict for limited water rights. Of vital importance to the resolution of such conflicts is the struggle to protect native rights against intrusion stemming from increased population demands and resource development.

Generally, Indian TRIBES and nations have sought protection of their water rights through court adjudications. Non-Indians have also pursued increased access to Indian waters, armed with legislative actions and statutory laws from state governments. While the federal courts have traditionally sided with Indian interests, the politically sensitive executive and legislative branches of the federal government have undermined the effectiveness of some federal court rulings by instituting programs and policies that have proved to be more beneficial to powerful non-Indian interests. These developments, along with ever-increasing population demand on water in the West, have created a legal quagmire from which simple, affordable, and fully just solutions are unlikely to emerge.

The seminal case for Indian water rights litigation is *Winters v. the United States* (1908). The U.S. Supreme Court ruling held that the creation of an Indian RESERVATION automatically, if implicitly, creates a water right for that reservation. The ruling was of particular importance in the West; not only were most reservations and trust lands there, but also the scarcity of water resources there was problematic. Because of the aridity of the West, most states had adopted the "prior appropriative" doctrine of water management. This method of water allocation involved a chronologically arranged hierarchy for water rights. "Senior appropriators" of water are given specified allocations for "approved beneficial uses," and all other appropriators are eligible for remaining water resources according to the chronology of their claims. The *Winters v. the United States* decision, by insisting that reserved water rights were inherent in the establishment of the reservations, rendered native water claimants as senior appropriators, because their claims dated from the times reservation lands were ceded to the tribes and nations.

Though the Supreme Court had protected Indian water rights, federal executive and congressional policies made use of the water resources by Indians difficult. Without political and financial power, tribal peoples saw non-Indian water projects divert both resources and economic improvement away from them. Indeed, careful study of concurrent federal Indian policies and water resource development projects shows that politically sensitive decision makers in the government were disinclined to encourage or assist Indians with water projects.

The overall effect of such inattention to Indian water rights, and the accompanying encroachment and reliance on entitled waters, has severely complicated resolution of water rights claims. Further, the passage of time and ongoing development have yielded a Supreme Court whose vision is less assuring to Indian interests. An important result of this is the trend toward negotiated settlements as opposed to litigation. While many Indians view negotiations as suspect in both intent and impact, others see them as the only means by which they can maintain their treaty-entitled rights.

SUGGESTED READINGS. See Lloyd Burton's *American Indian Water Rights and the Limits of the Law* (1991); Daniel McCool's study *Command of the Waters* (1987) investigates water resource rights history and analyzes settlement processes. For Indian perspectives on water rights negotiations, see the *Tribal Water Management Handbook* (1988), published by the American Indian Resources Institute.

American Indian weapons. *See* **Weapons—American Indian**

American Indian witchcraft. *See* **Witchcraft—American Indian**

American Indian women: The roles of American Indian women in their tribal cultures were long interpreted by observers, nearly always male, from European backgrounds who only partially understood the nature of those roles. Indian women have therefore historically been misunderstood and relegated to minor and unimposing cultural roles. This perception finally began to change in the 1970's. Moreover, in the second half of the twentieth century, American Indian women themselves became known in various fields, from tribal leadership to the visual arts to literature. Among them are Wilma MANKILLER, the first woman to become principal chief of the CHEROKEE Nation of Oklahoma, artist Elizabeth Woody, and writers Louise ERDRICH and Leslie Marmon Silko.

Early Views and Stereotypes. Scant attention was

paid to American Indian women in writings before 1900, which were usually from the perspectives of missionaries, trappers, or traders. Their observations tended to be uninformed and culturally biased; they represented an ETHNOCENTRIC and patriarchal point of view. These distorted interpretations set the stage for hundreds of years of mythologizing American Indian women into two general stereotypical categories: the princess and the squaw.

These two denigrating depictions shaped the views of the general American public, but they also colored the perceptions of scholars in the field. The simplified distortions became entrenched in mainstream culture as the closing of the western frontier combined with

this misguided perception.

The squaw stereotype evolved primarily from accounts written by missionaries, trappers, and traders who frequently misunderstood the behavior of American Indian women as they misunderstood many aspects of the native cultures. Among many TRIBES, women were expected to, and did, voice their opinions on community concerns. They were active guardians of their group's survival. Intense physical work was often seen by Europeans and white Americans as dull, brute drudgery, so the hard work performed by American Indian women was often construed as evidence that they were accorded a low status in their cultural milieu.

Two Cherokee women join a male friend at a powwow in Hunterdon Country, N.J. (Jeff Greenberg, Unicorn Stock Photos)

popular dime novels and then with early motion pictures to create a sentimental view of the vanishing "red" race. Even in scholarly works, the sheer volume of material on princesses such as POCAHONTAS and SACAGAWEA and on nondescript, voiceless squaw drudges are strong indicators of the pervasiveness of

The Indian princess STEREOTYPE is equally problematic; it reinterprets the behaviors of Indian women in order to establish a willingness on the part of native peoples to welcome the European invaders to their lands. Much of the scholarly inquiry devoted to Indian princesses (such as Doña Marina, or La Malinche,

Hernán Cortés' consort, as well as Sacagawea and Pocahontas) has failed to consider adequately the motives these women may have had. Consideration of the true roles the women played as members of their tribes has been absent, allowing the mythologizing of the Indian princess to occur.

Changing Perspectives. With the maturation of anthropology, and particularly with Margaret MEAD's *The Changing Culture of an Indian Tribe* (1932), new focuses and methodologies replaced the flawed and biased observations of the past. Still, most scholars of American Indian women held fast to certain limited topics about tribal women. These studies included accounts of native "customs" regarding menstruation, MARRIAGE, and ceremony. Little attention had yet been given to women as active and dynamic facilitators of tribal and cultural continuity. Though study of some Indian cultures, most notably the Iroquois, involved an examination of matriarchy, or a women-centered worldview, few researchers sought or examined other cultures that shared this trait. Additionally, much of the early examinations of matriarchal, matrifocal cultures perceived them in a culturally biased perspective, doubting both their functionability and their likelihood of survival. To Western or Eurocentric observers, tribal societies wherein women held prominent and active decision-making roles were nearly incomprehensible.

Studies of American Indian women continued to mirror trends in mainstream social science research. Scholarly endeavors frequently avoided undertaking culturally contextualized research, mostly because of the mythologized concept of the "vanishing Indian." The 1940's work on American Indian women reflected then-current academic interest in psychoanalytic inquiry and in public health. This, in turn, led to studies on fertility and contraceptive behaviors that continued through the 1960's and 1970's. Anthropological inquiries continued to emphasize puberty, child-rearing, and maternal behaviors. Scholars, while managing to avoid the ingrained princess or squaw stereotypes, still

Onlookers observe the intricate choreography of a traditional tribal dance in which a young woman takes center stage. (James L. Shaffer)

examined American Indian women through isolated, limited roles, with little or no attention to the necessary cultural contexts.

In the 1970's, corresponding with the rise of the WOMEN'S MOVEMENT, both women scholars and, increasingly, American Indian women writers began work that shifted the focus from American Indian women as objects of study to a revitalized and dynamic inquiry of women in and of the tribal world. Retrospective analysis of historical and ethnographic studies as well as a new emphasis on contemporary Indian women was finally underway.

Integral to this continuing research is the study of native women within cultural frameworks. American Indian cultures and Native traditions endure, despite intentional GENOCIDE, forcible ACCULTURATION, RACIAL DISCRIMINATION, and the divestment of tribal lands. This endurance is partly attributable to the integrity of American Indian women who, while holding to gynocratic tribal traditions such as sharing, nurturing, acceptance of diversity, and the absence of punitive means of social control, have enabled their cultures to survive.

Notable American Indian Women. American Indian women have become well known in a number of fields. Three women who have been involved in tribal leadership or political actions are Sara Winnemucca Hopkins, Anna Mae Pictou Aquash, and Wilma Mankiller. Hopkins, born about 1844 and descended from Paiute leaders, was an early activist for justice for her people. Aquash, born in 1945, was an activist with the AMERICAN INDIAN MOVEMENT (AIM). She participated in the AIM occupation of the Washington headquarters of the BUREAU OF INDIAN AFFAIRS and the 1973 confrontation at WOUNDED KNEE. Aquash was found dead of a gunshot wound in February, 1976, and her murder has never been solved. Wilma Mankiller, the first woman to become principal chief of the Cherokee Nation of Oklahoma, credits the AIM OCCUPATION OF ALCATRAZ ISLAND with providing the inspiration for her work on behalf of her people. She has been actively working for health care, economic development, and self-governance since the early 1970's.

American Indian artists include Dat-So-La-Lee, Maria Montoya Martinez, and Elizabeth Woody. Washo Indian Dat-So-La-Lee developed innovative designs based on traditional concepts. Constantly experimenting with new techniques, she became famous for her flame motifs and basketmaking artistry.

Martinez was a celebrated Pueblo potter who brought new attention to traditional Pueblo pottery; since her death in 1980, her descendants have carried on her legacy. Woody's reputation is multifaceted: Born in 1959, she first gained a reputation as an essayist and poet, and later achieved fame as a visual artist.

Among well-known writers and scholars are Louise Erdrich, Leslie Marmon Silko, Ella Cara DELORIA, Paula Gunn Allen, and Beth Brant. Erdrich, a poet and novelist, is one of the preeminent American Indian authors and has won numerous awards. Her novels *Love Medicine* (1984), *The Beet Queen* (1986), and *Tracks* (1988) employ multiple narrators to recreate a mesh of perspectives and identities that authenticate the intermingling of mainstream and American Indian cultures. Leslie Marmon Silko, a novelist, essayist and poet, won outstanding praise for her debut novel, *Ceremony* (1977). Silko uses photographs, traditional tales, poetry, and autobiographical narrative to fashion a twentieth century version of the oral tradition of native people. Deloria is a leading scholar and preservationist of SIOUX culture; Allen, a writer herself, is a leading authority on American Indian writing and writers. Brant, a writer and activist against the appropriation of Indian religious practices by non-Indians, compiled an important collection of American Indian women's writings entitled *A Gathering of Spirit* (1984).

SUGGESTED READINGS. For further study of American Indian women see Paula Gunn Allen's *The Sacred Hoop: Recovering the Feminine in American Indian Traditions* (1984), Allen's edited volume *Spider Woman's Granddaughters* (1989), and her work *Grandmothers of the Light: A Medicine Woman's Source-book* (1991). Also of importance are Rayna Green's edited volume *That's What She Said* (1984) and Beth Brant's edited collection *A Gathering of Spirit* (1984). Finally, for bibliographic sources on American Indian women, see Gretchen M. Bataille's *Native American Women: A Biographical Dictionary* (1993), Rayna Green's *Native American Women: A Contextual Bibliography* (1983) and Bataille and Kathleen M. Sands's *American Indian Women: A Guide to Research* (1991).—*Sherrie A. Juras*

American Indians—contemporary social conditions: The situation of American Indians is unique among contemporary American ethnic groups. They are the "first Americans," proud descendants of people who inhabited North America for centuries before the arrival of Europeans. Their ancestors belonged to hundreds of individual cultures with their own systems of belief, ecological adaptation, and governance, as well as complex forms of music and art. Over the past five hundred years, however, Indian life and culture have been disrupted and radically transformed by the pressures of the DOMINANT CULTURE. Today, American Indians are the poorest ethnic minority in the United States, suffering from extremely high rates of unemployment, substandard housing, and a host of health problems. These problems are generally the worst on and near RESERVATIONS, where about half of all Indians live. As an ethnic group, Indians are poorly represented in HIGHER EDUCATION, the professions, and nontribal political office. In many parts of the country, they have become an invisible or forgotten minority.

This American Indian woman works as a data entry operator in Rochester, N.Y., but unemployment in the Indian population is often as high as 80 percent. (Don Franklin)

Some of the roots of these problems can be traced back to the early period of contact with Europeans. Wars and disease decimated the population from an estimated twelve to fifteen million at the time of first contact to a low of 210,000 in 1910, as recorded by

the U.S. Census. Along with the loss of life came significant loss of land as tribes were forced to give it up to European American settlers, farmers, and ranchers. The U.S. government, though officially dealing with TRIBES as sovereign nations, shifted its Indian policy at will, often disregarding Indian needs and culture as well as prior treaties. Policies of the BUREAU OF INDIAN AFFAIRS (BIA), established in 1824, have been controversial for the control they exert over Indians living on or near reservations. One example was the abrupt TERMINATION AND URBANIZATION of certain previously protected tribes in the 1950's and 1960's—an instance of a more recent circumstance that caused cultural disruption and social dislocation.

Despite this legacy, the American Indian population has managed to survive and even grow. Its numbers rose from 552,228 in 1960 to 1,418,145 in 1980. According to the CENSUS OF 1990, the Indian population was 1,878,285 or 0.8 percent of the total U.S. population. The BUREAU OF THE CENSUS also reported that the Indian population was growing at a rate of 37.9 percent, which could be explained by both a high birth rate (twenty-eight births per thousand Indians, compared to sixteen per thousand for all Americans) and the trend of more people claiming Indian ancestry.

Poverty. POVERTY is the rule rather than the exception among Indians. For example, the per capita income for NAVAJOS in 1984 was only $2,214 compared to $7,731 for Americans generally. Contrary to STEREOTYPES, Indians do not receive more money from the federal government than other Americans; according to a 1980 congressional study, they actually receive about 20 percent less. An Indian middle class is small to nonexistent, although some individual Indians have broken through barriers to economic success.

Unemployment is endemic, both in cities and on reservations, where it may reach as high as 80 percent. The reasons for this are complex. Reservations are often located in remote, arid areas with few natural resources and little economic development. Thus, available jobs are minimal, with the exception of government jobs on the reservation. Some Indians may not be motivated to work because of health problems, alienation from non-Indian culture, or dependance on FEDERAL PUBLIC ASSISTANCE PROGRAMS. They may also be impeded by lack of EDUCATION and job skills, particularly when they move to cities seeking work. Indians who were essentially pushed off their reservations during the termination period were sent to large cities where there were only minimal programs to help them get settled, employed, and adjusted to a vastly different way of life. Even in 1985, Indians living in LOS ANGELES—the country's largest concentration of urban Indians—had an unemployment rate of 40 percent, and many of the employed were in low-paying, low-skill jobs.

Problems finding work may relate to prior problems in education. Some Indian adults have bad associations with education because of the treatment they experienced at Indian boarding schools in the past and are therefore suspicious of public education. Some Indian children brought up in traditional communities often find it difficult to function in the competitive atmosphere of mainstream schools. Yet most Indian children attend public schools, and in 1990, an estimated seventy thousand were enrolled in colleges, including seven thousand at tribally controlled colleges.

According to the U.S. Census, Shannon, South Dakota, home of the Pine Ridge Sioux Reservation, has been the poorest county in the country for more than fifty years. In 1969, the U.S. government spent $8,040 per family there, while the median income per family was $1,910. Sixty percent of the population was unemployed, and one bureaucrat was in evidence for each family on the reservation. Statistics suggest further ironies. While the state of Washington spent up to $2,000 per salmon to protect the fish for sport and commercial catch, they refused treaty-guaranteed fishing rights to Indians, whose annual income there in 1979 was $1,500.

Since the trend toward self-determination in the 1970's, increasing numbers of tribes have set up economic enterprises to reverse the cycle of poverty. They have mobilized to tap natural resources such as uranium, coal, gas, and oil on Indian lands, as in the Navajo Kayenta Mine. They have started farming cooperatives, timber companies, fishing industries, and radio stations. With money paid to them in government land claims, they have invested in schools and health clinics as well as local businesses and lucrative hotels. The Agua Calientes, who lease their lands to the resort of Palm Springs, CALIFORNIA, are the wealthiest group of Indians in the United States. Yet even for those tribes whose enterprises are still struggling, such efforts have raised hope and self-esteem, particularly among the young. Meanwhile, in the cities, underfunded Indian centers try to stay open to continue providing social services to needy Indians.

Health and Living Conditions. Corollaries of Indian poverty are poor health and living conditions. About half of all Indians live in substandard housing, compared to about one-tenth of all Americans. One main cause of this on reservations is overcrowding; because of insufficient housing and traditional values of generosity, it is common for two or more families to live in and around a small dwelling, often in trailers, tents,

The 1970's trend toward Indian self-determination pushed many tribes to establish economic enterprises to reverse the cycle of poverty; this Hupa Indian works for a tribal timber company. (Ben Klaffke)

or cars. Sanitation is poor on some reservations, leading to diseases such as hepatitis. In remote areas, many Indian homes lack electricity or running water.

Indians have a number of health problems that distinguish them from other Americans. For example, in 1990, they had a death rate from accidents of eighty per hundred thousand—more than twice the national average. They are prone to high rates of diabetes which, with poor living conditions, poverty, and inadequate health care, is difficult to control. Malnutrition is also common among Indians, notably children and the elderly. Life expectancy for Indians in 1990 was an average of 71.1 years, according to the BIA, but traditionally Indians have had significantly lower life expectancy than non-Indians, especially on reservations.

By far the greatest health problem in Indian communities is ALCOHOLISM. A 1985 study by the Department of Health and Human Services found that one-third of all Indian deaths could be traced to alcohol, three times as many as the national average. For example, alcohol figured in most accidents and teen suicides. Fetal alcohol syndrome (FAS), which alcoholic mothers pass on to their babies, has only recently been recognized and treated in accordance with its epidemic proportions. Most Indian child welfare placements outside the home relate to parental alcohol consumption. Again, the reasons for the high rate of Indian alcoholism are complex. Government studies and Indian accounts point to the disruption of traditional life, the stress of trying to adjust to non-Indian society, and a widespread sense of depression and despair, particularly among young reservation Indians.

Since the late 1800's, the federal Indian Health Service (IHS) has been operating hospitals in reservation areas. Medical services were one of the things promised to certain tribes in exchange for land in nineteenth century treaties. The contemporary Indian population, however, remains widely dispersed and existing clinics and staff are insufficient. Alcohol detoxification programs, for example, cannot keep pace with the need. Hopeful signs since the 1970's are a gradual increase in the proportion of Indian staff working for the IHS and greater leeway for tribal control of health programs and policy.

Changing social conditions have taken a toll on Indian mental as well as physical health. In the late 1980's, suicides accounted for nearly 3 percent of all Indian deaths—more in some areas such as Alaska. Urban Indians often suffer from a loss of identity or culture shock, the urban counterpart to depression on the reservations. Both reservation and rural Indians draw on strong family and community ties as well as cultural resources for help. Some rely on the services of medicine men and other traditional healers in curing ceremonies. Young people take part in celebrations, dance competitions, and a renaissance in Indian arts and RELIGION generally. Urban Indian centers sponsor counseling programs and cultural events such as intertribal POWWOWS to help ease isolation and social dislocation.

The Indian rights movement has been another outlet for Indians seeking to improve conditions for their community. Beginning in the 1960's, activists began to publicize the plight of certain tribes through highly visible actions. The federal government responded by adopting a policy generally oriented to self-determination for Indians in the 1970's. Since that time, a number of tribes have benefited from the payment of claims to them for usurped land and broken treaties.

SUGGESTED READINGS. For historical background that relates directly to contemporary conditions, see *Now That the Buffalo's Gone: A Study of Today's Indians* (1982) by Alvin M. Josephy. The pamphlet "American Indians Today" (1991 edition) by the Bureau of Indian Affairs answers commonly asked questions. A useful summary of social conditions is contained in Judith Harlan's *American Indians Today: Issues and Conflicts* (1987). See also *The American Indian in Urban Society* (1971), edited by Jack O. Waddell and O. Michael Watson.—*Susan Auerbach*

American Indians—removal and relocation. *See* **Removal and relocation of American Indians**

American Indians—rural: American Indians living in rural areas can be divided into those who live on RESERVATIONS and those who live in nearby nonreservation areas. One of the principal factors governing the American Indian migration from reservations has been U.S. policy toward native land management. In 1887, the General Allotment Act (or DAWES ACT) established tighter federal control over lands previously set aside for various Indian nations. As articulated in the law, "mixed-blood" Indians were eligible for immediate ownership of individually subdivided land parcels, while the land of "full-blood" Indians was placed in federal trusts for twenty-five years. Once lands were allocated, the remaining land of affected reservations reverted to federal government control. By the 1930's, this process had repossessed about two-thirds of the lands originally reserved for native peoples, providing no land allocations for future generations.

As the American Indian population steadily grew in the early decades of the twentieth century, thousands were forced to move from reservations to lands in adjacent rural areas. This trend of migration to non-reserved rural areas continued and accelerated until WORLD WAR II. The war caused many Indians to move to urban areas, both because of available employment in the booming defense industry and because American Indians were subject to compulsory military service; after serving in the military, many remained in urban centers.

In the 1950's, federal "relocation" programs were enacted in order to continue the trend of Indian migration to the cities as an intentional policy of ASSIMI-LATION. Employment agencies and services in selected cities were instituted, while federal cutbacks curtailed social services on the reservations. The URBANIZATION of Indian peoples, which was virtually nonexistent at the end of the nineteenth century, became a major trend by the early 1960's, bringing nearly 30 percent of all Indians to urban areas. By 1980 the numbers had grown to roughly half of the native population of the United States, with the largest concentrations found in LOS ANGELES, California; Tulsa and Oklahoma City, Oklahoma; Phoenix, Arizona; and Albuquerque, New Mexico.

Indians often live in remote rural areas. (Jeff Greenberg, Unicorn Stock Photos)

Living conditions in rural Indian communities and particularly on reservations deteriorated even as tribal authority was undermined by continual interventions of the BUREAU OF INDIAN AFFAIRS (BIA). Increasingly, non-Indians gained rights to reservation land through leasing rights ceded by government authorities, often without consent from Indians themselves. While American Indians who have migrated to cities have escaped the controlling influence of the BIA, they have struggled to survive in the face of the complex problems characteristic of American cities. Those Indians who live in nonreservation rural areas remain greatly influenced by arbitrary actions taken by the BIA.

SUGGESTED READINGS. Curtis E. Jackson and Marcia J. Galli's *A History of the Bureau of Indian Affairs and its Activities Among Indians* (1977) is a detailed but uncritical chronology of federal Indian policies. A more critical analysis is provided in Sar A. Levitan and Barbara Hetrick's *Big Brother's Indian Programs, with Reservations* (1971) and Vine DELORIA, Jr., and Clifford M. Lytle's *The Nations Within: The Past and Future of American Indian Sovereignty* (1984). Donald Lee Fixico's *Termination and Relocation: Federal Indian Policy, 1945-1960* (1986) offers additional information on federal legislation history, while Stephen E. Cornell's *The Return of the Native: American Indian Political Resurgence* (1988) highlights the struggles of the Indian rights movement.

American Indians and bison. *See* **Bison and American Indians**

American Indians and missionaries. *See* **Missionaries and American Indians**

American Indians of California: Because CALIFORNIA is a large state with many different types of habitats, the Indians that once lived throughout what is now California varied considerably in their subsistence patterns and cultural traditions. The traditional Californian Indian habitat varies from the moist, cool, forested Shasta region of the north to the hot, dry desert region of the south. On the west it is coastal; to the east it is mountainous. Among the many groups of Californian Indians were the northern Shastas, Yukis, and Pomos; the central Salinans, Yokuts, and Chumash; and the southern Serranos, Yumas, and Diegueños. The northern groups had more in common with INDIANS OF THE PACIFIC NORTHWEST than with TRIBES in the southern regions of California. Along the Oregon border there was a rich culture based on canoes, woodland hunting, and fishing. In the arid south there existed a corn-and-mesquite bean lifeway.

In California, tribes did not exist as large cohesive social units. Groups were small and were based on extended family ties and attachment to a particular location, stream, valley, or drainage territory. There were, however, hereditary chiefs throughout the region, their power resembling that of civil officials.

The gathering of acorns was an important subsistence activity in many areas. In the south, mesquite beans were crushed with a stone pestle in a stone mortar. The dough was patted into a cake, covered with wet sand, and baked. Some groups, such as the Mohaves, planted pumpkins, watermelons, cantaloupes, and wheat. A variety of pottery and basketry skills were practiced, using leaf or fishbone designs. Indeed, basketry was the most developed art of the entire region, with that of the Pomos possessing a worldwide museum reputation. They utilized lattice twining, coiling, and wickerwork in an exceptionally fine, tight weave.

Pomo arithmetical faculties were also highly developed; Pomos counted on long strings of beads. The clothing style among Californian Indians was usually a short two-piece skirt for women and a folded skin for men. The skirts were sewn from buckskin or from woven plant fibers such as the shredded inner bark of trees. In rain and wind, a skin blanket was draped over the shoulders; the best of these were of sea otter fur.

Houses varied from the rectangular plankboard house of the north to the light conical brush house of the Pomos and Chumash; this is often dug out a few feet. Among the Yokuts, large communal houses sheltered several families.

California Indian life was adversely affected by the Spanish incursions in the 1600's and the establishment of presidios and missions in the 1700's. In the 1800's California became a province of Mexico, leading to greater repression than had existed during the earliest period of settlement. The discovery of gold in 1848 saw the end of Indian tradition; many groups disappeared altogether. The largest groups remaining in the early twentieth century were the Shoshonean-speaking

AMERICAN INDIANS OF CALIFORNIA

Monos (1500), the Pomos (1200), the Maidus (1100), the Yuman-speaking Mohaves (1050), and the Wintuns (1000), with the rest totaling about 10,000—down from an estimated 133,000 in 1770.

This population loss had many causes. Between 1849 and 1860 the western foothills of the Sierra Nevada were overrun by gold miners, and from 1860 to 1865 by silver miners. This changed Indian food patterns and disrupted tribal boundaries. Between 1855 and 1865 there were raping and killing expeditions against the California Indians, particularly in counties of Trinity and Mariposa. White settlers kidnapped Indian children and sold them into peonage, and they tried to pass indenture laws binding slaves to buyers.

Whites also brought disease; by the 1850's, smallpox, typhoid, and cholera were found among the Wiyots, Hupas, Maidus, Miwoks Yanas, Pomos, and Yokuts.

After Indians became less of a threat to white settlers in the late 1800's, white treatment of them gradually became more benign. In 1970 the Hupas of northern California made $1 million from timber leases and concessions. In the same year in Sonoma County, the Pomos founded their Ya-Ka-Ama Project, funded by the U.S. Department of Labor, to train Indians in modern AGRICULTURE; it features an annual spring festival with games and dances. Pomo leaders are active in the Inter-Tribal Council of California and the Indian Board of Cooperation. On the Marongo reservation, the Cahuillas established the Malki Museum, which offers language classes. By 1980 California had the largest Indian population of any state because of immigration from Oklahoma, and the Southwest. More than half live in the large metropolitan areas and follow white lifestyles.

SUGGESTED READINGS. For further reading see Alfred

Louis Kroeber's *Handbook of the Indians of California* (1970), Sherburne F. Cook's *The Conflict Between the California Indian and White Civilization* (1976), and James J. Rawls's *Indians of California: The Changing Image* (1984). *Ishi in Two Worlds: A Biography of the Last Wild Indian in North America* (1961) by Theodora Kroeber describes the life of Ishi, the sole survivor of California's Yahi Indians.

American Indians of the Great Lakes: Great Lakes tribes are usually considered to include tribes inhabiting the Great Lakes region; tribes in the "lake areas" of Minnesota, Wisconsin, and southern Manitoba; and the Iroquoian-speaking peoples located near Lake Ontario. Among the Great Lakes tribes are the Ojibwas (Chippewas), IROQUOIS NATION tribes, Winnebagos, and Algonquins.

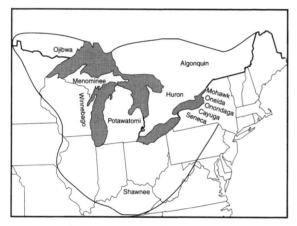

AMERICAN INDIANS
OF THE GREAT LAKES

This area was inhabited by Indian tribes of diverse cultural patterns. One of their most important developments was the Iroquois Confederacy (or IROQUOIS LEAGUE), which antedates European discovery. This was composed of five separate tribes—the Senecas, Cayugas, Oneidas, Onondagas, and Mohawks—and was governed under a council composed of fifty sachems, male representatives (chiefs) of the five tribes. In approximately 1722, the Tuscarora tribe was added to the council to make six tribes (the SIX NATIONS). The council had no authority over the internecine business of each tribe, but rather adjudicated matters pertaining to war and peace or to common problems of the members.

Awarding titles to war heroes was a responsibility of the council, with the "Pine Tree Chiefs" the highest honor accorded. Controlling the actions of young warriors, ambitious for awards, became a serious problem for the council. The AMERICAN REVOLUTION ended the military authority of the confederacy, since the tribes had divided allegiances, and the American westward expansion created further hostilities. After a campaign led by George Washington in 1779, the Iroquois forces were weakened considerably, until treaties in 1784, 1785, and 1786 deprived them of their land and forced them onto reservations in New York.

The Iroquois lived in rectangular longhouses with gabled roofs, which were shared by several individual families. The longhouses were controlled by the elder females; when people married, the husband moved into his wife's family's longhouse. Kin groups among the Iroquois were matrilineal, and women therefore had more influence than in other cultures. Women also chose the chiefs and could depose them if they were unsatisfactory.

Religion and the supernatural world were central aspects of daily life. Iroquoian tribes personalized forces in nature and made references to a universal "Great Spirit," sought through dreams, vision quests, and ceremonial events. The supernatural also explained mental illness for the Iroquois: They believed that the Windigo, a spirit monster, claimed those who became psychotic.

The Ojibwas (Chippewas) occupied areas in the upper Great Lakes, principally Lakes Superior and Huron. Their's was a hunter and fisher society, though they also harvested wild rice. Although they once lived in patrilineal villages and clans of 100 to 150 people, these communities dissolved into much smaller groups in the eighteenth century. The most important ceremony that brought these groups together was the Midewiwin, or the Great Medical Society. This was a "curing society" with an elaborate death/resurrection ceremony for initiation; Ojibwas became members in order to cure an illness, but also to gain prestige.

Today the tribes of the Great Lakes live in both the United States and Canada, with reservations (reserves) in both countries. In the early 1990's, there were about 160,000 Ojibwas, the majority living in Canada. Since the 1950's there has been significant migration from reservations to urban areas in both Canada and the United States. As with many tribes, a movement began in the 1960's to save the traditional Ojibwa culture from the danger of being lost through ASSIMILATION into the DOMINANT CULTURE. About six thousand Algonquians were living in Canada and the United States in the early 1990's, with their numbers roughly evenly divided between the two countries.

There are two main groups of Winnebagos today, one on trust lands in Wisconsin, the other on a reservation in Nebraska. The Nebraska group established a constitutional government in 1934 under the guidelines of the Indian Reorganization Act. Subsequently, the Nebraska Winnebagos joined with other Nebraska

Canada: A Reader (1974), Elsie C. Parsons' *American Indian Life* (1922, repr. 1967), and Anthony F. C. Wallace's *The Death and Rebirth of the Seneca* (1969). Additional sources for information on the twentieth century include *The Iroquois Struggle for Power: World War II to Red Power* (1986) by Laurence Hauptman and *Native Americans in the Twentieth Century* (1984) by James S. Olson and Raymond Wilson.

An American Indian of the Great Lakes region in Wisconsin, 1991. (James L. Shaffer)

tribes and filed a $4.5 million claim with the U.S. government, which was finally settled in the late 1970's. The Wisconsin group faced worsening economic conditions after World War II until it organized under Indian Reorganization Act terms in 1962 and qualified for federal benefits. It also began to generate income from bingo and smokeshops. After internal power struggles, a new level of stability had been reached by the 1980's.

SUGGESTED READINGS. For further information, consult Harold F. McGee's *The Native Peoples of Atlantic*

American Indians of the Great Plains: Native inhabitants of an area from northern Alberta, Canada, to the Rio Grande in Texas, and from the Rockies to approximately the present-day Minnesota-North Dakota border. Tribes include the Blackfeet, Crows, CHEYENNES, COMANCHES, and Pawnees. There was never a common language among the Plains Indians, though an elaborate system of sign language enabled trade and communication. Because these tribes inhabited such a vast living space, it is impossible to generalize about Great Plains culture. Two distinct representative tribes, the Mandans and the Sioux, provide examples of the wide range of social organizations, religions, and living styles that once thrived on the Great Plains.

The Mandans, located in central North Dakota, were traditionally a sedentary tribe, dependent on farming for subsistence. Crops cultivated included maize, beans, squash, pumpkins, sunflowers, and tobacco. Although maize was the main vegetable crop, tobacco was considered sacred and was planted and harvested with ritual and annual celebrations. The seriousness of the religious festival implies the importance of agriculture to the culture. Surplus crops were used by Mandans for intertribal trading, in which they excelled. A French fur trader wrote the Mandans "are sharp traders and clean the Assiniboins out of everything they have in the way of guns, powder, balls, knives, axes, and awls."

The material culture of the Mandans reflected their sedentary life patterns. They lived in large earth-covered lodges, with an opening on the top that allowed smoke to escape. Their houses surrounded a space for the Sacred Ark, a mythical wooden tower that had saved ancestors from the Flood. The central area was where tribal games were played and ceremonies held. Perhaps the most notable Mandan invention was the "Bull Boat," a circular boat made of bent willows and covered with bison hide, used for navigating the Missouri River.

During the years of white WESTWARD EXPANSION, Mandan lands were limited to a reservation in North Dakota. Then, in the 1880's, at the urging of the BUREAU OF INDIAN AFFAIRS, the Mandan reservation was divided into individual allotments. Mandans pursued ranching and farming. Some, frustrated by this risky business in the northern climate, leased their lands to non-Indians. In 1934 the Three Affiliated Tribes, including the Mandans, formed a constitutional government with an elected council; they also have a tribal court system. By the 1990's, most reservation land had been sold to non-Indians. Mandans are involved in a variety of occupations.

In 1950, government and private interests decided to build a dam on the Missouri River that would submerge Indian land. The Mandans and Hidatsas were virtually forced to sign away rights to land on the river. The dam flooded the bottomlands, where the tribes had lived on traditional village sites for more than a thousand years.

Unlike the Mandans, the Sioux were nomadic, following the huge bison herds, their principal source of food. The men stalked bison (often incorrectly called "buffalo") both on foot and on horseback, and the women skinned the animals, tanned the hides, and preserved the meat for consumption through the year. The bison hunt was critical: If the hunters were unsuccessful, the tribe would starve. The bison also provided the Sioux with skins for tipis and clothing; bones for making weapons and tools; skulls for religious ceremonies; and horns for everything from spoons to toys.

AMERICAN INDIANS OF THE GREAT PLAINS

The Sioux traditionally lived in tipis (from the Dakota word for "they dwell," or "dwelling"). These were portable, bison-skinned, conical-shaped dwellings with a vented top; they ranged from 12 to more than 30 feet in height. The tipis could be quickly disassembled and dragged by horses, the most important domesticated animal of the Sioux.

Popularly remembered today for their colorful clothing, the Sioux took great pride in artifice. Paintings often covered the surface of tipis and bison-skin robes; dyed quills and beadwork were attached to clothing. They also did featherwork with an elaborate symbolic sign structure. Although full war bonnets were unusual—relegated to highly respected war leaders—single feathers, such as that of the sacred eagle, represented achievements in warfare.

After being placed on reservations in the nineteenth century, the Sioux turned to ranching and farming in the early twentieth century. The GREAT DEPRESSION, however, proved disastrous; many Sioux eventually decided to lease their land to non-Indian interests. Some Sioux operate small businesses, but most of the large businesses near reservations are owned by non-Indians. The Teton Sioux have been governed by tribal councils since 1934.

There are a number of Sioux reservations in the northern Midwest as well as many reserves in Canada. The Teton Sioux is the largest group of Sioux, with an estimated population of about sixty-five thousand in the early 1990's, and many live on reservations in South Dakota. The Pine Ridge Sioux reservation is the second-largest reservation in the United States. Many Sioux, however, have left the reservations and moved to urban areas. There are large Sioux populations in Rapid City, South Dakota; LOS ANGELES; SAN FRANCISCO; CHICAGO; and Denver.

SUGGESTED READINGS. For further information on this vast subject, see *The Native Americans* (1965) by Robert F. Spencer, Jesse D. Jennings, et al., Robert M. Utley's *The Indian Frontier of the American West, 1846-1890* (1984), and Robert H. Lowie's *Indians of the Plains* (1954). For information on the twentieth century, see *Native American Testimony: A Chronicle of Indian-White Relations from Prophecy to the Present, 1492-1992* (1991), edited by Peter Nabokov, and *Native Americans in the Twentieth Century* (1984) by James S. Olson and Raymond Wilson.

American Indians of the Northeast: At the time of contact with Europeans, the culture of the American Indians living in what is now the northeastern United States and southeastern Canada had been evolving for many thousands of years. The ancestors of the modern Micmac, Maecite, Penobscot, Passamaquoddy, Abenaki, Pequot, Munsee, Lenape, Mohawk, Oneida, Cayuga, Seneca, and Wyandot tribes settled in the region some twelve thousand years ago.

Organized into many bands, tribes, and confederacies, they spoke many different dialects and sublanguages, which linguists have grouped into families. Many of the language families disappeared in early colonial times. Only two, perhaps three, of the families have survived: the Algonquian, Iroquoian, and perhaps Siouxan languages.

The Indians of the Northeast were gardeners, and those in Canada carried agriculture to its northernmost geographical limits. They had been slowly altering plants by artificial selection for more than four thousand years before the arrival of Christopher COLUMBUS in the New World. Among the cultivated or semicultivated plants that they artificially selected were black plums, goosefoot, and pigweed herbs. Many of their dwarf short-season plants are still grown, and some are now named varieties of plants.

There is little evidence of prehistoric warfare or feuds among the northeastern Indians. By the sixth century, however, population pressures had begun to provoke intertribal feuds, leading to the fortification of villages. This situation worsened until the fabric of society was threatened. Around the thirteenth century, leaders emerged who countered the violence with institutionalized peacemaking rituals. These rituals drew tribes together into enlarged kinship groups within which the carnage could be prevented. Efforts were not entirely successful, because the tribes and federations proved unable to control their warriors completely. Nevertheless, the Five Nations Confederacy generally managed to keep peace throughout the Northeast by linking tribes through adoptive kinship patterns, and enforcing a code of kinship responsibility.

AMERICAN INDIANS OF THE NORTHEAST

The appearance of Europeans violently disrupted the evolution of the native society. The newcomers brought a catalog of new infectious diseases with them; some tribes were entirely destroyed by disease.

The northeastern Indian tribes taught the Europeans hunting, among other survival skills: This Wampanoag Indian has successfully hunted for a meal (as portrayed by workers at Plimouth Plantation in Plymouth, Mass). (Cleo Freelance Photo)

The Europeans also brought firearms, which wrought another new type of destruction. Tribes were soon caught up in the Europeans' struggles (first between the French and the English, then between the colonists and the English), and then were pushed off their land as more Europeans arrived.

In the nineteenth and twentieth centuries, all American Indians were subject to the whims of shifting governmental demand and policies. Eventually, Indian groups became active in protesting, then bringing lawsuits against, government policies. The Senecas, for example, protested the flooding of their land by the Kinzua Dam project in the late 1950's. The tribe was compensated by the government but was unable to stop the project, which violated one of the oldest treaties between Indians and the government. In the 1970's and 1980's, tribes began to bring land claims in court, demanding that the government return land that had been taken from Indians even though promised them by treaty. In one case, the Penobscot and Passamaquoddy tribes of Maine recovered title to a huge area of more than 300,000 acres and received a trust fund of $27 million.

In the twentieth century, northeastern American Indians live modern lifestyles, both on and off reservations. Many are Christians, although native religions also remain strong. Tribal languages are still spoken by many, especially among the Wyandots, Oneidas, Mohawks, and Senecas. Some divide their time between working in large cities and spending weekends in reservation communities. Population patterns vary widely among tribes; fewer than 10 percent of Mohawks live on reservations. Large Indian populations now live in the NEW YORK CITY area, including northern New Jersey. Brooklyn, New York, has a sizable Mohawk population, some of whom originally moved to the city to work in the construction industry, particularly in high-rise construction.

The tribes who survived the arrival of the Europeans have been victims of ill-advised federal policies, PREJUDICE, and institutional RACISM. There has also been strife among and within tribes themselves. On the St. Regis Mohawk reservation in New York, for example, a bitter schism has existed between a minority of traditionalists and the tribal majority; the traditionalists believe the majority to be so ACCULTURATED to non-Mohawk values that they are a threat to the continuation of Mohawk culture. Other divisive issues include the proper places of the gambling and tax-free cigarette businesses run by tribal members.

SUGGESTED READINGS. An introduction to the topic may be found in *Handbook of North American Indians* (vol. 15, 1978), edited by Bruce T. Trigger. Introductions and guides to the archaeological literature include Jesse D. Jennings' *Ancient Native Americans* (1978) and Brian M. Fagan's *Ancient North America* (1991). Information on more recent conditions is included in *Native Americans in the Twentieth Century* (1984) by James S. Olson and Raymond Wilson and in *The Iroquois Struggle for Survival: World War II to Red Power* (1986) by Laurence M. Hauptman.

American Indians of the Pacific Northwest: The Pacific Northwest, a distinctive maritime and heavily forested culture area, is bounded in the north by the Tlingit town of Yakutat in southeastern Alaska and in the south by Cape Mendocino (home of the Wiyot Indians) in Northern California. It is warmed by the Japanese current and includes hundreds of offshore islands and navigable waterways. Languages spoken include Tlingit, Haida, Tsimshian, Haisla, Bella Coola, Kwakiutl,

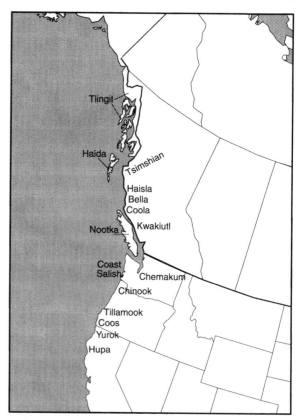

AMERICAN INDIANS OF THE PACIFIC NORTHWEST

Nootka, Coast Salish, Chemakun, Yurok, Hupa, and others.

The climate brings even temperatures and heavy rainfall. Before white settlement encroached on Indian lands, the ocean and rivers offered plentiful means of subsistence, such as salmon, halibut, cod, whale, sea lion, sea otter, and waterfowl, while the land held deer, elk, goat, bear, beaver, and mink.

The unified Indian culture area of the Northwest, first studied by anthropologist Franz Boas, is characterized by highly developed carpentry and wood-carving. The traditional dwelling was the rectangular planked house (often on pilings) with carved posts, gabled roofs, and multifamily occupancy. Large war canoes of red cedar were hollowed out with an adz; boiling water widened the hull.

Unlike other Indians, this group did not make tailored skin clothing but wore conical robes, ponchos, and aprons of woven goat wool. Wide-brimmed hats protected them from rain and bore signs of status. Tattooing was common, with face paint added for ceremonies, of which there were many.

Pacific Northwest Indians were highly socially stratified, with hereditary chiefs, noblemen, commoners, and slaves. Genealogy was critical. In the north, descent was through the female line. Rank and clan membership were formally validated at the social POT-LATCH (feast), featuring spectacular displays of carved totemic crests (such as Raven, Eagle, Wolf, Bear, Salmon, and Killer-Whale) and the dramatic re-enacting of clan CREATION MYTHS.

Important at the potlatch, a lavish feast at which gifts were exchanged, were large rectangular metal plaques, called coppers, of great symbolic and monetary value. Potlatches propitiated animal and guardian spirits, with the SHAMAN as intermediary with the supernatural. He also dealt with soul-loss, spirit possession, and WITCHCRAFT.

Northwest art is stylized, forceful, and derived from Indian mythology. Designs are space-filling, and three-dimensional figures are often represented by splitting and laying flat the subject, as one would a skin. Traditional designs continue to inspire both Indian and non-Indian artists in the region.

Songs, which may be inherited, are traditionally considered important personal property. They are sung in group unison and accompanied by rhythmic drumming, generally with spectacularly costumed dance.

Social change and modern lifestyles have entered Indian life in the northwest. For example, while the

witnessing of status-validation ceremonies used to be performed by opposing matrilineages, the women's auxiliary of the Anglican church now "stands in" for them at life-cycle rites. Many Haidas fish or work at canneries. Haida woman Mary Ellen Barnes became a militant leader elected to the United Fishermen and Allied Workers' Union; she advocated Indian welfare and fishing safety, leading to a wildcat strike in 1964.

Oregonian Indians dance at a powwow. (Gail Denham)

For the Tlingit, Tsimshian, and Haida in Alaska, the 1971 ALASKA NATIVE CLAIMS SETTLEMENT ACT brought land ownership and millions in cash, enabling the formation of large corporations. The Alaska Native Brotherhood established education programs funded by the Johnson-O'Malley Act and sponsors cultural aides in the schools.

SUGGESTED READINGS. See Philip Drucker's *Cultures of the North Pacific Coast* (1965), Erna Gunther's *Art in the Life of the Northwest Coast Indians* (1966), and Viola E. Garfield and Paul S. Wingert's *The Tsimshian Indians and their Arts* (1979). Other good overall views are presented in Karen Liptak's *Indians of the Pacific Northwest* (1991), and Robert H. Ruby and

John A. Brown's *Indians of the Pacific Northwest* (1989).

American Indians of the Southeast: "Five Civilized Tribes" of Cherokees, Creeks, Seminoles, Choctaws, and Chickasaws. In 1542, the Spanish explorer Hernando De Soto captured and killed many Creeks, Choctaws, and Chickasaws as he searched the Southeast for gold. Contacts between white Europeans and American Indians in the region were increasingly frequent, though little different than they had been with De Soto, until in 1784 the Cherokees made their first treaty, giving up land for white settlement and sovereignty. This set the stage for the westward movement of the Five Civilized Tribes.

During President George Washington's administration, the Shawnee warrior Tecumseh urged the southeastern tribes to oppose white settlement. The Cherokees went their own way, becoming farmers instead of hunters. The Creeks, meanwhile, surrendered land and then united with the Seminoles to follow Tecumseh against the white soldiers of President

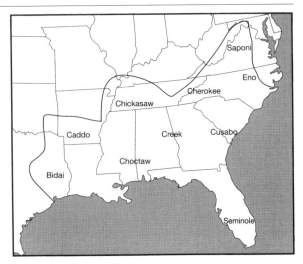

AMERICAN INDIANS OF THE SOUTHEAST

Thomas Jefferson. After Tecumseh's death in 1813, Creeks and Choctaws were massacred at Horseshoe Bend by Andrew Jackson's soldiers with help from Cherokees.

In 1821, white residents in Georgia, Alabama, and

Choctaws honor their ancestors on the commemorative Choctow "Trail of Tears Walk," in June, 1992. (Elaine S. Querry)

Mississippi persecuted local tribes, forcing the Choctaws into the territory later called Oklahoma. Most of the people in the remaining tribes of the Southeast eventually joined the Choctaws there, although many of the Seminoles followed their chief OSCEOLA into the swamps of Florida, where they

for settlement and railroads. Finally, in 1907 the Oklahoma Territory and Indian Territory merged to become the new state of Oklahoma, leaving the five tribes with no sovereignty and little identity to continue the traditions of the ancient people who once had lived in the American Southeast.

A Seminole woman with her craft in Tampa, Fla. (D & I MacDonald, Unicorn Stock Photos)

fought and hid for generations. The Creeks left their homes in 1831, some Cherokees left in 1835, and the remainder in 1838, on the infamous "TRAIL OF TEARS," when they were forcibly removed by the soldiers of General Winfield Scott. The Chickasaws left peacefully in 1837-1838.

In the area west of the Mississippi that was known as INDIAN TERRITORY, the five tribes quickly settled and began to prosper. The Cherokees set up a government with a Supreme Court in Tahlequah, and all the tribes except the Seminoles adopted written constitutions. The CIVIL WAR left the Indians of the territory in chaos and poverty from which they were unable to recover as various white governments seized their land

Remnants of tribal identities in the Southeast can be found in place names such as Chattanooga, Tennessee, and Tuscaloosa, Alabama. New organizations in Oklahoma, especially at the University of Oklahoma at Norman, have assured a continuing special identity for Indians of the Southeast. For example, the multitribal Oklahomans for Indian Opportunity was formed to sponsor community projects throughout the region to preserve traditional values of the Five Tribes while encouraging youth education and training. Such efforts have been necessary to combat the near total ASSIMILATION of descendants from the tribes of the Southeast. One notable achievement has been the leadership of Cherokee Principal Chief Wilma MAN-

KILLER, who has drawn widespread attention to the concerns of all Indians whose ancestors were once scattered throughout the Southeast.

SUGGESTED READINGS. James Adair, the British agent who lived among the Indians of the Southeast in the mid-eighteenth century, published his *History of the American Indians* in 1775. Another English writer, William Bartram, comments on the Southeastern Indians he encountered in his *Travels* (1792). Biographies of famous Southern American Indians include Glenn Tucker's *Tecumseh: Vision of Glory* (1956), Grant Foreman's *Sequoyah* (1938), and Rachel Eaton's *John Ross and the Cherokee Indians* (1914). Angie Debo's study, *A History of the Indians of the United States* (1970), is authoritative and comprehensive. Other useful sources are Paul Conklin's *Choctaw Boy* (1975), J. Leitch Wright, Jr.'s *The Only Land They Knew: The Tragic Story of the American Indian in the Old South* (1981), and Alvin M. Josephy's *Now That the Buffalo's Gone: A Study of Today's American Indians* (1982).

American Indians of the Southwest: Among the largest tribes in the Southwest are the PUEBLOS, HOPIS, APACHES, and NAVAJOS; there are also many smaller tribes and groups, including the Pimas, Papagos, Mohaves, and Yumas. There were three major ancestral peoples of these tribes. The Hohokam were ancestral to the Pima, Papagos, and Mohaves; the Athabascans to the Apaches and Navajos; and the Anasazi to the Pueblos and Hopis. The city-building Anasazi (Navajo for "ancient ones") were among the earliest inhabitants of the region.

The name Hohokam comes from a Pima word meaning "those who have gone." The Hohokam inhabited the bleak, arid area of southern and central Arizona continuously for some nine thousand years. Their culture was conspicuously rich and has attracted the attention of anthropologists by a series of rarely paralleled achievements. The period of continuous occupation alone is unusual, not to mention the sophistication of their agriculture, buildings, irrigation systems, medicine, and way of life. The Hohokam practiced pacifism and cooperation. Related to and influenced by the Mexican cultures to the south, they built complex cities centered on great ball courts and developed watering systems of astonishing proportions. Their artistry was especially remarkable: In stone and shell inlay, pottery, and engraving, they developed techniques that are still unrivaled.

By the time of the Spanish EXPLORATIONS of the sixteenth century, however, the Hohokam culture had

The artistry of southwest Indians is especially remarkable, as seen in this Pueblo village of Taos, N. Mex.. (Library of Congress)

declined to the point that the conquistadors did not even identify them in their records. By the time of significant contact with American settlers moving westward, the descendants of the Hohokam consisted of smaller tribes such as the Pimas, Papagos, and Mohaves. Between 1875 and 1925, the land still belonging to these tribes was incorporated into reservations. In the 1930's the tribes and reservations adopted constitutions, modeled on the U.S. Constitution. In some ways reservation life is typical small-town life; the reservation headquarters is analogous to "downtown," and villages or allotments represent neighborhoods. Gift-giving remains an important aspect of the culture. Pottery and basketry, traditional arts, are still practiced, but the works are made largely for sale to white buyers rather than for Indian trade or use.

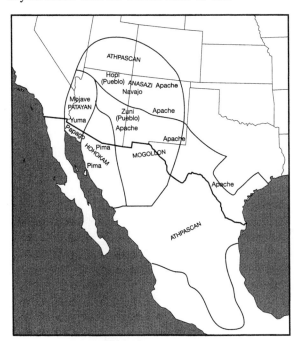

AMERICAN INDIANS OF THE SOUTHWEST

The Athabascans, forerunners of the modern Apaches and Navajos, invaded the area during the thirteenth and fourteenth centuries from the far Northwest. Their principal characteristic was a striking adaptability, a talent for accommodating themselves to any survival strategies they encountered and making them their own. The modern Navajos, for example, are renowned for silverwork, yet they turned to this craft only in the nineteenth century, learning it from tribes who had practiced it since the seventeenth cen-

tury. This trait is characteristic. All of the signs by which they are known—their hogan dwellings, elaborate weaving, basketry, and dancing—were acquired from other peoples. Similarly, of all the desert tribes, they were the people most affected by the inroads of the Spanish. As usual, they transformed the Spanish horses and mules into products of their own. Navajos were the only southwesterners to rival the Plains tribes in horsemanship.

SUGGESTED READINGS. Extensive accounts of Hohokam and Athabascan peoples appear in Alice Marriott and Carol K. Rachlin's *American Epic: The Story of the American Indian* (1969); William Brandon's *The Last Americans: The Indian in American Culture* (1974); and Angie Debo's *A History of the Indians of the United States* (1970). The best overview of the development of these divergent cultures is in Harold E. Driver's *Indians of North America* (1969).

American Jewish Committee: Organization devoted to defending the rights of Jews and other minorities. It was founded in 1906, in response to the proliferation of pogroms (massacres of Jews) in Russia. Its stated purpose was "to prevent the infraction of the civil and religious rights of Jews, in any part of the world." Based in New York, the committee has worked to liberalize immigration laws; assist the victims of war and persecution; prosecute Nazi criminals; and combat ANTI-SEMITISM in the United States, Germany, the Soviet Union, Muslim countries, and South America. It publishes the influential monthly magazine *Commentary* and the annual *American Jewish Year Book*. In 1973, the committee formed the Institute for American Pluralism to study the role of ETHNICITY in American life and bring together diverse ethnic groups on issues of common concern.

American Legion: Organization established and chartered by Congress in 1919 as a patriotic self-help community service organization for wartime veterans who were honorably discharged. By the early 1990's it served more than three million members. The organization's original emphasis on the welfare of children of deceased and disabled veterans has expanded to include programs involving teen suicide and drug-abuse prevention, missing children, and child safety. The American Legion had a reputation for being strongly anti-Communist during the COLD WAR and for general political CONSERVATISM.

American nationalism. *See* **Nationalism—American**

American Protective Association: Anti-Catholic political lobby founded in 1887 to combat the IMMIGRATION of Roman Catholics into the United States. Other goals included prohibiting immigrants from voting, reversing taxation laws that exempted CATHOLIC CHURCH properties, and maintaining a watchful eye on widespread political corruption. The group was defunct by the 1920's.

American Revolution (1775-1783): War waged by the thirteen English colonies in North America against England. It was caused by opposing ideals, by conflicting interests, and by ignorance and misunderstanding. By 1750 the colonists in North America had modified their inherited English religious, cultural, social, and political institutions. English people considered the colonists inferior, both socially and intellectually. The colonists and the English could not agree on questions of taxes, restrictive mercantilistic regulations, and other issues.

Each colonial assembly considered itself a local parliament with more powers within its colony than London was willing to concede. The colonial assemblies centered their attention on local concerns; they were not particularly interested in protecting and promoting the interests of the English ruling class, royal officials, or imperial interests. Yet as long as the British administration of the colonies was lax, harmonious relations prevailed.

In 1763, England adopted a policy of centralizing administration, increasing tax collections, reducing expenditures, and enforcing laws more harshly. The colonists resisted by organizing protests, congresses, and petitions as well as economic boycotts against English goods. Popular protests began to lead to violence and the two sides became more and more alienated. Then, on April 19, 1775, British authorities attempted to arrest two well-known colonial leaders, Samuel Adams and John Hancock, and to capture military stores at Concord, in Massachusetts. Minutemen fired upon the British troops, beginning the American Revolution.

The colonists, however, quickly found that they could not agree among themselves whether to support the rebellion or remain loyal to England. There were wealthy and educated colonists on both sides in all areas. A majority in Georgia and South Carolina remained loyal to the Crown. New England was regarded as the center of patriotism. The backcountry of Pennsylvania, Maryland, and Virginia, peopled largely by SCOTS-IRISH and GERMANS, supported the patriot cause. The western parts of North and South Carolina, also settled by SCOTS-IRISH, were loyalist. Many Irish and German regiments fought for independence, but a German regiment from New York and an Irish one from Boston fought for King George. Even American Indian involvement in the war was divided. In New York the Mohawks fought alongside the British, but other Iroquois support was considered essential to the patriot cause.

African Americans, both freemen and slaves, fought in the revolutionary war, most of them in the Continental Army and Navy. Some slaves assisted the British army as laborers; however, most slaves remained loyal to their American masters. Until November, 1782, the British offered emancipation to all slaves (belonging to patriots) who escaped to British lines. More than twelve thousand slaves, approximately 40 percent of whom were women, took advantage of the British offer. At the end of the war these blacks were evacuated to other parts of the British empire.

Wealth, class, ethnic origin, race, and residential location do not seem to have been primary factors in an individual's support of one side or the other. Religious affiliation did play more of a role, especially among the clergy. The QUAKERS, Moravians, and MENNONITES attempted to remain neutral. Most Anglican clergy were loyalists, and most PRESBYTERIAN clergy were patriots.

With only a few exceptions, men fought the war. Women, however, played an important role by taking over the outdoor work, running farms, and managing properties when their menfolk went to war. Women also provided food and clothing for the army. Some women accompanied their husbands to war and performed cooking, laundering, and nursing services at little or no pay.

SUGGESTED READINGS. Merrill Jensen, in *The Articles of Confederation* (1940, repr. 1970), views the revolution as a struggle between radicals and conservatives, with the radicals winning. Edmund S. Morgan, in his article "Conflict and Consensus in the American Revolution," in *Essays on the American Revolution* (1973), edited by James H. Hulson, finds conflict within the colonies but sees sectionalism as more important. Mary Beth Norton describes women's experiences in *Liberty's Daughters: The Revolutionary Experience of American Women, 1759-1800* (1980). The traditional economic interpretation is Charles A. Beard's *An Economic Interpretation of the Constitution* (1913, repr. 1956).

The battles of the American Revolution pitted different ethnic groups against each other in a war that also forced them to choose ultimately to support the Old World or their New World in America; this scene depicts a violent confrontation in Boston, Mass., on March 5, 1770. (Imagefinders)

Americanization: Process of inculcating the values and behaviors of the DOMINANT CULTURE on the foreign-born—roughly equivalent to "ASSIMILATION." During the early twentieth century, immigrants were urged—even commanded—to give up their traditional ways and become more "American." Efforts were focused on educational and social service programs, where Americanization was also known as Anglo-conformity. Proponents debated whether all immigrant groups were suitable for Americanization, pinpointing groups that they believed were unassimilable. Because there are so many different religions, customs, and ways of life recognized as "American" in different parts of the country—and because immigrants did not think all aspects of the American personality worthy of imitation—the idea was a vague one at best. After WORLD WAR I, groups such as the KU KLUX KLAN used the term to press for the deportation of undesirable non-Americans while liberals developed the model of CULTURAL PLURALISM, and the term "Americanization" fell out of favor.

Americans with Disabilities Act of 1990: Landmark federal law that provides comprehensive protection of the rights of Americans with disabilities. The act, which became effective in January, 1992, extends or increases constitutional protection of Americans with disabilities in EMPLOYMENT, transportation, public accommodation, state and local government, and telecommunications. It also provides greater remedies for violations of their rights. Title II of the Americans with Disabilities Act (ADA) requires state, county, and municipal governments to make "reasonable modifications" in policies, practices, and procedures that deny equal access to individuals with disabilities. Title III allows persons with disabilities the remedy of lawsuit, including jury trial, as well as the ability to seek punitive and compensatory damages—avenues that did not exist under the previous REHABILITATION ACT of 1973.

Americans with Disabilities. Americans with disabilities represent 17 percent of the population of the United States, according to a 1986 Interim Report of

President George Bush signs the Americans with Disabilities Act of 1990 into law. (AP/Wide World Photos)

the U.S. BUREAU OF THE CENSUS. The ADA defines a person with a disability as someone with a physical or mental impairment that substantially limits a "major life activity," someone with a record of such an impairment, or someone who is regarded as having such an impairment. Examples of disabilities include dis-

1 percent are Asian Americans. Forty-two percent are OLDER AMERICANS (sixty-five years of age or older), 8 percent are under nineteen years of age, and 50 percent are of working age. Disabilities contribute significantly to the barriers already experienced by persons because of ethnic, racial, gender, or age

Legislation has helped to remove many of the barriers that impede people with disabilities from finding employment. (Mary M. Langenfeld)

eases and conditions such as orthopedic, visual, speech, and hearing impairments as well as autism, cerebral palsy, epilepsy, muscular dystrophy, multiple sclerosis, cancer, heart disease, diabetes, mental retardation, emotional illness, specific learning disabilities, human immunodeficiency (HIV) disease (whether symptomatic or asymptomatic), tuberculosis, drug addiction, and alcoholism. Disabilities are not, however, limited to these examples. Major life activities include functions requiring self-care such as walking, seeing, hearing, speaking, breathing, learning, and working.

Nearly 10 percent of persons with disabilities are African Americans, 3 percent are Latinos, and about

STEREOTYPES. Nearly 60 percent of working-age persons with disabilities are unemployed. Yet studies indicate that 56 percent of workers with disabilities are not prevented from working because of their disability alone. For people with disabilities, barriers to employment include lack of basic education or skills training, loss of comprehensive Medicaid insurance, inadequate transportation to or accommodation in the workplace, inaccessible work sites, and the need for help with self-care activities at home or at work.

Not surprisingly, there is a link between disability and POVERTY. The *1979 Annual Housing Survey* of the U.S. Bureau of the Census determined that 70 percent of American households with a disabled family member rely upon one or more forms of public assistance as their primary source of income. Similarly, the *1986 Census Analysis* found that 40 percent of families with an annual income of $7,200 have a family member with a disability. These statistics reflect the consequences of the historic exclusion of persons with disabilities from mainstream educational and employment opportunities. The ADA attempts to confront these inequities and provide remedies for change.

Historical Background. Passage of the ADA grew out of the political activism of the DISABILITY RIGHTS MOVEMENT in the 1960's and 1970's. Political pressure won the passage of landmark protective legislation such as the Rehabilitation Act (1973) to train employable people with disabilities; the establishment of the National Developmental Disabilities Council (1974) to advocate for people with developmental disabilities (with onset from birth to age eighteen); the Education of All the Handicapped Act (1978), guaranteeing free public education; and the ARCHITECTURAL BARRIERS ACT (1968), mandating that public buildings be accessible to people with disabilities. The Civil Rights Act of 1991 extended the 1978 Civil Rights Act to include persons with disabilities. The ADA also built upon previous legislative foundations with a wider scope to its protective measures.

Political Impact of the ADA. Congress ruled that the fundamental purpose of the ADA was the integration of individuals with disabilities into the mainstream of society. As of January, 1992, public entities could no longer provide services or benefits to individuals with disabilities through programs that were separate or different, unless the separate programs were necessary to ensure that such benefits and services were equally effective. Individuals with disabilities thus might choose to accept a different program but could not be compelled to accept it.

Additionally, state and local governments were required to ensure effective communication with individuals with disabilities by providing such appropriate auxiliary aids as qualified interpreters, assistive listening headsets, television captioning and decoders, telecommunications devices for deaf persons (TDD's), videotext displays, readers, and taped texts, as well as materials in BRAILLE and large print. Public entities cannot charge individuals with disabilities for such aids. Telephone emergency services were required to provide direct access to individuals with speech or hearing impairments. In addition to these protections,

Congress further appointed the Coordination and Review Section of the Civil Rights Division of the U.S. Department of Justice to receive complaints of violations of the ADA.

SUGGESTED READINGS. Commentary on and reaction to the ADA have been plentiful. Of particular interest are the following articles which address the impact of the ADA on the workplace and the courts: "Work for Americans with Disabilities: Affirmative Action Revisited," by Walter Y. Oi, in *The Annals of the American Academy of Political and Social Science* 523 (September, 1992), p. 519; "Farewell, Dumb Blonde: Litigation, Americans with Disabilities Act," in *The Economist*, August 1, 1992, p. 21; and Arlene Vernon-Dehmke's "ADA Do's and Don'ts" in *Management Review* 82, no. 8 (August, 1992), p. 7. Alice LaPlante's article "Attitudinal Barriers," in *Computer World*, July 27, 1992, p. 83, analyzes the fears of the working community of people with disabilities over difficulties in enforcing the act.—*Barbara Langell Miliaras*

Amish: Highly sectarian religious and ethnic minority descended from the MENNONITES, or Anabaptists (rebaptizers), of the Protestant Reformation in Europe. The Swiss Mennonites of the sixteenth century practiced pacifism and adult baptism, as opposed to the infant baptism mandated by civil and state church authorities of the day. For these practices and their insistence that church membership be voluntary and church matters free of state control, they were persecuted as heretics and subversives. Many were tortured and killed by drowning, burning, and imprisonment. In the 1690's, a minister named Jacob Amman accused the Mennonites of laxity in church discipline and tried to restore a strict ban on wayward members. When most refused to follow him, he led a breakaway group that has been called Amish ever since.

European Amish immigrants settled in Pennsylvania, Ontario, Indiana, and Ohio during the 1700's and 1800's. Approved standards of church life and behavior expected of all baptized adult members are called the *ordnung*. These differ slightly between Amish church districts. Almost everywhere the Amish worship in homes instead of church buildings; use horse-drawn transportation; speak the German dialect called Pennsylvania Dutch; follow a modest and severe dress code; and prohibit electricity and HIGHER EDUCATION. They have a strong preference for farming and related occupations, allowing them to live in somewhat self-sufficient rural communities with their own private

The Amish use horse-drawn transportation and follow a modest dress code. (Pennsylvania Dutch Visitors Bureau)

schools. They feel that modern technology and "worldliness" would lead them away from true Christianity, and thus they try to minimize contact with outsiders, called "English," except for necessary business transactions. Some church districts permit alcohol and tobacco use, and the Amish in Iowa and Kansas permit tractors for farm work. The Beachy Amish, a more liberal group, permit the use of automobiles, preferably black, and electricity but not television in homes.

Strictly endogamous (in-marrying) and highly patriarchal, the Amish maintain exceptionally strong kinship ties which reinforce their rigid religious and lifestyle commitments. Common family names, almost all of German and Swiss-German origin, are Miller, Yoder, Hostetler, Kauffman, Swartzentruber, Stoltzfus, Bontrager, and Beiler, with some variations in spelling.

Conflicts with the larger society have arisen over Amish resistance to public school attendance requirements and colored marking requirements for their buggies. Problems are also presented by the hordes of camera-toting tourists who frequent Amish communities, oblivious of or insensitive to the Amish prohibition of photographs. Hollywood has exploited interest in the Amish with productions such as the film *Witness* (1985). Encroaching URBANIZATION also threatens their communities, especially in eastern Pennsylvania. This has resulted in increased outmigration and the establishment of new Amish settlements in locations where land prices are lower, such as upstate New York, Wisconsin, Kentucky, and Missouri.

Large average family size allows for continued growth despite limited attrition of disaffected members. By 1990, the Amish numbered around 100,000. Appearing outdated and quaint to outsiders, they are a thriving subculture that is not at all likely to disappear.

SUGGESTED READINGS. See John A. Hostetler's *Amish Society* (1963 and later editions), Hostetler's *Amish Life* (1952), and Donald B. Kraybill's *The Riddle of Amish Culture* (1989) for more information. John M. Zielinski has captured the Amish, not always with their permission, in photography books such as *The Amish Across America* (1983).

Amistad slave revolt (1839): Mutiny by captive Africans on a slave ship in Cuban waters. The revolt precipitated one of the most publicized judicial battles over

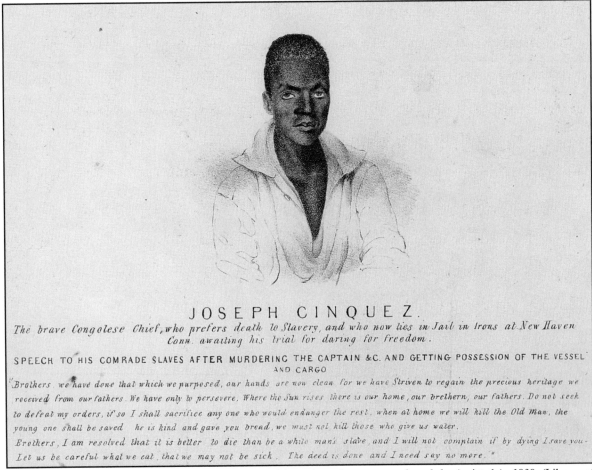

The captured African slave Joseph Cinque led a successful revolt against captors aboard the Amistad *in 1839. (Library of Congress)*

SLAVERY in the United States, ending in a great legal victory for American ABOLITIONISTS.

By 1839, the international slave trade was illegal; if caught, slaver captains and crew were charged with piracy. This penalty, however, did not deter many fortune seekers, and a highly lucrative covert slave trade existed, especially between Africa and Cuba.

In June of 1839, a slaver from Africa landed in Havana, Cuba, with its human cargo. Government officials receiving kickbacks provided paperwork declaring the Africans on board to be second-generation Cuban slaves, making their sale legal. Forty-nine Africans purchased by Don José Ruiz were loaded onto the schooner *Amistad,* where they were joined by Don Pedro Montes and four African children he had bought at the same sale. The *Amistad* set sail for Puerto Principe, a few days' journey away. En route, the slaves, led by a charismatic African named Cinque (originally Singbe), took over the ship, killing the captain and cook with cane knives. The Africans demanded that they be returned to Africa. For almost two months, the slaveholders pretended to comply; during the day they sailed southeast, stopping at islands to scavenge for food and water, but at night they turned north, in hopes of finding help. The Africans, knowing nothing about navigation, did not realize they were being duped.

The schooner slowly tacked up the eastern seaboard of the United States, where its by-now decrepit condition aroused suspicion. On a stop to search for food, it was spotted by a U.S. surveying brig. The brig's captain ordered the suspect ship boarded, and the Africans—near starvation and unable to resist—were taken into custody. Ruiz and Montes filed suits to have their slave property returned to them; the commander of the surveying brig claimed salvage rights to the *Amistad* and its cargo; the Spanish government that ruled Cuba demanded the fugitives be handed over to it; and American abolitionists clamored for the Africans to be set free.

The case was a complicated one. Slavery in Cuba was legal, and Ruiz and Montes had paperwork documenting their ownership; there were international treaties to be considered as well as precedents from earlier slaver incidents. Moreover, the case carried grave implications for the issue of slavery in the United States. The legal proceedings took eighteen months, as the case worked its way from circuit court to the U.S. Supreme Court, where former U.S. president John Quincy Adams argued on behalf of the Africans. The

Court ruled that Africans brought to Cuba illegally were not property; that as illegally held free men, they had a right to mutiny; and that the Africans should therefore be released.

The Africans, who had learned English, went on a lengthy speaking tour arranged by abolitionists to raise money for their return to Africa, which they finally accomplished in November, 1841. The *Amistad* decision was a great victory for the abolitionist movement, which in turn fed secessionist sentiments in the southern states.

SUGGESTED READINGS. Contemporary accounts of the incident have been collected in John Warner Barber's *A History of the Amistad Captives* (1840, repr. 1969). Both Christopher Martin's *The Amistad Affair* (1970) and Howard Jones's *Mutiny on the Amistad* (1987) are full-length examinations of the affair in its historic context.

Anasazi: Aboriginal ancestors of the PUEBLO and HOPI nations of the desert Southwest and Rio Grande Valley, named by later NAVAJOS the "ancient ones" and known for their communal pueblo housing. The Anasazi arrived in the area of the four corners of New Mexico, Colorado, Utah, and Arizona in the early fourth century from the south. They were originally called "the Basketmakers"

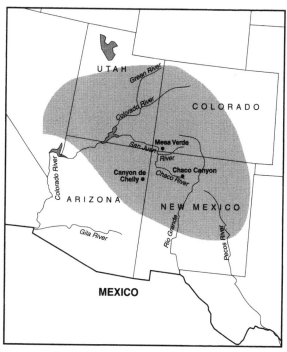

ANASAZI TERRITORY

because of their use of woven basketry as all-purpose vessels for cooking, carrying, and storing foodstuffs. The central Anasazi social unit was a married woman living with her married daughters and children. Discipline and direction were provided by the woman and her brother, while the husband performed that function for his own sister.

Although their earliest dwellings resembled those of the related Hohokam in being centered on pits dug out below the living areas, the Basketmakers eventually developed the communal, joined-wall housing and matrilineal clan organization still practiced by their descendants. The first joined houses were made of log and adobe, but stone quickly became the preferred material. By the seventh century, Anasazi dwellings had evolved into multiroomed, multistoried villages that housed the entire related community, the pueblos by which the people are known. The pits of the early structures developed into the subterranean excavations known as kivas, the centers of tribal ritual.

The Anasazi remained in the four corners until around 1200, when a drought combined with pressure from other migrating tribes to force a move. (Some Hopi cities in Arizona, however, have been continually occupied.) A few cities abandoned around this time are among the most spectacular, such as Canyon de Chelly, Arizona; Chaco Canyon, New Mexico; and Mesa Verde, Colorado. Permanent settlement was less characteristic of the Anasazi than easy ASSIMILATION and adaptation. Their history records repeated relocations and recombinations; their true genius lay in making the adjustments best suited to survival. Neighbor tribes and peoples often profited from association with the Anasazis.

The migrations of 1200 transferred the center of Pueblo culture from the four corners to the Rio Grande Valley, to isolated villages further west, and to areas east as far as the Pecos River. The villages founded in these areas survive, although the ancient way of life has largely faded.

For centuries the Anasazis thrived through cultivation of maize, squash, and beans for food, of cotton for clothing, and of tobacco for ritual. They developed a system of democratic government that proved stable and evenhanded; their social practices encouraged cooperation and assistance. Surrounded by hostile, predatory tribes, they were widely respected for pacifism and nonaggression. Their oldest and best-known tribal emblem, Kokopelli, the flute-playing fertility god in their petroglyphs, shows their love of music and esteem for harmony.

SUGGESTED READINGS. William Brandon's *The Last Americans: The Indian in American Culture* (1974) contains a chapter on Anasazi culture, as does Alice Marriott and Carol K. Rachlin's *American Epic: The Story of the American Indian* (1969). Angie Debo's *A History of the Indians of the United States* (1970) is also useful. The most thorough treatment is Jesse D. Jennings' *Prehistory of North America* (1968).

Anaya, Rudolfo A. (b. Oct. 30, 1937, Pastura, N. Mex.): Latino writer. Anaya taught in Albuquerque public schools before becoming an English professor at the

Latino writer Rudolfo Anaya focuses on the Chicano experience in New Mexico. (AP/Wide World Photos)

University of New Mexico in 1974. His acclaimed first novel, *Bless Me, Ultima* (1972) was followed by *Heart of Aztlán* (1976), *Tortuga* (1979), and *A Chicano in China* (1986). His writing focuses on the Chicano experience in New Mexico, exploring themes of growing up, faith, and death. In 1980, Anaya received a New Mexico Governor's Award for Excellence and was a National Endowment of the Arts literature fellow. He has lectured widely and edited several collections of Chicano stories and plays.

Anaya, Toney (b. Apr. 29, 1941, Moriarty, N. Mex.): Latino politician. Anaya was graduated from the Georgetown University School of Foreign Service in 1964 and the American University College of Law in 1968. He was legislative counsel to Senator Joseph MONTOYA of New Mexico after graduation. Returning to New Mexico in 1970, Anaya served as New Mexico's attorney general from 1975 to 1978. Anaya was elected governor of New Mexico in 1982 and served for one term. He became the center of controversy in 1986 by commuting the sentences of all of New Mexico's death row prisoners prior to leaving office. He returned to private practice in 1987 but continued to be politically active, becoming a member of the Democratic National Committee in 1988.

Politician Toney Anaya. (AP/Wide World Photos)

Ancestor worship: Form of religion that stresses the continuity of the family over generations, the influence of deceased relatives on the living, and reverence for the wisdom of elders. Ancestor worship is very ancient, dating from at least 1000 B.C.E in China. It is practiced in many different cultures in Asia and tropical Africa as well as among the PUEBLOS in North America and the Aztecs in Mexico. Ancestor worship also existed, to a lesser extent, in ancient Rome and Egypt.

Ancestor worship, based on the teachings of Confucius (551-479 B.C.E.), became a major component of Chinese culture. In the CONFUCIAN scheme of social organization, ancestor worship served to cultivate kinship values such as filial piety, family loyalty, and the continuity of family lineage. A major component of Chinese ancestor worship involved sacrifice, a form of ritualistic behavior toward the gods and spirits that included the burning of candles, incense, and papers; the offering of food and drink; following many taboos; kneeling in front of ancestral tablets in the home and ancestral temples; and offering prayers to garner ancestral protection and approval. In traditional China, sacrifices to the parents continued long after the three-year period of mourning, for according to Confucius, "It is not when a man's father is alive but only after he dies that the son can be judged dutiful." Ritual sacrifice, even among the very poor, who could ill afford it, based on the hope of supernatural help and the fear of supernatural punishment, was a powerful influence in stabilizing the kinship system.

A man's most important duty, according to Confucianism, is to his parents. The family became the central institution in Chinese culture, and maintaining family lineage was extremely important. According to Mencius, an ancient Confucian scholar, the biggest crime for a son is not to produce an heir.

Among ASIAN AMERICANS, ancestor worship, in some form, remains an important influence in their lives. Early Chinese immigrants expressed intentions of returning home to continue their duties to their ancestors. They also made arrangements that, if they should die in the United States, they would have their bones sent back to China to be interred on ancestral land. Although ritual sacrifice is no longer widely practiced, filial piety and respect for parents and elders is highly valued. VIETNAMESE AMERICAN families often gather on the anniversary of an ancestor's death to celebrate, an occasion called *ngay gio* in Vietnamese.

Confucius directed children to "behave in such a way that your parents' only concern for you will be your health." Family members try to honor their parents and ancestors by living virtuously. For children to achieve high marks in school, an advanced degree, a successful career (especially for males), and a happy family, particularly if there is a male child, reflects well on the parents. A poor education, a low-status job, the lack of a family heir, or divorce brings embarrassment on the parents.

As Asian Americans become ever more acculturated into American culture, the practice of ancestor worship

Filial piety and respect for parents and elders is highly valued among Asian Americans. (Gail Denham)

and strong parental influence over grown children are fading. While some family members still seek parental approval for major decisions such as marriage, career choice, and large financial purchases, many assert their independence and make their own choices.

SUGGESTED READINGS. For an excellent introduction to ancestor worship from an anthropological perspective, see William H. Newell's *Ancestors* (1976). For a more general introduction to Asian American family life and acculturation, see Stanley Karnow and Nancy Yoshihara's *Asian Americans in Transition* (1992). An excellent, if somewhat dated, introduction to Asian philosophies is James K. Feibleman's *Understanding Oriental Philosophy* (1976). For an in-depth look at Confucianism and ancestor worship, see Patricia Buckley Ebrey's *Confucianism and Family Rituals in Imperial China* (1991).

Anderson, Marian (Feb. 27, 1902, Philadelphia, Pa.— Apr. 8, 1993, Portland, Oreg.): African American classical singer. Born into a poor family, Anderson began singing with the local Baptist church choir at age six. At twenty-eight she toured Europe, and six years later had her debut in New York. When in 1939 she was prohibited, because of her race, from singing at Constitution Hall in Washington, D.C., a protest group led by Eleanor ROOSEVELT held a huge concert featuring her at the Lincoln Memorial. At age fifty- three Anderson became the first African American singer to appear at the Metropolitan Opera (1955). She was also a delegate to the United Nations in 1958 and a civil rights activist.

Anderson, Mary (1872, Linkoping, Sweden—Jan. 30, 1964, Washington, D.C.): Trade union activist. Anderson emigrated to the United States from Sweden with her sister at age sixteen. She found a job working at a shoe factory in Illinois and in 1894 became a member of the International Boot and Shoe Workers Union, rapidly reaching the position of local branch president. In 1914 she was involved in a research project studying women's war work. In 1920 she became the first director of the WOMEN'S BUREAU OF THE DEPARTMENT OF LA-

BOR. Even after her retirement in 1944, she continued to lecture and aided officials in investigations into labor laws and enforcement.

Angel Island: Site of the Angel Island Immigration Detention Center, established in 1910. After passage of the CHINESE EXCLUSION ACT of 1882, a detention center in San Francisco was needed to process the entry applications of new Chinese immigrants as well as determine the entry eligibility of other Asian immigrants. Conditions at Angel Island were appalling—poor sanitary facilities, inadequate food, crowded living spaces, harsh interrogations—and some people were held as long as two years before their cases were decided. Many inmates died or were traumatized.

After a fire in 1940, the center was closed and has since been preserved as a museum. Its walls are covered with poetry and other writings expressing the fear and loneliness of the detainees.

Angelou, Maya (b. Apr. 4, 1928, St. Louis, Mo.): African American writer, poet, and actress. Angelou's varied early career included singing, dancing, editing, civil rights activism, university work in Ghana, and teaching music and drama. She gained national attention with her lyrical autobiographical volume, *I Know Why the Caged Bird Sings* (1970), which details both racism and personal trauma. Eight subsequent books are mostly poetry and autobiography. She was named Woman of the Year by the *Ladies' Home Journal* (1976), acted in the 1977 television version of Alex Haley's *Roots*, and has been a professor at Wake Forest University (1990-1991).

Anglo-Saxons in colonial America: Of the many ethnic groups that contributed to the European settlement of the New World, the Anglo-Saxons prevailed in endowing the United States with its primary language, its system of government, and its system of justice. Indeed, the very diversity of motive and character which brought

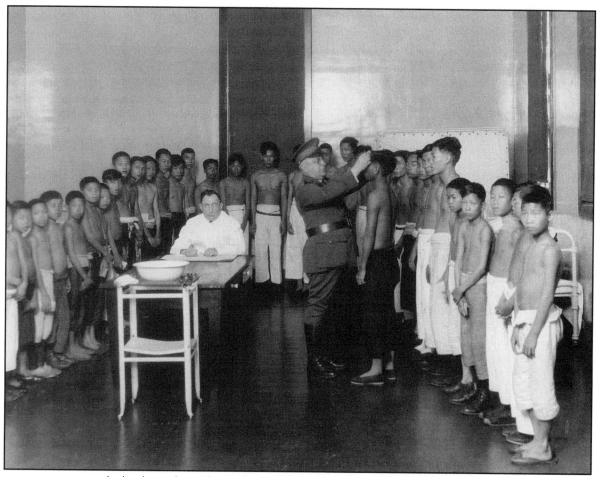

An immigrant inspection station at Angel Island, circa 1920. (National Archives)

differing Anglo-Saxon companies of colonists to North America ultimately helped establish the acceptance of diversity in political and religious prerogatives. This openness attracted widely diverse numbers of continental European refugees to American shores in the eighteenth and nineteenth centuries. The phenomenon continues but has become global, multiracial, and multicultural in its dimensions.

The tolerance of early Anglo-Saxon immigrants did not generally extend to those whose ethnic or racial heritage was not European. At the first sign of American Indian armed resistance to their presence in Virginia and New England (for perceived violations of agreements), the settlers staged reprisals that were typically swift, summary, and intense. Similarly, while the earliest Anglo-Saxon response to the importation and enslavement of Africans was negative, the first ship bearing human cargo sailed into Jamestown Harbor in 1619, and in 1661 the Virginia House of Burgesses declared African SLAVERY to be a legal institution.

Early Encounters: The Sixteenth Century. Anglo-Saxon settlement of the New World did not begin until the last decades of the sixteenth century. In 1583, Sir Humphrey Gilbert, half-brother of Sir Walter Raleigh, set off from England to found the first Anglo-Saxon colony beyond the Irish Sea in Newfoundland. For a hundred years, it remained little more than a fishing outpost. One year later, under Raleigh's sponsorship, a new company sailed farther south and claimed all territory north of Florida for the British crown, naming it Virginia in honor of their queen. On Roanoke Island, off the coast of North Carolina, they established the first real English or Anglo-Saxon colony in the future United States.

Adverse conditions of climate and disease so discouraged them that one year later they sailed for home. Two years later, a second company of 125 colonists set out. These settlers suffered an even worse fate, vanishing into the wilderness without a trace and leaving legends which discouraged any new efforts at colonization for nearly twenty years.

The First Permanent Settlements. In December, 1606, under charter from the London Company, a third group of colonists set sail for Virginia. Landing on April 26, 1607, at the entrance to Chesapeake Bay, they established the first permanent colony of Anglo-Saxon immigrants in North America at Jamestown. The colonists owed their survival to the legendary John Smith, who used his natural resourcefulness on their behalf. Negotiating with the American Indian chief POWHATAN, he obtained food and advice that carried the settlers through the first winter. Nevertheless, more than half the original colonists died. During Smith's absence on voyages of exploration, idleness set in among the colonists and morale sank. Like their predecessors, they had resolved to return to their homeland; they were about to set sail for England when the arrival of Sir Thomas Gates with three ships bearing three hundred new colonists prevented their summary departure.

Anglo-Saxon–American Indian Relations, 1608-1700. Indians living along the southern Atlantic coast were openly hostile and suspicious of settlers' ventures owing to early encounters with the Spanish conquistadors, who had plundered the New World and enslaved or exterminated its inhabitants. Along with their arms, European adventurers had brought with them the plagues of smallpox and measles, diseases that resulted in the extinction of many of the tribes up and down the Atlantic Coast. Like the Spaniards and French before them, English arrivals failed to honor the natives' right to dominion over their own territories. When offers of purchase or barter were refused or revoked, the new settlers pushed the Indians out of their own territory by force, despite the fact that they owed their very survival in the beginning to the sympathetic support of local tribes.

In New England, both Pilgrims and PURITANS alike enjoyed friendly relations with the Wampanoags and the Narragansets at first. Yet by 1675 relations had worsened, and the outbreak of King Philip's War changed the course of Anglo-Saxon–American Indian relations forever. Relations between the two groups in the South fared even worse. Tribes rankled at violations of their customs and their territories, and they defended themselves by force of arms. Colonists took reprisals and, through their superiority of numbers and weaponry, exterminated tribes or drove them west.

Anglo-Saxon Women Immigrants. Both men and women were among the lost colonists of Roanoke Island. The disappearance of that colony resulted in the exclusion of women from the first London Company ventures—a fact which may have contributed to the settlements' failure. In 1619, however, the first ships with Anglo-Saxon women aboard arrived in Jamestown Harbor, where they were courted and claimed as brides by their male compatriots.

Colonial laws were much more supportive of the rights of women to equal justice before the law than were those of the later republic. Women owned and operated businesses, pursued professions and even political offices, and served as teachers in all the regions colonized by Anglo-Saxon settlers. Even among the PURITANS, women preachers such as Anne HUTCHIN-

Women were subservient to their husbands within marriage, but in society they enjoyed the same rights and privileges due their spouses' rank.

Anglo-Saxon Immigration and Slavery. Meanwhile, the rigors of colonization and capitalization of the

A German sketch depicting an American Indian village being attacked by Europeans. (Library of Congress)

SON were openly tolerated until they ran into conflict with the tenets of CALVINISM. Hutchinson's early example led to the exclusion of women from preaching to the congregation in church or from any public platform. No such exclusion was imposed by other dissenting sects, such as the QUAKERS, and women enjoyed full equality in Pennsylvania as well as in New York, where the tolerant customs of the Netherlands prevailed. In the South, the rights of women were directly related to their class and marital status, and reflected the prevailing tenets of the Church of England.

southern crop economy created the need for a steady source of cheap and submissive labor. The concepts of INDENTURED service, lifetime bondage to the land, and bondage by sale or captivity are unfortunate global phenomena that date to prehistory and continue to this day. While no African slaves accompanied the early Anglo-Saxon immigrants to the New World, many indentured European bondservants did. Their duties were contractual and were of fixed term. In the South, underpopulation was a continuous problem, and disease was endemic and debilitating. Moreover, the region's plantation economy lessened its appeal for the independent small farmer, fisherman, or tradesperson who sought the greater religious freedom and economic opportunity of the Northeast.

Thus, in spite of royal and colonial policy against SLAVERY, a Dutch ship bearing twenty African slaves sailed into Jamestown harbor in 1619. Many later shipments of slaves made their way north. The institution was viewed with distaste by most Anglo-Saxons, and the first antislavery law to be passed in the colonies was issued in Rhode Island in 1652. This was countered by a 1661 edict of the Virginia House of Burgesses which recognized slavery as a legal institution. In 1667 the Virginia law was amended to read that African slaves and their descendants would remain in bondage even when converted to Christianity unless freed by their owners in their lifetime or by slaveowners' will.

The founding of Georgia by James Edward Oglethorpe in 1732 presents an interesting footnote on the ambivalence of Anglo-Saxons toward slavery. Founding the colony upon humanitarian principles as a haven for economic refugees from the poverty of English cities and the harshness of English debtor prisons, Oglethorpe specifically outlawed the formation of large estates, prohibited the sale of hard liquor, and forbade the importation of African slaves. All these constraints were violated from the beginning by the plantation owners. The offspring of the original 120 colonist-debtors who arrived in Georgia, however, formed the nucleus of the small, backcountry farmers who tilled the red clay of Georgia without slave labor. Thus were sown the CLASS divisions and suspicions that characterized the evolution of segregation in the Deep South through the twentieth century.

Religious Dissent and Cultural Diversity. Early dissension among the religious refugees in the Massachusetts Bay Colony led to permanent settlements of Anglo-Saxon colonists in New Hampshire, Rhode Island (led by Roger Williams), and Connecticut (Thomas Hooke). Roger Williams, exiled from the orthodox band of Massachusetts PURITANS because of his radical religious views, negotiated with the Narraganset tribe and purchased the land which he named Rhode Island and the Providence Plantations. It was the first European colony founded in the New World that granted religious freedom to Jews as well as to Christians and the only colony to live in peace with its American Indian neighbors throughout its colonial history. The toleration that the Dutch extended to all

religious groups was continued when Nieuw Amsterdam became New York as a settlement of the War of Austrian Succession.

The principle of religious tolerance prevailed outside the Massachusetts Bay Colony as well as in the South. Various associations of immigrants, joined in fellowship by diverse motives, established colonies in New Jersey, Pennsylvania, Delaware, Maryland, Virginia, North and South Carolina, and Georgia. Each colony was settled by Anglo-Saxons armed with charters espousing a variety of visionary purposes. From this diversity sprang the seeds of religious tolerance and, ultimately, the very cultural diversity that characterizes the modern United States, as religious refugees from central and eastern Europe and, later, from all continents, flocked to the New World and its freedom.

SUGGESTED READINGS. Contemporary accounts of the multicultural nature of Anglo-Saxon immigration include Aaron Fogleman's "Migrations to the Thirteen British North American Colonies: New Estimates," in *The Journal of Interdisciplinary History* 22 (spring, 1992), pp. 691-709. Joseph W. Alsop and Adam Platt's "The WASP Ascendancy," in *The New York Review of Books* 36 (Nov. 9, 1989), pp. 48-56, provides an assessment of continuing Anglo-Saxon influence on the shaping of American opinion. Other aspects of Anglo-Saxon immigration are covered in Daniel J. Boorstin's Pulitzer Prize-winning study *The Americans* (3 vols., 1958-1973), and in Isaac Azimov's *The Shaping of North America from Earliest Times to 1763* (1973).— *Barbara Langell Miliaras*

Anthony, Susan B. (Feb. 15, 1820, near Adams, Mass.—March 13, 1906, Rochester, N.Y.): Women's suffragist and teacher. In 1850 Anthony met Elizabeth Cady STANTON, prominent suffrage leader. Together they published *The Revolution* (1868), a magazine which backed not only women's suffrage but also labor rights, antidiscrimination laws, reformed divorce laws, and equal pay for women. Anthony traveled and lectured on these topics for more than thirty years. In 1892 she was the president of the National American Woman Suffrage Association. By 1902 she had published the first four volumes of *The History of Women's Suffrage.* In her lifetime, she saw four states open their polls to women voters. She died in 1906, fourteen years before passage of the NINETEENTH AMENDMENT giving women the right to vote.

Anti-Asian violence, contemporary: *(See also Anti-Chinese Violence)* Assault, vandalism, and murder directed at Asian Americans continue to occur across the United States. Many Asian Americans are also subjected to anti-Asian bigotry, including ignorant and insensitive remarks, stereotypical MEDIA PORTRAYALS, and name-calling. Like other minorities, Asian Americans are also the targets of organized hate groups, such as the KU KLUX KLAN, NEO-NAZI skinheads, and the anti-Indian "Dotbusters" in New Jersey.

Racially motivated violence against Asian Americans has occurred across the United States, affecting many different Asian groups. Despite the passage of the 1990 Hate Crimes Statistics Act, underreporting of HATE CRIMES by victims and difficulties in police identification of racially motivated crimes have prevented the collection of accurate statistics for hate crimes directed against Asian Americans. Police reports from several cities, however, indicate that anti-Asian violence accounts for between 15 and 60 percent of all hate crimes in the United States.

A number of factors contribute to anti-Asian violence. These include stereotypical perceptions of Asians, racial prejudice, displaced anger caused by wars and economic competition with Asian countries, economic competition among ethnic minorities, inaccurate media coverage of minorities, resentment of the real and imagined successes of Asians, increased immigration, racial integration of neighborhoods, cultural and linguistic barriers, ignorance of the cultural and religious customs of Asian Americans, and inadequate police response to as well as media coverage of hate crimes against Asians.

Anti-Asian violence has occurred in many places, such as schools, universities, bars, pool halls, city streets, and workplaces, in addition to homes and neighborhoods. Anti-Asian posters and newsletters advocating boycotts of Asian-owned businesses have circulated in communities from Bensonhurst, New York, to Castro Valley, California.

In the 1980's and 1990's, anti-Asian violence has often resulted in death. In Detroit in 1982, Vincent CHIN, a twenty-seven-year-old Chinese American, was beaten to death by two auto workers who mistook him for Japanese, a group they blamed for the loss of jobs in the auto industry. In 1987, Navrose Mody, an Asian Indian American, was likewise killed by a group of eleven youths during an outbreak of anti-Indian violence in New Jersey. In Raleigh, North Carolina, in 1989, Jim Ming Hai Loo, a twenty-four-year-old Chi-

nese American, was murdered by Lloyd and Robert Priche, who were angry about Americans killed in the Vietnam War. Five Southeast Asian children were killed and thirty wounded at Cleveland Elementary School in Stockton, California, in 1989, when Patrick Edward fired into the playground; he was reportedly driven by a hatred of racial and ethnic minorities and frequently made resentful comments about Southeast Asian refugees. In Houston, Texas, in 1990, Hung Truong, a fifteen-year-old Vietnamese American, was beaten to death by Derek Hilla and Kevin Michael Allison, who were well known for their racist views and connections to skinhead organizations.

Racial tensions between KOREAN AMERICANS and AFRICAN AMERICANS in Los Angeles and New York have led to several incidents. In 1991, in Los Angeles, African Americans killed seven Korean Americans. In March, 1991, a Korean American store owner, Soon Ja Du, shot and killed an African American teenager, Latasha Harlins, whom she accused of stealing a bottle of orange juice. In 1992, during the LOS ANGELES RIOTS following the Rodney King verdict, several Korean American stores in black neighborhoods were looted and burned. Lyrics in rap music such as Ice Cube's "Black Korea" ("Pay respect to the black fist or we will burn your store right down to a crisp") have caused concern in the Asian American community.

Asian Americans are often the victims of violence, not only from whites and other ethnic groups, but also from Asian GANGS. For example, Vietnamese American gangs from Little Saigon, an area south of Los Angeles, armed with knives and guns, often rob Asian-owned stores and extort payments from merchants. An official 1990 investigation found that Chinese criminal gangs, based in Hong Kong and Taiwan, extorted money from 81 percent of the restaurants and 66 percent of other businesses in New York's Chinatown.

SUGGESTED READINGS. An excellent overview of contemporary violence and discrimination against Asian Americans is provided in the United States Commission on Civil Rights report *Civil Rights Issues Facing Asian Americans in the 1990's* (1992). An excellent historical account of anti-Asian violence is provided in Ronald Takaki's *Strangers from a Different Shore: A History of Asian Americans* (1989). A brief account of Asian Americans is provided in Stanley Karnow and Nancy Yoshihara's *Asian Americans in Transition* (1992).

Major States of Chinese Settlement
and
Locations of Severest Anti-Chinese Violence, 1870–1900

CANADA

Skagit

Port Townsend
Seattle
Issaquah
Olympia
Tacoma

Havre

Great Falls

Pierce

Butte
MONTANA

WASHINGTON

Portland
Newberg
Mt. Tabor

La Grande

Salmon

OREGON

Broadford

IDAHO

Jacksonville

WYOMING

Eureka
Redding
Anderson
Chico

Promontory

Rock Springs

Ukiah
Santa Rosa
Nevada City
Rocklin
Napa
Sacramento
Auburn
Grass Valley
Truckee

Unionville

Gold Hill
Carson City

Petaluma
Sonoma
Dixon
Roseville
Placerville
San Francisco
Martinez

NEVADA

UTAH

San Jose
Merced
Hollister
Fresno
Visalia
Tulare
Panamint City

Tonopah

CALIFORNIA

Santa Barbara
Ventura
Los Angeles
Pasadena
Compton
Redlands

Kingman

ARIZONA

Yuma

Clifton

Tubac
Tombstone
Nogales
Bisbee

PACIFIC OCEAN

MEXICO

Source: From John Wilson, *Chinese Americans,* American Voices series, p. 11. Vero Beach, Fla.: Rourke Corp., 1991.

Anti-Chinese violence: By the 1870's, the Chinese immigrant population, which soared from 25,000 in 1851 to 105,000 in 1875, accounted for 25 percent of all male workers on the West Coast. When the economic crisis of the 1870's hit California, creating widespread unemployment, the Chinese made easy scapegoats. Demagogues such as Dennis Kearney, of the Workingman's Party of California, insisted that "the Chinese must go! They are stealing our jobs."

Anti-Asian violence had appeared against Chinese miners as early as the 1850's. By 1862, a committee of the California state legislature recorded at least eighty-eight murdered Chinese. The earliest documented mob violence against the Chinese, however, occurred in Los Angeles in 1871. In the early evening of October 24, a white police officer was shot near the Chinese quarter. When he asked for help, a large crowd gathered and started to shoot at the Chinese and loot their homes. By 9:30 P.M., the police found fifteen Chinese hanged, four shot, and two wounded. Eight men were convicted, but they were released after only one year in jail.

In 1877, five Chinese farmers were killed in Chico, a small town in the Sacramento Valley; another riot burned wash houses as the Chinese fought for their lives. Forty-one other major anti-Chinese incidents erupted in western locations before the passing of the CHINESE EXCLUSION ACT in 1882. Thereafter, anti-Chinese violence became more organized. The most notorious riot took place in Rock Springs, Wyoming Territory, in September, 1885. When six hundred Chinese coal miners refused to join European American laborers striking for higher wages, a white mob set fire to all seventy-nine of the Chinese workers' huts. Twenty-eight Chinese were killed, and fifteen were wounded; losses reached $147,000. Although Chinese diplomats protested, the U.S. government refused to take responsibility for the territorial event. It ultimately paid $150,000 for compensation. Outbreaks of violence accompanied attempts to expel Chinese people in Tacoma and Seattle in Washington Territory, while riots occurred in Compton, Fresno, Redlands, Truckee, and Ukiah in California. Violence also occurred in Oregon, Nevada, and Alaska.

In response, many Chinese moved to the Midwest, the eastern seaboard, and Hawaii; by 1890, Chinese had settled in every state and territory. Anti-Chinese sentiments continued, but the Chinese tried to engage in occupations that posed little threat to white Americans; for example, some negotiated their own niches

among blacks and whites in the rural South.

As immigration dropped drastically after the Exclusion Act, anti-Chinese violence died down. Eventually, World War II led to more positive portrayals of the Chinese as allies against the Japanese—a goodwill that faded with the Communist victory in Beijing in 1949. Prejudice can still erupt in ways that underscore cultural intolerance. This was made evident in the death of Vincent CHIN, who was killed in Detroit by two white unemployed automobile workers who mis-

A mob attacks Chinese people in a vulgar display of racially motivated violence in Denver, Colo., in 1880. (Library of Congress)

took him for a Japanese. This event was the subject of a powerful documentary by Christine Choy and Renée Tajima entitled *Who Killed Vincent Chin?* (1989).

SUGGESTED READINGS. Historical roots of the treatment of Chinese people in the United States can be found in Stuart Miller's *The Unwelcome Immigrant* (1969). More recent and comparative treatments appear in Ronald Takaki's *Strangers from a Different*

Shore: A History of Asian Americans (1989) and Sucheng Chan's *Asian Americans* (1991) as well as Hum Mark Lai, Joe Huang, and Don Wong's *The Chinese of America, 1785-1980* (1980).

Anti-Defamation League (ADL): Legal and educational organization created to safeguard the rights of Jews and others and to improve relations among all ethnic and religious groups. It was founded in 1913 in reaction to growing ANTI-SEMITISM within the United States. Originally a project within the Jewish service organization B'NAI B'RITH, the ADL uses education and litigation to combat bigotry and is especially vigilant in countering demeaning stereotypes.

Antifeminism: Political position that rejects women's claim to equality. It reflects conservative views on women's legal status, promotes the traditional male-dominated family, and claims Christian religious beliefs as its justification. Antifeminism usually emerges during times of social change, in reaction to improvements in

Antifeminist Phyllis Schlafly contends that women have all the equality that they need during this 1977 rally. (AP/Wide World Photos)

women's status and shifts in family roles and structure.

Antifeminist political conservatism in the nineteenth century opposed extending the vote, rights to property, and other civic responsibilities to women on the grounds that the authority of the husband in the home would be undermined. According to this view, women are different from men not only in their physical ability to bear children but also in emotion, capability, and mental traits such as reasoning. Women's "different" qualities included nurturing, domesticity, and emotional frailty; these were considered valuable virtues which needed protection. Women's sphere was meant to be home and hearth, while public participation, including rights of citizenship, were seen as unnecessary and dangerous. A specific interpretation of Christian religion and the Bible was used to justify subordination of the wife to her husband and children to father, paralleling man's subordination to God. This view of women's status was challenged by advocates of women's rights, including Sarah Grimké, who contended that it was a false interpretation of the Bible to use it to attack women's individual rights. Sarah and Angelina GRIMKÉ were also committed abolitionists who likened women's oppression to that of African American slaves.

In the later twentieth century these themes also made up the antifeminist view regarding women's natural place. New Right conservatives believed that the American moral fabric was unravelling and that the chief cause was the deterioration of the traditional family. They favored a specific form of family, with the father having authority over wife and children and responsibility for their support. The wife's place was to be a full-time mother, rear children to be moral and obedient, and provide emotional support for her husband. The New Right saw danger in the increasing numbers of women working outside the home, since this undermined the authority of the father. They successfully blocked passage of a federal EQUAL RIGHTS AMENDMENT (ERA) in the 1980's that would have guaranteed that "equality of rights under the law" not be "denied or abridged on the basis of sex." Since LESBIANS supported the ERA, the New Right considered that to be sufficient proof that the proposed law was harmful for women and the family structure. Antifeminists such as Phyllis SCHLAFLY contend that women already have all the equality they need. Rather, women are in need of protection, especially from immoral forces that threaten their traditional role at home in the family.

Another issue that concerns antifeminists is sexuality. They are against sex outside marriage; they also condemn homosexuality as unnatural and deviant. They oppose sex education in schools and tried throughout the 1980's (unsuccessfully) to get a "family protection act" passed that would have prohibited school textbooks that did not support "traditional family roles," meaning the male-dominant family.

SUGGESTED READINGS. For an example of antifeminist thinking, see Phyllis Schlafly's *The Power of the Positive Woman* (1977). For a discussion of the New Right and antifeminism from a feminist perspective, see *Feminism and Sexual Equality* (1984) by Zillah R. Eisenstein.

Antimiscegenation laws: Prohibitions on interracial marriage. The concept developed during the American colonial period as a way to ensure property rights in the ownership of African slaves. It was well-known that slaveowners produced children by having sex with their slaves. Such children became the property of the slaveowner. When a free white woman produced a child by a black slave, however, the law was unclear. In response, the first law prohibiting mixed marriages was passed in Maryland in 1664. Other states, such as Massachusetts (1705), Delaware (1721), and Pennsylvania (1726) passed similar laws. By 1858, thirteen states had passed such laws, and by 1932, thirty-two states had antimiscegenation laws on their books. The penalties for violating the law ranged from fines of $200 to $2000, and/or imprisonment from a few months up to ten years.

Whereas the early laws were apparently prompted by legal issues raised by the institution of SLAVERY, later laws became more of an issue of RACISM. The laws had evolved to bar intermarriage between whites and other racial groups. The statutes varied in their definition of persons who were not white. For example, the Georgia law referred to persons with an ascertainable trace of African, West Indian, Asiatic Indian, or Mongoloid (Asian) blood. Thirteen states specifically prohibited marriage and fornication between white persons and members of the Mongoloid race. Most of the states that forbade marriages between Caucasians and Mongolians were in the West, reflecting growing fear in that region of the rising Asian population. In 1872, California passed a law prohibiting marriage between blacks and whites, and later amended it to include marriages between whites and "Mongolians."

Antimiscegenation laws generally resisted attacks on their legality. By 1948 a number of states had repealed their antimiscegenation laws, but the U.S. Supreme Court consistently refused to address the issue until 1967 in *Loving v. Commonwealth of Virginia*. The case involved two residents of Virginia—Mildred Jeter, a black woman, and Richard Loving, a white man. The two were legally married in Washington, D.C., but upon returning to Virginia were charged and convicted of violating the law against interracial marriage and sentenced to one year in jail. A number of organizations supported the Lovings, including the AMERICAN CIVIL LIBERTIES UNION (ACLU), the NATIONAL ASSOCIATION FOR THE ADVANCEMENT OF COLORED PEOPLE (NAACP), and the JAPANESE AMERICAN CITIZENS LEAGUE, with the latter noting that there were more than one thousand Japanese living in Virginia who would be affected by the Virginia law.

After a lengthy appeal, the Court ruled unanimously that the Virginia law was in violation of the FOURTEENTH AMENDMENT guaranteeing equal protection to all under the law. As a result, all the remaining states with antimiscegenation laws on the books eventually repealed them.

SUGGESTED READINGS. For an examination of intermarriage among a variety of ethnic groups, see *Mixed Blood* (1989) by Paul R. Spickard. Other worthwhile sources include *Intermarriage in the United States* (1982), edited by Gary A. Cretser and Joseph J. Leon, and—for a historical view—*Northern Attitudes Towards Interracial Marriage* (1987) by David H. Fowler.

Antioch College (Yellow Springs, Ohio): Independent, coeducational liberal arts college founded in 1852 and open to all students regardless of gender or race from its inception. Antioch's first president was Horace Mann, an American educator who received national recognition for his organization of the Massachusetts public school system. A work-study curriculum, instituted in 1921 during the presidency of Arthur E. Morgan, divides the school year into alternating study and work sessions, and places students in positions of business and industry throughout the world. The college is well known for its support of experimental approaches to education and support for progressive political causes.

Anti-Semitism: Acts and attitudes that show hostility toward the Jews as a religious or ethnic group. It is frequently qualified by an adjective denoting the specific cause, nature, or rationale of a manifestation of anti-

Jewish Gamblers Corrupt American Baseball

"The Cleanest Sport" Near Its Doom From "Too Much Jew." Baseball Has Passed Under Control of "the Sport Spoilers." Can It Be Saved?

THERE are men in the United States who say that baseball has received its death wound and is slowly dying out of the list of respectable sports. There are other men who say that American baseball can be saved if a clean sweep is made of the Jewish influence which has just dragged it through a period of bitter shame and demoralization.

Whether baseball as a first-class sport is killed and will survive only as a cheap-jack entertainment; or whether baseball possesses sufficient intrinsic character to rise in righteous wrath and cast out the danger that menaces it, will remain a matter of various opinion. But there is one certainty, namely, that the last and most dangerous blow dealt baseball was curiously notable for its Jewish character.

Yet only lesser Jews were indicted. Inevitably the names of other Jews appeared in the press accounts, and people wondered who they were. A Jewish judge presided. Jewish lawyers were prominent on both sides of the cases. Numerous strange things occurred.

But strangest of all is the fact that although American fans felt that something epochal had happened in baseball, few really know what it is.

There has been time enough for others to tell the truth if they were so disposed. Many sport editors have come as near telling it as their newspapers would permit them. But it becomes daily more evident that if the whole matter is to be laid bare, so that Americans may know where to look for danger, THE DEARBORN INDEPENDENT will have to do it.

Jews Are Not Good Sportsmen

AND this is not of our own choosing. Baseball is a trivial matter compared with some of the facts that are awaiting publication. It is possible to see the operation of the Jewish Idea in baseball as clearly as in any other field. The process is the same, whether in war or politics, in finance or in sports.

To begin with, Jews are not sportsmen. This is not set down in complaint against them, but merely as analysis. It may be a defect in their character, or it may not; it is nevertheless a fact which discriminating Jews unhesitatingly acknowledge. Whether this is due to their physical lethargy, their dislike of unnecessary physical action, or their serious cast of mind, others may decide; the Jew is not naturally an out-of-door sportsman; if he takes up golf it is because his station in society calls for it, not that he really likes it; and if he goes in for collegiate athletics, as some of the younger Jews are doing, it is because so much attention has been called to their neglect of the sports that the younger generation thinks it necessary to remove that occasion of remark.

And yet, the bane of American sports today is the presence of a certain type of Jew, not as a participant but as an exploiter and corrupter. If he had been a sportsman for the love of sport he might have been saved from becoming an exploiter and corrupter, for there is no mind to which the corrupting of a sport is more illogical and even unexplainable than the mind of the man who participates in it.

Exploiting and Corrupting Clean Sports

THERE will be a very full case made out in justification of the use of the above terms "exploiter" and "corrupter" with regard to baseball. But it would be just as easy to make out the same sort of case with regard to wrestling and horse-racing. Wrestling is so completely ruled by Jews as to have become an outlawed sport. The story of wrestling is not only the story of the demoralization of a sport, but also the story of the wholesale bunkoing of the public.

The same is true of horse-racing. The whole at-

VOLUME two of this series of Jewish Studies is now off the press. It is entitled "Jewish Activities in the United States," being the second volume of "The International Jew," twenty-two articles, 256 pages. Sent to any address at the cost of printing and mailing, which is 25 cents.

and nearly destroying our cleanest, most manly public sports.

It is worth noting that in Chicago, where the Jewish Anti-Defamation League has its headquarters, there was not a word of reproof sent out from Jews to the Jewish culprits, chiding them for their activities. Not a word. But at the same time the pressure of the Anti-Defamation League was heavy on the whole American newspaper press to prevent the public statement that the whole baseball scandal was a Jewish performance from end to end.

Baseball had a close call for its life back in 1875. Rowdyism, gambling, drinking and general disorderliness on the baseball fields brought the sport very low in public estimation, so low that attendance at the games fell heavily.

In this year 1921 there is another public rebuke being administered baseball by the same means—a very heavy reduction of public support in attendance at the games.

The storm began to be heard as far back as 1919. The Cincinnati Nationals had defeated the Chicago Americans in the World Series of that year, and immediately thereafter the country became a whispering gallery wherein were heard mysterious rumors of crooked dealing. The names of Jews were heard then, but it meant nothing to the average man. The rumors dealt with shady financial gains for a number of Jew gamblers of decidedly shady reputation.

But "they got away with it," in the parlance of the field. There was not enough public indignation to force a show-down, and too many interests were involved to prevent baseball being given a black eye in full view of an adoring public.

Some Strange Occurrences Favor Jews

HOWEVER, not everyone forgot the incident. Some who had the interest of honest sport at heart, and a regard for facts as well, kept on the trail—long after the trail grew cold, long after the principal wrongdoers forgot their early caution. Where money had once been taken successfully, the gang would be sure to return.

Time went on until the 1920 season began to wane. One day when the Chicago and Philadelphia National League teams were engaged in a series at Chicago, strange messages began to reach the office of the Chicago club. The messages were dated from Detroit and informed the Chicago club and management that several "well-known" Jews were betting heavily on Philadelphia. The bets involved large sums of money, and as the contest was only the ordinary run of daily game, not an important contest at all, the unusual stress of Jewish plungers attracted attention. At the same time it was observed that money began rolling into the pool rooms on Philadelphia.

Chicago club officials called a hasty conference on receipt of the messages. They called in Grover Cleveland Alexander, explained the situation to him, and told him it was up to him to save the game. It was not Alexander's turn to pitch, Claude R. Hendryx hav-

the first one. Two of these men were Carl Zork and Benny Franklin who were just as much implicated at the time of the first grand jury as at the second, but the prosecutor's office did not try to secure their indictment. Why? Because Replogle, the attorney representing the prosecution, said there were enough men indicted without Zork and Franklin. These two St. Louis Jews were represented by Alfred S. Austrian, a Jewish lawyer, of Chicago.

This second grand jury also indicted Ben and Louis Levi and their brother-in-law, D. A. Zelser, gamblers from Des Moines. Their indictment was not secured at the first grand jury investigation directed by Replogle, assistant to Hoyne who was then acting for the state of Illinois. Between the first and second grand juries a political change had occurred, and the public interests in the second grand jury were in the care of a new prosecuting attorney, Robert Crowe, a former judge.

"Who's Who" of Jews in Baseball

IT BECOMES necessary at this point in the narrative to give a brief "Who's Who" of the baseball scandal, omitting from the list the names of the baseball players who are sufficiently known to the public. This list will comprise only those who have been in the background of baseball and whom it is necessary to know in order to understand what has been happening behind the scenes in recent years.

For the first name let us take Albert D. Lasker. He is a member of the American Jewish Committee, was recently appointed by President Harding to be chairman of the United States Shipping Board, and is known as the author of the "Lasker Plan," a widely heralded plan for the reorganization of baseball, which practically took the sport out of non-Jewish control. He is reputed to be the second richest Jew in Chicago and was head of the advertising agency which became famous under the Gentile names of Lord & Thomas. Moreover he is a heavy stockholder in the Chicago Cubs—the Chicago Nationals.

The so-called "Lasker Plan" has been attributed to Mr. Lasker, although it is not here intimated that he has specifically claimed to be its originator. The intimation is not made for the reason that to do so might be putting Mr. Lasker in the position of claiming what is not true. Until he makes the claim, the term "Lasker Plan" must remain merely a designation, and not a description of its origin.

This matter brings us to the name of Alfred S. Austrian, a Jewish lawyer of Chicago, who is a warm friend both of Mr. Lasker and of the Replogle aforementioned. It is said that Mr. Austrian was really the originator of the "Lasker Plan" which for certain reasons was handed to Mr. Lasker who was not averse to publicity and who knew the art of self-advertising. Now, it appears that Austrian was also the legal representative of Charles A. Comiskey, owner of the Chicago Americans, and that he was also, if he is not now, the legal adviser of William Veeck, president of the Chicago National League Club, in which it has just been said that Lasker is a heavy stockholder. It was this club which was touched by the questionable game of August, 1920, and which afterward released Hendryx, the pitcher chosen for and withdrawn from that game. The Chicago National League Club has never explained why it released Hendryx and he has never demanded redress.

Meet Mr. Rothstein—"Real Estate Man"

MR. AUSTRIAN'S further activities will appear when the narrative of the investigation and trial is resumed.

Then there is Arnold Rothstein, a Jew, who describes himself as being in the real estate business but who

Anti-Semitism often infiltrates the mainstream press in the guise of a "hard news" story, such as this blatantly anti-Semitic investigation of corruption in American baseball from Henry Ford's Dearborn Independent *in the 1920's.* (Library of Congress)

Jewish sentiments or policy. For example, there is economic anti-Semitism (barring or restricting economic activity among Jews or imposing such measures as quotas on them in education and the free professions); social anti-Semitism (compelling Jews to live in special ghettos or neighborhoods, minimizing their contact with the dominant society); and racial anti-Semitism (STEREOTYPED depictions of Jews as dangerous to society and culture, as powerful financiers, dishonest merchants, and as a people with special distinguishing personality and physical characteristics). Each of these types can be found at various periods of American history, especially in the twentieth century.

From Settlement to the Civil War. In 1811, Rabbi Gershon Mendes Seixas of New York wrote that the United States is perhaps the only place where the Jews have not suffered persecution but have, on the contrary, been encouraged and indulged in every right of citizenship. Unlike Europe, the United States did not have a medieval heritage of religious anti-Semitism. Since the United States is a young society, formed on the foundations of religious tolerance and cultural pluralism, anti-Semitism has generally been less harsh in the New World, devoid of pogroms and other violent manifestations.

Yet while American anti-Semitism did not attain the virulence and tragic consequences of European anti-Semitism, an undercurrent of anti-Jewish prejudice—sometimes overt, more often subtle—has existed throughout American history.

The early colonial settlers in America brought with them the old stereotype of the Jew as the mysterious outsider, heretic, and despoiler. These prejudices, however, were rarely translated into direct anti-Jewish activity. The first Jewish settlers in New Amsterdam (1654) did confront a challenge when Peter Stuyvesant, the Dutch governor, sought to expel them. Overruled by the Dutch West India Company, the governor had no choice but to grant them the right of residency.

Anti-Jewish prejudice from the American Revolution in 1776 until the Civil War, while evident in the form of the Shylock image, did not affect the legal rights of the small Jewish community. The 1840's and 1850's witnessed a sizeable immigration of GERMAN JEWS, but by 1860 there were still fewer than 200,000 Jews in a population of thirty million. The invisibility of the Jews, the availability of other targets of discrimination, the all-absorbing issue of slavery, and the enormous economic growth of the nation combined to reduce the symptoms of anti-Semitism.

From the Civil War to World War I. During the Civil War (1861-1865), anti-Jewish agitation emerged in both the North and South, where political leaders accused the Jews of aiding the enemy, smuggling essential goods, profiteering, and draft-dodging. Nevertheless, the unpleasant episodes of this period could not obscure the reality that American Jewry—mostly SEPHARDIC and German Jews—were freer than any Jewish community in the world at the time. No price or conditions had been exacted from them or imposed in return for complete political independence, as had been the case in post-1789 revolutionary France. Official or governmental discriminatory measures emulating the European model were also totally absent.

American anti-Semitism gained momentum following the arrival of the masses of YIDDISH-speaking EASTERN EUROPEAN JEWS beginning in the mid-1870's and early 1880's. Between 1880 and 1925, approximately 2,500,000 Jews from eastern Europe arrived in the United States. These immigrants swelled the already thriving urban Jewish community of former central Europeans and Sephardim.

On the one hand, the "new" Jewish immigrants and their children failed to assimilate as rapidly as their Sephardic and German counterparts had. Many eastern Europeans were highly religious Jews from poor, village backgrounds, who lacked the skills to survive in big American cities such as New York. Their persistence in "Old Country" ways and language fueled anti-Semitic sentiments. Furthermore, during the very nationalistic 1890's, an ideological anti-Semitism began to emerge as a by-product of American nativism and in reaction to the perceptible cultural gap between the settled population and the massive influx of Jewish immigrants. Henry Adams, representing Eastern patrician intellectuals, and Ignatius Donnelly, representing Western agrarian radicals, while far apart in basic orientations, both viewed the Jew as conniving and grasping and as the cause and symbol of their discontent. The anti-Jewish STEREOTYPE that emerged clearly during this period contained elements of the earlier Christian anti-Semitism and associated Jews with the Shylock image; the feared, hated city; and the wielding of excessive power through manipulation of gold.

On the other hand, since the Russian Revolution of 1917, the eastern European immigrants and their children were portrayed by American anti-Semites as Bolsheviks on the grounds that Jews were leaders of radical movements in the Soviet Union and Europe as well as in the United States. For example, Jews were active in American trade unions in the early 1900's. In the United States of the early twentieth century, Jews were not banned from academic life; however, quotas limited the numbers of Jews that could enroll in institutions such as medical schools and graduate schools. Similarly, the number of Jews hired for faculty positions was severely limited.

The Interwar Period. Right-wing extremists believed that the American Jewish community was then led by elements who were determined to enforce social change in order to realize their own advancement. An anti-Semitic countertheme was the populist identification of Jewish bankers—the very few that there were—with Wall Street interests. In the 1930's, in the midst of the Great Depression, with Adolf Hitler already entrenched in power and controlling vital parts of Europe, anti-Semitism posed a somewhat veiled threat to American Jewry. Yet Jews were still not free to apply to certain schools, practice certain professions, live in certain neighborhoods, or join certain social organizations.

It is noteworthy that *The Protocols of the Elders of Zion*, a forgery alleging a Jewish conspiracy to take over the world, won widespread circulation in the United States in the 1920's and 1930's under the title *The Jewish Peril* (1920). Its notoriety was particularly fostered by a weekly newspaper owned by auto magnate Henry Ford. The latter published a series of articles on the "international Jew" and printed them as a separate pamphlet; he was eventually sued for libel in the 1920's. Non-Jewish White Russian immigrants were also active in the United States in fomenting anti-Semitic propaganda. The Ku Klux Klan, having renewed its activity during the interwar years, added the Jews to its list of "enemies of America." Yet, even during the 1920's and 1930's, American anti-Semitism never took on the dimensions of a large organized public movement.

The intensification of anti-Semitism before World War II alarmed American Jews to the point that they fortified their national "defense" organizations, such as the American Jewish Committee, the American Jewish Congress, the Anti-Defamation League, and the Jewish Labor Committee. With the added intervention of local and national Jewish Federation leaders, efforts to coordinate Jewish action resulted in the formation of the Council of Jewish Federations. This body constituted a formal framework to combat prejudice and protect Jewish rights.

The Holocaust and Beyond. World War II, which vanquished Hitler's anti-Semitism, and the war's immediate aftermath did not bring automatic relief from anti-Semitism and other aspects of bigotry in the United States. Yet direct anti-Semitic agitation was, for the most part, confined to isolated fringe groups that were then declining in numbers and influence. Among the active exponents of anti-Semitism were groups such as the Columbians and the American Nazi Party and publications such as Gerald L. K. Smith's *The Cross and the Flag*, which began in 1942. Such groups had claimed during the war that Jews were either avoiding military duty or finding their way into rear-echelon jobs, despite the fact that Jews constituted 10 percent of the American force. In 1946 the Jewish Welfare Board, which had served Jewish soldiers in all theaters of war, felt compelled to publish two volumes of lists of Jews who had distinguished themselves in combat.

The war had brought about a new awareness of and sympathy for Jews, six million of whom had been killed in the Holocaust. During the late 1950's, at the height of the Eisenhower era, American Jewish leaders began to sense that anti-Semitism, while by no means a relic of the past, was nevertheless declining in American life. Public surveys during the years 1948-1970 generally supported this view. Whereas 63 percent of the American public attributed "objectionable traits" to the Jews as a group in 1940, only 22 percent did so in 1962.

Meanwhile, as second-generation Jews became well educated and moved into newly opened professional fields, their success aroused resentment among some Americans. Despite their small numbers—generally around 2 percent of the population—Jews were disproportionately represented in some areas, such as academia, and were accused of dominating American business, media, and culture. In the 1960's anti-Jewish sentiments were expressed not only by white extremist individuals or groups but also among segments of the African American community. Active Jewish participation in the Civil Rights movement of the 1950's and 1960's did not deter Gus Savage, the former Chicago congressman, or Louis Farrakhan, leader of the Nation of Islam, from speaking of "Jewish money," the "Jewish lobby," and "pro-Israel money," or from describing Judaism as a "gutter religion" (the latter attributed to Farrakhan). These attitudes won some support beginning in the 1970's in the African American community among those who were concerned with the rapid socioeconomic advancement of the Jews. Mean-

Anti-Semitism Time Line

1654	First 23 Jews arrive in American Colonies; turned back by authorities in New Amsterdam until intervention by West India Company
1658	Jewish Dr. Jacob Lumbrozo charged but not convicted under Maryland blasphemy law (penalty would have been death)
c. 1800	Most state constitutions bar Jews from holding political office with a requirement of belief in Jesus
1850	Rumor of ritual murder by Jews leads to mob wrecking of New York synagogue
1862	General Order No. 11 from General Ulysses S. Grant forbids Jews from engaging in trade during Civil War (accused of trading with the enemy South)
1877	Banker Joseph Seligmann, most prominent Jew of his day, and family denied lodging at Grand Union Hotel in Saratoga Springs resort on grounds of race; considered start of modern American anti-Jewish social discrimination
1913	Anti-Defamation League (ADL) formed to combat anti-Semitism, especially in portrayals of Jews in the mass media
1915	Mob in Georgia lynches Jewish factory owner Leo Frank after governor commutes his death sentence for allegedly murdering a thirteen-year-old employee
1920's	Auto magnate Henry Ford begins seven-year campaign against Jews in his national newspaper, the *Dearborn Independent*, alleging an international Jewish conspiracy to control the world; convicted of libel in 1927
	Revival of Ku Klux Klan in South, including terrorizing of Jews
	Restrictive covenants flourish banning Jews from living in certain neighborhoods
	Jews excluded from jobs in most corporations and in industries such as banking, insurance, and public utilities; wealthy Jews also kept out of prestigious social clubs
	Official and unofficial admissions quotas for Jews begin at many colleges, universities, and professional schools
	Immigration laws passed in 1921 and 1924 severely restrict Jewish arrivals
1930's	Father Charles Coughlin's national radio program and political campaigns promote anti-Semitism and fascism
	Majority of Americans polled and members of Congress oppose admitting refugees from Nazi oppression to the United States (until after 1944)
1939	German-American Bund rally of nineteen thousand people sports swastikas, cheers Hitler, denounces Jews
	S.S. *St. Louis* loaded with 900 German Jewish refugees refused entry into U.S. harbors
1941	Congress members and aviator Charles Lindbergh accuse Jews of forcing United States into World War II
1948	Greater American awareness of anti-Semitism helps win passage of Displaced Persons Act (admitting 400,000 World War II refugees) and Supreme Court decision saying federal and state courts cannot enforce restrictive covenants
1950's	Jews accused of fostering Communism
1960's	Jews charge some members of Black Power movement and New Left with anti-Semitism for their stands against Israel and Zionism; organizations such as Nation of Islam perpetuate notion of Jewish "conspiracy"
	Swastika epidemic in 1960: 643 incidents of desecration of Jewish buildings
1965-1970	165 American synagogues vandalized or desecrated
	Official meetings of Christians and Jews to address anti-Semitism and improve interreligious relations
1970's	Growth of movement to discredit the Holocaust, as in efforts by Institute of Historical Review (est. 1979)
	Rise of Jewish-African American tensions especially, in incidents in Brooklyn, New York
1980	377 anti-Semitic incidents reported by ADL, including ten arsons and four fire bombs
1984	Anti-Semitic rhetoric by black political and religious leaders Jesse Jackson and Louis Farrakhan sparks furor
1985	Coy Ray Phelps convicted for series of synagogue bombings on the West Coast
mid-1980's	Growth of white supremacist survivalist camps in isolated areas
1989	Former Klan leader and neo-Nazi David Duke elected to Louisiana state legislature
1991	Hasidic yeshiva student Yankel Rosenbaum killed by African American mob in Crown Heights, Brooklyn, New York, in disturbances set off by Hasidic motorist killing a young black pedestrian

Sources: Data are from the Anti-Defamation League (ADL) as well as Paul Grossen and Edwin Halpern's *Anti- Semitism: Causes and Effects.* 2d. ed. New York: Philosophical Library, 1983, and Nathan Belth's *A Promise to Keep: A Narrative of the American Encounter with Anti-Semitism.* New York: Times Books, 1979.

while, moderate leaders, who constituted the bulk of the African American leadership, vigorously condemned anti-Semitism.

Widespread Jewish support for ZIONISM and the state of Israel has also fueled what some Jews perceive as anti-Semitism. One of the leading spokesmen of the political right and a contender in the Republican presidential primaries of 1992, Patrick Buchanan, remarked in 1991 on a television program that there were only two groups beating the drums of war in the Middle East of the post-Cold War era: the Israeli Defense Ministry and its "amen corner" in the United States—the Jews, who were attempting to drag the United States into war. On other occasions, Buchanan challenged American Jewish leaders to behave like Americans and not as representatives of Israel's interests.

Despite these developments, continuing tension in JEWISH-AFRICAN AMERICAN RELATIONS, and occasional hate crimes or incidents of vandalism against synagogues, American Jewry had never fared better than in the late twentieth century. In 1992, the Anti-Defamation League, together with the Boston firm of Martilla and Kiley, published a poll on American race relations. Surveying 1,101 adults nationwide, the poll revealed a decline in anti-Semitic attitudes since the 1960's. The poll indicated that anti-Semitic attitudes are most prevalent among persons older than sixty-five; those who have a high school education or less; and blue-collar workers. These data suggest that the vast majority of Americans reject anti-Semitic stereotypes.

A full assessment of the extent of anti-Semitism in the United States is a highly complex task. For example, notwithstanding its poll showing a decline in anti-Semitic attitudes, the ADL counted an increase in violent crimes against American Jews from 1,432 incidents in 1989 to 1,879 in 1991. Many American Jews continue to define themselves as a minority in terms of the anti-Semitism they or their ancestors have experienced, and they remain concerned about unforeseen events that could trigger an upsurge in anti-Semitism in the future.

SUGGESTED READINGS. For firsthand accounts of anti-Semitism and Jewish life in the United States, see Arthur Gilbert's *A Jew in Christian America* (1966); *Black Anti-Semitism and Jewish Racism* (1969), edited by Nat Hentoff; Arthur Hertzberg's *The Jews in America: Four Centuries of an Uneasy Encounter* (1989); "Anti-Semitism in the United States," in *Encyclopedia Judaica* (1972), edited by Cecil Roth and Geoffrey Wigoder; Charles Herbert Stembler's *Jews in the Mind of America* (1966); Joshua Murovchik's "Patrick J. Buchanan and the Jews," in *Commentary* 91 (January, 1991), pp. 29-37; and Arch Puddington's "The Question of Black Leadership," in *Commentary* 91 (January, 1991) pp. 22-28.—*Michael M. Laskier*

Apaches: American Indian peoples of the Southwest. Derived from the Spanish term for enemy, *apíche,* the Apaches share several cultural characteristics with the NAVAJOS. Like the Navajos, the Apache peoples spoke Athabascan and migrated from Canada to the southwestern United States. In the process they adopted Plains Indian traits such as tipi dwellings, called *wickiup* by the Apaches. Meat eaters, hunters and gatherers, and never as numerous as the Navajos, the Apaches traced ancestry through the mother and divided themselves into political bands with tribal leaders but no tribal chiefs. These bands formed groups termed by the Spanish the Chiricahua, Mescalero, Jicarilla (divided into Hoyero, or "mountain people," and Llanero, "plains people"), Nednhi, Warm Springs Apaches, and the Western Apaches, made up of the Cibecue, San Carlos, Tonto, and White Mountain peoples.

The Apaches resisted Spanish harassment, fought COMANCHES, endured Mexican domination in the early 1800's, and in the mid-1800's, with increased American occupation of their lands, ceased their friendliness toward the United States. With their Navajo enemies, some four hundred Mescalero Apaches were interned at Bosque Redondo (Fort Summer, New Mexico) in 1863-1864. Hostilities with the U.S. military (a tragic saga which recalls the names of Apache leaders such as COCHISE, LOCO, Nachez, Nana, and Victorio) ceased finally on September 4, 1886, when the Chiricahua leaders, GERONIMO and Nachez, sons of Cochise, surrendered to Brigadier General Nelson A. Miles. Miles had replaced General George Crook, a longtime friend of the Apaches, in command of the Department of Arizona the previous April. After a twenty-seven-year confinement as prisoners of war in Florida, Alabama, and Fort Sill, Oklahoma, Geronimo and his Chiricahua Apaches were given the choice of relocating on the Mescalero Indian Reservation near Alamogordo, New Mexico, or accepting land in Oklahoma. A majority chose the former option.

Currently, Apache populations are slowly rebounding from lows in the early 1900's. The Mescalero-

APACHE TERRITORY

Chiricahua Apaches are concentrated at Mescalero, New Mexico, where they are governed by the Mescalero Tribal Business Committee and receive incomes from industry, livestock raising, and timber sales. The Jicarilla Apaches, with more than 2,000 tribal members, live on a reservation near Cuba, New Mexico, and, like the Navajos, are noted as raisers of livestock, especially sheep. The Jicarilla also receive income from gas and oil wells on their reservation and filmmaking (they financed the 1971 motion picture *A Gunfight*). The chief Western Apache groups dwell in RESERVATIONS near Glove and White River in southeastern Arizona, with income from cattle and timber. The San Carlos group experienced high unemployment in the 1970's. Contemporary Apaches, regardless of group, are devoted to improving their educational, employment, and housing opportunities.

SUGGESTED READINGS. Excellent discussions of the Apaches can be found in Bertha P. Dutton's *American Indians of the Southwest* (1983), especially helpful on Apache ceremonies and religious beliefs, and Dolores A. Gunnerson's *The Jicarilla Apaches* (1974). An excellent, though somewhat dated, source for a narration of late nineteenth century U.S. military incursions on Apache *rancherias* (farmlands) is Frank C. Lockwood's *The Apache Indians* (1938, repr. 1987).

Apollo Theater: Located at 125th Street and Eighth Avenue in Harlem, New York City, the theater opened January 26, 1934. Until financial difficulties forced it to close in 1976, it featured the best in jazz, rock and roll, and soul; many world-famous African American performers first achieved recognition there, including Sarah Vaughan, Jackie "Moms" Mabley, Bo Diddley, Stevie WONDER, and Ella Fitzgerald. On May 19, 1985, the theater reopened following extensive renovation financed by black executive Percy Sutton's Inner-City Broadcasting Corporation. A star-studded cast of performers recorded a three-hour television show commemorating the event. The remodeled theater now contains a state-of-the-art recording facility as well as satellite links.

Arab Americans: The word "Arab" refers to a person whose native language is Arabic. Before the spread of Islam and, with it, the Arabic language, "Arab" referred to any of the largely nomadic Semitic inhabitants of the Arabian Peninsula. In modern usage, it embraces any of the Arabic-speaking peoples—MUSLIMS and Christians—living in the vast region from Mauritania, on the Atlantic coast of Africa, to southwestern Iran, including the entire Maghrib of North Africa, Egypt, Sudan, the Arabian Peninsula, Syria (including Lebanon and Palestine), and Iraq. Arab Americans are thus a diverse people in terms of national origins and religion.

Early Immigration. Arabs emigrated in the late nineteenth and early twentieth century for a number of reasons. Many were Christians who had been exposed to Western ideals and education during the European colonial penetration of Greater Syria since the latter half of the nineteenth century; they were motivated politically and economically to settle in Western countries. Another "push factor" for leaving their homeland was the hardships imposed upon Arabs

ARAB WORLD

by Ottoman rule, including the requirement of military service, provision of clothing for the troops, and heavy taxation. Muslim Arab farmers, on the other hand, came to the United States for purely economic reasons, to escape their mounting financial difficulties.

Between 1890 and the Great Depression, the Arab American population increased from several hundred to well over 100,000. Large-scale immigration to the United States during this period included Arab immigrants from the Middle East and North Africa, mostly from Greater Syria. This region then incorporated Syria, Lebanon, pre-1948 Palestine, and Jordan—all of which had been an integral part of the former Ottoman Empire since the early sixteenth century. From the early 1920's until the mid-1940's, Syria and Lebanon were under French Mandates, Palestine and Jordan under British Mandates.

The early Arab immigrants, mostly Christians, were religiously devout. Between 1890 and 1895, New York Arabs founded churches for each of the three major sects represented among them—Melkite, Maronite, and Greek Orthodox—and imported priests to serve them. In the next three decades more than seventy additional Arab American congregations founded churches, with mass conducted in Arabic and Syriac. As more than half of these churches were then in the East, this meant that many Arabs in the more remote settlements were not yet served by any ethnic church. Consequently, numerous Arab families attended American churches, both Roman Catholic and Protestant.

Like other religious and ethnic groups before 1920, the original Arab immigrants encountered people whose language and customs were completely dissimilar from their own. The early Arab immigrants possessed few, if any, industrial skills, and they lacked a good command of the English language. Their dignity and cultural traditions, the very factors alienating them from the dominant culture, were the source of their cultural perpetuation and pride. As was the case with Italian, Irish, and Jewish immigrants, New York was the initial center of absorption for incoming Arabs. Many then moved into other parts of the United States.

The isolationist politics of the post-World War I period affected immigrants in the United States. The National Origins Act of 1924 restricted general immigration to 2 percent of the foreign-born who had lived in the United States in 1890. By 1927, this number was cut to an absolute limit of 150,000 yearly—a mere trickle. Immigrants such as Arabs felt like second-

class citizens who had to struggle against innumerable barriers of social discrimination. The act also separated family members who had hoped to be reunited in the United States.

Fragmentary records indicate that as much as 47 percent of the Arab immigration before the 1924 restrictions was male. Numerous Arab males who entered the country prior to 1924 regarded themselves as transients and hoped eventually to return to their countries of birth.

The overwhelming majority of the Arabs, perhaps 90 percent before 1914, began earning their living in the United States as peddlers. This was a specialization they embraced only after immigration. In their homelands, peddling was largely confined to minorities such as the Greeks, Armenians, and Jews, while the indigenous Arab Christians were businessmen, large-scale merchants, or peasants and rural landowners. As peddlers in the United States, the Arabs covered the entire nation, often working a distant territory or route for weeks or even months before returning to their base. As it had been for Jews earlier, peddling was most often a transitory occupation. The peddler had to acculturate rapidly. Unlike those immigrants who spent their lives in ethnic enclaves and worked in ethnic job markets, the Arab peddlers had an economic stake in learning English and American customs.

Arab Americans in general underwent assimilation and Americanization processes during the 1940's and subsequently. Spoken Arabic and the Arabic press receded in favor of the English language and the American press. Christian Arabs of the Catholic EASTERN RITE CHURCHES, still the majority of the community in the 1940's, lost members to the more popular ROMAN CATHOLIC and PROTESTANT churches. Third-generation Christian Arabs intermarried and became more assimilated. More Arab women began to immigrate, usually as members of families.

From the Post-World War II Period to the 1990's. The post-1945 period, especially the 1950's and 1960's, inaugurated a new influx of Arab immigrants from Egypt, Israel, Palestine, Syria, Iraq, and the two Yemens. These immigrants were, in many instances, better educated than their predecessors and often bilingual. They preferred to settle in communities and cities where members of their families were already established. Many members of this group were MUSLIMS who were more politicized than the immigrants of the pre-1945 period, demonstrating strong pro-Arab

Lebanese American James Thaber of Michigan listens to a 1958 radio broadcast of President Eisenhower's decision to send American troops into Lebanon; Thaber's son (in picture) is in the U.S. Army. (National Archives)

nationalist, anti-ZIONIST tendencies.

The immigrants arriving in the mid-1960's promoted the reawakening of an ethnic consciousness among Arab Americans. This ethno-nationalist reawakening process was also stimulated in part by the American Civil Rights movement and the ETHNIC HERITAGE REVIVAL of the 1970's, which affirmed the value of cultural pluralism and ethnicity. The Arab-Israeli War of June, 1967, further heightened Arab American political solidarity with their brethren in the Arab world. The war and the Arab defeat by the Israelis gave birth to Arab American political lobbying in an effort to counter the influence of American Jewish organizations active on Israel's behalf.

It is estimated that in 1970 the Arab American community reached 1,662,000, of whom 1,080,000 were over the voting age of eighteen. The largest Arab American concentrations were found in California (258,000), New York (195,000), Ohio (117,000), Illinois (116,000), Pennsylvania (115,000), Michigan (95,000), Texas (90,000), and Massachusetts (62,400). In 1984, the Arab American population exceeded 2,500,000, an increase of 33.5 percent in less than fifteen years. The population of the 1980's was heavily concentrated in California, New York, Illinois, Michigan, Ohio, and Massachusetts. Detroit had witnessed considerable Arab demographic growth since the early 1970's. By 1984, there were 250,000 Arabs in that city out of an ethnically diverse population of 4,700,000. The Christian denominations among Detroit's Arabs included Maronites, Greek Orthodox, Antiochian Orthodox, Egyptian Coptic, and Chaldeans. The rapidly increasing MUSLIM population in Detroit and other American cities included Sunnis, Shiites, and Zaydis, the latter category mostly Yemenis.

Arab Muslims. The MUSLIM population in the United States includes Arabs, Turks, Pakistanis, Eastern Europeans, and African American converts. The rapid demographic expansion of the Muslim American community has occurred over the years since the 1960's in response to the liberalization of U.S. immigration laws and the demands of the labor market. The majority of the Muslim newcomers are laborers and university graduates, part of the "brain drain" of for-

Prior to 1945, most Arab immigrants were Christians, but the new wave of immigrants after World War II were predominantly Muslims. Pictured here are Muslims bowing in supplication during a call to prayer. (Richard B. Levine)

eigners who joined the ranks of American professionals.

Most sociologists, demographers, and contemporary historians agreed that Islam was the fastest growing religion in the United States by the 1990's. It was unclear exactly how many Muslims there were in the country and even more uncertain how many of them were Arabs from the Middle East or North Africa. Estimates ranged between 1,200,000 to as many as 3,300,000 in the early 1980's. If the latter figure is correct, that estimate would have represented 3 percent of the total American population. By the late 1980's, there were about six hundred mosques/Islamic centers across the country as well as numerous Muslim parochial schools, two Islamic colleges, hundreds of weekend schools, women's organizations, youth groups, and professional and civic organizations, many involving Arab Americans.

According to Yvonne Yazbeck Haddad, a leading scholar of Arab Muslims in the United States, this population comprises two main categories. First are the majority group, who envision themselves primarily as Arab Americans. Though Muslim, they are generally secularists who see religion as a personal matter between the individual and God. They emphasize an ethnic identity based on heritage and linguistic affinity, which includes Christians and Jews from Arab lands. Some can be called American Muslims—that is, persons who are consciously both American citizens and members of the community of Islam who seek to hold the United States accountable to its ideals and values. Others are what might be called the "unmosqued"—those who are nominally Muslim but find their identity in ethnic or political organizations. These include Arab Americans who have decided to reach out to other ethnic groups and work together for a better America. They include a large number of American-born Muslims of the second-, third-, and fourth-generations. Arab American Muslims take exception to the portrayal of Islam as having a different value system from the Judeo-Christian tradition of the dominant culture, as well as to the frequent accusation that Islam espouses violence.

The second major category of Arab Americans, according to Haddad, are those who might be called Arab Muslims. They are often alienated from American culture and identify strongly with the culture and society of their homeland.

The Yemeni Muslims: A Case Study of Recent Arab Settlers. Although some Yemeni immigrants reached the United States in the 1920's, the majority came after 1970. Attempting to escape economic misery in Northern and Southern Yemen, they sought employment in American steel and automobile industries, as well as in California's vineyards and other agricultural sectors. They could be found in Detroit, New York City, Buffalo, and California's San Joaquin Valley. By the late 1970's, as many as twenty thousand Yemenis, mostly males, lived and worked in the United States, including two thousand farm workers in California.

Home for the Yemenis in the United States is usually a single, poorly furnished room or low-rent apartment shared with other men from the same family, village, or district. The men often sleep in shifts so that two can use a single bed. The rooming house or apartment is usually in a working-class or poor neighborhood in a heavily industrialized area. Most Yemenis who live this way work in the auto or steel industries or as migrant labor; they intend to return to the Middle East.

Whether in California, New York, or Michigan, Yemenis have increasingly gone into business for themselves. In concert with their brothers, cousins, or fellow villagers, they have purchased small grocery stores, newsstands, or candy stores. Often in the poorer sections of New York City, Buffalo, Detroit, or Oakland, these labor-intensive businesses require twelve to fourteen hours of work a day.

Thus, the Yemenis in the United States are both sojourners and settlers. Some temporary migrants have matured into a settled population, bringing over their wives, children, and older relatives.

Arab American Lobbying and Political Involvement. Since the late 1960's, several important Arab American organizations have been created to promote Arab American interests. Chief among these are the National Association of Arab Americans (NAAA), the Association of Arab American University Graduates (AAAUG), and the AMERICAN-ARAB ANTI-DISCRIMINATION COMMITTEE (ADC).

The ADC was created in 1980 as a direct result of the campaign by the Federal Bureau of Investigation (FBI) to have its agents trap a number of members of Congress by posing as Lebanese "sheikhs" offering bribes. This affair, known as "Abscam," prompted James G. Abourezk, a former Arab American senator, to form the ADC in order to counter stereotypes associated with anti-Arab racism. Modeled to some extent on American Jewry's ANTI-DEFAMATION LEAGUE (ADL), the ADC became an advocate, providing immigrant assistance, protesting harassment of Arab Americans, and calling for a congressional investigation of alleged improper treatment of Arab Americans and Arab Canadians at the U.S.-Canadian border.

In the early 1980's ADC began to manifest solidarity with other ethnic American groups in the fight against RACISM and discrimination. In the summer of 1983, ADC chapter members from across the nation participated in the march on Washington organized by the Coalition of Conscience for Jobs to commemorate Martin Luther King, Jr.'s historic march on that city twenty years earlier.

The year 1990 posed many challenges to Arab Americans in the wake of Iraq's annexation of Kuwait. As the media's interest in the Middle East increased during the Gulf War, so did threats and acts of violence against Arab Americans by individuals and hate groups. ADC condemned Iraq's violation of Kuwait's territorial integrity but also opposed the deployment of U.S. troops to challenge Iraq's President Saddam Hussein militarily. The committee also worked with elected officials to raise a public outcry against anti-Arab RACISM.

Arab Americans in the later twentieth century have promoted a reawakening of ethnic consciousness within their community. (Cleo Freelance Photo)

ADC's efforts to win Temporary Protected Status (TPS) for Lebanese and Kuwaitis residing in the United States were successful when the Department of Justice announced that it would grant TPS to more than fifty thousand Lebanon, Kuwait, and Liberia nationals. This allowed those from the designated countries to stay and work in the United States on a temporary basis until conditions in their homelands improved. Since TPS was implemented in the spring of 1991, more than six thousand Lebanese and Kuwaitis have benefited from it, including Palestinians.

Cultural Contributions. The most important area of Arab cultural preservation besides religious beliefs in the United States is the Arabic literary and historical heritage. The pioneers in these areas were mainly immigrants from Egypt and Lebanon. The most noted among the immigrants were Khalil Gibran (1883-1931), a native of Lebanon who settled in Boston at the beginning of the twentieth century and published extensively in American Arabic literary circles; Ameen Rihani (1876-1940), who arrived in New York from Lebanon in 1888, having published forty books in Arabic, which were translated into fifteen languages; and the historian and orientalist Philip Khûri Hitti (1886-1978). Born in Lebanon, Hitti settled in the United States in 1913.

After receiving his Ph.D. from Columbia University, Hitti began a distinguished career as a professor of Arabic history, culture, and language at Princeton University. He published many books, including *The Syrians in America* (1924), *History of the Arabs* (1937), *History of Syria (1957), Lebanon in History* (1957), and *The Near East in History: A 5,000 Year Story* (1961).

In 1944, Professor Hitti became chairperson of the Department of Oriental Languages and Literatures at Princeton. The following year, he served as adviser to the Arab delegates to the United Nations organizational meeting in San Francisco and was also a consultant to several American government agencies and corporations.

Arab Americans made equally significant contributions in other sectors. Faruq El Baz, born in Egypt in 1938, participated in planning and evaluation of NASA's Lunar Orbiter missions and served as a research director at the National Air and Space Museum of the Smithsonian Institution. Consumer rights advocate Ralph Nader was born in Connecticut in 1934 to Lebanese parents. An attorney, author, and lecturer, Nader founded numerous consumer protection groups, among them Public Citizen and Congress Watch.

Arab Americans are also well represented in the entertainment industry. Among the most noted are Casey Kasem, of Lebanese origins, an actor, host, and producer of radio shows; Paul Anka, born to Syrian parents, a well-known singer and composer; Michael Ansara, of Lebanese descent, an actor in stage productions, films, and television; and Danny Thomas, born in Michigan to Lebanese parents, an internationally acclaimed actor, comedian, film producer, and civic leader. He was best known for his television series Make Room for Daddy, which received five Emmys.

Several Arab Americans have distinguished themselves in American politics, among them John H. Sununu, the former governor of New Hampshire; James Abdnor, former senator from South Dakota; and James G. Abourezk, also from South Dakota, who was the first Arab American elected to the U.S. Senate (1972-1979).

SUGGESTED READINGS. For firsthand accounts on Arab Americans, their socioeconomic and political status, immigration/demographic trends and acculturation, see especially the articles by Mary Ann Fay and Alan Dehmer in *Taking Root, Bearing Fruit: The Arab American Experience* (1984), edited by James Zogby and published by the ADC. Two other edited collections to consult are Yvonne Yazbeck Haddad's *The Muslims of America* (1991), and Jonathan Friedlander's *Sojourners and Settlers: The Yemeni Immigrant Experience* (1988). An account of early Arab immigration can be found in Alixa Naff's *Becoming American: The Early Arab Immigrant Experience* (1985).—*Michael M. Laskier*

Arapahos: American Indian tribe of the Great Plains. The tribal name of this people of Algonquian linguistic stock may come from the Pawnee *tirapihu* (buyer, trader), referring to the Arapaho role as middlemen in Plains trade, or it may derive from a Crow word meaning "tattooed." The Shoshone-Comanche term *sariteka*, or "dog eater," was commonly applied to the Arapahos on the southern plains. They call themselves *Hinono'eino*, "the people."

Arapaho origins are obscure. Tribal legend places them between Lake Superior and the Mississippi head-

Artist's depiction of an Arapaho Ghost Dance ceremony. (National Archives)

waters, living a sedentary life as corn farmers. Pressure from Siouan and Algonquian peoples to the east (ultimately from Euroamerican settlement) apparently forced the Arapahos westward. A French trader's journal from 1795 shows them east of the Black Hills and for a decade afterward they appeared at various times in South Dakota, Nebraska, Wyoming, Montana, and Colorado. At some point they began a lasting friendship with another Algonquian group, the CHEYENNES, and the tribes continued southwestward more or less together.

As horse Indians on the High Plains, the Arapahos specialized in trading between northern and southern tribes. Their business depended on friendly relations with the farming Mandans, Hidatsas, and Arikaras along the upper Missouri River and with the horse-rich COMANCHES and Kiowas in Texas. Though a stable peace between the latter peoples and the Cheyennes and Arapahos was made only in 1840, some Arapahos customarily wintered in Comanche country by 1813. Others remained near the Colorado Rockies, giving rise to a dual north-south tribal organization paralleling that of the Cheyennes. Central Colorado, where the two Arapaho divisions periodically met, became the tribal heartland.

The Arapahos continuously warred against the UTES, Pawnees, and Shoshones, but they were reluctant to fight the encroaching white Americans. At the 1867 Medicine Lodge Council, the southern division agreed to a joint Cheyenne-Arapaho reservation in what is now Oklahoma and remained inactive during the hostilities of the 1870's. Their reservation was opened to white settlement in 1892, and the Indians took individual allotments. The Northern Arapahos were assigned to live with their traditional Shoshone enemies on the Wind River Reservation in Wyoming in 1876; this reservation remains intact.

True to their mediating role, the Arapahos were instrumental in spreading the 1890 GHOST DANCE RELIGION across the Plains. This nativistic movement, originated by a Paiute prophet in Nevada, promised world renewal if worshippers would sing and dance themselves into a trance. It involved most of the Plains tribes before gradually fading; Ghost Dance elements remain in other Arapaho ceremonies.

SUGGESTED READINGS. Perhaps because of their more peaceful disposition, there are fewer books on the Arapahos than on most Plains tribes. A narrative history is provided by Virginia Trenholm in *The Arapahoes, Our People* (1970). Alfred Kroeber's *The Arapaho*

(1983) is a superb description of tribal ceremony and decorative arts. *Arapahoe Politics, 1851-1978* (1982) by Loretta Fowler is a model ethnohistorical study focusing on political symbolism on the northern reservation. Donald Berthrong's *The Cheyenne and Arapaho Ordeal* (1976) covers the reservation era in Oklahoma. Sources on the Cheyennes usually include information on the Arapahos.

Architectural Barriers Act (1968): Set standards to make public buildings accessible to people with disabilities. In 1959, President Dwight Eisenhower's Committee on the Employment of the Handicapped joined with the National Easter Seals Society, the Veterans Administration, and others in launching a nationwide campaign to eliminate architectural barriers to people with physical disabilities. Throughout American society, curbs, narrow doorways, stairways, narrow aisles, and other structural elements made many buildings, mass transit systems, and other facilities inaccessible to those with impaired mobility. In 1965, Congress amended the VOCATIONAL REHABILITATION Act to create the National Commission on Architectural Barriers to the Rehabilitation of the Handicapped.

The commission studied the progress being made toward the elimination of barriers and recommended to Congress in 1967 that legislation was necessary. Senator E. L. Bartlett of Alaska introduced a bill that eventually became the Architectural Barriers Act (ABA) of 1968. Mandating standards for new buildings and selected alteration of old ones, the ABA stated, "Any building constructed or leased in whole or in part with federal funds must be made accessible to and usable by the physically handicapped."

Three agencies were made responsible to issue guidelines following the standards already established by the American National Standards Institute. The Department of Housing and Urban Development dealt with residences; the Department of Defense with military facilities; and the General Services Administration (GSA) with other public facilities, by far the largest percentage of facilities involved. Full compliance was to be achieved, according to the ABA, by January 1, 1977.

To monitor compliance, Congress passed Section 502 of the 1973 Rehabilitation Act, establishing the Architectural Barriers and Transportation Compliance Board. The board included representatives of eight cabinet departments and was headed by the Secretary of Health, Education, and Welfare. It was empowered to investigate compliance and initiate legal proceedings against ABA violators. By 1974, following the federal lead, all fifty states and the District of Columbia had laws requiring handicapped access for new buildings.

In 1975, however, a General Accounting Office (GAO) study of three hundred buildings uncovered numerous loopholes and inadequacies in the ABA and the guidelines it engendered. Thus, in 1976, Congress amended the ABA to include the U.S. Postal Service as a fourth guideline-setting agency to expand the definition for leased buildings. The following year, the GSA issued new, more specific rules for access to public buildings and transit.

In 1980, a second GAO study reported on remaining inadequacies in the ABA. The election of President Ronald Reagan led to criticism of the compliance board as costly and excessive. In 1982, the Office of Management recommended eliminating the board altogether, but it survived, revising its minimum guide-

lines in response to pressure from the administration.

In 1984, the four government agencies responsible for compliance guidelines jointly issued the Uniform Federal Accessibility Standards. Throughout the 1970's and 1980's, more and more public and private

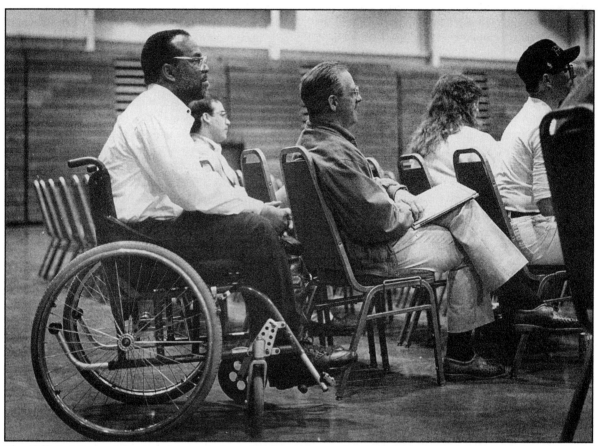

The 1968 Architectural Barriers Act required any building constructed or leased with federal funds to be accessible and usable by persons with physical disabilities. (James L. Shaffer)

entities came to understand the demands of the ABA and the need for accessibility for that part of the U.S. population (up to one-fifth) that can be said to have mental or physical disabilities.

SUGGESTED READINGS. Two excellent sources on the movement to remove architectural barriers are *Disability, Civil Rights, and Public Policy* (1989) by Stephen L. Percy and *The Quiet Revolution* (1979) by James Haskins with J. M. Stifle. Practical approaches can be found in Charles D. Goldman's *Disability Rights Guide* (1987); *Rethinking Architecture* (1987), edited by Raymond Lifchez; and *Design for Independent Living* (1979) by Lifchez with Barbara Winslow.

Architecture—Spanish influence: American architecture reflects the diversity of styles and traditions of the nation's multicultural origins. Spanish traditions were introduced during the sixteenth century as part of the discovery of the New World. Exploration and colonization in the Spanish Empire were impelled by several factors, including economic profit, missionary zeal, and territorial acquisition. Fortified towns and SPANISH MISSIONS were established to further these objectives. Both the location and design of Spanish settlements illustrated the importance placed on the achievement of these goals.

Fortifications. The first building efforts, part of the effort to control territory, were designed primarily as strategically located fortifications. ST. AUGUSTINE in Florida was the first site for the establishment of a Spanish presence. The succession of simple timber forts initially constructed there was eventually replaced by a permanent stone fort, the Castillo de San Marcos, between 1672 and 1676. This fortification was similar to other Spanish forts located along the Gulf of Mexico. The position of the chapel within the fort is testimony to the importance given to the Catholic religious mission underlying Spanish expansion. Later, Fort Matanzas was added as further security for the garrison. Materials used included stone, wood, and stucco. Several important stylistic features marked this construction, which saw the introduction of domes, molded corbeling, and casings.

In addition to forts, Spain constructed presidios, or garrisons, for troops assigned to protecting missionaries and their missions against attacks by disaffected American Indians. In the Southwest, the state of Texas was the site of several garrisons: Presidio Nuestra Señora de los Dolores de los Tejos (1716), Presidio Nuestra Señora del Pilar de los Adaes (1721), Presidio Nuestra Señora de Loreto de Bahia (1722), and Presidio de San Luis de las Amarillas (1757) are some which have partially survived the ravages of time.

Alta California, the site of several missions located along the Camino Real from San Diego to San Francisco, was also richly endowed with presidios to enhance the security of these religious establishments. Most of these, including the presidios of San Diego (1769), Monterey (1770), San Francisco (1776), and Santa Barbara (1782), were rather hastily constructed and poorly equipped to withstand a prolonged siege. Despite the impressive geometric uniformities in design, the materials used, such as timber, sod, and earthworks, detracted from the purpose of these garrisons.

From the perspective of design and function, the development of presidios resembled that of forts. Uniformity of concept was prevalent throughout: a walled enclosure with strategically sited bastions, barracks for the troops, storerooms for supplies, a chapel, and passages for access under cover to various sections of the enclosure. Presidios came to represent the determination of the Spanish to prevail in their colonial objectives of occupation and conversion.

CITY HALL

Pasadena, California's city hall building reflects the influence of Spanish architecture; important stylistic features are domes, molded corbeling, and casings. (Valerie Marie)

Towns. Spanish settlements were often designed with defensive considerations in mind. Towns were symbolic of territorial possession and also representative of the cultural origins of the colonial power. Elaborate care went into the planning and building of the settlements, which were authorized by charters from the Spanish Crown. The basic plan, inspired by the Greco-Roman tradition that was followed in Spain, usually consisted of a quadrangular street pattern focused on the plaza mayor. The plaza was the central meeting place for the community, and surrounding it were several public buildings, such as the cabildo

The Spanish-influenced Cathedral of St. Vibiana adds architectural diversity to the Los Angeles skyline. (David Fowler)

(town hall), the prison, and the church. The residences of prestigious townsfolk and officials were located close to the center. They were usually spacious, well-designed homes distinguished by tile roofs, arched colonnades, and sometimes inner courtyards. Less affluent residents lived in more modest structures. Generally, Spanish towns of North America were not as elaborately conceived, nor as durable, as those in Central and South America.

Monterey, which was the colonial capital of Spanish California, is representative of the finest traditions in Spanish town building in North America. Many of the original houses have survived to identify the Monterey style as two-storied adobe houses with wood balconies and verandas. Instead of the traditional tile roofs that sloped on two sides, the Monterey adobes possessed four-sided sloping roofs in a unique adaptation of the New England Cape Cod tradition. Small, inner garden courtyards continued to be a feature of the homes in the area. Casa Amesti, the Merrit house, and the Larkin adobe are examples of this style of architecture that was to be copied by several other towns such as San Juan Bautista.

Missions. Extensive mission building was a major characteristic of the Spanish presence in the New World. In style as well as in construction techniques, missions revealed another facet of colonial architecture. A number of regional variations emerge in these structures depending on geographic location and local craftsmanship. The Franciscans pioneered the settlement of the southwestern United States and established many distinctive missions in the area. Benefiting from the techniques of the pre-existing PUEBLO architecture of the region, the Franciscans were quick to adopt features such as adobe brick and build units that could accommodate expansion at a later date. The Spanish contributed the practice of forming square adobe blocks to this process of cultural exchange. Formerly room size had been determined by the length of the roof beam spans; the Spanish, with their more efficient tools, were able to cut larger lengths and expand room size.

Generally, Franciscan mission architecture reflected the austerity of the order itself. The incorporation of PUEBLO Indian styles, as a result of the American Indian labor involved in the construction of the missions with Spanish technology and design, gave rise to a distinctive architectural style known as the Spanish-Pueblo. This is characterized by extensive use of adobe walls of mud brick and straw, earth floors, and

Women apply adobe mud to an exterior church wall in Rancho de Taos, N. Mex. This type of architecture was practiced by the Pueblo Indians. (Elaine S. Querry)

rooms arranged around inner patios for security and to minimize the impact of wind and sun. Sometimes floors were paved with thin stones placed over a prepared earthen surface. Instead of glass panes, windows were equipped with shutters and wood grills. Both windows and doors operated on wooden rather than metal pivots, since metal was a scarce commodity. Fireplaces were another recognizable feature.

Texas alone has a number of missions constructed during the late seventeenth and early eighteenth centuries. The area of El Paso has four missions, one of them actually established by Tiwa Indians fleeing from the PUEBLO REVOLT OF 1680. The ALAMO, actually named San Antonio de Valero, is the best known of the five San Antonio missions established during the early 1700's. Forever associated with the heroic stand against Mexican General Antonio López de Santa Anna, it is actually one of the more modest missions of the Spanish style. The most magnificent of the Texas missions is San Jose y San Miguel de Aguayo, located five miles south of the Alamo area, distinguished by its elaborately decorated front and baptistery windows.

The seventeenth century was also a great building period in New Mexico. The rapidly increasing number of converts to Christianity impelled the mission-building process; by the mid-1600's there were at least twenty-five missions in the area. As in Texas, the Spanish depended heavily on Indian labor for the construction of the missions, and inevitably this was reflected in the introduction of Indian stylistic features into Spanish colonial architectural forms. This felicitous combination of cultural traditions may be seen in the adaptation of modern southwestern architecture.

The first California missions were founded by Jesuit priests; they were the main Spanish presence in the area for more than seventy years until their expulsion in 1767 by the Spanish king, Charles III. The Franciscan Order inherited their mission and continued the task of spreading Christianity among the native population. The Franciscans proceeded to build churches in California in order to limit the expansion of the Russian presence from north to south, as well as to commemorate the founder of their order, Saint Francis. Of the original missions constructed in the state, more than twenty have survived in various stages of restoration. The relative geographical isolation of the area hampered the movement of materials and influences from outside the region and partially explains the simplicity of style.

This was not the case further down the coast in Mexico, where the elaborate church architecture reflected the stylistic changes sweeping Spain itself. Only in rare instances is it possible to identify one or two features that represent Mexican influence on mission design. Mission Santa Barbara (1786) was originally a relatively simple church, however when the 1812 earthquake damaged the adobe structure, a new sandstone building was designed. This new mission (1820) had twenty feet square towers that rose to a height of 78 feet. The façade possessed many classic features, such as Ionic volutes and dentils adorning the columns. Another impressive church is the Mission San Luis Rey (1798), with its distinctive bell tower two stories high and embellished with arches, that was to serve as a model for other structures. The California missions are distinguished by their terraced bell towers and arcaded corridors, as well as inner courtyards and gardens with fountains influenced by Spain's Moorish legacy. These motifs permeated domestic architecture as well during the Spanish revival period.

Spanish Revival. The Columbian Exposition of 1893 in Chicago provided an opportunity for architects to present a variety of styles in pavilion design. California selected the Spanish mission style for its exhibition pavilion. This was the beginning of a wave of revivalist architecture that appeared in buildings in San Francisco; Riverside, California; Albuquerque, New Mexico; and in a series of railroad stations and hotels commissioned by the Southern Pacific and Santa Fe railroads. The style was clearly distinguishable by its red tiled roofs, arches, smooth plastered walls, towers, balconies, and a general simplicity of ornamentation, if not an entire absence of elaborate detail. Among the architects of the period who practiced this form were A. Page Brown, Bernard Maybeck, Irving Gill, and E. R. Swain.

During the 1920's there was a Spanish colonial revival that retained some of the features of the mission style but also added significant modifications. Among the features retained were the low-pitched red tiled roofs, plastered walls, and balconies. Arches were sparingly introduced and more ornamental detail was favored, especially around doorways and windows. The ornamentation of this period shows distinct Mexican influence. This transformation of domestic architecture was especially noticeable in areas where the Spanish style already prevailed. It was also introduced to new locations, particularly to areas with warm, dry climates, for which the style was suited.

The revival of the Spanish style, especially in Florida, was in large measure the work of Addison Mizner (1872-1933). His early training in Guatemala, Spain, and in the firm of Willis Polk—a Californian who promoted the Spanish mission style—influenced Mizner in his interpretation of the Spanish Revival. In Palm Beach, he designed several villas in the Mediterranean tradition with strong Spanish overtones. The Everglades Club was typical of his unique design. The entire city of Boca Raton was planned along colonial lines. Mizner established the Mediterranean tile roof and arched corridors as well as the inner courtyard as characteristic of Florida architecture. His influence extended as far north as Brookville, New York, where he continued to design buildings in the Spanish style.

SUGGESTED READINGS. Trent Elwood Sanford's *The Architecture of the Southwest* (1950) is both a history of settlement and a history of design in a region of North America that is home to three traditions: Indian, Spanish, and Anglo American. Donald W. Curl's *Mizner's Florida: American Resort Architecture*

(1984) chronicles the contribution of this significant architect in interpreting the Spanish tradition of design and town planning. *Master Builders: A Guide to Famous American Architects* (1985), edited by Diane Maddex, is the best concise introduction to important architects, most informative on the revival of different styles. *What Style Is It? A Guide to American Architecture* (1983) by John C. Poppeliers, S. Allen Chambers, Jr., and Nancy B. Schwartz is a brief and useful explanation of the terminology of architecture and style.—*Sai Felicia Krishna-Hensel*

Architecture and dwellings—American Indian: Indigenous architecture varied from region to region, but the two most common traditional methods of construction involved compressing earth or ice, creating a frame, and either covering it or walling it in. The American Indians of the Arctic and subarctic regions compressed ice, snow, and earth in order to form their housing, as in

be covered with hides or mats made of reeds and brush. The frame might also be used to support walls made of earth, skins, wood, or a combination of all three. Some common examples of these types of housing are the Great Lakes tribes' wigwams and the Northwest coastal tribes' plank houses.

This variety of materials and forms was reflected in the variety of uses of American Indian structures. Some were meant for living purposes, such as keeping their inhabitants protected from the environment. Other dwellings, however, served important social purposes, such as housing the tribe's government members. Some dwellings also fulfilled sacred religious functions. These dwellings were home to the religious leaders of the tribe and contained their medicine and other sacred items.

Tradition dictated who could build the dwelling, how it was to be built, and by whom it could be owned. Tribal religious beliefs and worldviews also

A Pawnee lodge in Loup, Nebr., in 1873. (National Archives)

the well-known igloo. The American Indians of the Southwest compressed earth and brush to form their pueblos and kivas.

Another type of dwelling was made by constructing a frame of wood, tree limbs, or bones tied together with sinew or softened bark. This frame would then

presented guidelines on how to arrange dwellings into villages. Most often, the arrangement was both significant and complex. Some villages were intended to mirror the human body, while others were meant as a representation of the universe. Social stratification could also be seen in this organization. Council lodges and religious dwellings were often placed away from the housing of the general public and oriented in specific ways according to the directions and movements of the sun and moon.

While it is often noted for its practicality, American Indian architecture was deeply sacred to the Indians themselves. Many believed that a house had a spirit of its own and that the dwelling and its inhabitants had to become comfortable with each other's presence. This sacredness is also evinced in Indians' attention to form and arrangement in the light of the tribe's tradition, mythology, and religion.

SUGGESTED READINGS. Peter Nabokov and Robert Easton's *Native American Architecture* (1989) gives a thorough survey of the subject. The Smithsonian's multivolume *Handbook of North American Indians* (1978-1990), edited by William C. Sturtevant, and Ed-

ward S. Curtis' series *The North American Indian* (1907-1930) contain valuable information on the American Indian culture in general as well as on architecture specifically.

Arden, Elizabeth (Florence Nightingale Graham; Dec. 31, 1878?, Ontario, Canada—Oct. 18, 1966, New York, N.Y.): Pioneering woman entrepreneur. Graham and partner Elizabeth Hubbard opened a beauty salon for women in 1909 in New York. Hubbard went her own way, leaving Graham with the salon. At that point she changed her name and, as Elizabeth Arden, introduced COSMETICS to upper-class women, setting a new standard for women in the corporate world. An extremely adept businesswoman and a creative advertiser, Arden eventually opened salons in over one hundred locations throughout the United States and Europe that offered a

In the early to mid-1900's, Elizabeth Arden (left) introduced cosmetics to a consumer group of upper-class women; she is shown here in 1956 with actress Irene Dunne. (AP/Wide World Photos)

full range of products and services, from wholesale Elizabeth Arden makeup to fashion tips.

Arendt, Hannah (Oct. 14, 1906, Hanover, Germany—Dec. 4, 1975, New York, N.Y.): Political theorist and philosopher. Arendt's studies in philosophy began with Martin Heidegger and Karl Jaspers. After imprisonment by Hitler's Gestapo for collecting material on anti-Semitism, Arendt fled to Paris, where she married Heinrich Blucher, a working-class activist. They moved to New York, where Arendt wrote political columns for the German Jewish paper *Aufbau.* In 1951 she published *The Origins of Totalitarianism,* and in 1959 she became the first full-time woman professor at Princeton University. Her numerous articles and books, including *Between Past and Future: Six Exercises in Political Thought* (1961) and *On Revolution* (1963), attempt to define the bridge between politics and philosophy by clarifying political language.

Philosopher Hannah Arendt became Princeton University's first full-time woman professor. (AP/Wide World Photos)

Argentinean Americans: Argentineans come from many backgrounds. Before Europeans arrived in the sixteenth century, Argentina had an Indian population of about 300,000. Argentina was a Spanish colony from 1580 until it became independent in 1816. As a new nation in the nineteenth century, Argentina attracted immigrants from many lands. Its population has included Nobel Prize winners, famous authors, musicians, statesmen, and the first woman president in the Western Hemisphere. Argentineans have also immigrated to the United States, where they have added to the diversity of the growing Latino population.

History. In 1580, Spanish military leader Juan de Garay founded the city of Buenos Aires. The city, surrounded by grassy plains called *pampas,* developed slowly. Spain only became concerned about the southern reaches of its empire in the eighteenth century when the British took the Malvinas (Falkland) Islands. In response, the Spanish created the viceroyalty of La Plata in 1776, and Buenos Aires, its capital, began to grow.

In 1808 Napoleon deposed the Spanish king and placed his brother, Joseph, on the throne. In response, an open town meeting was held in Buenos Aires on May 25, 1810, to oppose Bonaparte and demand local self-government. Independence was formally proclaimed on July 9, 1816. Both dates are celebrated as national holidays in Argentina.

The junta of Buenos Aires attempted to retain all the territory of the old viceroyalty, but lost Paraguay and Upper Peru (Bolivia) in military defeats. José Francisco de San Martín, a native of northern Argentina, returned from Spain to lead an army against Spanish forces in the Americas. He proved to be a military genius, crossing the Andes and defeating Spanish armies in Chile in 1817; he is now regarded as the liberator of southern South America. From 1816 to 1852 Argentina experienced periods of political instability and dictatorship. Juan Manuel de Rosas became the governor of the province of Buenos Aires in 1829. He achieved a closer federal union among the region's provinces, but after 1835 he became a virtual dictator.

The second half of the nineteenth century brought stability to Argentina. Justo José de Urquiza defeated Rosas in 1852. A new constitution was written, and Argentina became a federal republic. Buenos Aires was recognized as the capital city. Elections were held, although the right to vote was severely restricted.

From the 1860's to 1930, Argentina experienced nearly continuous growth. Domingo Faustino Sarmiento, president from 1868 to 1874, favored immigration and education. Beginning as a trickle in the 1870's, European immigration into Argentina would become a flood by the end of the century. Most of the immigrants came from Spain and Italy, but others were from Russia, Syria, England, and Germany. Many of these immigrants remained in Buenos Aires. The city's population increased from 500,000 to more than one million between 1889 and 1909.

Political reforms in 1912 led to the victory of a middle-class political party in the 1916 presidential elections, but the government was overthrown by the military in 1930. The military-dominated governments of the 1930's severely repressed political opposition.

ARGENTINA

The Modern Era. After a military coup in 1943, Colonel Juan Domingo Perón emerged as a leading member of the new government. Perón used his position in the government and the popularity of his second wife, Eva (Evita), to build a political coalition with labor and the masses. They voted Perón into the presidency in 1946. He was reelected to a second term but was later overthrown by the military in 1955.

From 1955 until 1983, all elected civilian governments in Argentina ended in military coups. Periods of economic development alternated with periods of repression and economic stagnation, prompting many Argentineans to leave the country, often for the United States.

In 1973 Juan Perón was allowed to return from exile and was elected president. He died in office the next year. His third wife and vice president, Isabel Perón, became the first woman head of state in the Western Hemisphere. In 1976 she was removed from office by the military after economic turmoil and increasing violence brought the country to the verge of chaos. Argentina then entered a period known as the "Dirty War," a virtual civil war waged by leftist guerrillas and government-supported death squads. Guerrillas assaulted army bases, ambushing soldiers and stealing weapons. Death squads kidnapped, tortured, and killed thousands of suspected leftist sympathizers, who suddenly "disappeared" from their homes in the middle of the night. Additional thousands of Argentineans fled to Europe or the United States, many never to return.

In an attempt to gather popular support and resolve a long-standing dispute with Great Britain over the Falkland (Malvinas) Islands, the military government authorized an invasion in April, 1982. The U.S. government condemned Argentina's aggression and supported Great Britain. The ensuing war lasted several weeks, and Argentina was defeated. In the aftermath of the war the military permitted national elections and a return to civilian rule.

Argentineans in the United States. Argentinean immigration to the United States has been caused by both economic and political problems in Argentina during the modern era. In the 1960's there was a steady flow of skilled workers, medical doctors, and scientists. During the "Dirty War" and terror of the 1970's, more than three thousand Argentineans immigrated to the United States annually. Since 1980 the figure has remained about two thousand immigrants per year.

Argentineans have contributed to American culture in a variety of ways. Many Argentinean immigrants are academics who teach or do research at major universities. For example, Luis Angel Caffarelli is a mathematician at the Institute for Advanced Study in Princeton, New Jersey, who came to the United States in 1973. He has taught at the University of Minnesota and the University of Chicago and was the recipient of a Guggenheim fellowship. Physicist Leopoldo Maximo Falicov, who came to the United States in 1960, teaches at the University of California, Berkeley. He is the author of *Group Theory and Its*

Physical Applications (1966). Enrique Anderson-Imbert is an emeritus professor of Hispanic literature from Harvard University who came to the United States in 1947. In addition to teaching at Smith College and the University of Michigan, he authored numerous literary studies, including works on Domingo Faustino Sarmiento and Ruben Dario.

renowned Argentinean writer Jorge Luis Borges taught at Harvard and the University of Texas in the 1960's and continues to enjoy a faithful following in U.S. literary circles. Manuel Puig's *Kiss of the Spider Woman* (1976) was made into a successful American film.

Many Argentinean Americans have worked in the

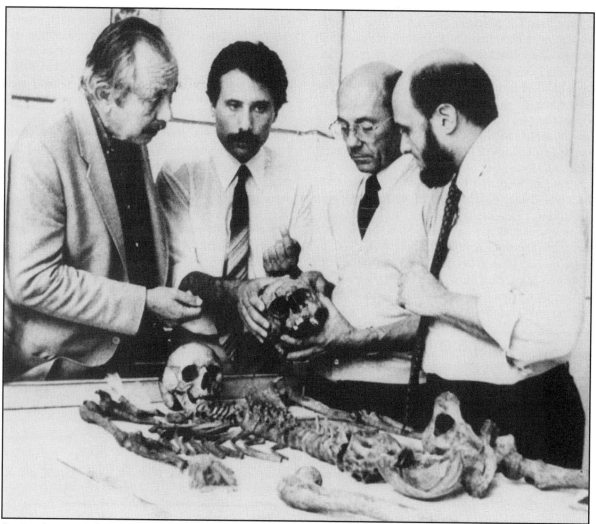

During the twentieth century many Argentineans immigrated to the United States to escape political unrest and repression in the homeland. Here, forensic experts in Buenos Aires, Argentina, examine the bones of victims of political repression. (AP/Wide World Photos)

Other Argentineans are well-known in the arts. For example, Geny Dignac is a prize-winning sculptor who has exhibited her works of light and fire at the Corcoran Gallery of Art in Washington, D.C., and in Venezuela. Tito Capobianco founded the San Diego Opera Center and the Pittsburgh Opera Center as part of an international career as an opera director. The

field of medicine. For example, dermatologist Irma Gigli taught at the Harvard Medical School and the New York University Medical Center before becoming chief of the division of dermatology at the University of California, San Diego.

Argentineans live throughout the United States. The largest Argentinean American communities are in the

New York, Washington, D.C., and Los Angeles metropolitan areas. There are several associations that link the two countries. The Argentine-American Chamber of Commerce in New York City promotes business contacts between Argentina and the United States and publishes a weekly newsletter. The Argentine Information Service Center, also in New York City, was founded in 1976 to monitor the human rights situation in Argentina. The Argentine-North American Association for the Advancement of Science, Technology and Culture, with offices in New York City, promotes scientific and cultural exchange. Finally, the Argentine Association of Los Angeles serves the large Argentinean population of that city, celebrating the national holidays of May 25 and July 9 and reminding Americans of the contributions of the Argentineans to the culture and society of both their native and adopted lands.

SUGGESTED READINGS. The *Harvard Encyclopedia of American Ethnic Groups* (1980), edited by Stephan Thernstrom, offers detailed descriptions of many ethnic groups, including case studies of individual Latin American families. Yearly statistical tables can be found in *The Chosen People* (1990) by Guillermina Jasso and Mark R. Rosenzweig. James Scobie's *Argentina: A City and a Nation* (1971) is an excellent overview of Argentina's history, although *Argentina,*

1516 to 1987: From Spanish Colonization to the Falkland War (1987) by David Rock is more up-to-date.— *James A. Baer*

Ariyoshi, George Ryoichi (b. Mar. 12, 1926, Honolulu, Hawaii): Japanese American politician. Ariyoshi attended the University of Hawaii, Michigan State University, and the University of Michigan, receiving his J.D. in 1952. He entered private practice in Honolulu, but soon became active in politics. He was elected as the territorial representative from Hawaii from 1954 to 1958 and served in the Hawaiian senate from 1959 to 1970. He was lieutenant governor from 1970 to 1973 and governor from 1973 to 1986. As governor, Ariyoshi served as chair of the Western Governors' Conference from 1977 to 1978. He has received honorary degrees from universities in the United States, Guam, and the Philippines, and was awarded Japan's Order of the Sacred Treasury in 1985 and the Emperor's Silver Cup Award in 1986.

Armenian Americans: Armenian Americans are a proud and diverse people who are part of an international Armenian diaspora. Many of them still have strong attachments to their historical homeland, which is located in an area shared by three contemporary countries: Turkey, Iran, and the Armenian Republic (formerly part

ARMENIA

of the Soviet Union). This sense of ethnic identity persists even among Armenians who came to the United States from Lebanon, Paris, or Iran. Central to this identity is a belief in the greatness of traditional Armenian culture and the injustices suffered by the Armenian people at the hands of the Ottoman Turks in the early 1900's.

Historical Background. Armenian national claims to an ancient homeland are based on the existence of an independent Christian Armenian kingdom between the second century B.C.E. and the fourth century. Collapse of this state under Persian attack eventually made the Armenians subjects of Persia on the one hand and Rome on the other. Although Armenians lived throughout the nineteenth and early twentieth century as a minority population under Russian, Persian, and Ottoman Turkish rule, it was under the latter empire that they endured the most extreme repression. It was, therefore, from Turkey that most Armenians first emigrated to the United States.

The major waves of Armenian emigration to the United States corresponded to periods of violence carried out against them by the Turks in the last stages of the Ottoman Empire. Although there is no certainty about the numbers of Armenians killed in any of the three most violent repressive campaigns, it was during World War I—when the Ottoman Turks most feared subversion of their rule by minority nationalities looking for aid from the Allied powers—that levels of attacks against Armenians were highest. Counterclaims continue to be exchanged as to the numbers of Armenians killed in the worst year of the war (1915). Most Armenian Americans believe that their ancestors were victims of a GENOCIDE that saw the massacre of one to two million Armenians. Despite politically sensitive and controversial divisions of opinion on the subject, there is no doubt that numerous Armenian communities were wiped out and many thousands killed.

High expectations came with the break up of the Ottoman Empire under provisions of the Treaty of Sevres (1920), which promised to establish an independent Republic of Armenia. Postwar complications associated with the establishment of a firmly nationalist Turkish Republic (1924), however, and imposition of the Soviet Socialist Republic of Armenia in areas further east dashed such hopes. Large numbers of Armenian refugees fled into Syria and Lebanon, where a French mandate regime was then being established. The effect of this movement of Armenians into neighboring Syria is visible in the fact that both Syria and Lebanon have substantial minority Armenian populations of their own. The overall pattern of emigration to the United States, therefore, includes elements of "second-stage" movement of Armenians from other areas where they originally took refuge from Turkish persecution.

Immigration. Armenian immigration to the United States took place in stages beginning in the 1890's, when about 71,000 entries were recorded, and continuing through the peak years of immigration in the early 1900's. By the 1960's, upwards of 400,000 Armenians had become part of the ethnic makeup of the United States. Since no Armenian nation-state existed, this flow came from various countries with Armenian minorities, such as Turkey, Syria, or parts of Europe, as part of their U.S. immigration quotas.

The earliest communities of Armenian immigrants from Turkey and other areas of the former Ottoman Empire were established in cities on the East Coast. Immigrants from the area that became the Armenian Soviet Socialist Republic tended to enter the United States via Canada. Many of the latter group formed the early nucleus of Armenians in California, especially Southern California. Eventually the two main centers of Armenians in California would be in Fresno and Los Angeles.

The demographic pattern established by early immigrants continued as the numbers of second- or third-generation Armenian Americans grew and additional immigrants came after immigration laws were liberalized in the 1960's. By the mid-1970's, out of an estimated total of between 350,000 and 450,000 persons of Armenian descent in the United States, 45 percent lived in the Middle Atlantic states and New England, 25 percent in California, and 15 percent in the four Midwestern states of Michigan, Illinois, Ohio, and Wisconsin. New arrivals since that time have tended to boost the number of Armenians in the western United States, particularly in the Los Angeles area.

Like some other national groups in the United States, Armenians have been affected by world political upheavals in the late 1900's. Many began to come to the United States, especially the Los Angeles area, as a result of the civil war in Lebanon in the 1970's, the revolution in Iran in the 1980's, and violence and the break-up of the Soviet Union in the late 1980's and early 1990's. The latter group had some of the benefits of refugee status. These new waves of Armenian immigrants have had an impact on the culture, religion, and politics of the older Armenian American

Many Armenian Americans follow political developments in Armenia with great interest. This man was one of 1.5 million Armenians who joined in a general strike in Yerevan in 1988. (AP/Wide World Photos)

community. In the future, they may well alter the traditional images and attitudes of the hundred-year-old Armenian American community.

Political and Religious Identity. Many early Armenian immigrants were concerned with the cause of political justice for Armenians who were left behind. Because Turkish violence against Armenians occurred during an era of rising revolutionism that would culminate in the overthrow of the Russian czar, some Marxist and socialist elements could be found in certain Armenian political organizations that emerged in the same period. At one end of the spectrum were members of the Armenian Progressive League of America, which was associated with Communist Party in the early to mid-1900's. Much more representative of moderate Armenian opinion in that heyday of nationalist consciousness were supporters of Ramgavar, the Armenian Democratic Liberal Party.

The early Armenian community in the United States also had to determine how developments affecting their religious status in and around their historical homeland might affect their American communities. A problem was posed in particular for the Armenian Apostolic (or Gregorian) church, whose leader, known as the Catholicos, remained at his seat "in captivity" in Etchmiadzin, Soviet Armenia. Militantly nationalistic Armenian Americans, especially those sympathizing with the Dachnag movement, have tended to refuse to recognize the Catholicos' legitimacy and have founded alternative Armenian churches in their diaspora. These churches honor the Armenian patriarch who presides over the See of Cilicia, which is recognized in Lebanon.

The significance for Armenian Americans of this historical division in the institution of their church is considerable. Of the 115 Armenian churches in the United States by the early 1990's, fifty-three, organized under the Eastern and Western Diocese of the Armenian Church of North America, remained under the jurisdiction of the Holy See of Etchmiadzin. Twenty-eight others, organized under the Eastern and Western Prelacy of the Armenian Apostolic Church of America, followed the Holy See of Cilicia, located in Antelias, Lebanon. The division between the two rival sectors of the Armenian church has created significant political tensions in the Armenian American community since 1933, when Archbishop Tourian, sent by the See of Etchmiadzin to assume spiritual leadership of all Armenians in the United States, was murdered in New York. In addition to these traditional Armenian American church communities, there are twenty-eight Armenian American Protestant communities, most notably in the Los Angeles area.

Organizations and Publications. Armenian group identity in the United States has been fostered by a number of organizations, ranging from religious, social, and charitable associations to groups sponsoring particular political causes or informational publications. There are numerous local social and cultural activities in Armenian American communities. These range from church picnics featuring traditional dishes and folk dance ensembles to memorials to the Armenian GENOCIDE. Various organizations provide wider visibility for Armenian culture through exhibits and festivals. The Armenian Art Society of America located in Montebello, California, for example, sponsors concerts and poetry readings, while the Armenian Film Foundation hosts an annual Armenian film festival and disseminates copies of rare films in Armenian to smaller audiences. At a national level, the American-Armenian Friendship Foundation in Washington, D.C., is active in publicizing special activities held in local Armenian American communities and in interpreting the importance of religious and cultural traditions to the general public.

The Armenian American community has always had a wide choice of media. Among the oldest Armenian publications were newspapers representing clear political causes, such as the *Yeritasard Hayastan* ("Young Armenia"), founded in New York in 1903 to represent the views of the Social Democratic Armenian Party. The even older paper *Hairenik* ("Fatherland"), first published in Boston in 1899 by the Armenian Revolutionary Federation of America, tended to shift from political and ideological analyses to items of general informational interest to Armenians, as did many papers founded in the interwar years. A long tradition of nonpartisan informational journalism followed the model of *Asbarez* ("Arena Stage"), a semiweekly paper published in Los Angeles continuously since 1908.

In contrast to the more popular medium of daily or weekly newspapers, some of which reflect localized concerns, the post-World War II period saw the rise of more specialized nationally distributed monthly or quarterly magazines that covered cultural issues.

Contributions. In general, Armenian Americans have tended to work in small business ventures in suburban areas or in factories in larger cities. According to a 1993 study of Armenian American communities in the greater New York area, for example, nearly half of all adults were college graduates and almost a quarter had attended graduate or professional schools. Occupations in this sample were split between nearly a quarter in traditional professions, another quarter in business, slightly over 14 percent in white collar employment, and 10.6 percent in blue collar employment. There are also geographical pockets where Armenian emigrants took up important agricultural pursuits, such as the raisin industry in Fresno, California.

One field of traditional commercial endeavor among Armenian Americans has remained unique. Not only have the most important importers and retailers of "Oriental" carpets in the United States generally been of Armenian heritage but the introduction of carpet mills in the United States for production of both Oriental and western style carpets has also attracted considerable Armenian capital and artisan skills.

Armenian Americans have made important contributions to American society and culture that have gained them national recognition. A few examples from a long list would range from high-ranking officers in the U.S. Army, such as General Haig Shakerjian, through popular entertainers such as Arlene Francis and accomplished artists such as Paolo Ananian of the Metropolitan Opera. In the field of literature, the novels and plays of William Saroyan (1908-1981) capture the flavor not only of mid-century Armenian American life but also of small town American life in general.

SUGGESTED READINGS. Sources on the Armenian American experience are numerous. The richest body of practical information on Armenian culture in the United States, including a very extensive bibliography, is Hamo B. Vassilian's *Armenian American Almanac* (1985). On cultural identity as expressed in literature, see Margaret Bedrosian's *The Magical Pine Ring:*

Culture and the Imagination in Armenian-American Literature (1991). Numerous books and articles on the early twentieth century Armenian persecutions are listed in a scholarly bibliography, Richard G. Hovannisian's *The Armenian Holocaust* (1980). On Armenian immigration to the United States, see Gary A. Kulhanjian's *The Historical and Sociological Aspects of Armenian Immigration to the United States, 1890-1930* (1975), James H. Tashjian's *The Armenians of the United States and Canada* (1947; repr. 1970), and Anny Bakalian's *Armenian Americans* (1993).—*Byron D. Cannon*

Louis Armstrong treats Parisian firefighters to some American jazz. (AP/Wide World Photos)

Armstrong, [Daniel] Louis "Satchmo" (July 4, 1900, New Orleans, La.—July 6, 1971, Queens, N.Y.): African American jazz trumpet virtuoso, singer, and bandleader. The name "Satchmo" denotes ultimate artistry in American jazz. Armstrong first learned to play the cornet in a New Orleans detention home for "colored waifs." As a young musician, he joined Joseph "King" Oliver's band in Chicago in 1922 and quickly became known for his vocal and horn improvisations. In the 1920's he gained fame in New York, and after 1929 he organized bands of his own, often touring abroad. In the United States, he made numerous recordings and appeared in jazz festivals, Broadway shows, and film roles.

Army Nurse Corps: Nursing division of the U.S. Army. The SPANISH-AMERICAN WAR demonstrated the need for trained nurses, leading to the formation of the first Army Nurse Corps in 1901. Army nurses served during both world wars and the conflicts in KOREA and VIETNAM. African American women were part of the corps, but through the 1950's they were assigned to racially segregated units where they treated only black servicemen. Nurses gained the right to the same rank as male Army officers following World War I, but they did not win fair wages and benefits until World War II. Men began joining the corps in 1955.

Arnaz, Desi (Desiderio Alberto Arnaz y de Acha; Mar. 2, 1917, Santiago, Cuba—Dec. 2, 1986, Del Mar, Calif.): Cuban American bandleader and actor. Arnaz emigrated to Miami, Florida, with his mother in 1933. He began playing music with such figures as Xavier Cugat and, by 1938, led his own band. In 1939 he moved to California, where he married actor Lucille Ball in 1940. Arnaz acted in films, including *Bataan* (1943) and *Cuban Pete* (1946). In 1950, Arnaz and Ball formed Desilu Productions, which pioneered the three-camera film technique that soon became standard in television. Their show, *I Love Lucy*, featuring Arnaz as bandleader Ricky Ricardo and Ball as his zany wife, Lucy, ran from 1951 to 1961 and became a classic of television situation comedy. It was the first television show to feature a multiethnic marriage, portraying the marriage of a Cuban American man, whose heavily accented English often gave way to Spanish, and a Scottish American woman whose real maiden name was MacGillicuddy.

Desi Arnaz receives kisses from I Love Lucy *costars and Emmy recipients Vivian Vance (left) and Lucille Ball.* I Love Lucy *featured television's first multiethnic married couple.* (Hearst Newspaper Collection, University of Southern California Library)

Art and artists: Multicultural and feminist art and art history, which have become such integral components of American art, were spawned by the CIVIL RIGHTS MOVEMENT and the WOMEN'S LIBERATION MOVEMENT of the 1960's. As the United States awoke to the realization that the country would not, as predicated, become a melting pot where all peoples would merge into a single culture, the significance of the artistic expression of women and minorities was underscored.

Con Safos in San Antonio, Texas, and The Royal Chicano Air Force in Sacramento, California, but there was one in almost every major city of the Southwest. Chicano art in Los Angeles was fostered by Sister Karen Boccalero, an artist-nun who returned from Rome in 1972 and started Self-Help Graphics, a workshop with silk screen equipment, in the EAST LOS ANGELES barrio.

The Museum of African Art and the Frederick

The Chicano mural movement that began in the 1970's provided work for many Chicano artists and trained young people in mural techniques. Here a mural enlivens the street scene in a midwestern city. (James L. Shaffer)

History. Females and members of minority groups had been artists for generations in the United States, but they were often excluded from training, recognition, and patronage. The late 1960's and early 1970's saw the blossoming of the arts of women and minorities and efforts to incorporate them into the mainstream art world. Artists of color and women came together with new purpose, MUSEUMS were founded to preserve their contemporary art and past heritage, and exhibitions were mounted to bring recognition to this material. Asian American artists, for example, formed the Kearney Street Workshop in San Francisco, California, in 1968, and the Basement Workshop in New York in 1970. Numerous Chicano artist groups were started; prominent early examples were

Douglass Institute was founded in 1964 in Washington, D.C., for the preservation of African and African American culture. Other centers followed including the Museum of the National Center of Afro-American Arts in Boston, Massachusetts, the Studio Museum in Harlem, New York, and the Ile-Ife Museum of Afro-American Art and Culture in Philadelphia, Pennsylvania. In 1974, Chicano art was exhibited for the first time at a major public museum, the Los Angeles County Museum of Art. The Institute of American Indian Arts was founded in Santa Fe, New Mexico, in 1962, and by the late 1960's the innovative work of Fritz Scholder (Luiseño) and his student T. C. Cannon (Kiowa/Caddo) opened the way for individual and interpretive Indian art.

The feminist art movement, which emerged from the WOMEN'S LIBERATION MOVEMENT, provided physical and psychological space for women artists to interact, exhibit, and perform. The first women's art organization, Women Artists in Revolution, began in New York in 1969, followed by the Ad Hoc Committee of Women Artists in 1970 and Women in the Arts in 1971. Centers in Chicago (Artemisia and Arc Galleries) and Los Angeles (Womanspace and the Los Angeles Woman's Building) were all formed in 1973. In 1971, African American women artists formed their own organization, called Where We At. Meanwhile, feminists staged demonstrations at major museums that rarely, if ever, exhibited women artists, and Judy Chicago made history with her installation *The Dinner Party*, featuring images of great women in history dining together.

developed to promote these new artistic directions. Art historians and critics of all cultural backgrounds began to study, teach, and publish the work of women and artists of color. With the exhibition "The Evolution of the Afro-American Artist: 1800-1950" at the City University of New York in the mid-1960's, African American art shows for the first time moved out of churches and social centers. Paralleling the new examination of artists of color, art historian Linda Nochlin's seminal 1971 article, "Why Are There No Great Women Artists?" prompted scholars to investigate the past and examine the present for art by women.

This new activity was aided by the spirit of the CIVIL RIGHTS ACT OF 1964 and the Equal Employment Opportunity Act of 1972. Under affirmative action, most federal, state, and local organizations, including arts agencies, had to initiate plans to increase

Judy Chicago, shown speaking here in 1979, galvanized the feminist art movement with provocative works such as The Dinner Party. *(AP/Wide World Photos)*

Museum shows and gallery exhibitions focusing on African American art, Japanese culture, the Mexican American experience, and the past and present artistic endeavors of many other peoples proliferated. Journals

the proportions of their female and minority employees until they became equal to the proportions existing in the available labor force. At universities and colleges, people of color and women had to be represented among both faculty and students. National Endowment for the Arts initiated programs such as Expansion Arts and Folk Arts to target diverse communities' artistic efforts, and other art-oriented funding organizations began to seek "minority" art and artists.

By the 1980's MULTICULTURALISM was a major force in the art world, with increasing power and funding in the hands of artists of color. In 1990, the Wight Gallery at the University of California, Los Angeles (UCLA), inaugurated a major traveling exhibition of Chicano art curated for the first time by Chicanos. In 1989, the largest collection of American Indian art and objects in the world, held by the Museum of the American Indian in New York, was transferred to the Smithsonian Institution and refounded as The National Museum of the American Indian on the federal mall. Legislation was also passed for the establishment of a National African American Museum within the Smithsonian. In 1990 the first book devoted to multicultural American art, Lucy R. Lippard's *Mixed Blessings: New Art in a Multicultural America*, was published.

Individuality. Within this milieu, artists of many different cultures and backgrounds have felt freed to observe their own lives, heritages, ideas, joys, and pains, defining their own artistic views and approach, rather than having their positions interpreted by others. Their voices, together and individually, have come to be a vibrant cry. Their views have been clear and vocal, but above all they have been independent and diverse.

There is no one category or categories which provides a window through which to examine all of these artists and their work; there is no one definition or look to multicultural art or feminist art. It should never be assumed that all artists of a similar cultural background or nationality, or all women, have a similar view of their cultural identity or of their place in relation to European Americans or male artists. Artists may be influenced by traditions not their own; Sylvia Lark, for example, a Seneca Indian artist, has drawn on the arts and settings of Asia. Some artists of color have adopted mainstream artistic styles and concerns; they believe that cultural identity has no place in defining their art. There are artists, generally born in the United States, who want to be defined simply as American and have no special attention brought to their ancestry or heritage. Many artists continue the traditional arts and styles of their culture or gender; some women, for example, weave or sculpt with clay in traditional forms. It is the artists who push at the

barriers, however—those making political and social statements—who receive the greatest publicity. Thus, Effie Tybrec (Sioux), who beads tennis shoes, receives more attention than an Indian artist who beads more traditional objects.

Since the civil rights, ethnic pride, and feminist movements of the 1970's and 1980's, many artists have wished to be known as American Indians, African Americans, Asian Americans, Latinos, or women as they increasingly identify with their cultural heritage and a history of oppression. Their art often reacts against a legacy of European Americans' disregard not only of cultural differences but of individuality as well. Since the earliest days of European conquest, there has been a tendency to objectify all people of color, assuming similarities across social class, education, personal taste, degree of assimilation, country of birth, and dozens of other factors. American Indians, for example, have been seen as descendants of one monolithic "primitive" culture rather than acknowledged as individual members of the Cherokee, Sioux, Tlingit, or other nation. The Diegueño/Luiseño artist James Luna took the ultimate step in illustrating this objectification of non-European peoples in 1986 when he put himself on display, with the appropriate labels, as an Indian artifact (*The Artifact Piece*) in San Diego's Museum of Man.

Shared Concerns. Many minority artists share a sense of community resulting in part from a common history. They are aware of the past, and often the present, manipulation of their land, religion, culture, and social position at the hands of the politically and economically dominant culture. The majority of artists of color have strong feelings and stored pain and anger about the treatment of their ancestors, their peers, and themselves, and use their art to express this. Thus, certain themes run through or across the work of a particular group or nation. Indian artists have been particularly sensitive in their work to the destruction of the environment—the lands of their ancestors. Phil Young in *Glen Canyon Desecration 1* (1991) scrapes and defiles his painting and creates a rough surface by the inclusion of sand to re-create the treatment of sacred American Indian sites at the hands of European Americans. When she discovered that the water in her raisin-growing California hometown had been contaminated for more than twenty-five years, Ester Hernandez substituted a skeleton for the cheerful figure on a box of Sun Maid raisins and called her product *Sun Mad* (1981).

African American artists have used various media as a vehicle for interpreting the history of slavery and discrimination. John Outterbridge has created, as a way of remembering, a series of bound slaves (1978-1982), depicted both as elegant in the remains of their native clothes and as mutilated from their torture. In a set of small welded steel pieces which he directly titles *Lynch Fragments* (1988-1989), Melvin Edwards turns the past chains of oppression into objects of strength. Similarly, Chinese American artist Bing Lee makes reference to the 1989 student massacre in Tiananmen Square in China in *Under the Black Flag: China Star 6/4 and Pants on Fire.*

Much multicultural art relies on pointed symbolism and textual elements. Jaune Quick-to-See Smith (Flathead/Shoshone/Cree) addresses past maltreatments of Indians in *Paper Dolls for a Post-Columbian World with Ensembles Contributed by U.S. Government* (1991). Two sets of clothes made for paper dolls are labeled "Special Outfit for Trading Land with the United States Government for Whiskey with Gunpowder in It" and "Matching Smallpox Suits for All Indian Families After U.S. Government Sent Wagon Loads of Smallpox Infected Blankets to Keep Our Families Warm." African American Carrie Mae Weems photographs the personal pain of many in *Mirror, Mirror* (1986-1987), where reflected in the mirror held by an African American woman is an older European American woman. The caption reads: "Looking into the mirror the black woman asked, 'Mirror, mirror on the wall, who's the finest of them all?' The mirror says 'Snow White, you black bitch, and don't you forget it!!!.'" In *The Good Doctor's Bedside* (1983), Lance Belanger (Maliseet) documents the continuing insensitivity of some European Americans; the work shows how a physician had actually sewn the operation scar of an American Indian woman with beads as a reference to traditional native bead work.

Cultural STEREOTYPES have left uncomfortable if not painful marks. Some artists of color feel their art as well as their person is subjected to stereotyping. The Los Angeles artist Gronk (Glugio Gronk Nicandro) noted that if he does a wall painting it is called a mural, rather than a painting or an installation, because he is a Chicano and because murals are deemed a Mexican art form.

David Hammons has reoriented objects found in African American communities that are often

Twentieth century African American artist Jacob Lawrence paints his heritage, as depicted in this painting on black labor. (National Archives)

the material of African American stereotypes, such as fried chicken, liquor bottles, boomboxes, hair, sparerib bones, and grease, into artworks, thereby forcing viewers to look at them in a unique way. Other African

American artists have reactivated the ongoing stereotyped caricature of Mammy, that mythical rotund, content servant from the days of the plantation South, who lives on today in the smiling face of Aunt Jemima. In 1964 Joe Overstreet depicted *The New Aunt Jemima* as a revolutionary with an automatic rifle whose syrup container becomes a grenade. Murray

López challenges expectations for Mexican American women in a self-portrait (*The Guadalupe Triptych: Victoria F. Franco, Our Lady of Guadalupe; Portrait of the Artist as the Virgin of Guadalupe*, 1978), in which she bursts forth from the trappings of an image of the Virgin of Guadalupe. Japanese American artist Ben Sakoguchi in the mid-1980's revived Asian ste-

Navajo artist R. C. Gorman (center) has become one of the most popular and critically acclaimed southwestern artists. One of his paintings hangs behind him. (Elaine S. Querry)

DePillars several years later (*Aunt Jemima Section 22*, 1968) has her blasting from her pancake box, now adorned with clenched fists and African American history lessons. In 1972 Betye Saar presented her work, *The Liberation of Aunt Jemima*, in which Aunt Jemima holds a broom in one hand and a rifle in the other. Similarly, the Chicana artist Yolanda

reotypes such as Fu Manchu and Charlie Chan in a series titled *Bananas*. The name is intentionally ironic as Asians who too energetically model themselves after whites are referred to as "bananas," ("yellow on the outside, white on the inside"). There is sometimes considerable wry humor in artists' confrontation of stereotypes, as when the Mohawk artist Shelley Niro in a hand-tinted photograph draws on conventional images of the Beautiful Indian Princess and the Matronly Squaw as she poses her mother coquettishly as *The Rebel* (1987) on the trunk of the family car.

In a significant turnabout, some artists of color have produced stereotypes of European Americans, with the tourist emerging as a primary topic. Decades before the Civil Rights or Indian rights movement, American Indian artist Woodrow Cumbo depicted in *Land of Enchantment* (1946) three white tourists staring at a Navajo mother and daughter selling blankets and pottery. The huge, overbearing wife, too large for her clothes, gawks through her lorgnette while the wispy husband, with camera and briefcase, and son stare through large round glasses. Harry Fonseca (Maidu/ Portuguese/Hawaiian), pictured the Indian culture hero, Coyote, at Taos Pueblo in 1979 in *Snapshot, or, Wish You Were Here Coyote*, clad in the tourist regalia of Hawaiian shirt, sandals, and camera.

Because of cultural and linguistic differences as well as discrimination, artists of color often share feelings of living simultaneously in two worlds. Some Indians live literally in two distinct places as they commute between their "American" home and their ancestral tribal home. These feelings of duality often emerge in self-portraits. Joe Feddersen, a Colville/ Okanogan Indian, often halves his face—each half in a distinct world, different yet the same. Linda Nishio, a Japanese American, feels so fractured by dual cultures that in one work, *Kikoemasu Ka* (*Can You Hear Me*) (1980), she cries out her history in an attempt to be heard and appears to be pressing against a pane of glass as she tries to be seen.

Other artists address the disparities between cultures. Japanese American Masami Teraoka has gained attention by putting contemporary American objects such as fast-food hamburgers and snorkels into the realm of elegant figures from nineteenth-century Japanese prints—humorous but telling comments on both cultures. In *New Views of Mount Fuji: La Brea Tar Pits* (1980's), ancient animals in the Los Angeles area loll in the tar, now below Mount Fuji, as Teraoka plays off of the Japanese artist Hokusai's *Thirty-six Views of Fuji* (1823-1829).

Cultural Strength. As a counterthrust to feelings of alienation in the United States, many artists have looked to the art and culture of their past and present—whether in America or elsewhere—as a source of ideas, spirituality, and strength. The energy of the

BARRIOS or GHETTOS may become the basis for powerful art, as when wall GRAFFITI provided the foundation for much of the California Chicano mural tradition. Judy Baca, a Chicana artist, has drawn on the Mexican mural tradition to present a history for those written out of history: *The Great Wall of Los Angeles* covers half a mile of flood channel in Los Angeles with scenes from various ethnic histories. Faith Ringgold weaves stories of the present into quilts, linking generations, as both her mother and great-grandmother, a domestic slave, were African American quilters. Kazuko, who was raised in Japan, draws inspiration for her installations from the art of Japanese braided or woven string. Puerto Rican Jorgé Rodriguez in *Orisha/Santos* (1985) draws on both Puerto Rican *santos* (wooden figures of saints) and the ancient gods of the Yoruba of Nigeria. Though some multicultural artists show strong influences from the FOLK ART of their culture, their contemporary works reach a different audience through the world of galleries and MUSEUMS.

Multicultural art is an ever-expanding canvas playing to an equally pluralistic audience. Cultural community as a creative force continues to explore, unleash, and create the world anew.

SUGGESTED READINGS. Lucy R. Lippard's *Mixed Blessings: New Art in a Multicultural America* (1990) is an excellent general source. The fall, 1992, issue of *Art Journal* (vol. 51) is dedicated to contemporary American Indian art. On Chicano art, see the monumental catalog *Chicano Art: Resistance and Affirmation, 1965-1985* (1991), edited by Richard Griswold del Castillo et al., from the Wight Art Gallery at the University of California, Los Angeles. David C. Driskell's *Two Centuries of Black American Art* (1976) and Elsa Honig Fine's *The Afro-American Artist: A Search for Identity* (1982) are useful sources. On Asian American art, see *A Place in Art/History: Six Contemporary Asian American Artists* (1988) by Fay Chiang and Margo Machida. A thorough history of the feminist art movement is detailed in "The Feminist Critique of Art History" by Thalia Gouma-Peterson and Patricia Mathews in *Art Bulletin* 69 (Sept., 1987), pp. 326-357.

Arts and crafts—American Indian: To speak of the aesthetic achievements of more than two thousand cultural groups, whose languages lack a word for the European concept of "art," is fraught with unique difficulties. Not the least of these is attempting to make a meaningful distinction between the categories of "art" and "craft." Many people still believe that the arts of Indians were and are "primitive," belittling the aesthetic and philosophic complexities of these art forms. To call these objects mere "artifacts" is to succumb to two pervasive reactions: condescending curiosity or fear of potential danger in the unfamiliar. Even when true status as "art" has been granted by the dominant culture, the term has frequently been modified with either "ornamental" or "decorative."

The intricate beadwork in this dancer's tail feathers characterizes "tribal art"—art created by and for members of a particular group. (Elaine S. Querry)

Indian arts can be usefully classified according to four categories: tribal art, created by and for members of a particular group; ethnic art, created by Indians for another ethnic group, usually motivated by the need for income and showing a mixture of native traditions and foreign expectations (such as the art found in commercial "Indian shows"); Pan-Indian art, unbound by traditional values, customs, and media, cre-

ated by artists who consider themselves as artists in a mainstream art market (such as the artworks found at powwows); and mainstream contemporary art, the production of artists whose Indianness may very well be incidental to their works (such as artwork found in galleries and MUSEUMS).

Meaning and Function. First to be understood is the essential principle that Indian art forms, materials, and subjects are culturally coded, expressing complex signals within a particular tribal group, usually with distinct spiritual meanings. The more familiar concept of "beauty" denotes pleasure for the senses, whereas in virtually all traditional Indian cultures the term would connote balance, harmony, and the proper order of things, as well as unity between the individual and society, the natural and supernatural, and the physical and metaphysical. A work of art is one that is fully integrated into society and environment, functional, with both social and religious purposes. Key to this view is the idea that all of creation is infused with spirit without distinction or hierarchy; a human has neither more nor less spirituality than an animal, a plant, or a rock. Art that reflects such a worldview is profoundly ecological in both its origins and philosophic assumptions. While a particular work can certainly be beautiful and give pleasure, such effects are secondary to its reason for being. Indeed, the act of creation is frequently more important than the object itself, as in the case of NAVAJO sand paintings, which are part of elaborate healing (or "balancing") ceremonies and whose component materials must be returned to the earth from which they came in order to effect the requisite "cure." Similarly, many works of Indian art created for ceremonies and burial rituals are intended for purposeful destruction and decay.

Traditional Arts. In the traditional visual arts, several motifs and concepts prevail, uniting the diversity of Indian cultures. SHAMANIC qualities and animal imagery related to the personal quest for spiritual vision, guidance, and direction are found in many precontact—and some modern—art forms. Directionality and numerology are also common elements, as in the number four signifying the cardinal directions, the races of humanity, or essential virtues and six representing the zenith and nadir (or Mother Earth and Father Sky), sometimes with a final central point representing both self and tribe or unified parts of a tribe.

Traditional Indian arts functioned (then as now) in five basic ways: as a system of public communication and communion; as a means of sharing symbols and their culturally specific meanings; as a way of confirming and reinforcing systems and values; as a means of adding to the visible dimension of beauty and spirit (all creation having both external and internal entity); and as a way to affirm the animate nature and bonds of reciprocity among peoples, their works, and their environments.

edged and respected within the culture, even if their names have failed to be recorded. Though they seldom functioned within the tribal group as "professional" artists, their contribution was seen as only one of the many that each member added to the well-being of the tribe or nation.

Uninformed observers have assumed a static notion

The wares these American Indians are displaying are examples of "ethnic art"—art created for another ethnic group, usually motivated by the need for income and showing a mixture of native traditions and foreign expectations. (Jay Foreman, Unicorn Stock Photos)

Non-Indians have often made unfair distinctions between technical mastery (for an "artifact" or "craft") and aesthetic quality (for "a work of art"). The latter is dependent on values and standards set by the group in a particular time and place. Good design and execution, in whatever medium—painting, sculpture, pottery, weaving, leatherwork, beading, quillwork, jewelry, and the like—are the rules, not the exceptions. The apparent anonymity of the artist is a false notion fostered by several factors, including cultural ignorance and chauvinism as well as the vicissitudes of history. Masters of a medium were always acknowl-

of "tradition" and its immutability, yet Indian cultures have always been dynamic, embracing evolution and change in many arenas. Also neglected are the effects on Indians of various cultural contacts and the profoundly holistic nature of native arts. For example, as a result of trade with European settlers and the availability of beads, quillwork painstakingly made with porcupine quills was largely replaced by intricate beadwork to ornament Indian clothing among some tribes. Perhaps no factor is more significant than the history of collection and preservation of Indian art.

Collection and Preservation. Native arts were often

preserved for being typical rather than extraordinary, as in the systematic efforts of Captain James Cook's third voyage to the South Pacific in 1776-1778. Early collections were formed from what outsiders selected as war trophies, personal souvenirs, or ethnographic relics. Still, as early as 1520, European artist Albrecht Dürer expressed immoderate joy in viewing what "treasures" Cortés and his followers had brought back to Europe from the "New" World. Another early reaction was provoked by the "curiosities" (including people) that Christopher Columbus presented to the Spanish court. For the most part, Indian arts were viewed and treated for centuries as curios of strange and unknowable heathens.

Recognition of the aesthetic dimension of Indian art works came only recently, flourishing between 1900 and 1930. This was linked to the early preservationist movements of the twentieth century and a relaxation of the federal policy of assimilation for native peoples. Increased tourism gave rise to a new curio industry at the same time that the Navajo woven blanket was being recognized for its inherent artistry. Ironically, this period gave rise to the glorification of several master artists, such as Maria Martinez at San Ildefonso Pueblo in New Mexico. She resurrected and redirected the traditional pottery of her people, eventually commanding high prices and thus legitimacy for her work and her entire medium of expression, which was then largely divorced from its traditional cultural context. This, in turn, gave rise to difficult questions about the secularization of the sacred, commercial merchandising, and the very nature of "Indianness" in art, which continue to be debated.

In 1932, the U.S. government funded the first Indian art school, The Studio in Santa Fe, New Mexico, which eventually evolved into the Institute of American Indian Arts in 1962. In 1925, the Denver Art Museum was the first to exhibit former Indian "curiosities" as fine arts. A 1931 exhibition curated by John Sloan and Oliver LaFarge (fresh from his Pulitzer Prize in 1929 for *Laughing Boy*) in New York gave impetus for this new appraisal.

After World War II, national attitudes again favored ASSIMILATION. Only devotees of the INDIAN HOBBYIST MOVEMENT maintained any serious interest in native arts; their attempts to emulate Indian ways of life also added much technical knowledge about the means and methods of artistic creation. By the mid-1960's, however, with that period's emphasis on cultural diversity, Indian arts again began their ascendance from deni-

gration to their rightful position, in which they are now secure. Federal legislation in 1991, the Indian Arts and Crafts Sales Act, has helped to protect legitimate Indian artists and artisans who work in traditional forms. Tribal councils since the 1980's have asserted their rights to the return of art works and "artifacts" that were appropriated by museums. The works of contemporary Indian artists are among the most sought-after in international art collection and acquisition. Fritz Scholder, Harry Fonseca, R. C. Gorman, Frank LaPeña, and Richard Glazer Danay, among countless others, are in the forefront of contemporary American art.

SUGGESTED READINGS. Many serious studies of American Indian arts and crafts are available, a good beginning point being Peter T. Furst and Jill L. Furst's *North American Indian Art* (1982) and Christian F. Feest's *Native Arts of North America* (1980). More complete considerations can be found in the University of California at Los Angeles (UCLA) American Indian Studies Center's *Sharing a Heritage: American Indian Arts* (2d ed., 1991) and *The Arts of the North American Indian: Native Traditions in Evolution* (1986), edited by Edwin L. Wade. Essential for an understanding of contemporary accomplishments is Jerry Jacka and Lois Essary Jacka's *Beyond Tradition: Contemporary Indian Art and Its Evolution* (1988).—*Rodney Simard*

Ashe, Arthur R., Jr. (July 10, 1943, Richmond, Va—Feb. 6, 1993, New York, N.Y.): African American tennis professional. Ashe was the first black athlete to gain prominence in tennis. Mentored by Dr. R. W. Johnson, a black physician, Ashe was nationally ranked in high school and went to UCLA on a tennis scholarship. He went on to win the U.S. Amateur and U.S. Open Championships and to defeat such world greats as Pancho GONZALES, Jimmy Connors, and Bjorn Borg. He was the first black to play on a Davis cup team, and he helped crack open sports in apartheid-bound South Africa. Also a sports commentator and author, Ashe retired in 1980. The same year, he was infected with the human immunodeficiency virus (HIV) during treatment for heart disease, a condition he made public in 1992.

Ashkenazic Jews: Jews of central and eastern European origin. The Hebrew word *Ashkenaz* designates the first relatively compact geographical area of settlement of Jews in northwestern Europe, initially on the banks of the Rhine. The term became identified with, and denotes in its narrower sense, Germany and German Jewry. In a broader sense it denotes the Ashkenazic Jewish cultural complex, comprising its ideas and views, lifestyle, and mores, legal issues, and sociocommunal institutions. The Ashkenazic cultural legacy, emanating from northern France and Germany, later extended into eastern Europe and came to embrace modern Jewish settlements all over the world, in clear contradistinction to the traditions of SEPHARDIC JEWS.

Although the Sephardim constituted the majority of American Jews until 1720, after that year GERMAN JEWS and eventually eastern European Ashkenazim predominated through massive immigration waves. In 1826 there were only six thousand Jews in the United States, the majority Ashkenazim; by 1880, on the eve of the great wave of eastern European Jewish immigration, there were as many as 280,000 Jews, the majority, once again, being central European Ashkenazim from Bohemia, Bavaria, Hungary, and Posen.

Between 1880 and the 1930's, the number of Ashkenazim in the United States rose about eighteenfold, from 250,000 to approximately 4,500,000. Vast numbers of Ashkenazim moved during this period from eastern Europe into the world's fastest-growing economy and were automatically emancipated from the legal discrimination to which they had been accustomed in the Russian Empire.

Besides the anti-Jewish pogroms of 1880-1883 and 1903-1907, the expulsion from Moscow in 1890, and Russia's years of war and revolution, there were other stimulants and incentives for the eastern European Ashkenazic immigration. Perhaps the most significant cause was the dramatic demographic growth of eastern European Jewry in Romania, the Russian Empire, and Austrian Poland from 1,500,000 in 1800 to 6,800,000 in 1900. This phenomenon generated nearly insoluble questions of sheer physical survival.

Despite the renewed Sephardic immigration of the post-1900 period, as well as later immigration movements of Sephardic Jews and Jews from the former

An Ashkenazic rabbi discusses the Torah with Jewish schoolchildren. (James L. Shaffer)

Ottoman Empire, Iran, and Israel, the majority of American Jews are of Ashkenazic background. Their numbers in 1992 ranged between estimates of 4,700,000 and 5,900,000. As a result of large-scale immigration from the former Soviet Union, the United States absorbed 84,564 more Ashkenazic Jews between 1977 and 1983. After the fall of communism in parts of eastern Europe in December, 1989, tens of thousands more Ashkenazic Jews settled in the United States.

The major American Ashkenazic communities include New York City, Los Angeles, Chicago, Philadelphia, San Francisco, Boston, Baltimore, Atlanta, Milwaukee, Cleveland, and Detroit. They are divided into congregations of the ORTHODOX, CONSERVATIVE, REFORM, and RECONSTRUCTIONIST movements of Judaism. Many Ashkenazim in the contemporary United States are secular and unaffiliated with a synagogue or any of the denominational movements.

SUGGESTED READINGS. For comprehensive accounts on the Ashkenazim in the U.S., see Arthur Hertzberg's *The Jews in America: Four Centuries of an Uneasy Encounter* (1989) and *Being Jewish in America: The Modern Experience* (1979), and Jonathan S. Woocher's *Sacred Survival: The Civil Religion of American Jews* (1986). These studies cover the status of Ashkenazic Jews in American society at large and within the Jewish community.

Asia-Pacific Triangle: Component of revised U.S. immigration policy in the immediate post-World War II period, providing for small numbers of Asians to immigrate to the United States after a long period of exclusion. Initially proposed in 1948 by Congressman Walter Judd, who had led the successful fight to repeal exclusion of Chinese immigration in 1943, the Asia-Pacific Triangle encompassed most of South and East Asia. Nations within this region were eligible for annual QUOTAS of at least one hundred immigrants to the United States. The Asia-Pacific Triangle was eventually passed by Congress in 1952 as part of the IMMIGRATION AND NATIONALITY ACT OF 1952 (McCarran-Walter Act), remaining in force until the national origins system was abolished by the IMMIGRATION AND NATIONALITY ACT OF 1965.

Asian American population—diversity within: Asian Americans are those individuals residing in the United States whose ancestors, or who themselves, were born in Asian countries. Asian Americans have been in the United States for more than 150 years. Their American experience can

roughly be divided into two distinct parts: old Asian immigration, from the mid-eighteenth century to the early 1960's, and contemporary Asian immigration, since 1965. Most of the early Asian immigrants came as laborers to work in Hawaii's plantations and to help develop the American West. Asian immigration to the United States steadily declined, however, from the late 1800's to the early 1960's as a result of a series of Asian exclusion laws.

The Asian American population has been fast-growing and increasingly visible since the 1960's because of the liberalized IMMIGRATION AND NATIONALITY ACT OF 1965 and the U.S. withdrawal from Indochina in the mid-1970's. By census count, the Asian American population increased by 687 percent in thirty years: from 877,934 in 1960 to 6,908,638 in 1990, representing nearly 3 percent of the total U.S population. Asian Americans in 1990 comprised, in order of size, 1,645,472 CHINESE, 1,406,770 FILIPINOS, 847,562 JAPANESE, 815,447 ASIAN INDIANS, 798,849 KOREANS, 614,547 VIETNAMESE, 149,014 LAOTIANS, 147,411 CAMBODIANS, 91,275 THAIS, 90,082 HMONG, and 302,209 persons from other parts of Asia not specified by the 1990 U.S. Census. That census also reported a total of 365,024 persons under the PACIFIC ISLANDER label. This group includes 296,145 Polynesians (native Hawaiians, Samoans, and Tongans), 63,348 Micronesians (mostly Guamanians), and 5,531 Melanesians. The Pacific Islanders, however, are not generally considered Asian Americans.

The term "Asian American" is essentially one of convenience for administrative agencies and scholarly researchers rather than a term based on the real experiences of the group so labeled. The variety of the ethnically distinct subgroups far exceeds the similarities they share. Asian Americans as a group encompass not only differences in national origins, history of immigration, socioeconomic status, and cultural traits but also variations in patterns of settlement, length of residence in the United States, and degree of ASSIMILATION into mainstream U.S. culture.

Chinese. The Chinese were the first Asian group to enter the United States in significant numbers. Early Chinese immigrants were predominantly from the rural southern part of Guangdong Province and were mostly sojourners seeking to make money and return home. They were initially contracted to work in mines in California in the 1850's and later turned to work on the CENTRAL PACIFIC RAILROAD between Sacramento, California, and Promontory Point, Utah, in the

The Chinese were the first Asian group to enter the United States in significant numbers; they concentrated in Chinatowns, like this one in San Francisco around 1900. (Library of Congress)

1860's. When the railroad was completed, the Chinese laborers branched out into a variety of economic activities in the West, working in construction, agriculture, and light manufacturing. They worked in woolen and knitting mills and in small-scale manufacturing of books, shoes, and cigars.

The visible presence of cheap Chinese labor in California was perceived as a threat to the white working class during the 1860's and 1870's. Violent anti-Chinese movements at that time resulted in the CHINESE EXCLUSION ACT of 1882, one of the few federal laws to exclude a whole group of people based merely on national origin. This act subsequently led to a series of exclusionary and discriminatory immigration laws regarding Asians, such as the GENTLEMAN'S AGREEMENT of 1907; the IMMIGRATION ACT OF 1917, which designated an Asiatic barred zone to exclude immigration from countries in the Asian-Pacific Triangle; and finally the National Origins Act of 1924, which assigned limited quotas to non-European immigrants.

As a result, Chinese immigration to the United States dropped from 123,203 in the 1870's to 4,928 in the 1930's. Those already in the United States retreated to CHINATOWNS to continue to pursue their sojourning dreams.

After 1965, the Chinese American population increased rapidly—from 435,062 in 1970 to 1,645,472, in 1990, a rise of 278 percent. Unlike the earlier Chinese immigrants, who were poor laborers, the Chinese Americans in the 1980's were socioeconomically heterogeneous. The 1980 U.S. Census reported that 63 percent of Chinese Americans were foreign-born, 19 percent spoke only English at home, 31 percent had completed four years or more of college education, and 33 percent were in managerial and professional occupations. Chinese Americans shared a median household income of $19,561, which was higher than that of "non-Hispanic whites."

While many Chinese, particularly newer immigrants, were still concentrated in Chinatowns in major

U.S. cities in the West and Northeast, by 1990 a sizable number had spread out into the suburbs and other parts of the country. In 1990, 43 percent of the total Chinese American population resided in California, and another 17 percent lived in New York. There were also sizable communities in Hawaii, New Jersey, Texas, Illinois, and Massachusetts.

Japanese. Japanese Americans constitute another of the oldest Asian subgroups in the United States. They first arrived as contract laborers to work on sugar plantations in Hawaii in the late 1880's; others came to work as agricultural workers in California. Like their Chinese counterparts, Japanese Americans were discriminated against by law and by sheer RACISM. For example, Japanese were restricted to free immigration to the United States by the GENTLEMAN'S AGREEMENT negotiated between the respective governments in

riod of exclusion, Japanese Americans established strong communities to shield themselves from ethnic hostility.

Japanese Americans tend to be the most ASSIMILATED of the Asian Americans. They have produced a sizable second and third generation, most of whom resemble the white population in socioeconomic status. In the 1980 U.S. census, 28 percent of Japanese Americans were foreign-born, 56 percent spoke only English at home, 23 percent had completed four years or more of college education, and 28 percent were in managerial and professional occupations. They had a median household income of $22,517. In 1990, the vast majority of Japanese Americans were concentrated in California (37 percent) and Hawaii (29 percent), comprising more than one-fifth of the total Hawaiian population.

In May, 1942, the Mochida family, like other Americans of Japanese ancestry, prepared for evacuation by the War Relocation Authority; they are wearing identification tags to avoid separation. (National Archives)

1907. The most outright display of racism was the INTERNMENT of Japanese Americans during World War II, which cost more than 110,000 Japanese Americans their homes, jobs, and freedom. During the pe-

Filipinos. Filipino immigration to the United States dates back to 1903, shortly after the United States took control of the Philippines in 1899. Before the U.S. conquest, Filipinos in the United States included a small group of colonial government-sponsored students and a group of seamen who deserted their Spanish ships. The real wave of Filipino immigration did not occur until the early 1900's, when cheap labor was needed on Hawaiian sugar plantations. From 1906 to the early 1930's, more than 112,000 Filipinos were contracted out by the Hawaiian Sugar Planters Association. During the 1930's, Filipinos made up 75 percent of all plantation workers in Hawaii. One-third of Filipino plantation laborers returned home after completion of their contracts, while the rest stayed or moved to California.

Early Filipino immigrants were mostly agricultural workers. During the winter, they came to cities to take odds jobs that nobody else wanted such as domestic service, gardening, and dish-washing. During the summer, they returned to the countryside to work in the fields. Unlike the Chinese and Japanese, Filipinos did not develop strong ethnic communities because of their highly mobile and seasonal employment patterns.

Filipino American children fish for candy from a ruptured piñata. (Ronald R. Smith)

Filipinos were also unique in having the greatest familiarity with American culture of all Asian immigrants as a result of former colonial relationships.

Filipino immigrants arriving after 1965 included a significant number of well-educated professionals and highly skilled workers, such as doctors, engineers, teachers, and nurses. According to the 1980 census, 65 percent of Filipino Americans were foreign-born, 33 percent spoke only English at home, 20 percent had completed four years or more of college education, and 25 percent were in managerial and professional occupations. They had a median household income of $21,926. In 1990, about 25 percent of Filipino Americans were concentrated in California and 12 percent in Hawaii. They were also highly visible in New York, New Jersey, Illinois, and Washington.

Koreans. Koreans are another Asian subgroup who arrived in the United States in significant numbers only after 1965. The Korean American population increased from 69,130 in 1970 to 798,849 in 1990 through immigration. Like the earlier Japanese and Filipino immigrants, Koreans first came to Hawaii to work in sugar plantations around 1902. In 1905, the Korean government stopped emigration because of complaints of ill treatment of its nationals in the United States. Unlike other early Asian immigrants, the Koreans who stayed in Hawaii and moved to the mainland were mostly Christians. They organized churches as a way to preserve their own culture and language, and they took an active part in politics of their country of origin. Their churches later became the backbone of Koreatowns, which function not only as residential enclaves but also as cultural and business centers.

Korean immigrants who came after 1965 were almost uniformly from urban Korea and had a Protestant, middle-class background. Upon arrival, many engaged in small business ventures, such as the grocery trade and wig manufacturing. Many Korean entrepreneurs started their business within three years of arrival in the United States, with little prior business experience in Korea. They did so to avoid being trapped at the bottom of the American economic structure. The Korean American ethnic economy has tended to be strong in the inner city, aggravating Korean American–African American relations.

Korean Americans are known for their tenacity, strict adherence to the work ethic, commitment to educational achievement, and entrepreneurial spirit. According to the 1980 U.S. Census, 82 percent of Korean Americans were foreign-born, 20 percent spoke only English at home, 39 percent were U.S. citizens, 27 percent had completed four years or more of college education, and 25 percent were in managerial and professional occupations. They had a median household income of $18,145. In 1990, about 33 percent of Korean Americans were located in California; 12 percent lived in New York. Others were found concentrated in Illinois, New Jersey, Texas, Maryland, and Virginia.

Asian Indians. Like the Koreans, Asian Indian Americans are a relatively recent immigrant group. Long before arriving in the United States, Asian Indians had emigrated to the West Indies as indentured laborers in the nineteenth century, to East Africa as traders and entrepreneurs at the beginning of the twentieth century, and more recently to Great Britain as factory and transport workers.

Most Asian Indian immigrants came to the United States as professionals or skilled workers. In the 1980 U.S. Census, 70 percent of them were foreign-born, 31 percent spoke only English at home, 46 percent had completed four years or more of college education, and 49 percent were in managerial and professional occupations. They had a median household income of $20,598. In 1990, about 23 percent of the Asian Indian Americans were concentrated in New York and 20 percent in California. Others were found concentrated in New Jersey, Florida, Illinois, and Texas.

Southeast Asians. Unlike other Asian immigrants, most Indochinese arrived in the United States as REFUGEES after the VIETNAM WAR. According to U.S. immigration records, 150,266 Vietnamese were admitted into the United States as refugees between 1971 and 1980, and 324,453 came between 1981 and 1990; 7,739 CAMBODIANS were admitted between 1971 and 1980 and 114,064 between 1981 and 1990; and 21,690 LAOTIANS were admitted between 1971 and 1980 and 142,964 between 1981 and 1990. The United States admitted 1,241 THAIS as refugees between 1971 and 1980 and 30,259 between 1981 and 1990. Included in these numbers are many HMONG people, the Hmong are an ethnic minority primarily from Laos.

The official label of refugee conceals differences not only between national groups but also within each of them. The first-wave Vietnamese departees, for example, had little difficulty in validating their claim of political persecution. They were also distinguishable from the later arrivals known as the "BOAT PEOPLE" in that they were from more affluent and better-

Most Asian Indians came to the United States after 1965 and a majority were professionals or skilled workers, like this pathologist. (Ben Klaffke)

educated middle-class backgrounds. The later waves of refugees, on the other hand, were mostly from disadvantaged socioeconomic backgrounds. Poverty rates among refugees from Southeast Asia have been particularly high. In 1980, one-third of all Vietnamese, half of Laotians, and two-thirds of Cambodians living in the United States were poor. Almost all Indochinese refugees began their American lives on welfare or

ethnic communities. After a decade since arrival, however, many Southeast Asian Americans experienced a significant trend toward secondary migration, directing them to traditional Asian-concentrated locations. In the 1990 census, 46 percent of all Vietnamese, 46 percent of Cambodians, 39 percent of Laotians, 35 percent of Thais, and 52 percent of Hmong people were concentrated in California.

An influx of Southeast Asian refugees sought asylum in the United States during the 1970's. This Cambodian monk accepts offerings in Oakland, Calif. (Eric Crystal)

some form of government assistance. Some have been able to rise from poverty within a relatively short period of time with the help of strong families, ethnic networks, and hard work.

The settlement and adaptation patterns of Southeast Asian Americans are different from those of other Asian Americans. The refugees were forced out of their homeland because of the threat of political persecution. They left hastily, without adequate preparation or much control over their final destination. Their place of resettlement was decided by U.S. government authorities and private agencies rather than by existing

Asian Americans have become an important part of American society. Within a relatively short time, Asian Americans, nearly two-thirds of whom were foreign-born and more than a quarter of whom immigrated after 1975, have exhibited remarkable socioeconomic achievement. Except for the Indochinese refugees, CHINESE, JAPANESE, FILIPINO, ASIAN INDIAN, and KOREAN AMERICANS have achieved levels of educational attainment and median household income higher than the national average levels for non-Hispanic whites in the 1980 census. It is important, however, to abandon attempts to consider these groups as a uniform entity and instead to seek to understand their distinct nationalities, cultures, and ethnic identities.

SUGGESTED READINGS. For a more detailed account of Asian Americans, see Ronald Takaki's *Strangers from a Different Shore: A History of Asian Americans* (1989), Roger Daniels' *Asian America: Chinese and Japanese in the United States since 1850* (1988), Nathan Caplan, John K. Whitmore, and Marcella H. Choy's *The Boat People and Achievement in America: A Study of Family Life, Hard Work, and Cultural Values* (1989), and Joan M. Jensen's *Passage from India: Asian Indian Immigrants in North America* (1988).— Min Zhou

Asian American studies programs: Academic departments, units, or organizations devoted to the scholarly investigation of the history and culture of people of Asian ancestry living in the United States. Asian American studies programs are usually located on college and university campuses. In some cases, college students may major in Asian American studies; in others, they may obtain an Asian American studies emphasis while pursuing a degree within another department. Asian American studies programs are sometimes administered within a larger ETHNIC STUDIES center or department. Individual faculty members are most often specialists in other academic disciplines, such as sociology, history, anthropology, or social work.

Asian American studies programs should not be confused with general Asian studies programs or other area-studies academic units. The latter programs traditionally focus on the study of the history, politics,

The discipline of Asian American studies grew directly out of the unrest caused by the Vietnam War, the women's liberation movement, and the Civil Rights movement of the late 1960's. (James L. Shaffer)

and cultures of contemporary Asian peoples living in Asia. Besides having a much longer history in American academics, Asian studies programs are generally larger, better funded, and more visible than the newer and smaller Asian American studies programs.

History. The discipline of Asian American studies grew directly out of the unrest caused by the VIETNAM WAR, the WOMEN'S LIBERATION MOVEMENT, and the CIVIL RIGHTS MOVEMENT in the late 1960's. On many college campuses, minority students marched and picketed, occupied administrative buildings, and demanded greater social relevance in the university curriculum. Traditional American institutions and mainstream values—that is, belief systems that were perceived to be exclusively white, male, and upper-class—were increasingly challenged by young women, African Americans, Latinos, and Asian Americans. The war in Vietnam and the rest of Indochina made Asian Americans especially sensitive to issues of power, dominance, and cultural imperialism. The war also had significant racial and CLASS overtones for many American people of color.

The Third World Strike in 1968 at San Francisco State University and the University of California at Berkeley instigated the first courses on Asian American studies in the United States. As with most ethnic studies programs, the early period was difficult, and funding and institutional support were often only reluctantly given. There was also some administrative resistance from those who were unclear about the goals of an Asian American studies program, and some faculty members were uncertain if a rigorous academic department would ever develop. Still, by the early 1970's there were scores of Asian American studies courses and programs across the country. Usually these early courses were taught by graduate students, existing faculty members, or local Asian American community leaders.

Programs and enrollments gradually increased throughout the 1970's and 1980's and then leveled off. In the early 1990's there were twenty-one Asian American studies programs in the United States, including thirteen in California. Programs in California include four departments in the University of California system (Los Angeles, Berkeley, Davis, and Santa Barbara); four in the California State University system (Fresno, Sacramento, Long Beach, and Dominguez Hills); the San Francisco State, San Jose State, and San Diego State universities; and the University of Santa Clara and East Los Angeles College. Other Asian American studies programs are found in New York (Cornell University, Queens College, and City College of New York), Ohio (Oberlin College), Hawaii (University of Hawaii, Honolulu), and Washington (Washington State University at Pullman and University of Washington, Seattle). In addition, there is active interest in Asian American studies at Hunter College in New York City, the University of Massachusetts in Boston, New York University, and the University of Pennsylvania in Philadelphia.

San Francisco State and the University of California at Berkeley have the largest programs, with more than two dozen courses usually offered each year. UCLA's program, while slightly smaller, is extremely active in research and public service, and publishes several journals and papers. UCLA offers an M.A. in Asian American studies, and Berkeley offers a Ph.D. in ethnic studies. Most programs, however, are substantially less ambitious. The average program or department has a director, a few staff members, and several instructors or professors. Only a few schools have full-time faculty positions exclusively dedicated to Asian American studies. Small as they may be, however, these Asian American studies programs have become institutionalized at their universities and colleges and are now vital parts of the general education curriculum.

Goals and Agendas. Asian American studies programs pursue a variety of goals. Each program is different in size, community, and philosophy, so it is difficult to generalize about them; however, the following are probably important missions of most Asian American studies programs.

Despite their concern with contemporary social problems, most Asian American studies programs retain an interest in traditional scholarship and research on Asian American history and culture. There is also an attempt to expand the methodological and theoretical basis of this work. As one scholar said, there is more to Asian American studies than Chinese railroads and Japanese concentration camps. Asian Americans are becoming increasingly involved in music and the visual arts, and there is now a very large body of literature by and about Asian Americans. Thus, Asian American studies may be seen as part of the humanities as much as a social science.

Asian American studies programs have generally tried to educate the general public about Asian American affairs and concerns through curriculum development and other efforts. Courses and materials on Asian

American culture are designed to integrate the Asian American experience into the greater pageant of American history. Asian American studies courses, for example, tell how Asians (as much as immigrants from Africa and Europe) helped build the United States. Many such classes have become a critical part of the college general education courses.

For many Asian Americans, however, the American dream remains elusive. For recent newcomers such as Southeast Asian REFUGEES, there are financial, linguistic, and cultural barriers that are extremely difficult to overcome; often, they must rely on public assistance for a long time and cannot easily take advantage of educational opportunities.

Asian American studies programs are often the center of academic, cultural, and social life for many Asian American students. (James L. Shaffer)

Another important goal of most Asian American studies programs is the elimination of Asian racial stereotypes such as the "MODEL MINORITY" and "Madam Butterfly" myths. Many Asian Americans believe that they are shut out from mainstream society and are increasingly being denied benefits accorded to most other Americans. On one hand, they are depicted as the "model minority": hard workers and good students who hold strong family values. On the other hand, they are often discriminated against because they are thought to be "curve breakers," overachievers, and social misfits. Ironically, it is their very success that causes them to be envied by others.

ASIAN AMERICAN WOMEN commonly complain of another pervasive stereotype in which women of Asian ancestry are seen as exotic, rare, Oriental beauties: charming yet mysterious; subservient yet erotic. The "Madam Butterfly" stereotype, essentially a product of the Western male imagination, impedes interaction by objectifying Asian American women.

In the 1980's and 1990's there was continuing debate concerning Asian American ADMISSIONS policies among several of the most selective universities in the United States. Some people, including members of Congress and the Department of Education, have claimed that certain elite schools—such as the University of California at Berkeley and Harvard University—have tried to restrict their admissions of Asians and Asian Americans in an attempt to create ethnic balance. Indeed, throughout the 1980's, these schools did have lower freshman admission rates for Asian Americans than for white applicants. The controversy centers on whether a school should accept students purely on the basis of merit or should try to achieve a mix of students that reflects the makeup of society at large. Those involved in Asian American studies programs generally feel that it is their duty to try to educate the general public and politicians about the fairness of these admissions quotas. As Asian Americans are the fastest-growing ethnic group in the United States, this issue may be even more critical in the future.

Fair employment for Asian Americans is another primary concern. Most programs provide job search networks to help students find employment and utilize their special skills. Also, most Asian American studies programs are naturally extremely concerned with civil rights and job discrimination issues. Asian American faculty tend to be paid significantly less than non-Asian American professors; moreover, they are adequately represented only in the mathematics and engineering fields.

One of the initial stimuli for the development of Asian American studies programs was a desire to cultivate relationships with local Asian American communities. Programs hoped to participate in local cultural affairs; teach classes; and provide assistance, information, and resources to the community for political and social activities. With new Asian immigrants coming to the United States in increasing numbers, Asian American studies programs can often provide assistance in governmental processing and act as a technical information clearinghouse.

It should be noted, too, that Asian American studies programs are often the center of academic, cultural, and social life for many Asian American students. There are more than fifty active Asian American student organizations on U.S. campuses where students meet and address issues of mutual concern.

Ultimately Asian American studies programs serve as resource centers for students, scholars, and the community. Most units collect and distribute information—both locally and nationally—and many Asian American studies programs produce their own newsletters or newspapers. The reading room at the UCLA Asian American Studies Center, for example, has a collection of more than 350 specialized newspapers and newsletters such as the *Asian New Yorker, Asian Pacific Communityline*, and *Newsletter of the National Association of Asian Pacific Americans in Education.*

Educational Reform and Research. Asian American studies programs, especially in the early years, were instrumental in exposing institutional PREJUDICE, unquestioned racial STEREOTYPING, and covert bias on American campuses. These programs have educated faculty, students, and administrators about the lifestyles, customs, and concerns of Asian Americans. As several critics have warned, however, Asian American studies programs should not be seen as only compensatory education, belatedly rectifying gaps in an outmoded, biased curriculum. Nor should they be seen merely as an attempt to increase minority enrollment or simply provide Asian American students with a convenient way to learn about their heritage. Asian American studies programs should be thought of as a legitimate part of major pedagogical reform, making American education more inclusive, equitable, and democratic.

In this sense, Asian American studies is part of the newer trend toward MULTICULTURALISM in the social sciences, history, and literary theory, in which concerns with issues of cultural domination, resistance, and power are paramount. In terms of theory and method, research conducted at Asian American studies centers has been at the forefront of the social sciences. For example, such research has demonstrated some of the problems of the sociological theory of ASSIMILATION (seeing America as the "melting pot"). Closer examination of Asian American statistical data has shown that the "MODEL MINORITY" thesis is also questionable. Asian American social scientists have also been creative in their use of primary sources, such as oral histories and documents.

SUGGESTED READINGS. There are numerous books and articles concerning Asian American issues, but the literature on Asian American studies programs is less extensive. A good place to begin is with three books published by Washington State University Press at Pullman: *Reflections on Shattered Windows: Promises and Prospects for Asian American Studies* (1988), edited by Gary Okihiro et al.; *Frontiers of Asian American Studies: Writing, Research, and Commentary* (1989), edited by Gail Nomura et al.; and *Asian Americans: Contemporary and Global Perspectives* (1991), edited by Shirley Hune et al. A special issue of *Change: The Magazine of Higher Learning* 21 (November/December, 1989) has a number of articles on Asian American studies programs. The Asian American Studies Center at the University of California at Los Angeles publishes two excellent periodicals, *Amerasia Journal* and *Crosscurrents: Newsmagazine of the UCLA Asian American Studies Center.—James Stanlaw*

Asian American women: Asian American women represent a number of diverse ethnic and national groups with marked differences in language, occupation, religion, culture, and immigration patterns. According to the U.S. Census, the more than 3.5 million Asian Americans are made up of twenty-eight groups, the largest constituencies being CHINESE, FILIPINO, JAPANESE,

Asian, PACIFIC ISLANDER, and Southeast Asian heritage.

These women of color cannot be described as a single, homogeneous group in terms of class, economic status, cultural practices, educational levels, immigration trends, or historical experiences. Although past research has grouped all nonwhite immigrant women's experiences together and contrasted them with the white and European American majority, studies show that women of color do not identify themselves in such terms. Asian American women define themselves in terms of their national or cultural origin. There is, however, a common thread that runs through the tapestry of their differing experiences: the Asian American woman's roles within the contexts of family and work.

Chinese American woman and girls carry a Buddha during a Chinese New Year celebration in Los Angeles. Many Asian American women believe it is their social and religious duty to maintain a strong sense of womanhood. (Claire Rydell)

ASIAN INDIAN, KOREAN, and VIETNAMESE. Other sizeable racial ethnic groups include LAOTIAN, THAI, CAMBODIAN, PAKISTANI, INDONESIAN, and HMONG. Hence, Asian American women are of Japanese, Chinese, South

Bicultural Existence. Traditionally, Asians share a common set of ingrained cultural values, sanctioned by societal norms and religious beliefs and teachings. Often these values stand in direct opposition to Ameri-

Some women leave their Asian homelands to escape limited social and economic options; retreat from war, poverty, and persecution; and search for freedom from discrimination and restrictions within male-dominated family and social structures.
(Richard B. Levine)

can values: fate versus personal control; tradition versus change; hierarchy versus equality; collective versus individual interest; cooperation versus competition; formality versus informality; indirectness versus directness; and detachment versus materialism.

These cultural concerns are an integral aspect of Asians' overall identity, crossing both gender and class lines. Adherence to these values means that Asian American women believe it is their social and "religious" duty to maintain a strong sense of womanhood, devotion to extended family and society, sacrifice to others' advancement, self-control, delay of personal satisfaction, reliance on family and community support, and stability and harmony in interpersonal relations. It should come as no surprise, then, that when East meets West, traditional Asian values come into conflict with mainstream American values. For Asian American women, this dilemma can be confusing: On the one hand, immigration strengthens their allegiance to the national and ethnic identity of their native Asian culture; on the other hand, the United States offers them opportunities for self-fulfillment, cultural freedom, and personal advancement not often available to or acceptable for females in their lands of origin. Asian Indian writer Feroza Jussawalla confirms that Asian American women "are like 'chiffon saris'—a sort of cross-breed attempting to adjust to the pressures of a new world, while actually being from another older one."

Women leave their Asian homelands for a number of reasons: to escape the limited social and economic options available to them as females; to retreat from war, poverty, and persecution; and to search for freedom from discrimination and restrictions within male-dominated family and social structures. Although more Asian women are immigrating to the United States alone, most generally arrive with husbands or families. These immigrant women often find themselves dependent on their husbands; loyal to their familial roles of wife and mother; tied to the concerns of housework, pregnancy, and childrearing; and cut off from professional, educational, and other outside experiences. These women attempt the difficult task of balancing the old Asian values of group identity, work ethic, and hierarchy with American values of individualism, entrepreneurship, and equality. Their daughters and granddaughters, born and reared in the United States, seem to feel less of a dilemma as they are less bound to traditional Asian values—but these younger women, too, may struggle with biculturalism when dealing with older family members.

Family Roles. The family remains central in the lives of Asian American women. Considering themselves powerful forces within their homes, these women of color proudly identify themselves with devotion and loyalty to the family's well-being. A strong sense of duty to their husbands and children often takes precedence over any personal goals women may harbor. Their sense of obligation and sacrifice to family tends to overpower urges for self-promotion and self-expression.

Asian American women's responsibility of working in a family-owned business is compatible with their family identities as wife and mother. KOREAN retail shops, groceries, and service stations; ASIAN INDIAN family-managed hotels and motels; CHINESE restaurants and small businesses; and Asian-owned garment industry shops are staffed mostly by family and other close compatriots. The success of these self-owned businesses is largely attributable to the long hours and back-breaking labor of wives and women of the extended family. Some Asian American women consider themselves privileged to operate such businesses; while contributing to the family's welfare, they can continue to care for their children and oversee the household activities. Yet running a family business affords these women little opportunity to pursue school instruction, improve job skills, learn English, or develop friendships.

Roles in the Work Force. The contributions by Asian American women extend beyond the home and family-operated businesses. Employed women constitute more than 50 percent of the Asian American population. These women participate in the labor force at rates higher than any other group, including Anglo women, working full-time and year-round. Concentrated in areas where both income and cost of living are high, they have higher median earnings than comparable Anglo women. Those who pursue higher education, particularly FILIPINO AMERICAN, CHINESE AMERICAN, and JAPANESE AMERICAN women, surpass all women and men on college completion rates. More than 68 percent of Filipino women participate in the labor force compared with only 49 percent of Anglo women. In Southern California, between 25 and 30 percent of all Korean immigrant women operate small businesses. For Asian American women, employment outside the home is an essential element in economic and cultural survival.

This group is not exempt from discrimination in the

labor market. According to the 1980 U.S. Census, more than 40 percent of working Asian women are concentrated in the technical, sales, and administrative support occupations. As a whole, Asian American women are concentrated in less prestigious positions of file clerks, office machine operators, typists, and cashiers. They are less likely to obtain high profile positions as secretaries and receptionists. At least a

little access to upward mobility. Women make up 90 percent of the workers in California's Silicon Valley. Yet half of those employed are in production-related jobs; the majority of employees are Filipino, Vietnamese, and Korean women who work for minimum wage and work forced overtime. Many are faced with unhealthy working conditions, stress, and plant closures.

Hmong American refugee women found a market for their exquisite needlework and appliqué in many American cities in the 1980's that helped to supplement family income. (L. Gubb/UNHCR)

quarter work as restaurant servers, maids, and sewing machine operators. Even college-educated women are concentrated in select positions of the professional-managerial class.

Like women everywhere, Asian American women have faced the pervasive forces of RACISM, SEXISM, CLASS distinction, and economic inequity. Many female Chinese immigrants who arrived in the United States after 1965 found work in the small sewing factories of Los Angeles and New York City. With limited English language and job skills, many Chinese American women remain trapped in an industry of low wages, long hours, little job security, and no time to acquire advanced skills and instruction. In the electronics industry, too, Asian women find jobs but gain

Women's new economic independence brings new expectations. Wives expect more equal treatment from their husbands in the home, equal partnership in the marriage, and equal responsibility in child and home care. They complain that although their families are living in a society of less rigid gender roles and greater equity, their husbands are unwilling to share the duties of the household and childrearing. Many Asian husbands are disturbed by their loss of social and economic dominance, which can lead to abusive behavior, substance abuse, divorce, and psychological stress, as often happens with Southeast Asian refugees. Traditional Asian family structures and expectations are being challenged. Women's roles and domains may have changed, but men's attitudes toward and treatment of

Employers may wrongly stereotype Asian American women as submissive, obedient, and unambitious, and therefore often overlook these women for promotion. (Richard B. Levine)

women generally have not.

Professions and Cultural Contributions. The struggles and opportunities of professional Asian American women are different. Many work in positions of responsibility, visibility, and authority as attorneys, doctors, teachers, judges, and businesspersons. Yet they, too, experience the double-edged sword in their corporate environments, technical fields, and professional domains. Asian American women may gain easy access to entry-level management jobs, but then they hit their heads on the "GLASS CEILING," making little headway into the inner circle of the "good old boy" networks. They may also arrive on the job suffering from the stereotypes of "exotic Oriental" or "MODEL MINORITY." Asian American women are generally considered desirable employees. They hold a reputation of being conscientious, efficient, and hard-working. They are not perceived as difficult employees juggling career and home like the stereotyped Anglo "superwoman." At the same time, however, employers may view Asian American women as submissive, obedient,

and unambitious, and therefore often overlook these women for promotion or recognition. Movement up the ladder is further impeded by many Asian American women's inability to promote and assert themselves. All these factors help explain why Asian American women are underrepresented in positions of power in government, corporations, and private and public institutions.

In many professional contexts, Asian American women show a significant presence. In the field of broadcast journalism, Asian American women anchor news in the largest markets in the country: CONNIE CHUNG and Kaity Tong in New York, Tritia Toyota and Joanne Ishimine in Los Angeles, and Linda Yu in Chicago. Prominent Asian women filmmakers such as Mira Nair, Deepa Mehta, Christine Choy, LONI DING, and Emiko Omori are challenging Asian images and stereotypes in their work. Writers MAXINE HONG KINGSTON, Bharati Mukherjee, AMY TAN, and Wendy Wang are fast becoming internationally acclaimed authors who focus on themes of Asian American identity. More Asian American women are running for public offices, organizing action groups, and advocating legal rights and other social causes.

With such expansion, it is only a matter of time before Asian American women gain a stronger presence in the nation's economic, educational, and political systems. Although Asian American women are in a doubly disadvantaged position as members of a racial-ethnic minority group and as females, they can proudly claim their own unique identities, histories, voices, and contributions in American society.

SUGGESTED READINGS. For insightful accounts of the experiences and histories of Asian American women since the early 1970's, consult *Making Waves: An Anthology of Writing by and About Asian American Women* (1989), edited by Asian Women United of California. Two essential bibliographies to any research in Asian American studies are the "1991 Annual Selected Bibliography," in *Amerasia* 17, no. 3 (1991), pp. 83-169, and *The Immigrant Woman in North America: An Annotated Bibliography of Selected References* (1985) by Francesco Cordasco.— *Tamara M. Valentine*

Asian immigration and chain migration. *See* **Chain migration—Asian immigration**

Asian immigration and sojourners. *See* **Sojourners and Asian immigration**

Asian immigration to Canada. *See* **Canada—Asian immigration**

Asian Indian Americans: Asian Indians, or East Indians, trace their ancestry, either directly or indirectly, to South Asia or the Indian subcontinent. Unified by a common Indo-Aryan tradition, dating from 3000 to 2500 B.C.E., this quasi-racial/ethnic community exhibits complex diversity and incongruities. It includes people with dissimilar historical origins, racial roots, customs, cultural patterns, and practices. Asian Indians speak fifteen major languages comprising more than five hundred dialects, and they follow seven major religious orientations.

The arrival of "HINDUS," (as South Asians were then called, regardless of religion) on the West Coast

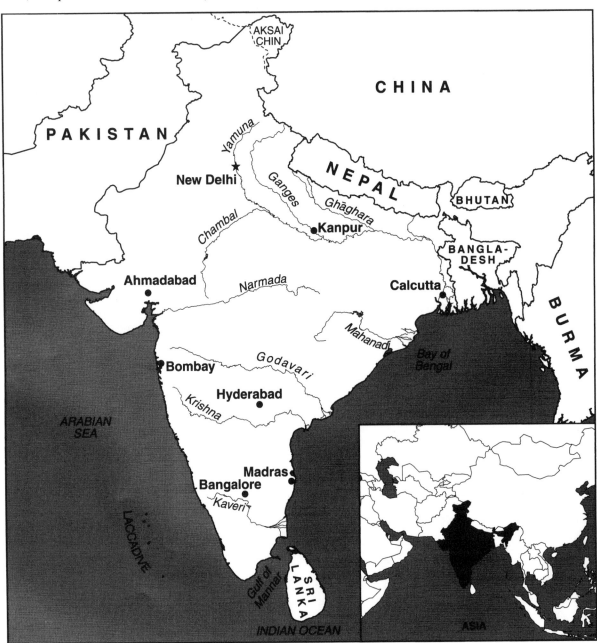

INDIA

was a by-product of Asian Indian emigration to Vancouver, British Columbia, in the first decade of the twentieth century. Most were farmers and laborers from Punjab. Coming to British Columbia at the rate of about two thousand per year, they quickly encountered opposition. After the Canadian government ended Asian Indian immigration in 1909, many immigrants returned to India or followed the path of others who had migrated earlier in small numbers to the United States.

The reports by various authorities of early East Asian arrivals in the United States were often conflicting. Careful examination of immigration data for the period 1899-1920, however, indicates that between 1899 and 1907 there were only 1,957 Asian Indians, mostly businesspeople and students who later became laborers, followed by 5,391 arrivals and 1,651 departures between 1908 and 1920. The dramatic growth of Asian Indian immigrants from eighty-four in 1902 to 1,710 in 1910 aroused hostility against them, especially in California. Their arrival gave fresh impetus to anti-Asian feelings created by the Chinese and Japanese immigration to the West Coast.

Anti-Asian Sentiment. The growth of the Asian Indian community was accompanied by resentment and discrimination; the anti-Asian Japanese and Korean Exclusion League changed its name to the ASIATIC EXCLUSION LEAGUE. Immigration officials began rejecting Asian Indian immigrants on grounds of sickness and the likelihood of becoming public charges. Anti-Asian violence directed at Asian Indians occurred in a few cities, including Seattle, Everett, and Bellingham, Washington. In the most publicized incident, at Bellingham in September, 1907, six hundred lumberjacks herded some two hundred "Hindus" out of town, with many immigrants suffering serious injuries.

In 1913, the California legislature enacted the ALIEN LAND LAW; while directed at the Japanese, it also affected the few hundred Asian Indians who were seeking to buy land in the Sacramento, San Joaquin, and Imperial valleys. Loopholes in the law made evasion possible; and land under the control of Asian Indians jumped from 20,000 acres in 1918 to 38,000 acres in 1920 in the Imperial Valley. In the Sacramento Valley, they operated 85,000 acres.

Beginning in 1917, laborers from Asia (except Japan) were barred from immigrating to the United States; in 1923, the Supreme Court ruled "Hindus" ineligible for citizenship. It was not until 1946 that Asian Indians were again allowed to immigrate and apply for citizenship.

The number of Asian Indian immigrants to the United States increased enormously after India became independent in 1947. Changes in immigration policies, reflecting the changing nature of American diplomacy, encouraged Asian Indian immigration. Between 1947 and 1965, approximately six thousand Asian Indians were admitted to the United States.

Many Punjabi Sikh immigrants in the 1930's worked as farmers on the Pacific coast; as the years passed, their careers diversified: This man is running for civil court judge in New York City. (Richard B. Levine)

Social and Political Conditions in the Early Immigrant Community. There were approximately forty-five hundred Asian Indians on the Pacific Coast by 1934. Three thousand were farmers, predominantly Punjabi Sikhs, who were easily recognized by their turbans, unshorn hair and beards, and distinctive dress. Most farmed on leased land because of the restrictions of the anti-ALIEN LAND LAWS. The rapid expansion of orchard holdings was made possible because of the early immigrants' ability to save and their willingness to live modestly. Many slept in fields or on hay in barns, cooking their meals over campfires and work-

Heavy investment and participation in higher education have provided Asian Indian Americans with viable avenues to mobility. These students are shown performing at a midwestern university. (James L. Shaffer)

ing ten to twelve hours a day, seven days a week, for a mere $1.50 a day. The early involvement of Asian Indians in agriculture continues to the present day in the Sacramento and Imperial valleys of California.

A love for the mother country and a concern for Indian national affairs set much of the agenda for the early immigrants. The Ghadr Party, formed in California between 1913 and 1914, was a semi-religious Sikh political association primarily concerned with raising funds for transporting men, arms, and ammunition to support revolutionary efforts to free India from foreign control. It published reviews of political, economic, social, and intellectual conditions in India. On the domestic front, early Asian Indians recognized the value of political action. For example, they obtained congressional sponsorship of a number of bills in the period after 1946 that allowed Indians to bring dependents to the United States as permanent citizens.

Newcomers to the Community. By 1980, it was estimated that about 387,000 Asian Indians were residing in the United States, 70 percent of them foreign-born. Much of this increase has been attributed to the IMMIGRATION AND NATIONALITY ACT OF 1965, which eliminated national quotas. From 1965 to 1975, thousands of Asian Indian professionals, including scientists, physicians, engineers, college professors, and businesspeople entered the United States. Between 1976 and 1986, however, revisions and amendments to the 1965 law modified the character of Indian immigration to the U.S., greatly minimizing the "brain drain" from South Asia.

By 1989, estimates of Asian Indians in the United States approached 700,000; by the year 2000, this number will be close to a million. The New York metropolitan area, the San Francisco Bay area, and the greater Los Angeles metropolitan area support the largest concentrations of Asian Indians. Communities of several thousand Asian Indians are also found in Illinois, Maryland, Massachusetts, Michigan, Ohio, Oregon, Pennsylvania, Texas, and Washington.

The community reflects the linguistic, ethnic, religious, and economic diversity characteristic of "Mother India." Major languages spoken within the community include, among others, Hindi, Urdu, Bengal, Gujarati, Punjabi, Tamil, and Telugu. The English language, however, remains the most common mode of communication among the linguistic groups, not only in the United States but also in India itself.

With their ability to read and write English, Asian Indians have generally made a smooth transition into the mainstream of American life. Heavy investment and participation in higher education have provided this community with one of the only viable avenues to mobility. Approximately 52 percent of all Asian Indians over twenty-five are college graduates, compared to only 16.2 percent for the U.S. population as a whole. Educational links to occupational profiles of Asian Indians are clear: Approximately 50 percent are managers and professionals (as compared to only 25 percent among white Americans), including an estimated 30,000 physicians and other medical professionals; 45,000 engineers; 25,000 scientists and professors; and 3,000 professionals in law, finance, and business. Approximately 30 percent of the United States' hotels and motels are owned and operated by Asian Indians. They are represented in virtually every occupational category, including small grocery store owners, restaurant operators, jewelers, farmers, and travel agents.

Religious Life. The religious life of the community distinguishes the Asian Indians from the dominant Anglo American society. They are adherents of four major religions: Sikhism, Hinduism, Islam, and Christianity. Sikhism, an integral part of life for the early Punjabi immigrants, continues to be the dominant belief system among the West Coast Asian Indians. As early as 1907, Stockton, California, had emerged as the major center for Sikhism, and by 1909 the Pacific Coast Khalsa Diwan Society had organized a *gurdwara* (temple). Since then Sikh temples have flourished in the Imperial Valley, the San Francisco Bay area, Los Angeles, and the Sacramento Valley area of California. Gurdwaras have served as centers not only for religious and cultural life but also for celebrations of political events.

Hinduism is a noninstitutional religious form, and much of the HINDU religious life has remained essentially private. Within each Hindu household, a small area is generally designated as a shrine for daily *pujas* (worship, prayers). Each shrine contains pictures and miniature statues of deities for whom incense and an oil lamp are lit and prayers are offered each morning and evening. The proliferation of American Hindu temples has created centers for Hindu cultural and religious life.

Masdjids (mosques) have become an important source of identity for the increasing number of Asian Indian Muslim immigrants mostly from Pakistan and Bangladesh. Religious, cultural, and social continuity have been maintained through *Namaz* (prayer services) and the celebration of two major religious festivals in the Muslim lunar year: the *Id al-adha* (festival of sacrifices) and the *Id al-fitr*, the festival of breaking the fast at the end of Ramadan.

Asian Indians immigrated to the United States in large numbers after India became independent in 1947. (James L. Shaffer)

Christianity has also found converts among Asian Indians, particularly those from southwest India and overseas Indian communities. They frequently participate in racially and ethnically integrated church services; however, Asian Indian Christian congregations are beginning to emerge among the West Coast communities. Jain and Parsis immigrants from the Bombay and Gujarat regions of India, while fewer in number and less visible, further contribute to the religious diversity of the Asian Indian community.

Preserving Their Ethnic Heritage. Cultural continuity in the United States has been a major goal for the immigrants. A number of linguistic, regional, and religious groups have formed organizations to promote social and cultural events. Annual festivals not only serve the social needs of the community but also transmit and maintain Indian cultural heritage. In every major metropolitan area, Asian Indian radio broadcasts, television programming, and the screening of Hindi films have further facilitated the continuation of a way of life reminiscent of the homeland. Furthermore, touring film stars and musicians from India continue to provide important cultural links with the mother country. Several Indian newspapers in the United States inform the immigrants of political events in the homeland and provide commentaries on American life, information on community activities, and advertising of marriage proposals. The maintenance of ethnic heritage is nowhere more visible than in the dietary practices within the community. Many observe the religious prohibitions against MUSLIMS eating pork and HINDUS eating beef. Evening meals often consist of *roti/chapati*, tortilla-like bread and vegetable curries spiced with turmeric, coriander seed/cilantro, cumin, cardamom, cloves, cinnamon, and chili peppers.

In many ways, Asian Indian immigrants have attempted to create a replica of their homeland in the United States, contributing much to a richly diverse multicultural society. Their greatest challenge is to assure the continuity of their heritage and cultural identity while participating in the mainstream of American society.

SUGGESTED READINGS. For an overview of the social and cultural history of Asian Indians, see Paul R. Brass's *The Politics of India Since Independence* (1990). Sathi S. Dasgupta's *On the Trail of an Uncertain Dream: Indian Immigrant Experience in America* (1989), Sriapati Chandrasekhar's *From India to America: A Brief History of Immigration: Problems of Discrimination, Admission, and Assimilation* (1982), and Partmatma Saran's *The Asian Indian Experience in the United States* (1985) provide commentaries on Asian Indian immigrants from India.—*Richard A. K. Shankar*

Asiatic Exclusion League: Group formed in San Francisco in 1905, made up of representatives of sixty-seven labor organizations. Resenting competition from Japanese laborers, who were often willing to work for less money than whites, members of the league worked to restrict opportunities for Japanese and Filipino immigrants. (Chinese immigrants were already severely restricted by law.) The league worked for restrictions on Asian immigrants through the courts, through propaganda, and through violence. Eventually, more than two hundred labor unions joined the league.

Assembly of First Nations: Intertribal Canadian Indian organization, also known as the National Brotherhood. The group represents more than 350,000 Canadian Indians. Its goals are to attain a measure of Indian sovereignty and to improve the conditions of Indian life. In order to achieve those goals, it is working to establish an independent, native-run justice system. Cree Chief Ovide Mercredi, a lawyer and staunch opponent of traditional government Indian policies, was elected the organization's leader in 1991.

Assimilation: Social and cultural adaptation and absorption of a minority group into the dominant culture. Whenever members of one racial or ethnic group come into contact with members of another, a principle must govern their relations. During the ancient Chinese, Mesopotamian, and Roman empires, for example, the principle was that one race should dominate others; genocidal war often resulted, leaving the subordinate group in a position of slavery. Gradually, in a change that some scholars have linked to the advent of capitalism in the West, the principle of domination became one of assimilation: the requirement that the subordinate group abandon its own culture, language, and traditions and conform to the culture, language, and traditions of the dominant ethnic group. In general, members of minorities were allowed a certain amount of upward mobility if they assimilated, whereas unassimilated minorities remained exploited.

Forms of Assimilation. Members of American minorities have learned that assimilation is not an all-or-nothing process. To complete the process, the enterprising minority individual must jump through several hoops. These forms of assimilation, or steps in the process, vary from the superficial (behavioral) to the most intimate (intermarriage), according to sociologist Milton Gordon.

ACCULTURATION (behavioral or cultural assimilation) involves adapting or borrowing aspects of another culture, such as modes of dress and speech. For example, older or rural men from Africa or the Indian subcontinent who move to the United States often abandon traditional dress for the conventional Western shirt and trousers. Young Southeast Asian immigrants are likewise quick to adapt mainstream American youth styles.

Asians for becoming "bananas" (yellow on the outside, white on the inside), or even "top bananas" when whites co-opt them to positions of leadership. Similarly, attitudinally assimilated African Americans may be called "Oreos," particularly if they are upwardly mobile, or "Uncle Toms" if co-opted by whites.

Choosing to adopt Western styles of dress rather than wear the traditional clothing of one's homeland is often an indication of assimilation. (Odette Lupis)

Identificational assimilation exists when members of diverse ethnic groups share a perception of common nationhood. Although American Indians may consider themselves to be members of the Cherokee, Navajo, or other tribe, one measure of their assimilation within the United States is whether they also consider themselves to be Americans. Attitudinal assimilation occurs when members of a subordinate culture shed their own value system in order to adopt the values of the dominant culture. Asian Americans who "think white" in the United States are sometimes chided by other

The road to acceptance can also involve structural assimilation, which entails the entrance of members of ethnic groups into secondary groups, such as the Boy Scouts, Girl Scouts, trade unions, and other voluntary organizations. The effects of black exclusion from trade unions still linger in the underrepresentation of African Americans in many of the skilled crafts today.

Civic assimilation occurs when members of a subordinate ethnic group no longer make special claims on the political system based on special needs of their ethnic group. This usually occurs when a group achieves an important measure of political power. The ascendancy of Irish Americans in Boston politics since the 1880's and of Japanese Americans in Hawaiian politics since the 1950's allowed both groups to jump through important assimilationist hoops. On the other hand, some African Americans and Latinos who have recently come to positions of power have discovered that their agenda of special demands is too lengthy to be satisfied in only one or two terms of office after years of political disfranchisement.

Marital assimilation exists when members of two racial or ethnic groups live together as spouses. In some cases, the children may celebrate their mixed heritage; for example, Polish-Italians may celebrate

Other forms of assimilation depend on the dominant culture's reception of a minority group. Attitude receptional assimilation exists when an ethnic group has reached the point where its members experience little or no prejudice. Groups that experience behavior receptional assimilation encounter little or no discrimination. Jews, subjected to ADMISSION QUOTAS in American colleges before the 1950's, formed the ANTI-DEFAMATION LEAGUE in order to fight both prejudice and discrimination. Their efforts may not have fully eradicated ANTI-SEMITISM, but they have eliminated religious quotas.

Ideologies of Assimilationism. Assimilationism has been a powerful force in American life, particularly in policies and attitudes toward immigrants in the

Government and private groups have tried to absorb newcomers as quickly as possible into American culture and society. These refugees and asylum seekers participate in an official orientation session in New York City. (L. Solmssen)

both Pulaski Day and Columbus Day in the United States. In other cases, the child may identify more with the ethnicity of the father or the mother. Light-skinned offspring with one African American parent and one white parent may even be encouraged to "pass" as white. Dinah Shore is a famous example of a part-black person who "passed" as white.

twentieth century. From Americanization campaigns in the early 1900's for the large influx of southern and eastern Europeans, to orientation programs for Vietnamese refugees in the 1970's, government and private groups have tried to absorb newcomers as quickly as possible into American culture and society.

Jumping through some hoops may be easier than

others. According to Robert Dahl, all ethnic groups will eventually join the mainstream; the most important step is to take advantage of economic opportunity, which affords the possibility of social mobility to all groups. Capitalism, according to Dahl, is by definition an economic system that provides equality of opportunity. Assimilating to the values of capitalism is thus the most crucial step in moving up the social ladder. Dahl's ideology, with which many have disagreed, may be characterized as laissez-faire assimilationism.

This form of assimilation does not always work for African Americans, who may assimilate attitudinally but encounter so much discrimination and prejudice that they are unable to accumulate sufficient capital to follow the path of upward mobility. According to Milton Gordon, when a group has structurally assimilated, all other types of assimilation will follow. His view is common among advocates of INTEGRATION as the solution to problems of diversity in multicultural societies. Integrationists argue that the principal barrier to assimilation is deliberate or inadvertent segregation; breaking down monoethnic patterns in education, employment, and social life is a precondition to assimilation.

Alternatives to Assimilationism. Both assimilationism and integrationism have many critics. Jewish playwright Israel Zangwill wrote a play entitled *The Melting Pot* (1914) to argue that all Americans are immigrants who should jump into a pot that would melt away the most shadowy attributes of their root cultures, while the most solid attributes would agglutinate to form a new amalgamated culture. The new American culture was to be composed of the best elements of the various ethnic groups that left homelands in turmoil for a new life. Zangwill's plea is for attitudinal and INTERMARRIAGE assimilation; his ideology, sometimes called amalgamationism, is thus assimilationism in disguise. Those urging the development of a unique amalgamated American culture during the twentieth century simply placed a new façade on assimilationist Anglo-conformity, according to William Newman.

Philosopher Horace Kallen, another Jewish immigrant, argued that a more realistic alternative to assimilationism is CULTURAL PLURALISM. His celebration of the feasibility of replacing monoculturalism with MULTICULTURALISM is based on the example of Switzerland.

Black Power advocates Stokely CARMICHAEL (Kwame Toure) and Charles Hamilton argued in 1967 that assimilationists and integrationists fail to understand that white society has no intention of treating African Americans equally; following the assimilationist agenda, in short, is an exercise in futility for blacks. Both authors believed that African Americans should work together to achieve political power, and then dismantle institutional racism. Whereas MALCOLM X advocated black separatism and an enclave economy at the peak of his career, Carmichael and Hamilton assumed that all ethnic and racial groups would interact together. Since these three black theorists expounded their ideologies, the success of African American politicians has outdistanced efforts to promote black capitalism. Yet research has shown that the mere election of African and Latino Americans to public office has not brought about a more equal society.

Contemporary Assimilationism. With increasing awareness of MULTICULTURALISM inside the United States and international interdependence outside, many people find assimilationist ideas passé. The capitalist marketplace that appeared to be the great equalizer of diverse ethnic groups has become an international bazaar. Corporations thrive if they can do business in many countries, take into account the diversity of the marketplace, and institute multiethnic employment at all levels. Forcing members of one ethnic group to conform to the culture, language, and values of another appears unprofitable and politically explosive, as seen in South Africa.

Meanwhile, leaders of poorer countries appear to have fewer options. Ethnic groups in the former Soviet Union and Yugoslavia prefer to pursue monoculturalist self-determination than to have ethnic groups compete for scarce resources in multiethnic states. Members of American minorities still differ as to what degrees of separateness or integration are desirable. Thus, the debate between assimilationism and its alternatives continues.

SUGGESTED READINGS. William McNeill's monumental *Polyethnicity and National Unity in World History* (1986) provides a broad historical perspective on the rise and fall of assimilationist policies. The most comprehensive treatment of the concept of assimilation in the United States is Milton Gordon's *Assimilation in American Life: The Role of Race, Religion, and National Origins* (1964), which compares blacks, Catholics, Jews, and Puerto Ricans. Robert Dahl applies laissez-faire assimilationism as an ideology in *Who Governs? Democracy and Power in an American City*

The AIAW has tried to better the opportunities for women in college sports. (Ken Layman/Photo Agora)

Association for Intercollegiate Athletics for Women (AIAW): Organization to promote gender equity in college athletics. The AIAW worked to open opportunities for women in college sports beginning in the early 1970's. Title IX of the Education Amendments of 1972 outlawed sex discrimination in institutions of higher learning that received federal aid. This created an opening for women's college sports to gain greater support and recognition. The AIAW estimated that, in 1972, women's college sports received 1 percent of the budget for men's sports. This figure had increased to 10 percent by 1979. In that year, the AIAW had 100,000 members. It disbanded in 1983 when women's sports were encompassed in the National Collegiate Athletic Association (NCAA).

Association of Puerto Rican Executive Directors (ASPIRA): Nonprofit private agency founded in 1961 with the aid of the National Puerto Rican Forum to help Puerto Rican youth finish high school and go on to study in a college or university. It was initiated in response to the high dropout rates among Latino youth and to the social and economic conditions found in the Puerto Rican community in New York City. ASPIRA has offices in six cities and assists more than fifteen thousand people each year through its programs.

(1961) and *Pluralist Democracy in the United States* (1967).

On the integrationist route to assimilation, see the works of sociologist Robert Park, especially *Race and Culture: Essays in the Sociology of Contemporary Man* (1950). Raymond Wolfinger applies integrationist assimilationism to the study of ethnic bloc voting in New Haven, Connecticut, in *The Politics of Progress* (1974), in which he refutes Dahl. Using Hawaiian ethnic bloc voting data, Michael Haas in turn refutes Wolfinger in *Institutional Racism: The Case of Hawai'i* (1992). To read about alternatives to assimilationism and integrationism, consult Stokely Carmichael and Charles Hamilton's *Black Power: The Politics of Liberation in America* (1967); Malcolm X's *The Autobiography of Malcolm X* (1965); Horace Kallen's *Culture and Democracy in the United States* (1924); and William Newman's *American Pluralism: A Study of Minority Groups and Social Theory* (1973).—*Michael Haas*

Assimilation of American Indians. *See* **American Indian assimilation**

Athletics and sport: The playing fields and sports arenas of the United States have offered opportunities for athletic achievement and financial success since the last decades of the nineteenth century. The fame and fortune associated with champions of the baseball diamond and football gridiron were based upon acceptance of these sports and their participants by a mass audience willing to pay to see the contests. For racial and ethnic minorities, the possibility of gaining acclaim and wealth through sports held an attraction that few individuals with the appropriate skills could resist. Yet the attention of the mass audience and the events on the field, both of which involved frequent interaction with people of the dominant Anglo-Saxon culture, did not mean equal treatment and social harmony. Many of the leading sports figures from minority groups attained their success in spite of encounters with discrimination.

The late nineteenth century crusaders for physical fitness did not anticipate the direction that their crusade would take. They promoted athletics—activities involving strength, stamina, speed, and usually teamwork—in order to build national character. Fictional hero Frank Merriwell and real-life advocate Theodore

Roosevelt held up as a model the vigorous life that included FOOTBALL and BASEBALL. In the early 1900's, however, the focus of athletics moved from the development of character and physique to an innovative form of public spectacle and private enterprise. The better athletes became the stars of mass spectator sports (leisure activities that usually did not involve exercise for onlookers). These sports catered to a broad audience with inexpensive admission charges to contests in which the fans greatly outnumbered the participants. Baseball, football, BASKETBALL, and boxing were also easily accessible to the mass media, which provided intensive coverage.

The combination of large arenas, massive crowds, and media coverage made for popular entertainment that cut across the boundaries of social status, wealth, and ethnic background. Crowd behavior at these events often befuddled and sometimes shocked foreign observers who were accustomed to the slow-paced dignity of England's cricket matches and the polite applause of Japanese baseball spectators. By contrast, American fans screamed their anger at baseball umpires and taunted rival players in language unacceptable in school and church. On occasion, fights and even riots broke out in the stands. Under these conditions, the entry of minorities into the arena often involved verbal abuse and the possibility of physical harm. In spite of these unfriendly conditions, people of diverse cultural backgrounds made important contributions to the history of athletics and sport as players, coaches, and business executives.

American Indians. American Indians began to participate in the national sports scene around 1900, largely through the CARLISLE INDIAN SCHOOL and its football team. Established as a vocational training school for young Indians, Carlisle's victories on the FOOTBALL field against major college teams soon captured the attention of a growing number of sports fans. Jim THORPE entered Carlisle in early 1904 at the age of sixteen and soon established himself as a superior performer in track and BASEBALL. In the fall of 1911, Thorpe became the dominant figure on the already successful football team through his speed as a runner and his extraordinary kicking ability. Newspapers and magazines portrayed him as the quintessential Indian athlete, while predominately white audiences cheered his record-making feats.

Thorpe and the Carlisle teams had found an acceptable place for American Indians in the mainstream of popular culture. This did not mean, however, that their

people had escaped prejudice. While the Carlisle team dashed to victories on the football field, most Indians remained confined to barren, poverty-stricken reservations. A more likely explanation of Thorpe's remarkable popularity was that the public saw athletic achievement as acceptable for young men whose ancestors were acknowledged masters of tracking and chasing the wildlife of forest and plain.

Jim Thorpe (of Sac, Fox, Chippewa, Potawatomie, Irish, and French descent) established himself as a superior performer in track, baseball, and football. (National Archives)

Thorpe was one of the first members of a minority to experience the adulation and anxiety of sports celebrity in twentieth century America. In the 1912 Olympics he won two gold medals; however, he was later denied amateur standing and lost these awards because he had received a few dollars for playing semi-professional baseball in 1910. A leading figure in the early years of professional football, Thorpe was the first president of the American Professional Football Association in 1920. Salaries were small in these years, however, so Thorpe had no financial security at the time of his retirement. He had difficulty with life off the playing field and suffered a series of misadventures in business. His later years served as a warning to aspiring young athletes that the world of

roundabout route from his home in a small Cahuilla village in California to Dartmouth College in 1904 to the minor leagues in 1905 and finally to the Giants four years later. His job as catcher was a demanding one; it required special skills, physical toughness, and the knowledge to select the type of pitch to throw to opposition hitters. The dependable Meyers helped to establish a path to the major leagues also taken by Thorpe (Meyers' roommate on the 1913 Giants), Charles Albert "Chief" Bender, Bob Johnson, and Allie Reynolds.

Athletics provide an opportunity for people of different backgrounds to come together as a team. (Jeff Greenberg, Unicorn Stock Photos)

modern mass sport brought no guarantees of personal security, no matter what the level of accomplishment on the playing field.

Other American Indians achieved a more stable if less prominent success in other arenas, especially baseball. John Tortes "Chief" Meyers was the regular catcher for the New York Giants from 1909 to 1915. His career was shortened because he did not reach the major leagues until the age of twenty-nine, taking a

Jewish Americans. The contribution of Jews to American sport is one the least-known aspects of multicultural U.S. society. Barney Ross, lightweight champion in world boxing in the 1930's, became a symbol of hope for aspiring Jewish athletes. In the 1920's and 1930's many young Jewish males played BASKETBALL and BASEBALL at both the college and professional levels. Basketball teams in large eastern cities such as New York and Philadelphia generally had substantial numbers of Jewish players and coaches. Moe Goldman, Red Holzman, and Eddie Gottlieb helped to establish the forerunner of the National Basketball Association in the 1930's under the most difficult of conditions. Long bus trips and cold, cramped gymnasiums during the northeastern winters made playing conditions difficult. Goldman, a six-foot, three-inch center for the South Philadelphia Hebrew Association ("Sphas" for short), was an outstanding defensive player in a league known for its rough style; some of his most painful moments came when he and his teammates encountered anti-Semitic taunts from fans in rival cities. Goldman retired in 1942. After World War II, professional basketball emerged as a major spectator sport in which Jewish players such as Max Zaslofsky and Dolph Schayes were outstanding performers.

A contemporary of Goldman was Henry "Hank" Greenberg, a New York-born baseball player who rose to stardom as a power hitter for the Detroit Tigers. His large frame and impressive strength alone did not guarantee a major league career. Handicapped by flat feet and awkwardness, Greenberg worked with great intensity to improve his running, fielding, and batting. The extent of his achievement can be measured in baseball statistics, which reveal that he hit fifty-eight home runs in 1938 (only two short of Babe Ruth's 1927 record) and drove in 170 runs in 1935 and 183 two years later. In spite of his exceptional record, Greenberg, like Goldman, encountered anti-Semitic comments in the playing arena. In 1941, at the age of thirty, he became one of the first professional athletes to enter military service in World War II. He returned to the Tigers in the 1945 season to lead them to the American League pennant and a World Series championship. After his retirement as a player in 1947, Greenberg became a baseball executive with the Cleveland Indians and the Chicago White Sox.

As impressive as Greenberg's accomplishments were, they were exceeded by those of another Jewish baseball star, Sandy Koufax. Koufax, a tall left-handed pitcher, began his major league career with the Brooklyn Dodgers in 1955. It was not until after the Dodgers moved to Los Angeles in 1959, however, that he developed into a star. From 1962 to 1966, Koufax used his overpowering fastball and nearly unhittable curveball to dominate hitters in an almost unprecedented fashion, leading the National League (NL) in earned run average each year and in strikeouts, shutouts, and victories three times each. Koufax won the Cy Young

Award as the league's best pitcher in 1963, 1965, and 1966 and won the NL's Most Valuable Player Award in 1963. In 1963 and 1965, he led the Dodgers to World Series titles. After the 1966 season, Koufax, though only thirty years old and at the height of his success, quit baseball to protect his pitching arm from damage; his brilliant career and unusually early retirement combined to elevate him to near-mythic status in the minds of many baseball fans.

In 1972, a twenty-two-year-old Jewish American swimmer, Mark Spitz, became the talk of the sports world when he captured the unprecedented total of seven gold medals at the Munich Olympic Games. Spitz set world records in each of his events and was named the Associated Press Male Athlete of the Year. His Olympic triumph was darkened, however, when Palestinian terrorists invaded the Olympic village and killed two Israeli athletes; it was feared that Spitz's Jewish heritage might make him a target as well, and he was rushed back to the United States. Handsome and articulate, Spitz was soon receiving large fees to endorse a variety of products and was featured on a best-selling pinup poster.

Another Jewish athlete who, like Greenberg, excelled in sports after his playing days were over was Arnold "Red" Auerbach. A hardworking, highly motivated basketball guard for George Washington University in the late 1930's, Auerbach finally managed to become a starter in his senior year. An astute analyst of the game, he grasped the potential of the fast-break offense and helped to develop that style of play at the professional level, first as coach of the Washington Capitols, then as coach and general manager of the Boston Celtics.

Eastern and Southern European Immigrants. Immigrants from eastern and southern Europe also encountered cultural barriers in the early 1900's. For many of their male offspring, FOOTBALL and BASEBALL fields presented an opportunity for friendships and, for a talented few, the possibility of a professional career. One of the first Polish Americans to gain prominence was Bronko Nagurski, a hulking six-foot, four-inch football player at the University of Minnesota. Often compared to Jim THORPE by enthusiastic sportswriters in the 1920's and 1930's, Nagurski inspired a new wave of popularity for the National Football League. He alternated between tackle and fullback for the Chicago Bears until his retirement in 1938. Another Polish American, Stan Musial, rose to baseball stardom with the St. Louis Cardinals in the 1940's and contin-

Though professional organized sports have at times discriminated on the basis of race, the youth of today face fewer obstacles in pursuing their dreams of being great athletes. (Jim and Mary Whitmer)

ued his productive career until 1963 with a remarkable total of 3,630 hits and a .331 lifetime batting average. Few fans realized that Musial, much like Greenberg, became a superb hitter through hard work and discipline. Only after an injury ended his brief pitching career did Musial perfect his unorthodox batting stance.

Nagurski and Musial led the way for young men of Polish and Slavic descent at the same time that the sons of southern European immigrants began to see their names featured on sports pages across the land. Sports fans from Tacoma to Tupelo found that the national games had a decidedly multicultural flavor. Nagurski's University of Minnesota was a member of the Midwest's Big Ten Conference, which included Slavic players such as Ted Kluszewski, Vic Janowicz, and Roger Zatkoff; Italians Leo Nomellini, Dante Lavelli, and Alan Ameche; and Greeks Pete Pihos and brothers Alex and Ted Karras. Baseball counted among its stellar performers the Italian Americans Tony Lazzeri, Ernie Lombardi, and the DiMaggio brothers (Joe, Vince, and Dom). Slavic baseball players included former football player Kluszewski, Whitey Kurowski, Gene Hermanski, Ray Jablonski, Rip Repulski, and Carl Yastrzemski.

Angelo Enrico "Hank" Luisetti, a versatile college basketball player of Italian parentage, symbolized one of sport's most significant revolutions in the twentieth century. Borrowing from innovations that originated in backyards and playgrounds, Luisetti brought together the jump shot and rapid movement offense to become a national celebrity. At a time when nearly all players planted both feet on the floor and launched arching, two-handed set shots, Luisetti used only one hand, often suddenly breaking his dribble and tossing the ball into the basket before his defender could react. He also used the jump shot, in which he released the ball at the top of a vertical leap. In a 1937 tour of Philadelphia and New York, Luisetti led the Stanford University team in an impressive series of victories. In a few decades his style of play would dominate the game.

African Americans. In spite of their impressive athletic abilities, African Americans encountered stubborn resistance in their efforts to enter mass audience sports. There is evidence that blacks and whites played FOOTBALL and BASEBALL together in the 1880's and 1890's. The emergence of organized college and professional sports in the last years of the nineteenth century, however, coincided with the rise of racial barri-

ers, or the so-called color line, in such events. A few colleges refused to establish discriminatory practices, thus allowing a handful of blacks to continue competing at the college level. For example, the multitalented Paul ROBESON was an outstanding football player at Rutgers from 1915 to 1918. Boxing provided the most dramatic challenge to the color line when the towering black heavyweight Jack Johnson became the acknowledged but highly controversial world champion from 1908 to 1915.

Two decades later Joe Louis found more tolerance and even public acclaim as heavyweight champion. His first bout with Nazi Germany's standard-bearer, Max Schmeling, brought painful defeat, but in the rematch Louis quickly knocked out Schmeling and became a national hero in a time of growing tensions between the two nations. He soon shared heroic status with the swift-footed Jesse Owens, a black athlete who defeated the representatives of Adolf Hitler's regime by winning four gold medals in the 1936 Olympic Games in Berlin.

While these were important breakthroughs, the color line remained in the professional team sports of baseball, football, and BASKETBALL. Other athletic events held many challenges, but this trio of spectator sports offered the greatest fame and fortune to athletes seeking professional careers.

For most of the first half of the twentieth century, black professional baseball players were restricted to competing in the NEGRO LEAGUES, a loose confederation of teams and organizations that spanned the Northeast, Midwest, and South. Such enormously talented players as Josh Gibson and Buck Leonard displayed their skills for years in the Negro Leagues but were never allowed into the white major leagues. The entry of blacks into the baseball major leagues in the late 1940's transcended the playing fields to anticipate the Civil Rights movement of the 1950's.

It was Jackie ROBINSON who finally broke the color line in 1947. An all-around athlete who excelled in football, track, and basketball as well as baseball, Robinson played at the University of California at Los Angeles (UCLA) before World War II. After three years in the army, he returned to civilian life in 1945 with the Kansas City Monarchs of the NEGRO LEAGUES, the source of employment for many of the great black players excluded from the major leagues.

Robinson's physical ability and personal maturity impressed many writers and scouts. Branch Rickey of the Brooklyn Dodgers was aware of the task he placed

Sprinter and long jumper Jesse Owens won four gold medals in the 1936 Olympic Games and set three Olympic records. (AP/Wide World Photos)

before himself and his franchise when, in 1945, he decided to bring Robinson into the major leagues. After one year of minor league experience with the Dodger farm team in Montreal, Robinson became a Dodger.

Fully aware of the burdens imposed by racial discrimination after his years in college athletics and the army, Robinson was still deeply dismayed by the racist epithets shouted at him by loud-mouthed spectators and opposition players. In a game where one of the primary duties of a position player is to hit a baseball hurled at speeds around ninety miles an hour from a mound only sixty feet six inches away, total concentration is a necessity. That Robinson weathered the storms of player and fan abuse to maintain a respectable .297 batting average, to steal twenty-nine bases, and to strike out only thirty-six times in 590 at bats testified to his strengths as a player and a person. He

was not without moral support from his teammates and other players. Within a few weeks of the beginning of his first season, white Dodgers, including many Southerners, rallied to his support. The legendary Hank Greenberg, a victim of anti-Semitism in the 1930's but by 1947 a member of the Pittsburgh Pirates, openly welcomed Robinson to the big leagues. A torch of hard-earned tolerance was passed between the veteran and the rookie player. Robinson's first year was Greenberg's last as a player.

While baseball integration was underway in the National League, racial prejudice still haunted the American League. Bill Veeck, the owner of the Cleveland Indians, had a more impulsive management style than the cautious Rickey. In 1947 Veeck purchased the contract of Larry Doby and, within a few days, the twenty-two-year-old black was playing with the Indians. Doby did not have Robinson's experience in integrated college athletics and minor league ball, and his performance in the field reflected his lack of preparation. In thirty-two at bats he registered only five hits and struck out eleven times. After such a disappointing performance in 1947, many experts predicted that Doby would not return to the major leagues. The 1948 season confounded these pundits, however; Doby returned to the Indians and, bolstered by the presence of Negro Leagues veteran Leroy "Satchel" Paige and the encouragement of manager Lou Boudreau and pitcher Steve Gromek, Doby helped to lead the Indians to the American League pennant with a .301 batting average and fourteen home runs.

Robinson, Doby, and Paige opened the way for black athletes in baseball and in other sports. Roy Campanella, Willie Mays, and Henry "Hank" AARON soon became stars of the diamond. Professional football accepted black players such as Robinson's teammate at UCLA, Kenny Washington, and defensive back Emlen Tunnell, who joined the New York Giants

in 1948 and was a key member of their innovative "umbrella" defense against the forward pass in the early 1950's. Blacks were numerous among the era's outstanding running backs. Marion Motley, Joe Perry, Ollie Matson, and Jim Brown all combined speed, size, and strength to frequently overwhelm rival defenses with memorable individual efforts.

Professional basketball also integrated gradually in the 1950's. Indeed, by the 1970's, blacks dominated the game. Such pioneers as Nat "Sweetwater" Clifton and Chuck Cooper were soon followed by the towering six-foot, ten-inch philosopher and practitioner of defensive basketball Bill Russell, and the even taller offensive powerhouse Wilt Chamberlain. These giants often overshadowed smaller but still important players such as Hal Greer, Oscar Robertson, and Elgin Baylor. Most professional black players arrived by way of college basketball, which also integrated in those years. A crucial event was the 1966 National Collegiate Athletic Association (NCAA) victory of an all-black starting five from Texas Western. In the 1970's the revo-

Latinos hold prominent positions in major league baseball. (Robert Fried)

lution in technique begun by the quick-moving, jump-shooting Italian American Hank Luisetti four decades earlier reached its culmination. Taller players with remarkable mobility and jumping ability made the game a stream of fast breaks, jump shots, penetrating drives, and slam dunks, with much of the action taking place at or above the ten-foot height of the basket.

Latinos. While the inclusion of blacks in major professional sports had a symbolic turning point with the appearance of Jackie ROBINSON as a Brooklyn Dodger in 1947, the arrival of Latinos was never so clearly defined nor dramatically focused. The reason for this perhaps has more to do with the nature of prejudice in the United States than with the sports themselves. Light-skinned Latinos endured ethnic stereotyping and prejudiced humor, but their presence did not cause public controversy on the scale that Robinson faced. These pioneers included two men of contrasting temperaments and styles. Vernon "Lefty" Gomez of Rodeo, California, was a pencil-thin, left-handed, twenty-year-old pitcher with a blazing fast ball and an irrepressible sense of humor. He strode out onto the hallowed turf of Yankee Stadium in 1930 to take his place beside Babe Ruth and Lou Gehrig. That same summer Alfonso Lopez, a serious twenty-two-year-old from Tampa, Florida, became the regular catcher for the Brooklyn Dodgers. No more than a competent hitter in his best years, Lopez lacked the flamboyance of Gomez, but he gradually earned a reputation as one of BASEBALL's great defensive catchers. The exciting and excitable Gomez won 189 games against only 101 losses for the Yankees, and also had a brief career as a stand-up comic in vaudeville. By contrast, Lopez became a thoughtful student of the game and channeled his experience into an impressive career as a manager, winning American League pennants with the Cleveland Indians in 1954 and the Chicago White Sox in 1959.

Neither Lopez nor Gomez had to break the color line, even in a society that was highly sensitive to skin pigmentation. That task went to Orestes "Minnie" Minoso, the first Latino player of widely acknowledged African ancestry. Minoso was well known to scouts and managers because of his fame in Cuba (where baseball was the national game) and his play for the New York Cubans of the NEGRO LEAGUES. He finally entered the major leagues in 1951 at the age of twenty-nine. He remained there for fifteen years, forever shattering the stereotype that Latinos could not hit top-level pitchers. An energetic player with great foot speed and batting ability, Minoso radiated an enthusiasm that infected fans, who cheered his hustle and dedication. Despite losing some of his most productive years because of his late entry into the major leagues, Minoso amassed 1,963 hits and three times led the American League both in triples and stolen bases.

Minoso seemed to transcend or, at least, to ignore the tensions surrounding the arrival of minorities in major league baseball, but Puerto Rican Roberto CLEMENTE could not. He made his debut with the Pittsburgh Pirates at the age of twenty-one in 1955 and played there for his entire major league career. With exceptional talent in every phase of baseball—running, throwing, and fielding as well as batting—Clemente, like Minoso, injected electricity into the game. Unlike Minoso, however, Clemente was unable to remain silent about the game's psychological and physical costs, which ran the gamut from overt ethnic insults and serious injuries to unintended slights. To the end, Clemente was a frustrated star, a four-time batting champion with a lifetime average of .317 who felt, with some justification, that his black Latino background had prevented him from receiving the credit he deserved.

Clemente's volatility diverted attention from his compassion and generosity toward those who needed help. For example, he introduced fellow Puerto Rican Orlando Cepeda to professional baseball in the United States. Cepeda went on to an outstanding career, mostly with the San Francisco Giants. In 1961 the two Puerto Ricans excelled among National League hitters. Cepeda led with forty-six home runs and 142 runs-batted-in, while Clemente led in batting average with .351. Sadly, Clemente's compassion played a role in his premature death. He died in a plane crash in 1972 on a mission of mercy to earthquake victims in Nicaragua.

Minoso, Clemente, and Cepeda established a path for many athletes from the Caribbean. Juan Marichal, Cepeda's teammate on the San Francisco Giants, emerged as a star pitcher from the talent-laden Dominican Republic. Known for an unusually high leg kick in his pitching delivery, Marichal used a baffling assortment of throwing motions that helped to make him one of baseball's most successful starting pitchers. After his retirement in 1975, Marichal participated in the development of young talent in his homeland that also sent to the major leagues the Alou brothers (Felipe, Jesus, and Matty), George Bell, Julio Franco, and Pedro Guerrero.

Women. The role of women in American college and professional sports was limited until the 1960's. This was largely because of the notion that women should play only a narrow, carefully circumscribed part in society. The duties of mother and housekeeper at home and secretary or schoolteacher on the job very nearly covered the spectrum of opportunities for women in the late 1800's and early 1900's. Educators discouraged even the most rudimentary forms of ex-

Young girls and women who aspire to be athletes have more and more women role models. (Betts Anderson, Unicorn Stock Photos)

ercise for adolescent females and young women. In the 1920's, however, a few exceptional women carried their daring achievements in athletics beyond traditional bounds. "Babe" Didrikson ZAHARIAS (born Mildred Didriksen) excelled in track and field events and set world records in the javelin throw, high jump, and hurdles in the 1932 Olympics. Although a sports celebrity while still in her twenties, Didrikson had to

face the limited options available to a female athlete. She decided to concentrate on golf which provided a rewarding outlet for her talents. She became a professional golfer in 1947 while collaborating in the creation of the Ladies Professional Golf Association. Her long drives, steady putting, and outgoing personality attracted many new fans to women's sports and helped to challenge the image of the passive, physically inactive female in American culture.

By the 1950's and 1960's, many skilled and determined young women turned to amateur and professional sports. Tennis became one of the first multiethnic events for women. Typically a "country club" sport that required access to expensive playing courts, tennis matches took place in front of stands located very close to the playing area. Under such challenging conditions, Althea GIBSON emerged as the first black American tennis champion in the 1950's, a decade of tension and violence surrounding the burgeoning Civil Rights movement. Gibson won the major tournaments in the United States and Great Britain in 1957 and 1958.

Chris Evert developed her tennis skills in the late 1960's and became a professional in 1972. An innovator in the use of a powerful, two-handed backhand stroke, Evert revealed an intelligence and tenacity to spectators in the stands and, by the late 1970's, to a much larger television audience. A calm performer in a sport known for dramatic and often frustrating near misses, Evert won championships in Great Britain, France, the United States, and Australia.

Meanwhile, a new generation of women began to take sports seriously both as a legitimate activity at the college level and as a career possibility in professional competition and coaching. Colleges and universities had large budgets for expensive FOOTBALL, BASKETBALL, BASEBALL, and track and field programs for men. Women began to demand and to receive a greater portion of the athletic budget in the 1970's, but inequities remained. Many women who excelled in college sports—especially track and field and swimming—went on to earn acclaim in the Olympics. Runner Florence Griffith Joyner, swimmer Janet Evans, and the multitalented Jackie Joyner-Kersee led the field in their respective sports in the late 1980's and early 1990's.

The Ambiguous Legacy. Mass-audience sports celebrate individual and team achievement in a way that often respects and even nourishes cultural identity. Millions of fans have come to accept and admire ath-

During a stay in New York City in 1933, Babe Didrickson donned a Rangers uniform and tried her hand at ice hockey. (AP/Wide World Photos)

letes from cultures quite different from their own. Jackie ROBINSON and Larry Doby quickly gained the support of most of their teammates, soon earned the respect of their competitors, and eventually won the allegiance of fans. Their acceptance as black athletes was not in the same category as Jim THORPE's recognition as an Indian athlete, which resulted to a large extent because the majority culture deemed it appropriate (according to the stereotypical view) for Indians to display great foot speed and elusive movement. By contrast, Robinson and Doby challenged the widespread prejudices against them and other blacks by going to work as members of integrated teams at a time when the nation was struggling with the larger problem of social integration. They arrived not as part of a stereotype that fit comfortably into the nation's dominant values but as members of a racial minority with an established identity.

An analysis of Jackie Robinson's first World Series (1947) by black sportswriter Wendell Smith exemplifies this acceptance of multiculturalism. Robinson acquitted himself well, but Joe DiMaggio, Cookie Lavagetto, and Al Gionfriddo made the decisive plays. In Smith's view, if race and ethnicity were to be considered in the distribution of kudos, "we'll have to pass the laurels to the players of Italian extraction. . . . In short, it's been a great series . . . no matter who your parents were."

The treatment of women and minorities in American sports reflects the nation's sometimes harmonious, sometimes discordant social history. Organized sports are based on rules in which all participants are to be treated equally; winning competition depends on a combination of talent and tenacity. In sports as a microcosm of American society, young people from minority groups have found social acceptance as respectable competitors and champions. Yet in the larger competitive arenas of business, politics, and education, members of minorities have often continued to encounter racial and ethnic barriers. Fairness and justice in these arenas are far more complex than on the playing fields, involving ideological and philosophical differences that have engaged national leaders in extended debates. In spite of the symbolic importance and popularity of sports and the accomplishments of diverse individuals in these sports, the United States remains a divided society in which much diligent and significant work is rewarded in a haphazard and sometimes prejudiced fashion.

SUGGESTED READINGS. There are few serious studies of multiculturalism in athletics and sports in spite of the popularity of those pursuits. Two of the most thorough are Jules Tygiel's *Baseball's Great Experiment: Jackie Robinson and His Legacy* (1983) and Peter Levine's *Ellis Island to Ebbets Field: Sport and the American Jewish Experience* (1992). Donald Mrozek's *Sport and the American Mentality, 1880-1910* (1983) and Allen Guttmann's *A Whole New Ball Game* (1988) offer thoughtful general views. The works of Harry Edwards are helpful, including his groundbreaking *The Sociology of Sport* (1973).—*John A. Britton*

Atlanta Compromise Address: Also known as the Atlanta Exposition Speech, delivered by Booker T. WASHINGTON in 1895 at the Cotton States and International Exposition in Atlanta, Georgia. The address was widely published in newspapers around the United States. Because Washington encouraged African Americans and whites to work together for economic advancement and did not demand political and social equality for African Americans, most listeners of both races received his ideas enthusiastically. W. E. B. DU BOIS, however, termed the speech a "compromise" because Washington asked African Americans to accept racial injustice in exchange for economic gains.

Attica prison riot: Occurred in the state prison in Attica, New York, over a four-day period beginning September 9, 1971. Approximately three hundred of the 2,250 inmates took thirty-eight guards hostage to protest unsatisfactory prison conditions ranging from brutal treatment by the guards to inadequate shower facilities. A majority of inmates were African Americans. After four days of negotiation, Governor Nelson Rockefeller and State Correction Commissioner Russell Oswald agreed to most of the prisoners' demands but not to complete amnesty. New York law enforcement officials, in an effort to regain control, attacked the prison, killing forty-two men, nine of them hostages, and injuring eighty-three prisoners seriously. Investigators uncovered evidence that prison authorities had manufactured stories regarding the treatment of hostages in order to mobilize support for the final police assault. Public attention focused on the inhumane conditions at the prison eventually led to the filing of a $2.8 billion civil class-action suit against four former state officials in 1991.

Attitude: Positive or negative evaluation held by an individual or a group. Members of a culture may share particular attitudes about ideas, places, people, objects, and other ethnic or racial groups. At its most simple, an attitude may consist simply of what a person or culture likes or dislikes. Attitudes do not always predict behavior; in other words, PREJUDICE against members of a particular ethnic group (an attitude) does not always translate into harmful behaviors such as discrimination. One of the challenges of multiculturalism is to eliminate racist or otherwise exclusionary attitudes.

Attorneys: The practice of law is arguably both one of the most admired and most reviled professions in the United States. Traditionally an elitist occupation open to a very few, attorneys in the United States are still mostly white males from middle-class or upper-class backgrounds. Women and minorities, however, have made steady inroads into the profession in the latter half of the twentieth century.

Training and Careers. The first institution devoted entirely to teaching the law operated in Litchfield, Connecticut, from 1774 to 1833. In 1817, Harvard University was the first university to establish a law school. In 1870, Christopher Columbus Langdell be-

came the first dean of Harvard Law School and introduced the case method of teaching law. This method trains students in legal reasoning by reading, analyzing, and discussing actual court cases. Virtually all American law schools still use this method.

In 1992, there were 175 accredited law schools with more than 127,828 students in the United States. Law school usually takes three years to complete and most schools only admit college graduates. Law school graduates are granted either a Bachelor of Laws (LL.B.) or a Juris Doctor (J.D.) degree. Upon graduation, prospective lawyers must pass a bar examination in every state in which they want to practice. A few states grant automatic admission to the bar upon graduation from an approved law school in that state.

Women and minorities have made steady inroads in legal careers, but attorneys in the United States are still usually white males from middle- to upper-class backgrounds. (Gerold Lim, Unicorn Stock Photos)

In 1992, there were 655,191 attorneys in the United States. Although in the past the main career for attorneys was private practice, contemporary attorneys have various options, such as government practice, solo practice, legal aid, or even law professor. The legal profession offers many different areas of specialization, such as corporate, patent, business, criminal, civil, bankruptcy, and tax law. Many lawyers use their legal education as a stepping stone to other careers, such as public office. Congress, state legislatures, and the administrative branches of the government draw more people from the law than from any other profession. For example, roughly three-fourths of U.S. senators are lawyers, and approximately two-thirds of all U.S. presidents have been lawyers. Like many other countries, the United States has an abundance of law-making bodies. Certain areas of the country have a surplus of attorneys. In the early 1990's, California had the most with about 82,000, closely followed by New York; the state with the fewest attorneys was Wyoming with about 900.

After practicing for many years, most attorneys aspire to become JUDGES. A judgeship is considered the highest honor in the legal profession. Unlike attorneys, who are often stereotyped as unethical, judges are highly regarded and respected by the public. One excellent trial attorney who reached this pinnacle was Thurgood MARSHALL, the first African American to sit on the U.S. Supreme Court. As an attorney, Marshall's most famous case was *Brown v. Board of Education*, which he argued successfully before the Court in 1954. This landmark case demolished the legal basis for segregation.

Fees and Legal Assistance. Attorneys may charge flat (usually for routine legal matters), hourly, or contingency-based fees. The latter is most common in personal injury cases, in which nothing is owed if the case is lost. If the client wins, he or she pays a percentage of the settlement. This system can be beneficial for low-income clients who do not have money and otherwise would never be able to pursue a meritorious case because of a lack of funds. Others argue that with this system attorneys only take cases that they will win and forgo other cases.

As the law has grown more complex, people have required more legal advice. This has increased the demand for attorneys in the United States. In the 1960's, legal aid clinics were set up to provide free or low-cost legal advice not only for poor people but also for people with disabilities or older people on a fixed income. At the same time, lower cost legal clinics began cropping up for middle-income Americans who do not qualify for legal aid services.

Legal clinics tend to be run by large groups of attorneys who specialize in the most needed areas of law. Since they can afford to advertise, many people turn to the clinics instead of seeking out a more expensive solo practitioner who has to charge more. In this way, Americans who never went to a lawyer before or only sought advice when there was trouble can afford to get legal advice, such as help in preparing a will.

Legal aid services and legal clinics have created an opportunity for poor and middle-class people to receive routine legal services at reduced rates. This has also opened the door for attorneys to practice in a nontraditional field of law. Many minorities and women have chosen this avenue as opposed to attempting to break down the resistant barriers at prestigious private law firms. Lawyers from all types of practices volunteer their time in *pro bono* work for various causes, ranging from arts and charitable organizations to cases being pursued by the AMERICAN CIVIL LIBERTIES UNION (ACLU) or the National Association for the ADVANCEMENT OF COLORED PEOPLE (NAACP). In addition, many lawyers serve on the boards of nonprofit organizations, offering legal advice.

Women Attorneys. The number of women in this traditionally white, male-dominated profession has grown over the years. The proportion of women in law school rose from 4 percent in the 1960's to 8 percent by 1970; it was 36.8 percent in the 1980's. In 1992, women comprised more than 40 percent of all students entering law school. Yet despite these gains, the majority of working attorneys are men; out of 655,191 attorneys in the United States in 1992, only 85,552 or about 13 percent were women. Some of this discrepancy may be the result of certain types of discrimination faced by women attorneys, including pressure to work long hours for less pay then men, to work in less lucrative fields, to work harder and wait longer for partnership offers, and to postpone motherhood and marriage.

Minority Attorneys: In the past there were limited opportunities for minorities to participate in any type of graduate studies, including law school. After various forms of racial segregation were struck down, some institutions in search of minority applicants admitted them with lower test scores than those of white students. This has resulted in ongoing controversy as to whether minorities are truly qualified to be in law school and work as attorneys. Minorities tend to be underrepresented in the top half of their respective law schools. The "rumor of inferiority" that permeates

American society regarding the intellectual capabilities of minorities has serious psychological effects on minorities not only while in school but upon taking their productive places in society.

In spite of racism, minorities' presence in law school is steadily increasing. In 1986-1987, for example, 1,054 Latinos and 1,735 African Americans earned a law degree. Nevertheless, minorities are seldom seen in certain areas of the law, especially in fields dominated by large prestigious law firms. The state of New Jersey in 1990 created The New Jersey Law Firm Group in an effort to recruit more minorities, but little progress has been made. In a survey of twenty firms in the state of New Jersey, there were only ten minority partners and forty-nine minority associates. In 1991 and 1992, only ten minorities were hired.

The presence and activity of a diverse pool of legal professionals helps to ensure the passage of legislation that serves to protect minorities. (Dennis MacDonald, Unicorn Stock Photos)

There are no African Americans among the nation's ninety-three U.S. attorneys despite the fact that African Americans comprise 3 percent of the nation's lawyers. Less than 6 percent of the sitting federal JUDGES are African Americans, and in the highest state courts only 4.5 percent of the judges are African Americans. At least fourteen state courts, including California, Michigan, and New York are studying the impact of this bias. In the 1980's and early 1990's, many observers such as Judge A. Leon Higginbotham of the U.S. Court of Appeals criticized the Reagan and Bush Administrations for their lack of minority judicial appointments. Various studies suggest that the American judicial system is biased against minorities, both in hiring personnel and in sentencing defendants. One survey conducted in 1987 revealed that 98 percent of judges and court managers perceived some bias against minorities in the justice system.

Image. Over time, the image of attorneys has slowly eroded. A popular STEREOTYPE persists of lawyers as sleazy "ambulance chasers" who will do anything to bilk money from their clients and the system. Attorneys are blamed for a host of social problems, such as soaring insurance rates. Yet in a highly litigious society in which many Americans sue each other, the profession that delivers legal services cannot be entirely to blame. As in any other profession, there are competent, ethical members as well as incompetent, unethical ones. This image can perhaps be traced to the enormous proliferation of legal malpractice suits during the 1970's and 1980's—suits which won large sums for attorneys. One Harris Poll found that only 18 percent of the American public had confidence in law firms—a lower approval rating than for garbage collectors, police officers, and business firms.

SUGGESTED READINGS. For a detailed study of the renowned African American attorney and judge, see Lisa Aldred's *Thurgood Marshall* (1990). Journalist Carl T. Rowan's biography, *Dream Makers, Dream Breakers: The World of Justice Thurgood Marshall* (1993) also provides fascinating insights. Gerald P. Lopez presents his own perspective on minorities in the legal profession in *Rebellious Lawyering: One Chicano's Vision of Progressive Law Practice* (1992). Cynthia Fuchs Epstein's *Women in Law* (1981) offers a historical perspective, while *Women Lawyers* (1984), edited by Emily Couric, contains various essays on the experience of women within the profession. Nicholas von Hoffman's article "Crossing the White-Shoe Line," in *The New Yorker*, May 10, 1993, pp. 54-58, profiles H. Jesse Arrelle, founding partner of the first minority-owned national law firm to specialize in corporate law.—*Valerie Hartman*

Australian Americans: Australia, like the United States, was colonized largely by people from England. The Australian colonies were settled later than the American colonies, however; settlement did not begin until 1788, and Australia did not become a unified commonwealth until 1901. Both lands were "new worlds" to which Europeans moved for various reasons, and so have been known primarily as places to which people move rather than from which people emigrate.

(In both countries, too, native populations were forcibly pushed aside by Europeans.) Nevertheless, Australians have immigrated to the United States, although they have only formed a tiny fraction of the U.S. population.

The first significant immigration from Australia came in 1849-1850, in response to the California GOLD RUSH. The period of greatest immigration from Australia occurred between 1900 and 1920, and numbers steadily declined from then until the 1950's, when

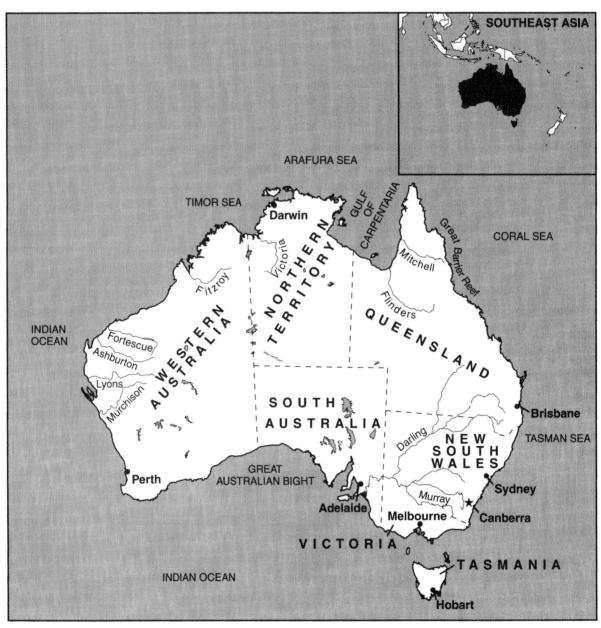

AUSTRALIA

they again began to rise. The exception to this pattern was the post-World War II period between 1945 and 1948, when a large number of Australians immigrated. Many of the immigrants were new brides of American servicemen who had been stationed in the Pacific.

It is estimated that between 10 and 13 percent of the nineteenth century gold-seeking immigrants were former convicts who had been sent from Great Britain to Australia to settle the colony. The most rough, lawless Australians living in San Francisco became nicknamed "Sydney Ducks," abhorred and feared for their violent behavior. The notorious waterfront area of San Francisco in which they lived was dubbed "Sydneytown" (later known as the Barbary Coast), and they developed their own form of organized crime there that catered to every vice. Civic leaders and vigilante groups alike tried to deal with the problem, but the most beneficial event, ironically, was the discovery of gold in Australia in 1851: A large number of felons simply moved back to Australia.

Twentieth century immigrants, especially since the 1940's, have been nothing like their nineteenth century predecessors, except for the fact that large numbers live in California. Since the 1960's, many Australian immigrants have been professional and technical workers. Because Australia is, like the United States, an industrialized, English-speaking country, Australians generally assimilate easily into American society and culture. Australians therefore have maintained less of a recognizable ethnic identity in the United States than have many other immigrant groups. Neverthe-

less, there are some organizations of Australian Americans, including the Australian and New Zealand Society of New York, the America-Australia Interaction Association, and the American Australian Association (a small business and political group) that promotes Australian-American cultural and business ties.

Austrian Americans: The story of Austrians in the United States is as complex as the history of that ancient Alpine country, which for centuries was one of Europe's most multicultural empires. Merely determining who in America was an Austrian—as opposed to a German, Tirolean, Czech, Slovak, or Bohemian—was long a daunting task. Many German-speaking Austrians were

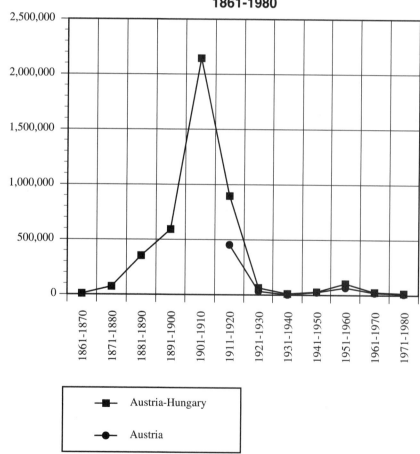

Immigration from Austria-Hungary and Austria: 1861-1980

Source: Data are from *Statistical Yearbook of the Immigration and Naturalization Service, 1986.* Table 2. Washington, D.C.: Department of Justice, 1987.
Note: Data for Autria-Hungary not reported until 1861. Austria not reported separately until 1911.

content with a German identity both in their homeland and in the United States. It was only late in the nineteenth century that a specific Austrian identity began to emerge.

At the time of the American Revolution in 1776, Austria under the ruling Habsburg family had been part of the Holy Roman Empire for five hundred years and was the core of a multinational empire in the heart of Europe. In the ensuing decades, this patchwork realm of more than a dozen nationalities—mostly Germans, Slavs, Hungarians, and Jews—slipped into decline. Meanwhile, the United States was becoming a world power in part by absorbing millions of European emigrants. Many of the most notable Austrians among them were combinations of German, Jewish, Slavic, or Hungarian stock.

Cataclysmic events in the forms of a failed revolution (1848), overpopulation and economic distress (1850-1910), world wars, and racial or ethnic persecution (1930's-1940's) prompted mass migration from the Austrian and Austro-Hungarian empires (1776-1918) as well as the First Republic (1918-1938). Ultimately, the Austro-Hungarian empire and its successor states provided 10 percent (4.2 million) of the swelling tide of immigrants that engulfed and enriched the United States between 1820 and 1960.

Early Settlers. In colonial America, German-speaking natives of the Austrian Empire were few. Most were members of the clergy, charged with spreading the CATHOLIC faith. German-speaking Jesuits were active in educating and converting American Indians in the Southwest. The Jesuits continued missionary work and exploration until the order was expelled from New Spain by Charles III in 1767 and replaced by the Franciscans.

Meanwhile, a group of Protestants fled persecution in the province of Salzburg and established the southernmost "German" settlement in the colonies at Ebenezer, Georgia in 1734. After moving to a more favorable location, they prospered until the revolutionary war. One of the settlers, Johann Treutlen, became the first elected governor of the state of Georgia.

After the AMERICAN REVOLUTION, relations between the fledgling democracy and the old absolute monarchy were strained. Formidable barriers were erected on both sides to prevent or discourage migration to the United States. The ruling Habsburgs originally prohibited emigration, and Catholics were among the least welcome of immigrants to the early United States. Thus, only a few thousand German-speaking Austrians were among the approximately 1.5

million immigrants to the new country between 1776 and 1846.

Despite adversity, including attacks on their Catholic religion, German Austrians managed to establish communities in the Yorkville section of New York City, as well as in Philadelphia and Allentown, Pennsylvania; some pioneers also went west.

The Growth of Austrian Immigration. The unsuccessful revolution in Vienna in 1848 compelled a small but illustrious group of political refugees to leave for the United States. These "FORTY-EIGHTERS" were radical reformers and free-thinking intellectuals, including many Jews. They joined the new Republican Party, supported Abraham Lincoln and the abolitionist cause, and distinguished themselves in various areas: music and law (Frederick and Louis Brandeis), medicine and journalism (Heinrich Börnstein and Julius Hausen), and architecture (John Smithmeyer). As emigration restrictions were lifted in the late nineteenth century, working-class immigrants began arriving en masse to take up jobs in a rapidly industrializing United States. The significance of the mass migration of the peoples of the Austro-Hungarian Empire to the United States can scarcely be exaggerated. It was these diverse nationalities, including German Austrians, which made up the largest single contingent (2.1 million) of immigrants during the peak decade of arrivals (1900-1910).

The newcomers enlarged and enriched established ethnic enclaves in burgeoning American cities such as New York, Philadelphia, Chicago, and St. Louis. They helped the United States assume a leading position in agriculture, mining, and manufacturing. For German Austrians, the greatest contributions were to be in music and film; in industries such as brewing, baking, and textiles; and in winter recreation. During this period Americans were introduced to delicatessens, beer gardens, pretzels, wieners, schnapps, and schnitzel. The Roman Catholic church underwent unprecedented growth, and the German and Austrian way of celebrating Christmas with carols and a tree became increasingly popular.

After World War II, before a smaller, more homogeneous Austria became one of the most prosperous countries in Europe, about 100,000 German Austrians emigrated to the United States. They came under the provisions of the DISPLACED PERSONS ACT of 1948 and a quota system permitting an additional 1,400 Austrian immigrants per year. Eventually, more than four million immigrants from the Austro-Hungarian

AUSTRIA

Empire and Austria found their way to American shores. In this total, German-speaking Austrians may be estimated at 650,000.

Austrians in the Arts. In the arts and sciences, entertainment and recreation, fashion, and many other fields, Austrians and Austrian Americans have enriched American traditional and popular culture.

As they have for centuries, the Austrians registered their most significant and enduring achievements in MUSIC. Austrian or Austrian American composers and MUSICIANS helped build some of America's most revered cultural institutions. Indeed, from the Metropolitan Opera to record-setting Broadway musicals, as American music came of age, Austrians often held the baton or performed at the keyboard. Gustav Mahler, Bruno Walter, Fritz Kreisler, Arnold Schönberg, and Rudolf Bing are but a few of the most prominent names on a long list of luminaries.

After music, the American film industry has been the greatest beneficiary of Austrian genius and talent. Austrians such as Fritz Lang, Erich von Stroheim, and Josef von Sternberg were among the most creative artists in early American cinema. Austrian Americans have won Oscars for best director (Billy Wilder, Otto Preminger, Fred Zinneman) and best actor (Paul Muni). Max Fleischer, a pioneer of the animated cartoon, was an Austrian.

Scientific Contributions. As in music, Austrians have a tradition of excellence in science and higher education. When the Nazis began persecuting Austrian Jews following Germany's annexation of Austria in 1938, many of the most outstanding Austrian scientists emigrated to the United States. All four Austrian Nobel laureates in physics lived and taught in the United States or became American citizens. The defense industry in particular greatly benefited from the work of Victor Hess, Karl Landsteiner, and Isidor Rabi. Many of America's finest universities welcomed Austrian Jewish scientists to their faculties. During World War II, Austrians as well as German émigré scientists worked on critical projects at the national laboratories at Los Alamos and Oak Ridge.

Similar contributions were made in the fields of chemistry, biology, and mathematics. Too numerous to mention are the many Austrian practitioners of psychoanalysis who emigrated to the United States and spread the influence of an Austrian named Sigmund Freud. Austrian émigré scholars also included notable philosophers of science and logical positivists.

Austrians in Business and Community Service. Austrians have left their marks on American journalism and manufacturing, as well as on the service sector. Personifying the multiculturalism of an earlier era, Joseph Pulitzer, part Jewish Hungarian, part German

Austrian, was a central figure in American journalism. Born in Hungary, he helped develop the German-language press in St. Louis, then moved on to greater enterprises in the 1880's as owner of the *New York World*. The most prestigious awards in journalism, the Pulitzer Prizes, bear his name.

The SPINGARN MEDAL for civil rights achievements is named for one of the founding fathers of the NATIONAL ASSOCIATION FOR THE ADVANCEMENT OF COLORED PEOPLE (NAACP), Joel Elias Spingarn, of Austrian Jewish descent.

The Kohler family built upon their success in the plumbing supply business to become one of Wisconsin's most prominent families. Two Kohlers have been governors of the state. August Brentano in books, John David Hertz in car rentals, and Frederick Praeger in publishing are only a few of the most famous Austrian Americans in business. Joining them in the 1980's was technological innovator Ray Kurzweil, who invented reading machines for the blind, text scanners, and digitizers.

Austrians have always been among the best skiers in the world. They helped spawn a new industry in the United States with the founding of two key resorts: Sun Valley, Idaho, in the West and Stowe, Vermont, in the East. Expert instructors, Austrians established ski schools in the 1940's and 1950's to introduce Americans to modern techniques and equipment.

For the most part, Austrian immigrants were assimilated into American society easily and without fanfare. Actor Arnold Schwarzenegger, for example, a native of the Styrian provincial capital of Graz, became one of Hollywood's biggest stars in the 1980's. Neither advertising nor concealing his origins, he is typical of the businesslike German Austrian Americans.

SUGGESTED READINGS. The most complete account of Austrians in the United States is E. Wilder Spaulding's *The Quiet Invaders: The Story of the Austrian Impact upon America* (1968). For a more recent concise overview, see Frederick Luebke's essay in the *Harvard Encyclopedia of American Ethnic Groups* (1980). A map and table with immigration data are provided in *The Ethnic Almanac* (1981) by Stephanie Bernardo Johns.—*Dave E. McClave*

Authoritarian personality: A personality type that was suggested, in the early 1950's, to advocate PREJUDICE. In *The Authoritarian Personality* (1950), Theodor Adorno and his coauthors put forth the idea that prejudice was the result of a "fascist" type of personality. Adorno theorized that this personality type was produced by authoritarian child-rearing practices. The idea that prejudice was created by individuals with a certain type of upbringing led to overly optimistic forecasts about the ease with which it could be reduced or eliminated. Such hopes were challenged by the concept of institutional RACISM that developed in the late 1960's. Institutional racism shifted the focus from prejudiced individuals to prejudices that are ingrained in the economic, educational, and political institutions of American society.

Aztlán: Legendary place of origin of the Aztecs, which was reportedly located "somewhere to the north" of the Valley of Mexico. It is believed that the Aztecs began a two hundred-year migration from Aztlán around the year 1111 that ended in the Valley of Mexico, where they founded Tenochtitlán (modern Mexico City). The CHICANO MOVEMENT has made frequent references to Aztlán, using it as a symbolic name for the southwestern part of the United States, where most Mexican Americans live, or for the metaphorical space that exists wherever Chicano culture flourishes.

B

Back to Africa movement: The concept of a return to Africa by black Americans had its inception in 1822 with the founding of Liberia on the west coast of the African continent. Liberia was primarily a white enterprise, supported by the U.S. government and intended as a homeland for former slaves living in the United States who might wish to emigrate. In the latter part of the nineteenth century, a similar undertaking was initiated by African Americans in response to the Berlin Confer-

Turner's ideological successor, Marcus GARVEY, was the man with whom the term "Back to Africa" came to be identified, not only as a call for large-scale emigration but also as a source of black pride and identity. Garvey, a Jamaican, founded the UNIVERSAL NEGRO IMPROVEMENT ASSOCIATION (UNIA) in Kingston in 1914. He came to the United States in 1916 and subsequently settled in New York, where, in 1917, he established the New York chapter of UNIA as a

A rendering of Monrovia, Liberia, a possible destination for former American slaves. (Library of Congress)

ence of 1884-1885, at which the major European powers met to agree upon the boundaries of their colonies in Africa. The conference determined that the only countries in the continent that remained under black control were Liberia and Ethiopia. In an effort to fight the potential loss of African culture and identity that this situation threatened, the prominent African American clergyman Henry McNeal Turner and others led a PAN-AFRICAN MOVEMENT to persuade American blacks to return to the African homeland.

result of the enthusiastic response he received in many cities during his tour of the United States.

Garvey's UNIA supported the central conviction that people of African descent living in America were essentially outsiders who would remain disenfranchised and powerless in a country where white supremacy was widely accepted as indisputable reality. An admirer of Booker T. WASHINGTON and the TUSKEGEE INSTITUTE, Garvey advocated wide-scale programs of education with the intention of creating a foundation for establishing economic power for black people. Such power would be instrumental to Garvey's fondest wish, the establishment of an independent nation that would be home to black people throughout the world. In this sense, Garvey's concept of an African nation is analogous to the Zionist view of Israel as a haven for the Jewish diaspora.

In 1922, Garvey sent a delegation to the League of Nations requesting that the colonies that had belonged to Germany prior to its defeat in World War I be turned over to the UNIA for colonization by the black people of the world. Although it was initially considered, nothing came of Garvey's petition. At the same time, Garvey was negotiating with President Charles D. B. King of Liberia for permission to establish UNIA settlements for African Americans in his country. In exchange for his support, Garvey promised King that the UNIA would bring large-scale development to the small African nation, offering, in grandiose fashion, to build schools, railroads, and various forms of commercial and industrial enterprise. By 1924, Garvey had convinced the Liberian government to grant permission for the establishment of a small settlement of several thousand people. Garvey's success, however, was short-lived. When a UNIA delegation arrived in Liberia that summer to make the necessary arrangements, President King had abruptly reversed his position and withdrew his permission. Garvey pleaded, without success, and the UNIA's Back to Africa movement came to an end.

SUGGESTED READINGS. For a brief but informative overview of Garvey and the UNIA, see *Marcus Garvey* (1988) by Mary Lawler and *Marcus Garvey and the Vision of Africa* (1974), edited by John Henrik Clarke. Tony Martin's *The Pan-African Connection: From Slavery to Garvey and Beyond* (1983) offers interesting insights into Garvey's enduring legacy. Although somewhat less than objective, *Garvey and Garveyism* (1963), written by Garvey's wife, Amy Jacques Garvey, includes a perspective on Garvey unavailable elsewhere. The salient documents of the UNIA are available in *Marcus Garvey: Life and Lessons* (1987), edited by Robert Hill and Barbara Bair.

Bacon's Rebellion: Campaign led by Nathaniel Bacon in 1676 to gain more power for freemen in the Virginia colony. Bacon and his followers believed that Governor William Berkeley was not protecting them adequately from American Indian assaults, so they randomly attacked surrounding tribes, killing many Indians.

Berkeley had Bacon arrested. When Bacon was later freed, he took control of the colony and forced the governor to flee. For three months, Bacon and his followers ruled, plundering the estates of wealthy landowners before Berkeley regained control. The rebellion is an example of early American class struggle between wealthy and middle-class people, with slaves and servants on both sides.

Badillo, Herman (b. Aug. 21, 1929, Caguas, Puerto Rico): Puerto Rican attorney and politician. Orphaned at age five, Badillo was sent to the United States in 1940 to live with relatives. After graduating with honors from the City College of New York and receiving a doctorate from Brooklyn Law School, Badillo served as commissioner of the New York City Department of Housing Relocation from 1962 to 1965 and then as borough president of the Bronx through 1969. Badillo was a member of the United States Congress from 1970 to

Badillo during a 1979 news conference. (AP/Wide World Photos)

1978. In 1972, he published *A Bill of No Rights: Attica and the American Prison System*. In 1978, Badillo was appointed to serve as deputy mayor of New York City under Edward Koch. Badillo returned to private practice in 1979, but he continued to be involved in public affairs, running unsuccessfully for New York state comptroller in 1986.

Báez, Joan (b. Jan. 9, 1941, Staten Island, N.Y.): Folk musician and pacifist. Báez neglected her studies at Boston University to sing in coffeehouses. In 1959 and 1960 she played the Newport Folk Festival, and soon after released her first album, *Joan Baez,* a compilation of traditional folk songs. When the United States entered the Vietnam War, she sang protest songs, often with songwriter Bob Dylan.

In 1965 Báez founded the Institute for the Study of Nonviolence, located in Carmel Valley, California, and in 1979 became cofounder of Humanitas, the International Human Rights Committee. Though Báez was most popular in the 1960's and early 1970's, she continued to record and to make public appearances on behalf of peace and civil and human rights.

Folk singer and peace activist Joan Báez. (AP/Wide World Photos)

Baha'is: Members of a religious sect devoted to spiritual unity and world peace. Founded in Iran in the nineteenth century, the sect has more than 100,000 adherents in the United States, with strong missionary programs to reach more converts. It is unique among American religions in recognizing not only its own historic leader, Bahá'u'lláh, but the leaders of all major world religions, such as Moses, Buddha, Jesus, and Muhammad, as legitimate vehicles for the revelations of a single "religion of God." The sect won many new converts in the 1970's, including a number of African Americans in the South. Besides world peace, Baha'is promote the elimination of racial and religious prejudice, the emancipation of women, and economic and political justice.

Baker, Houston Alfred, Jr. (b. Mar. 22, 1943, Louisville, Ky.): African American educator and scholar. A Phi Beta Kappa graduate of HOWARD UNIVERSITY (1965), Baker earned his master's (1966) and doctorate (1968) from the University of California at Los Angeles. He then taught English at Yale University, the University of Virginia, and the University of Pennsylvania, where he was also director of Afro-American Studies. His numerous publications since 1971 have focused on African American literature, culture, and aesthetics. Author of three volumes of poetry, Baker has received many academic awards.

Baker, Josephine (June 3, 1906, St. Louis, Mo.—Apr. 2, 1975, Paris, France): African American stage star. The energetic, vivacious Baker was a sensation in Paris in the 1920's, appearing in music hall acts that were considered bold, and playing the flamboyant eccentric offstage. She had begun dancing while still in elementary school, and she appeared at Radio City Music Hall in New York City before going to Paris as a principal in a jazz production troupe in 1925. Her international career later included film and television. She received the French Legion of Honor order in the 1940's and adopted a multiracial "rainbow family" of orphans in the 1950's.

Bakke case. *See* **Regents of the University of California v. Bakke**

Balch, Emily Greene (Jan. 8, 1867, Jamaica Plain, Mass.—Jan. 9, 1961, Cambridge, Mass.): Sociologist and social reformer. Balch was the second American woman recipient of the Nobel Peace Prize (1946). In 1896 she taught economics at WELLESLEY COLLEGE. Among other activities, she was cofounder and president of the Boston Women's Trade Union League (1902). Her most notable published work was *Our Slavic Fellow Citizens* (1910). In 1919 Wellesley refused to renew her contract because of her pacifist activities. At age fifty-two, Balch joined with London Quakers and helped establish the Women's International League for Peace and Freedom (WILPF), a major influence on the nascent League of Nations.

Baldwin, James Arthur (Aug. 2, 1924, New York, N.Y.—Nov. 30, 1987, St. Paul de Vence, France): African American author. Baldwin was a skillful, subtle prose writer from the early 1950's onward. His well-received first novel, *Go Tell It on the Mountain* (1953), fictionalized his Harlem boyhood. He worked mostly in France, producing other novels—notably *Giovanni's Room* (1956) and *Another Country* (1962)—along with essays and stories. Struggles with race and sexuality were recurring themes in his works. His essays in *Notes of a Native Son* (1955) and *The Fire Next Time* (1963) spoke powerfully for American blacks during a turbulent era.

An animated Baldwin one year before his death. (AP/Wide World Photos)

Ballet Hispanico: Leading Latino dance company and school in the United States, founded in 1971 in New York City by Venezuelan-born Tina Ramirez. The ballet company was established to promote an appreciation of Latino cultural heritage, to provide opportunities for professional training, to perform new works by Latino and Latin American choreographers, and to sponsor educational programs in public schools. Ballet Hispanico's annual operating budget is provided by grants and contributions from corporations, foundations, and individuals. In 1989 an abandoned warehouse was purchased and renovated to serve as headquarters for the school and dance company.

Banco Popular: Largest commercial bank in Puerto Rico, incorporated in 1984. Under a reorganization plan designed to create a bank holding company, it became owner of all shares of the older Banco de Ponce (established in 1917) through a share-for-share exchange in 1985. The interim holding company, named Ban Ponce Corp., merged with Banco Popular in 1990. Banco Popular conducts general banking business through its 194 branches in Puerto Rico. It also has twenty-two branches in New York City, one in Chicago, one in Los Angeles, and three in the U.S. Virgin Islands.

Banneker, Benjamin (Nov. 9, 1731, near Ellicott City, Md.—Oct. 9, 1806, Baltimore, Md.): African American inventor, mathematician, and almanac maker. Largely self-taught, Banneker is considered the first black scientist in America. He grew up a freeman in Maryland and had a limited formal education in an integrated school. Thereafter he made the first locally built clock in the country, and he predicted the 1789 solar eclipse. Beginning in 1792, he published an almanac that compiled data on tides, eclipses, and medicines—the first scientific publication by an American black. He also played an important role in the unique urban planning of Washington, D.C.

Baptists: While incorporating members of every race and ethnicity, Baptists have the single largest organization of African Americans of any church. Myriad churches within the Baptist family—many independent, others belonging to massive parent organizations—trace their roots to Calvinism and eighteenth century evangelicalism. Little else, however, appears universal. The Southern Baptist Convention, for example, is a dominant conservative influence in the South emphasizing often intolerant, white southern values. Simultaneously the interests of African Americans are served by Baptist churches throughout the country.

African American Baptist churches originated in the colonial South. Few African American slaves were Christianized before the early eighteenth century religious revival known as the GREAT AWAKENING. They

were prohibited by law and by social sanctions from learning to read and write and were viewed as subhuman—a moral position justified by biblical citations. Encouraged by the evangelicalism of the Awakening, however, by the mid- to late 1700's Baptist and METHODIST proselytizers from the western regions of the colonies began recruiting African Americans while espousing greater religious egalitarianism. Additionally, Baptist frontier churches emphasized emotionalism

Baptist ceremony in Immokalee, Fla. (Michael L. Kimble)

and personal religious experience while deemphasizing the relative intellectualism of then-dominant CONGREGATIONAL, PRESBYTERIAN, and EPISCOPALIAN churches. Their focus on emotionalism and a willingness to include African Americans among God's children made these churches uniquely alluring to slaves.

While most slaves initially attended churches with their masters, by the start of the nineteenth century, African Americans began forming independent congregations. The Baptist family of churches, which had been a minority religion throughout the colonial period, rapidly gained dominance. Black Baptist churches became a central focus for African American communities, incorporating unique blends of Christianity and African cultural and social traditions.

With twentieth century migrations of African Americans from the rural South to northern and southern urban regions, Baptist churches consistently provided community and continuity for African Americans. Whether housed in storefront churches or elaborate cathedrals, African American Baptist churches have adapted to individual community needs. The organization of Baptist churches consists of loose combinations at the regional or national level, with most belonging to one of three major organizations and others remaining entirely independent. Ideologies vary with some emphasizing mainstream middle-class experience and others a more traditional African American folk tradition.

Baptist churches historically have provided crucial training grounds for African American leaders, many of whom gained valuable speaking and leadership experience within their churches. Martin Luther KING, Jr., himself a Baptist preacher and preacher's son, culled much of his support for the Civil Rights movement from Baptist churches.

SUGGESTED READINGS. A cogent analysis of the nineteenth century rise to dominance of Baptist churches is found in Roger Fink and Rodney Stark's *The Churching of America, 1776-1990: Winners and Losers in Our Religious Economy* (1992). C. Eric Lincoln and Laurence H. Mamiya, in *The Black Church in the African American Experience* (1990), provide a history of African American Baptists in the broader context of African American religion, while James Melvin Washington's *Frustrated Fellows: The Black Baptist Quest for Social Power* (1986) focuses on the nineteenth century African American Baptist movement.

Bar/bat mitzvah: Ceremony that initiates young adults into the Jewish faith. The bar mitzvah (literally, "son of the commandment") also refers to a boy who is ready to take on the responsibilities of an adult in the Jewish community. After months of study, he appears in synagogue soon after his thirteenth birthday to read a portion of the holy Torah (first five books of the Bible) aloud in Hebrew and give an interpretive speech. The parallel ceremony for girls, the bat mitzvah ("daughter of the commandment") takes place after a girl's twelfth birthday. Jewish families celebrate bar and bat mitzvahs with elaborate festivities as well as religious observances.

Baraka, [Imamu] Amiri (LeRoi Jones; b. Oct. 7, 1934, Newark, N.J.): African American poet, playwright, and activist. A prolific writer and militant black nationalist leader, Jones began his career in the late 1950's with poetry and fiction palatable to white liberals. In the 1960's, his award-winning play *Dutchman* (1964) and subsequent works, along with his new Muslim name, proclaimed his revolutionary turn of mind. As coeditor of *Black Fire: An Anthology of Afro-American Writing* (1968), Baraka promoted a Black Arts movement that linked literature to the politics of African American separatism. An angry tone, strong language, shocking realism, and criticism of the mainstream culture characterize his writings.

Barnard College (New York, N.Y.): Women's college founded in 1889 as an affiliate of the all-male Columbia College (now Columbia University) in New York City. Its founder, Annie Nathan Meyer, resolved to create a college for women when her efforts to attend classes at Columbia were thwarted. Barnard required that women maintain the same rigorous academic standards as their male peers. This accounted for the small number of enrolled students initially, since there were few opportunities for women to prepare for college education. In 1900, Barnard incorporated with Columbia University, although it maintained a separate institutional structure. In 1983, Columbia began to accept women undergraduates; until then, women attending classes at Columbia were officially enrolled in Barnard College.

Barrio: Spanish term literally meaning "district." In the United States it is used to refer to a part of a city or town inhabited by Mexican Americans or other Latinos. Barrios have formed as a result of segregation as well as by choice. The term barrio has also come to have the connotation of slum or ghetto. In the United States, barrios have been characterized by widespread poverty, disease, substandard housing, limited city services, and neglect. Spanish is often the dominant or preferred language within the area.

Barrymore, Ethel (Aug. 15, 1879, Philadelphia, Pa.—June 18, 1959, Los Angeles, Calif.): Actor. In her prime, Barrymore was known as the first lady of the American stage; her career spanned stage, film, and television. Born into a prominent theatrical family, (Lionel and John Barrymore were her brothers), she had her acting debut at the age of fourteen. In 1895 she apprenticed under manager Charles Frohman, with whom she worked until his death in 1915. Her many notable performances included Alexandre Dumas' 1852 play *The Lady of the Camellias* (1917); Zoë Akins' *Déclassée* (1919), in which she sold out two hundred consecutive performances in New York and triumphed on tour; and W. Somerset Maugham's *The Constant Wife* (1926). One of her most memorable roles came in 1940 (and lasted three years), when she successfully played Miss Moffat in Emlyn Williams' 1938 drama *The Corn Is Green*.

Barton, Clara (Clarrisa Harlowe; Dec. 25, 1821, North Oxford, Mass.—Apr. 12, 1912, Glen Echo, Md.): Founder of the American Red Cross. During the CIVIL WAR, Barton went to the front to distribute medical provisions by mule, funding her efforts herself. In 1868 she attended the International Committee of the Red Cross in Geneva, Switzerland. In 1881, after a five-year campaign, Barton became president of the newly established American Association of the Red Cross, which provided relief for peacetime catastrophes as well as aid in wartime. During the SPANISH-AMERICAN WAR, she again aided troops by mule train.

Clara Barton, founder of the American Red Cross. (AP/ Wide World Photos)

Baseball: This distinctive American sport, which evolved from the British game of "rounders," reached the United States sometime after the American Revolution. By the mid-1800's, it had become well established among American youth. The two major leagues of modern baseball are the National League, formed in 1876, and the American League, begun in 1900.

Through much of its history, professional baseball was organized along strict color lines. The National Association, precursor to today's leagues, barred "Negro" players in 1867 from membership in the organization. The rule was only intermittently enforced, as blacks continued to participate with whites in professional baseball into the 1880's. The first African American player in the major leagues was Moses "Fleet" Walker, who played for Toledo of the American Association (then a major league) in 1884. As a result of the influence of Cap Anson, manager and part-owner of the National League's Chicago team, and other owners and players, an unwritten agreement developed that barred blacks from participating with whites in organized baseball. This agreement remained in effect until Branch Rickey signed Jackie ROBINSON to play for the Brooklyn Dodgers in 1947.

Negro baseball clubs and leagues were established in the late nineteenth century. Patterned after the white leagues, they provided a means for African American athletes to participate in the game at a professional level. Black players also formed "barnstorming" teams, traveling from city to city to play local teams. Often their opponents were white, and the black players could hold their own.

The first nationally successful black baseball league was the Negro National League, established in 1920. Other successful leagues included the Eastern Colored League (1923-1929) and the Negro American League (1929-1948). These leagues generally consisted of six teams; schedules allowed additional competition with semiprofessional opponents, often white teams. Eleven Black World Series were held. For many years, a black East-West all-star game was also held, often at Chicago's Comiskey Park. With the admission of African Americans to the white major leagues in 1947, the black leagues began to fold. The last of them, the Negro American League, continued playing until 1960.

Baseball was introduced into Latin America by touring professionals during the nineteenth century. The first Latino ballplayers appeared in professional baseball during the 1870's. Several dozen Latino ball-

"Fleet" Walker played for Toledo and was the first African American in the major leagues. (National Baseball Library, Cooperstown, NY)

players, all light-skinned, played in the major American leagues prior to 1947. Black Latinos were allowed to compete only in NEGRO LEAGUES. With integration, a large number of excellent Latino ballplayers have played professional ball. In general, these players came from countries in which baseball has been a prominent national sport: Mexico, Cuba, the Dominican Republic, Puerto Rico, and Venezuela. As with famous players from other ethnic and national groups, their success at the American national pastime boosted their group's image and bolstered the notion of an American melting pot.

SUGGESTED READINGS. An excellent history of the game can be found in the baseball trilogy by Harold Seymour; the third volume, *Baseball: The People's Game* (1990) is exceptional in its treatment of the sport outside the professional mainstream. The treatment of African American players is described in *Only the Ball Was White* (1970) by Robert Peterson. Short biographies for most "name" players are included in *The Ballplayers* (1990), edited by Mike Shatzkin.

Basie, Count [William] (Aug. 21, 1904, Red Bank, N.J.—Apr. 26, 1984, Hollywood, Fla.): African Ameri-

can jazz musician and bandleader. A keyboardist with a clean style and strong right hand, Basie began his career in vaudeville in the 1920's. He brought his own band to New York City in 1936. His popular group featured an outstanding rhythm section. For the next forty years, Basie's big band set the standard for American jazz bands. In 1957 Basie scored two "firsts" for black musicians: He performed for the Queen of England and played at the Waldorf Astoria Hotel in New York City. His band kept its style despite changing fads over the years. In the 1970's and 1980's, the ever-popular Basie continued to receive many accolades.

Legendary jazz musician Count Basie, in 1957. (AP/Wide World Photos)

Basketball: When James Naismith first nailed a peach basket to the wall of his Young Men's Christian Association (YMCA) in Springfield, Massachusetts, in 1891, he could hardly have envisioned the phenomenal growth of the game of "basket-ball" into a multimillion-dollar international industry. Besides being a popular sport, basketball has also become a significant aspect of minority culture in the United States, most predominantly in the African American community. In 1982, for example, African Americans represented 11.7 percent of the American population but made up about 70 percent of the players in the National Basketball Association (NBA). African American stars such as Bill Russell, Wilt Chamberlain, Elgin Baylor, Kareem Abdul-Jabbar, Julius Erving, Magic JOHNSON, and Michael JORDAN rank among the game's greatest players.

Three aspects of the game of basketball have helped to make it popular among members of minority groups. First, it can be played in a small area that requires minimal investment and upkeep (as opposed to the large grass fields that are necessary for such sports as BASEBALL, soccer, and FOOTBALL). Basketball courts are a common sight in urban playgrounds, parking lots, and driveways through-out the United States. Basketball is also popular on Indian reservations and among Alaskan Inuits, who play on hardened dirt, the goals supported by poles placed in fifty-gallon steel drums weighted with rocks. As few as two can play the game, and one person can enjoy solitary practice. Finally, the tremendous publicity given to the financial rewards of those who are able to play professional basketball make it an attractive goal for children in poorer neighborhoods, who usually have few successful professional role models other than athletes.

The deceptive financial lure of professional basketball makes it highly controversial with many African American leaders. Sociologists of sport point out that fewer than one high school athlete in twelve thousand will successfully enter professional sports. Despite the massive publicity given to black basketball heroes in the NBA, the total number of African Americans in the major U.S. professional sports of basketball, baseball, football, track, and boxing is merely a few thousand. This raises questions about whether professional sports are truly a significant source of economic opportunity for the millions of young members of racial and ethnic minorities in the United States. Nevertheless, ticket sales and television rights have become so essential to college and professional budgets that recruiters—not to mention sportswear manufacturers—have vested interests in perpetuating unrealistic expectations among vulnerable minority youth who see few other possibilities for escaping the economic disadvantages of their minority status.

Black leaders and college officials are concerned that seventy five percent of the African American athletes in American universities and colleges do not graduate after their four years of eligibility are concluded. They also fault the media for emphasizing the physical prowess of black basketball players—and, as a result, of African Americans in general—as opposed to emphasizing the academic and intellectual skills necessary for fullfilling economic and educational goals. Thus, some believe that professional sports may, in fact, serve to perpetuate racial stereotypes and complex racial barriers for African Americans.

Basketball is a popular game for all groups and a common sight in playgrounds, parking lots, driveways, recreation centers, and more. (Robert Fried)

SUGGESTED READINGS.
A helpful survey of the sociology of sport is found in "Sport and Society" by James Frey and D. Stanley Eitzen in the *Annual Review of Sociology* 17 (1991), pp. 503-522. One of the scholars known for his analysis of sports sociology and African American athletes in particular is Harry Edwards, who wrote *Sociology of Sport* (1973). See also Nelson George's *Elevating the Game: Black Men and Basketball* (1992) and

Arthur Ashe's *A Hard Road to Glory: A* History of the African-American Athlete (3 vols., 1988) for the trials and triumphs experienced by black basketball players.

Basque Americans: The Basque people live on the western border between France and Spain where the Pyrenees Mountains meet the Atlantic Ocean. They have fought against the domination of the national governments of France and Spain for centuries and are fiercely proud of their unique ethnicity. They call themselves *Euskaldunak*, which means "people who speak *Euskera*," the Basque language. This is the only language in the world that is not related to any other.

Basques have always been good sailors and have a long tradition of migration overseas. They gained high positions in the colonial Spanish government and were often assigned administrative positions in South America. In the early nineteenth century, Basque emigrants in Argentina began to raise sheep.

When GOLD was discovered in California in 1849, hundreds of Basques streamed into the state from South America, while French Basques came directly from Europe. Few got rich mining, and many of the immigrants subsequently moved to Southern California. There, they signed sheep-range lease agreements with the owners of vast cattle ranches. By 1860, Basques dominated the state's sheep industry.

By 1910, itinerant Basque shepherds had spread throughout the grazing ranges of the western United States. They came into conflict with powerful cattle ranchers, who considered the open land their own. In 1934, this rivalry was ended by the Taylor Grazing Act, which severely circumscribed Basque grazing

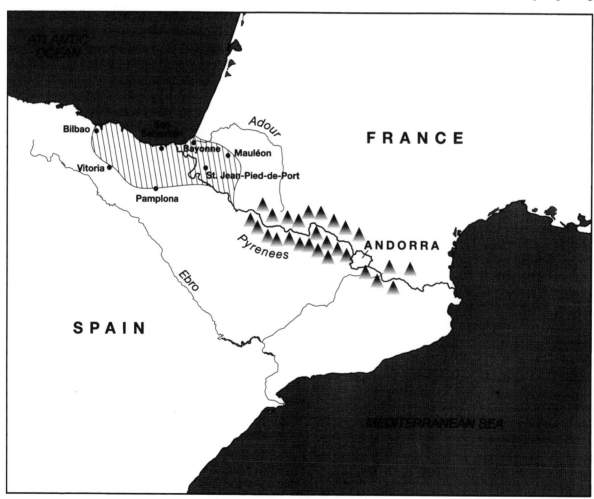

BASQUE REGION

rights. In the decades that followed, Basque American shepherding began to die out, but Basque American families branched out to other lines of work in ranching communities.

Basque American ethnic pride became evident at the first Western Basque Festival, held in Sparks, Nevada, in June, 1959. That event featured weightlifting and woodchopping, popular Basque pastimes, as well as FOLK MUSIC, FOLK DANCE, and a big Basque barbecue. Since then, annual Basque festivals have become popular, especially in Nevada, and smaller Basque American communities maintain their own organizations and dance troupes, especially since the ETHNIC HERITAGE REVIVAL of the 1970's.

Basque American sheepherder in Nevada. (Library of Congress)

Battle of the Little Bighorn. *See* **Little Bighorn, Battle of the**

Battle of the Washita. *See* **Washita, Battle of the**

Battle of Wounded Knee. *See* **Wounded Knee, Battle of**

Bay of Pigs invasion (Apr. 17, 1961): Invasion of Cuba by United States in effort to topple government of Fidel Castro. The abortive attack was the result of growing tension between the United States and Cuba, marked by a trade embargo and breaking off of diplomatic relations in the last days of President Dwight Eisenhower's administration. In 1960 Eisenhower had given the Central Intelligence Agency (CIA) the responsibility for a plan to overthrow revolutionary Cuban leader Fidel Castro. The CIA trained and armed some fourteen hundred anti-Castro Cuban exiles at camps in Florida and Nicaragua. John F. Kennedy inherited the Eisenhower plan when he became president in January, 1961. His political and MILITARY advisers persuaded him to proceed; however, Kennedy ruled out the use of U.S. forces or provision of air cover for the invasion.

The attack was launched on April 17 at the Bay of Pigs on Cuba's southern coast. The attackers were completely routed by Castro's troops within two days, and more than a thousand men were captured on the beaches. The invasion was badly planned and miserably executed. Kennedy was blamed for its failure since he did not permit any direct American involvement. The attack would probably have failed, however, even with greater U.S. military support. More than one landing site would have been needed for success. The CIA had faulty intelligence, and Castro reportedly not only knew of the invasion but also knew the planned landing site. The CIA failed to inform the noncommunist People's Revolutionary Movement, the largest and most effective opposition to Castro in Cuba, of plans for the invasion. By including supporters of former Cuban president Fulgencio Batista in the invading force, the CIA also gave Castro propaganda material that he effectively exploited.

The United States suffered a humiliating defeat and its international prestige declined. A year later, the Soviet Union placed nuclear weapons in Cuba, perhaps concluding that the United States was incapable of effective opposition. The Soviets congratulated Castro and extended assurances of their loyalty and continued support. China likewise proclaimed its support of Cuba's struggle against imperialism. The slogan "We are not alone" blazed in neon lights over the streets of the capital city of Havana.

The invasion led Castro to define the goals of his revolution and accelerate its institutionalization. Whereas before he had described the revolution as socialist, during the euphoria over Cuba's victory, Castro declared himself a Communist and announced a

Marxist-Leninist program. He also combined the 26th of July Movement, the Directorio Revolucionario, and the Communists into the Organizaciones Integradas Revolucionarias as the first step in creating a new Communist Party.

The Bay of Pigs invasion caused Cuba to seek

Draper discusses the invasion in the context of Cuban politics in *Castro's Revolution: Myths and Realities* (1962). For narrative accounts of the invasion, see Karl E. Meyer and Ted Szulc's *The Cuban Invasion: The Chronicle of a Disaster* (1962) and Peter Wyden's *Bay of Pigs: The Untold Story* (1979).

Cuban leader Fidel Castro (left) shakes hands with Soviet premier Nikita Khrushchev, signaling the close tie that the Bay of Pigs invasion helped to create. (AP/Wide World Photos)

closer ties with the Soviet Union. Cubans were convinced that the United States would attempt a second invasion, using U.S. military forces. A military and trade agreement between Cuba and the Soviet Union allowed the Soviets to place medium-range missiles in Cuba, which led to the Cuban Missile Crisis (1962).

SUGGESTED READINGS. For an account of the incident by its leaders, see *The Bay of Pigs: The Leaders' Story of Brigade 2506*, edited by Haynes Johnson (1964). The report of the special investigating committee, the Taylor Committee, is included in *Operation Zapata: The "Ultrasensitive" Report and Testimony of the Board of Inquiry on the Bay of Pigs* (1981). Theodore

Beauty pageants: Contests based on female physical beauty. They began in the United States in the late nineteenth century with photographic competitions introduced by impresario P. T. Barnum. Initially these competitions were popular with the public because contestants were judged on the basis of civic leadership or popularity in the community or were chosen to honor a male relative. Selection was made by photograph rather than in person, thus conforming to the late Victorian belief that women should not display themselves in public. Soon, such competitions became common publicity devices for carnivals and mass-circulation newspapers. As local civic and business ventures began to sponsor the contests, the American public grew to accept the idea of a competition based on physical beauty.

The formal beauty contest—originally a beach beauty contest—came to characterize the newly emancipated 1920's "flapper" during the same era in which modeling emerged as a respectable career for women. During that decade, contestants' qualities of "naturalness" were highly valued, but their attractiveness was

Marjorie Judith Vincent was crowned Miss America 1991 and was the second African American to gain the title. (AP/ Wide World Photos)

also considered to be composed of the liberated qualities of self-definition and assertiveness. In the context of the beauty contest, these qualities were shown in the display of one's body and an openly competitive spirit. The Miss America contest, held annually in Atlantic City, New Jersey, since 1921, began as a promotional effort by hotel managers to keep tourists in the summer resort past the Labor Day weekend, the

traditional end of summer. The pageant, which initially stressed the athletic abilities and natural, wholesome qualities of the contestants, became a national ritual. Prizes for the winners included scholarship money. In the 1990's, the Miss America competition offered $3 million in scholarship money for its winners, but not all modern pageants expect participants to have career plans and talents.

Feminists have frequently criticized beauty contests, seeing in these competitions opportunities to protest the open commodification of women in American culture. Described as a "cattle call" and an event that pits women against one another as men's sex objects, the beauty contest became the target of protests. One type of protest focused on the concentration and judging of male-imposed standards of beauty, while another centered on the exclusive ideal of beauty which the competitions espoused—an ideal that long excluded women of color, mothers, and married women. In many cases, beauty contests have become occasions for controversy; the first major public protest of the WOMEN'S LIBERATION MOVEMENT in the United States took place at the Miss America pageant of September 7, 1968.

In addition to major beauty pageants such as Miss America, Miss Universe, Miss Teenage America, America's Junior Miss, and Miss World, a host of local, regional, and state beauty contests exist, including contests specifically celebrating cultural and ethnic separateness. Indeed, beauty contests remain an integral part of many ethnic community festivals, from Guatemalan fiestas to Japanese American parades.

SUGGESTED READINGS. Discussions of the importance of beauty pageants in American culture can be found in Lois W. Banner's *Women in Modern America: A Brief History* (1974) and *American Beauty* (1983). Cheryl Prewitt and Katheryn Slattery's *A Bright and Shining Place* (1981) and Nancie S. Martin's *Miss America Through the Looking Glass* (1985) provide history and analysis of Atlantic City and the Miss America pageant.

Beecher, Catharine Esther (Sept. 6, 1800, East Hampton, Long Island, N.Y.—May 12, 1878, Elmira, N.Y.): Educator and author. After the sudden death of the man to whom she was engaged, Beecher went through a severe depression, the end result of which was a belief that her true calling lay in education. She opened two schools for women, but both collapsed. She published a number of pamphlets and books on child rearing and domestic management including *A Treatise on Domestic Economy* (1841), *The Domestic Receipt Book* (1846), and *The Evils Suffered by American Women and American Children: The Causes and the Remedy* (1846). She had no part in the suffrage movement and instead fought for the inclusion of domestic science in the higher education curriculum for women.

Belgian Americans: Belgians immigrants have generally assimilated well into American society. Though some suffered from anti-Catholic prejudice in the Midwest in the nineteenth century, Belgians in the United States suffer no discrimination based on their nationality.

The nation of Belgium was created in the 1830's as a buffer state between the Netherlands and France. It lies astride the northern border of the ancient Roman Empire. Citizens in the northern half of the country, known as Flanders, speak Flemish, a Germanic language that is very similar to Dutch. The southern Belgians, known as Walloons, were influenced by Latin culture and speak French. The Flemings and the Walloons share the Roman Catholic faith.

BELGIUM

The Belgians who emigrated to the United States between 1840 and 1900 came to escape a land shortage and the potato blight. They sought prosperity by farming the rich, arable land in the American Midwest. Many Belgian immigrants settled in Michigan, but others established farms in Indiana, Wisconsin, and Illinois. The Flemish and Walloon farmers lived in separate communities and rarely mixed with each other. The Flemings in Michigan found themselves rejected by their DUTCH AMERICAN neighbors, though they spoke a common language, because the Dutch Reformed Church was profoundly anti-Catholic.

Belgian immigration peaked in the years between 1900 and 1920. The new arrivals were not farmers, but craftsmen and tradesmen from cities such as Brussels and Antwerp. They came to seek their fortunes and to escape the devastation of WORLD WAR I.

Since Belgium is split into two distinct cultures, its early immigrants did not have a strong sense of national identity. That situation changed during World War I, when the people of Belgium joined in a courageous struggle against the Germans. This caused both Flemings and Walloons in the United States to feel pride in their mutual national heritage.

Since 1920, Belgian immigration to the United States has slowed, but its nature has remained the same. Twentieth century Belgian immigrants, including those who fled their homeland during World War II, have been mostly professionals. Belgian Americans have made outstanding contributions in the fields of science, engineering, medicine, business, and music. Those in science include Karel-Jan Bossart, known as the "father of the Atlas missile," and Leo Baekeland, who developed the synthetic resin Bakelite.

Belorussian Americans: The new country of Belarus, formerly the Belorussian Soviet Socialist Republic (also known as Belorussia or Byelorussia) lies between Russia and Poland. Belorussians are descended from several eastern Slavic tribes who were converted to Orthodox Christianity in the tenth century.

In medieval times, Belorussia was part of the Grand Duchy of Lithuania, which joined with Poland to form a commonwealth in 1569. At that point, about 20 percent of the Belorussian people became Roman Catholic. In the eighteenth century, the Polish-Lithuanian Commonwealth was destroyed and the Russian Empire absorbed the Belorussian territory.

Approximately 100,000 Belorussians emigrated to the United States in the last half of the nineteenth century and the early twentieth century to escape religious PERSECUTION and a land shortage. They settled in the industrial cities of the northeastern United States and took, for the most part, unskilled factory jobs. These early immigrants assimilated into already established Russian Orthodox or Polish Catholic communities. Early Belorussian Americans did not transmit

BELARUS

their Belorussian heritage to their descendants primarily because, prior to World War I, Belorussians had little sense of national identity.

Belorussia achieved independence briefly in 1918, but in 1921 the country was divided among Russia, Poland, Lithuania, and Latvia. After 1945, three-fourths of ethnic Belorussians lived within the boundaries of the Belorussian S.S.R.

During World War II, five hundred thousand Belorussians fled to the United States to avoid being put in forced labor camps in Germany. Tens of thousands more emigrated from refugee camps in Germany and

Austria after the war. These newcomers were distinctly different from the peasant immigrants who came before 1914. The new arrivals were educated people, artisans and professionals. They had experienced the renaissance of national pride of the 1920's and were aware of their heritage as Belorussians. They formed their own branch of the EASTERN ORTHODOX church and used it to promote the culture of their homeland, including language classes, traditional feast days, and observance of Belorussian Independence Day (March 25). Until 1990, Belorussian Americans worked to free Belorussia from Soviet domination.

Benevolent and fraternal organizations: Two of the most widespread types of social organizations in the United States. Generally, benevolent and fraternal organizations assist members, their families, and the community in times of need. They combine aspects of "good works" and community service with social programs, secret rituals, and efforts to promote religious or moral values. Some organizations are affiliated with religious organizations while others draw exclusively from certain ethnic or national groups.

In the 1830's, Alexis de Tocqueville, a visitor from France, observed the tendency of Americans to join groups: "In no country in the world has the principle of association been more successfully used or applied to a greater multitude of objects than in America." Perhaps the diversity of racial, ethnic, and religious groups in the United States makes its people more likely to seek organizational membership in order to protect their interests.

Incentives for Membership. There are a variety of benefits obtained from group membership. One advantage is purposive or expressive: Members may wish to work together in pursuit of some common cause. Ethnic groups have an interest in the well-being of their ancestral lands. There are also utilitarian and economic values from belonging to a benevolent or fraternal organization, much like the benefits of MUTUAL AID SOCIETIES. These include group insurance, funeral arrangements, travel services, health care (including care of the aged), legal services, and even credit cards at lower interest rates. Finally, there are solidarity incentives. Members gain a sense of belonging and camaraderie. Some people join to make friends or to enjoy the company of like-minded individuals of similar backgrounds. Others join because it is the expected thing to do—because one's family, friends, and associates are already members.

Not all Americans are equally likely to join these organizations. Those with higher income and education are more conspicuous as members. They can afford the dues, have the leisure necessary to participate, and have the organizational skills that groups seek. Competition from other types of leisure pursuits, however, has cut into lodge membership in the late 1900's.

Many ethnic-specific organizations, such as this one, grew out of a need for and a desire to help. (Center for Migration Studies)

Religious Groups. The primary concerns of religious benevolent and fraternal groups are religion, community welfare, and social activities. A significant area of their involvement may also be political. Historically, they fulfilled an ACCULTURATION function for migrants from other lands and from rural areas of the United States, helping them adjust to their new homes. For example, YOUNG MEN'S (AND WOMEN'S) CHRISTIAN ASSOCIATIONS provide educational, recreational, housing, and social outlets for their members.

The largest American Catholic fraternal organization is the Knights of Columbus. It was founded in 1882, and has 1.5 million members. Unlike many orders such as the Masons and Odd Fellows that have declined in membership or become extinct, the Knights continues to thrive. It meets the need for a fraternity of Catholic men that has the approval of the Catholic church. Ever since 1738, the pope has condemned secret societies; Catholics who entered Masonic lodges were excommunicated, while Odd Fellows and Knights of Pythias were denied the sacraments. Ironically, the Knights of Columbus is patterned after Freemasonry.

One of the groups affiliated with the National Council of Catholic Women is the Catholic Daughters of America. It was founded in 1903, and has more than 200,000 members in 1,500 local units. It supports religious and charitable projects.

The counterpart for Protestants (aside from auxiliaries of their churches) is the Masons. Masonic groups come in all varieties and sizes. Among those listed in the *Encyclopedia of Associations* are the Masonic Relief Association of U.S.A. and Canada, Modern Free and Accepted Masons of the World, Most Worshipful National Grand Lodge Free and Accepted Ancient York Masons, Ancient Egyptian Order of Scots, Conference of Prince Hall Grand Masters, Daughters of the Nile, and Federation of Eastern Stars. Freemasonry

A "Shriner" (or member of the Ancient Order of the Nobles of the Mystic Shrine, a spin-off of the Freemasons) and family. (Frances M. Roberts)

was organized in England more than 250 years ago, but in the early 1990's, four-fifths of the world's Masons lived in the United States. While Continental Masons were highly political, British and American Masonic orders stay out of politics. Members qualify for advancement to different degrees of exclusiveness. The Masons maintain hospitals and other philanthropic projects. The Masons remain controversial with organized religion; in 1993, the Southern Baptists received a recommendation that the decision to join the Masons should be left to individual choice.

Jews also produced their own groups, sometimes responding to exclusion from established groups (Knights of Pythias), sometimes to retain their unique identity (Young Men's/Women's Hebrew Association).

Among the GERMAN JEWS who founded B'NAI B'RITH in 1843 were members of the Masons and the Odd Fellows. Lack of hierarchical religious structure also led to the expression of Jewish values through voluntary associations. These groups undertook charitable, religious, educational, and social welfare activities. For example, the Workmen's Circle was founded in 1900 as a Jewish cultural and fraternal benefit life insurance society. It operates a resort, cemeteries, a children's summer camp, Jewish schools, and homes for the aged.

The Legacy of Discrimination. Fraternal orders generally had a rhetoric of equality. Yet they often excluded women, African Americans, and ethnic minorities. During the nineteenth century, for example, some fraternal orders were strongholds of anti-immigrant sentiment. Some lodges were established by foreign-language speaking immigrant groups, but the upsurge of NATIVISM in the 1880's led to their abolition. In the twentieth century, battles have been fought in the courts against exclusivity in fraternal and benevolent organization membership.

The Benevolent and Protective Order of Elks began in 1867. More than one hundred years later, it supports traditional American values and has a benefit program for members as well as the needy. Its white-only membership clause was finally removed in 1976 after several court battles.

The Fraternal Order of Eagles started in 1889 as a social organization. Over time it shifted its emphasis to fraternal service. It offers sick and funeral benefits to members, promotes social legislation, supports children's and retirement homes, and helps maintain medical research projects. In theory it does not bar non-whites; however, its blackball system for new members has made it difficult for nonwhite applicants to gain admission.

When SEGREGATION laws and practices prevented African Americans from being accepted into mainstream fraternal and benevolent groups, they formed their own counterparts. Examples were the Grand United Order of Odd Fellows and the Prince Hall Masons. When African Americans were barred from the Elks, they founded their own Improved Benevolent and Protective Order of Elks. It became one of the largest and most influential black lodges. Despite losing a 1912 lawsuit in New York against using the Elks name, the group continued to call itself "Elks" and to use names for its officers modeled on those of the white organization. In a similar case, the Loyal Order of Moose brought suit against the black Independent, Benevolent and Protective Order of Moose in 1925 to keep the latter from using the Moose name, emblem, ritual, and officer titles.

Fraternity and Diversity. Fraternal and benevolent organizations have been one of the ways people banded together in the United States to help themselves and others. Such groups have been an important part of the forging of community for individuals of similar religious or ethnic background. There is an apparent paradox: The organizations urge their members to acquire those aspects of the host society necessary for survival and prosperity (ACCULTURATION). At the same time, the groups' very existence is rooted in the preservation of a separate identity. Though the goals of identity and acculturation may seem antithetical, they are both coping mechanisms for survival in American society.

SUGGESTED READINGS. Among the sources which could be consulted for further information about the activities of fraternal and benevolent organizations are the *Encyclopedia of Associations,* a multivolume directory which is updated annually. Three general sources are William J. Whalen's *Handbook of Secret Organizations* (1966), Alvin J. Schmidt's *Fraternal Organizations* (1980), and Mary Ann Clawson's *Constructing Brotherhood: Class, Gender, and Fraternalism* (1989).—*Martin Gruberg*

Berenson, Senda (Mar. 19, 1868, Biturmansk, Lithuania—Feb. 16, 1954, Santa Barbara, Calif.): Advocate of physical education. Berenson's parents immigrated when she was a child. Because of a weak back, she was restricted from usual school activity. In 1890 she studied physical education at the Boston Normal School. Begin-

ning in 1892 she taught physical training to women at SMITH COLLEGE, introducing fencing, FOLK DANCE, field hockey, and—most notably—women's line basketball. She offered a new view on sports that did not center on competition and that favored intramural sports.

Berry, Chuck (Charles Edward Anderson; b. Oct. 18, 1926, St. Louis, Mo.): African American ROCK AND ROLL singer and composer. A pioneer of the rock and roll sound, Berry's songs helped define the style in the 1950's and influenced a whole generation of performers and composers. Such top-selling songs as "Maybellene," "Roll over Beethoven," "Sweet Little Sixteen," "Reelin' and Rockin'," and "Johnny B. Goode" earned him a Grammy Award and induction into the Rock and Roll Hall of Fame. Berry appeared in several films, including *Go, Johnny, Go!* (1958). Problems with the law in his teens and in later life led to several periods of incarceration.

The pioneering rock and roll musician Chuck Berry on stage in 1980. (AP/Wide World Photos)

Bethune, Mary McLeod (July 10, 1875, Mayesville, S.C.—May 18, 1955, Daytona Beach, Fla.): African American educator and activist. Bethune's parents were freed slaves. In 1904 she opened Daytona Normal Industrial Institute in Florida with almost no money and five student girls. In 1923 the school merged with the Cookman Institute in Jacksonville to include college courses. She was also involved with housing development programs, black voter registration drives, and the establishment of an African American hospital. In 1935 she was appointed to the National Advisory Committee of the National Youth Administration (NYA). She found an ally in Eleanor Roosevelt, whose eyes she opened to the problems of African Americans. In 1932 she founded the National Council of Negro Women.

Big Five: Collective nickname for the five huge companies that, from the nineteenth century to World War II, owned or controlled sugar production in Hawaii. Because sugar production was central to the Hawaiian economy, the Big Five also had near-complete control over all other important aspects of the economy, including railroads, banking, utilities, tourism, and pineapple farming. From the beginning, the companies were controlled by non-Hawaiians who employed and exploited cheap labor imported from China, Japan, Korea, and the Philippines. Native Hawaiians were made, in some ways, marginal residents of their own land. A number of factors led to a loosening of the Big Five's grip after World War II, although the companies remained powerful; among them were unionization of the workers and increased competition from outside interests.

Big Foot [Sitanka]: (c. 1825—Dec. 28, 1890): Miniconjou Sioux of the Cheyenne River Indian Reservation in South Dakota known for his role in the massacre at Wounded Knee. Following the death of Sitting Bull, a small number of his people joined with Big Foot to resist the U.S. Army. On December 23, 1890, Big Foot led about 350 followers toward Pine Ridge. Soldiers from the Seventh Cavalry soon surrounded them, causing them to surrender peacefully near Wounded Knee Creek. When the Indians refused to hand over their weapons, a scuffle broke out. What followed was the massacre at Wounded Knee (December 28, 1890), the last major battle of the Indian Wars, during which Big Foot was killed.

Bigotry: Intolerance or hatred of a racial, ethnic, religious, or other minority group. Bigotry implies attitudes of extreme prejudice that are deeply ingrained in an individual and are unlikely to change. Bigots are obstinate in their opinions, which are based on hearsay and racial or religious stereotypes rather than on the actual attributes of individuals who belong to the hated groups. Bigotry often leads to the practice of discrimination. Members of either dominant or minority groups can practice bigotry, although the term is most often applied to attitudes of majorities toward minorities.

Bilingual education: Instruction presented in two languages intended to provide equal educational opportunities for linguistic minorities. In bilingual education in the United States, one of the languages is English; the other is the student's first or native language. The general purpose of such an approach is to increase students' academic achievement in subject areas by using the first language while developing language proficiency in English. Many researchers maintain that students should develop basic language skills in their first language before being expected to master the same skills in English.

The number of bilingual education programs rose significantly during the second half of the twentieth century in response to increased Asian and Latin American immigration and the increasing numbers of school-age children of limited English proficiency (LEP). These students' lack of skills in English was thought to have considerable negative consequences on their academic achievement and job prospects. Bilingual education programs have often been funded by federal sources following the enactment of the Bilingual Education Act of 1968.

This act (Title VII of the Elementary and Secondary Education Act) authorized funding to support classroom programs, train teachers, and develop instructional materials. Surprisingly, however, it did not require schools to use a language other than English in funded programs. Additional support for bilingual education had come earlier with the passage of Title VI of the Civil Rights Act of 1964. This prohibited denial of equal educational opportunity on the basis of race, language, or national origin. In 1974 the U.S. Supreme Court's *Lau v. Nichols* decision placed an obligation on school districts to take action to assist students of limited English proficiency. Although that decision did not mandate bilingual education, it did suggest it as one of several available options.

In general, bilingual education does not advocate any one specific method or approach. It also does not attempt to prescribe an exact proportion of first or second language usage. Bilingual education programs fall into three broad categories: transitional, immersion, and developmental. Transitional bilingual education programs are designed to teach English to language minority students as quickly as possible so that students can be mainstreamed into regular, all-English classrooms. Little emphasis is given to the development of language skills in the first language. Immersion bilingual programs use the second language extensively so that students are "immersed" in a total

English and function well in a regular English-language environment.

Proponents of bilingual education point to positive effects beyond students' improved test scores in math and science. A decrease in the school drop-out rate, for example, is one effect commonly associated with successful bilingual programs.

In 1993, federal funding continued to be provided to bilingual programs, but the trend was toward programs that quickly move students into mainstream programs. There was also an effort to promote two-

Bilingual education at work in this Crystal City, Tex., classroom, using both audio and visual tools. (AP/Wide World Photos)

English-language environment for all subjects. Developmental bilingual programs (sometimes called maintenance programs) aim to teach English language skills while developing reading and writing skills in the first language.

ENGLISH AS A SECOND LANGUAGE PROGRAMS (ESL programs) are not strictly bilingual education, although they may be part of a bilingual program. ESL programs focus on teaching languages skills in English so that students can learn content areas in

way bilingual programs that would enable both language-minority and language-majority students to develop bilingual fluency within the same classroom. Opposition to bilingual education continues to stem from a fear that language maintenance will delay the ASSIMILATION into American society. Proponents argue that a valuable national resource will be lost if students are not encouraged to preserve and enhance their native language skills.

SUGGESTED READINGS. Kenji Hakuta deals with many

of the myths and misconceptions concerning bilingual education in Mirror of Language: The Debate on Bilingualism (1986). James Crawford provides a comprehensive look at the topic in Bilingual Education: History, Politics, Theory, and Practice (1989). *Bilingual Education: Issues and Strategies* by Amado Padilla, Halford Fairchild, and Concepción Valadez (1990) considers research and program design and strategies for classroom instruction. Finally, *Bilingual and ESL Classrooms: Teaching in Multicultural Contexts* (1985) by Carlos Ovando and Virginia Collier deals with the issues of language, culture, and instruction in subject areas such as social studies, music, math, and science.

Bilingual Education Act of 1968: Prototype for a series of laws requiring that students who speak little or no English be instructed in both English and their native language in American public schools. The act mandated that instructional materials, teacher training, and research be developed to allow these students to enter all-English classrooms as soon as possible. Pressure to support bilingual education grew out of the CIVIL RIGHTS MOVEMENT, specifically the Supreme Court decision in BROWN V. BOARD OF EDUCATION, which set a precedent for mandating equal educational opportunity. Activists in the CHICANO MOVEMENT in the 1960's also called for better educational options for Spanish-speaking students. The 1968 act led to the creation of various bilingual education programs around the country, supported by $626 million in federal funds for the first ten years. The concept of bilingual education was strengthened by the 1974 Supreme Court decision in LAU V. NICHOLS, which stressed the need for schools to ensure that educational programs were fully accessible to students of all language backgrounds.

Bilingualism: Ability to speak two languages. For centuries, North America has been multilingual. AMERICAN INDIAN LANGUAGES before European contact were as many and diverse as the tribes themselves. Canada's Royal Proclamation of 1763 gave equal recognition to

Chinese American student shares her language with an Anglo classmate. (Don Franklin)

the French and English languages. In the United States, English was never the only European language spoken: Spanish and French were present from the early years of European conquest.

American history provides important insights leading to an understanding of contemporary bilingualism. American ethnic groups are indigenous or immigrant. Indigenous groups include Indians or Latinos who already inhabited areas later taken over by the U.S. government. Immigrants may be voluntary, such as Polish and Chinese Americans, or involuntary, such as African slaves and Indochinese political refugees. Whatever the situation, the impact of immigrant and indigenous groups on the language status of the country has been considerable.

Early debate abounded about whether bilinguals were intellectually inferior to native English speakers, fueling anti-immigrant nativist arguments. John Adams' proposal to make English the official language of the United States failed in the early years of the republic. The idea gained greater support in certain states with the ENGLISH ONLY MOVEMENT of the late 1900's.

During World War I, German Americans bore the brunt of a rise in American nationalism and NATIVISM; World War II saw Japanese Americans interned and their schools closed. American Indians, Latinos, and various immigrants who used their native language at school have often been punished. In more recent years, however, there has been a growing recognition of the importance of bilingualism in education and intergroup relations. Modern research shows that bilingualism can enhance the cognitive development of a child rather than slow down language acquisition, as previously believed.

Ideas about what constitutes bilingualism are surprisingly varied. Most definitions stress the concept of native-like control of two languages. The degree of perfection that makes a person truly bilingual is a relative distinction. Bilingualism may be horizontal, as in Quebec, Canada, where English and French have equivalent status and considerable overlap in use in similar circumstances. Bilingualism may also be characterized as vertical, balanced (equilingual), consecutive (successive), infantile, and sequential, among other terms.

Whatever the type, in the United States the term "bilingualism" is often laden with connotations beyond the use of multiple languages. The term commonly connotes poor English-speaking skills and a need for remediation in school.

The United States has probably been host to more bilinguals than any other country in the world. Each new wave of immigrants bringing its own language, however, has seen native language deterioration in the face of English, which is implicitly if not explicitly acknowledged as an official language. No other country has as rapid a rate of native language decline.

Ethnic groups in the United States with significant numbers of bilingual speakers include Latinos (6.8 million), the fourth largest Spanish-speaking population in the world; Germans and Italians (3.9 million each); French (2.2 million); and Asian groups such as Chinese, Japanese, and Koreans.

Guatemalan American couple browse Spanish-language books at a fair in Flushing, N.Y. (Odette Lupis)

SUGGESTED READINGS. See Bilingualism and the Bilingual (1987), edited by Samuel Abudarham; Hugo Baetens Beardsmore's Bilingualism: Basic Principles (2d ed., 1986); Kenji Hakuta's Mirror of Language: The Debate on Bilingualism (1986); and *The New Bilingualism: An American Dilemma* (1981), edited by Martin Ridge.

Bill of Rights: Part of the U. S. CONSTITUTION guaranteeing individual liberties. It consists of not only the first ten amendments to the Constitution, but also many of the succeeding amendments (13, 14, 15, 19, 23, 24, and 26).

The Bill of Rights originated in the founding fathers' deep suspicion of a strong central government. Still fresh in their minds were the British Crown's callousness to colonists, and bloody chapters in European history.

George Mason of Virginia was one of three delegates to the Constitutional Convention in 1787 who refused to sign the document it produced. He cited the Constitution's lack of a bill of rights, and he vowed to oppose its ratification. Even some advocates of the Constitution buttressed their arguments for its adoption by promising that a bill of rights would be added. In the first session of Congress, a list of twelve amendments was sent to the states, and ten were approved, becoming a permanent part of the Constitution. Over the next two centuries, additional amendments specifically recognized the rights of African Americans, women, and many other groups.

These amendments supported court rulings that interpreted and enforced the rights of an enormous diversity of people. Ethnic and cultural groups played an especially significant role in this evolution of the Constitution. In response to their determined struggle for equal treatment, the Bill of Rights has been expanded and clarified, becoming an ever stronger underpinning for a truly democratic nation.

Amendments 1 Through 4. The broad First Amendment protects freedom of speech and press; freedom to assemble peaceably and to petition government for a redress of grievances; and freedom of worship. Civil rights protesters exercised these rights as they spoke and demonstrated against racial injustice in the 1960's at events such as the 1963 MARCH ON WASHINGTON.

The right to freedom of speech also permitted NEO-NAZIS to march past the homes of Jewish Holocaust survivors in Skokie, Illinois and allowed KU KLUX KLAN members to present their views on a public television channel in Kansas City. In *Meyer v. Nebraska* (1923), the Supreme Court decided that the First Amendment upheld the right of immigrants to have their children educated in their native language.

This amendment prevents censorship of the press. Press freedom can be limited only when a "clear and present danger" can be demonstrated. Nor can people sue their critics for libel unless it can be proved that the critics presented false information and acted out of malice. *New York Times Co. v. Sullivan* (1964) found a group of civil rights supporters innocent in such a libel suit brought by a Montgomery, Alabama, police commissioner.

Religious freedom and separation of CHURCH AND STATE have been important to many ethnic and religious groups which hold beliefs different from those of mainstream Anglo culture. The First Amendment has kept prayer out of schools and Christian symbols such as crèches off public property. In 1983, a federal court ruled that a proposed government road through sacred American Indian lands would violate a tribe's right to practice its religion. Religious freedom has

The First Amendment of the Bill of Rights protects freedom of the press; here, a woman and her child show off the newspaper published by their neighborhood group in Madison, Wis. (Mary M. Langenfeld)

also allowed AMISH children to be exempted from a high school education and JEHOVAH'S WITNESSES' children to refuse to salute the flag at school.

Amendments 2 and 3 provide for the right to bear arms and freedom from forced quartering of soldiers in private homes (a concern which grew out of colonial bitterness). Although many have argued that this guarantees the right of private citizens to own and use firearms, the courts have limited and regulated firearm use. The right to bear arms protects citizens in a collective sense, allowing states to maintain armed militias for the protection of civilians.

The Fourth Amendment protects Americans from unreasonable search and seizure by law enforcement authorities and guarantees their right to be safe in their homes. Police must present a search warrant clearly describing what is sought, and warrants must be based on reasonable evidence. Electronic eavesdropping is subject to the same standards, and illegally seized evidence cannot be used in court. There were sweeping violations of this right in a mass arrest of "suspected" members of the Communist Party, mostly without warrants, in 1920. More than 10,000 people, the majority of whom were immigrants, were unjustly jailed and deported.

Amendments 5 Through 10. Amendments 5, 6, 7, and 8 protect those accused of crimes and provide for some civil suits. Under these provisions, civilians arrested for serious crimes cannot be held for trial without grand jury indictment, cannot be tried twice for the same crime, and cannot be compelled to testify against themselves. Nor can a person's life, liberty, or property be taken without due process of law. The accused has the right to a speedy and public trial with an impartial jury. Accused people have the right to be informed of the accusations against them, to confront witnesses against them, to have compulsory means for calling witnesses in their favor, and to have counsel for their defense. They cannot be subjected to excessive bail or to cruel and unusual punishments. In some civil suits, litigants also have the right to a jury trial.

In *Brown v. Mississippi* (1936) the Supreme Court overturned the murder conviction of black defendants because their confessions had been obtained through torture. In the case of the SCOTTSBORO NINE (*Powell v. Alabama,* 1932), black defendants accused of rape had been denied due process because their court-appointed counsel was not given enough time to prepare a good defense; their conviction was overturned. In the case

---

MIRANDA WARNING

1. You have the right to remain silent.

2. Anything you say can and will be used against you in a court of law.

3. You have the right to talk to a lawyer and have him present with you while you are being questioned.

4. If you cannot afford to hire a lawyer, one will be appointed to represent you before any questioning, if you wish one.

Source: Courtesy of the Clinton, Iowa, Police Department.

Machetti v. Linahan (1979) a woman convicted of murder received a new trial because her jury had included only one woman. In *Miranda v. Arizona* (1966), the Court ruled that a person under arrest must be informed of constitutional rights before being questioned. "Reading of rights" is now a standard part of arrest procedure and still a matter of concern for those who defend the rights of undocumented aliens. During World War II, Japanese Americans lost property and jobs when they were shipped off to internment camps. Decades later, the Supreme Court found the action unconstitutional, violating the right to due process. These protections also extend to property being repossessed. In *Fuentes v. Shevin* (1972), the Court concluded that creditors could not seize property without a hearing. Similarly, a person's wages may not be garnished nor welfare benefits stopped without prior hearing.

Amendment 9 states that the enumeration of certain rights by the Constitution must not be construed to mean that other rights are not retained by the people. Court rulings have guaranteed some of those retained rights. In *ROE V. WADE* (1973), for example, the right to privacy was held to confer the right to ABORTION. *GRISWOLD V. STATE OF CONNECTICUT* (1965) struck down a state law which forbade contraceptive devices. The right to privacy also protected an Atlanta, Georgia, man who had been arrested for engaging in homosexual acts in his own bedroom with a consenting adult.

Amendment 10 states that powers not explicitly given to the federal government are retained by the states or the people. In the pre-Civil War period, states' rights advocates attempted to use this amendment to protect the institution of slavery. John C. Calhoun's doctrine of nullification was an argument that states could reject federal laws. In 1832, South Carolina sought, unsuccessfully, to nullify the Tariff Acts of

1828 and 1832. The southern states' attempt to secede from the union was also based in part on the Tenth Amendment. Succeeding events, both in court and on the battlefield, however, enforced the primacy of federal power over the states. For example, in Garcia v. San Antonio Metropolitan Transit Authority (1985), the Court ruled that state employees could receive the federally set minimum wage. These interpretations helped working people fight economic exploitation.

Citizenship and Equal Rights. Amendments 13, 14, and 15 outlawed slavery throughout the United States, declared persons born or naturalized in the United States to be citizens with the rights of citizens, including the right to vote, and guaranteed these citizens equal protection under the law.

Amendment 23 abolished poll taxes, which had become a requirement for voting in some states. These amendments freed African American slaves and reversed the Dred Scott decision (SCOTT V. SANDFORD (1857), which had stated that slaves were not citizens. Although these amendments initially seemed to provide protection for all races and ethnic groups, subsequent court rulings and law enforcement failures led to widespread discrimination.

In 1870, Hiram Revels of Mississippi became the first African American in the U.S. Senate, living proof of black suffrage. Soon, however, white supremacist terrorism and other kinds of repression began the de facto disfranchisement of southern blacks. In 1896, the Supreme Court in *PLESSY V. FERGUSON* made it legal to segregate blacks from whites. The "separate but equal" doctrine then became all-pervasive, segregating the races in schools, churches, restaurants, and virtually every other corner of society. Poll taxes, abuses of the LITERACY TEST, and terrorism prevented blacks from voting.

Other ethnic groups also faced DISCRIMINATION. In 1854, the California Supreme Court ruled that Asians could not testify against white defendants in court. In 1859, the California Superintendent of Education segregated nonwhite children from white children in school. Asians were denied citizenship and the right to own land and were singled out for unfair taxes. The case of Yick Wo v. Hopkins (1886), for example, protested a San Francisco ordinance designed to drive Chinese laundries out of business. Because of housing and job DISCRIMINATION, Asians lived in inner-city ghettos (as in San Francisco and New York Chinatowns) and were restricted to menial jobs, regardless of education or skills.

American Indians and Latinos fared just as badly. After the Mexican War, many Latinos lost their land through unfair legal practices, and many found job and educational opportunities closed to them. Many Indians were isolated on reservations, the victims of broken treaties and economic exploitation.

Struggle, legislation, and court battles were necessary before members of these ethnic groups gained more equal treatment under the law. The INDIAN CITIZENSHIP ACT (1924) assured citizenship to all American Indians, and the Fair Employment Practices Committee (1941) worked to eliminate discrimation in defense jobs. BROWN V. BOARD OF EDUCATION (1954) made racial segregation illegal, overturning *PLESSY V. FERGUSON.* Two CIVIL RIGHTS Acts (1957 and 1964) enforced voting rights, integration, and equal opportunity.

In 1986, a federal judge ruled that Yonkers, New York, had "illegally and intentionally" racially segregated its schools and public housing, and ordered sweeping changes. In Sweatt v. Painter (1950), the Court ruled that the University of Texas had to admit a black law student, despite the state's last-minute effort to set up a separate, inferior school for him. In 1957, federal troops escorted nine black students into LITTLE ROCK's Central High School. In 1964 (Heart of Atlanta Motel v. United States), the Supreme Court prohibited discrimination by businesses engaged in interstate commerce. School busing and AFFIRMATIVE ACTION led to further successes against discrimination.

Between 1930 and 1965, about 53 percent of executed criminals in the United States were black, although blacks made up less than 10 percent of the nation's population. The Supreme Court ruled that this situation did not constitute unequal protection under the law. Ethical concerns about this reality, however, were part of the impetus that led some states to abolish the death penalty.

The NINETEENTH AMENDMENT granted women the right to vote and led to widespread election of women to public office and greater attention to women's rights. The Supreme Court ruled that women must be included in juries. Congress passed the EQUAL RIGHTS AMENDMENT in 1972, though the states failed to ratify it. Many states adopted their own equal rights measures to protect women. The military services struggled against tradition to eliminate practices discriminating against women.

Amendment 26 granted eighteen-year-olds the right to vote, leading to greater concern for the rights of young people. In 1982, the Supreme Court upheld the rights of students to have "access to ideas" and forbade school board censorship of books in the school library (Island Tree Union Free School District No. 26 v. Pico).

SUGGESTED READINGS. The Commission on the Bicentennial of the U.S. Constitution produced an excellent, readable overview of the Bill of Rights, the thin but powerful *The Bill of Rights and Beyond: 1791-1991* (1991). Another excellent discussion of the history and meaning of the document is Milton Meltzer's *The Bill of Rights* (1990). For case histories see *In Our Defense* (1991) by Caroline Kennedy and Ellen Alderman.—*Barbara Glass*

Birmingham demonstrations (1963): Series of protests organized by the SOUTHERN CHRISTIAN LEADERSHIP CONFERENCE (SCLC) in order to integrate Birmingham, Alabama, the most segregated city in the United States. Disillusioned by their failure to integrate Albany, Georgia, during a 1962 campaign, Martin Luther KING, Jr., and the SCLC turned their attention to Birmingham, the South's largest industrial city. With the

support of Birmingham's African American leader, Reverend Fred Shuttlesworth, King and his advisers met for three days in early 1963 and laid out the initial plan to desegregate all the city's public facilities. Their intention was to mobilize the black community around a series of mass demonstrations and boycotts targeting Birmingham merchants. With 40 percent of the city's population, blacks wielded enough purchasing power to damage the economic base of Birmingham severely.

Several factors delayed the demonstrations. King had to convince some black city leaders that the plan would not backfire because of negative publicity. Birmingham was in the middle of a mayoral election pitting Eugene "Bull" Connor, the vicious SEGREGATIONIST police chief, against a more moderate candidate. To forge ahead ran the risk of turning the white electorate in Connor's favor. The SCLC eventually waited until Connor was defeated, but he contested the election results and remained commissioner of public safety, vowing to meet the nonviolent protests with a violent counterresponse.

On April 3, King issued a "Birmingham manifesto" calling for complete DESEGREGATION in public facili-

Antidemonstration commando station in Birmingham, Ala., 1963. (Library of Congress)

ties, more jobs for African Americans in local business and industry, and the formation of a biracial committee to set a schedule for desegregating other sectors of city life. Demonstrations, boycotts, and SIT-INS would continue until these demands were met.

Major department stores such as Woolworth's were the early targets. King also led followers on daily mass marches resulting in hundreds of arrests. As the campaign grew in intensity, the police had difficulty rounding up demonstrators, despite Connor's intention to put all of them in jail. After a court injunction against marching, King and Ralph Abernathy chose to be arrested. While in solitary confinement, King composed his famous "Letter from Birmingham jail," a rebuttal to white fellow clergy who had counseled him to be more moderate in his tactics. The letter became one of the most eloquent defenses of the nonviolent philosophy of the Civil Rights movement.

Needing a new strategy to bolster the movement's spirit, King and his organizers recruited school children for a massive march. On May 2, more than one thousand children as young as six years old marched through Birmingham's streets. Approximately nine hundred were arrested and carted to jail in school buses. When the marching continued the next day, Connor ordered police to attack the children with clubs, police dogs, and high-pressure water cannons. The ensuing brutal scene was covered by the many reporters who had descended on the city, and it was condemned worldwide. With the jails full, with Birmingham severely condemned in the court of world opinion, and with its economy feeling the effects of the protests, business leaders began serious negotiations with King's forces and soon agreed to desegregate all facilities.

SUGGESTED READINGS. For further details, see Taylor Branch's history of the Civil Rights movement, *Parting the Waters* (1988), and Stephen B. Oates's biography of King, *Let the Trumpet Sound* (1982). James H. Laue's *Direct Action and Desegregation, 1960-1962* (1989) is another useful source.

Birth control and family planning: Family planning is a broad term referring to ways that prospective parents can voluntarily determine the number and timing of their children via prevention or postponement of conception. Family planning is often used synonymously with the term "birth control." Contraception refers more specifically to various means that interrupt or change the normal chain of events involved in conception. Most methods of contraception involve either placing a barrier between the sperm and egg or preventing the production of a mature egg.

Both the concept of family planning in general and particular methods of birth control have sparked political controversy since the late nineteenth century. As social issues, they have divided legislative bodies and courts of law as well as members of religious, cultural, and family groups in the United States. Just as there are many methods of contraception, there are many cultural traditions and religious beliefs that have a great impact on which methods, if any at all, are acceptable to an individual belonging to a particular culture or religion.

One of the most common methods of birth control in the United States is the ingesting of oral contraceptives, commonly known as birth control pills. These contain hormones that suppress ovulation. Other methods include condoms, intrauterine devices (IUDs), diaphragms, cervical caps, and implants that release hormones. Some methods of birth control require no pills or devices; among them is the rhythm method. In this method, a man and woman have intercourse only during the period of the month in which the woman is not supposed to be fertile. The rhythm method is not as reliable as the others noted. It is the only birth control method other than abstinence, however, that is approved by the Roman Catholic church.

Sterilization (for women) and vasectomy (for men) are operations that confer permanent contraception. ABORTION is also considered by some to be a form of birth control; the issue of abortion has polarized various factions in the United States. (Abortion cannot be considered contraception, because it takes place after the sperm and egg have united.)

History of the Birth Control "Movement" in the United States. "Voluntary motherhood" was a concept invoked by the early American feminist movement as early as 1870. Basically, feminists who held this position supported natural means of contraception such as abstinence and the rhythm method. In the Victorian era, supporting methods that would allow sexual activity without conception was seen as an attack on the family. Contraception was believed to make prostitution more viable, encourage "loose morals" in women, and separate procreation from sexual intercourse in opposition to the Judeo-Christian tradition. Methods of contraception were known to some and even written about in the early 1900's, but communication about birth control was risky because of an obscenity

Margaret Sanger (front row, left) is charged with maintaining a birth control clinic, in violation of New York law (1929).
(AP/Wide World Photos)

law known as the Comstock law forbidding the passage of such information through the mail.

The climate in the United States during World War I was opposed to family limitation. Policymakers were worried that educated people were not having families as large as they had in the past; large families were considered necessary to "serve the government" and protect the nation. President Theodore Roosevelt called family limitation selfish and immoral. Probably the most important figure in the modern birth control movement in the United States was Margaret SANGER. A former nurse, Sanger became convinced that birth control information needed to be in the hands of the masses. After gathering information at home and abroad from 1912 to 1914, she published papers entitled "The Woman Rebel" and "Family Limitation" and began to advocate contraception, which she called "birth control." The legality of some of her publica-

tions was questioned, and both she and her husband were convicted under the Comstock law in 1915.

In October, 1916, Sanger and others opened a clinic in Brooklyn. They distributed a flyer in three languages offering information on birth control. They were often harassed by police and threatened with lawsuits as they were accused of distributing "obscene literature." Sanger publicized birth control in the periodical *The Birth Control Review* and in two books she wrote in the 1920's. She and her supporters formed numerous organizations to mobilize efforts for the cause, but most were short-lived and fractious.

In the 1920's, Sanger established the American Birth Control League (ABCL), which had a platform of education, research, and legislative reform. It used physicians to speak to medical societies and sponsored a symposium in 1925. Because of these efforts and other societal changes, health professionals became involved in birth control clinics and organizing, helping the cause shift from a "radical" or underground position to a professional association-controlled movement.

By the 1930's, birth control had emerged from the taboo era to become an international social movement. In 1938, the Comstock law was overturned, removing federal bans on birth control. At that time, however, many states had their own laws prohibiting birth control clinics or means of distributing birth control information.

In 1938, the two major organizations active in birth control efforts joined to form the Birth Control Federation of America. This organization changed its name in 1942 to the PLANNED PARENTHOOD FEDERATION OF AMERICA. Its centralized efforts to promote birth control and family planning ended the infighting that had characterized the earlier period. Over the years, Planned Parenthood led efforts to make contraception and information on family planning available to all Americans regardless of education or income.

In the early 1990's, nearly 90 percent of sexually active women in the United States used some form of birth control, according to the Alan Guttmacher Institute and the Planned Parenthood Federation. The most popular method of contraception was sterilization (35.3 percent), followed by birth control pills (27.7 percent).

Cultural Values Affecting Family Planning. Cultural values held by various religious and ethnic groups support and mitigate against family planning and birth control. It is helpful to examine both pro and con positions on this issue from a cultural viewpoint in order to understand why some people are more willing than others to accept birth control practices.

A number of cultural values that support birth control as a part of family planning tend to be associated with middle-class white Americans. These include the desire of parents for their children to have a better, happier life than their own through having more material possessions per person in smaller families. Women, more than men, may favor birth control in recognition of physical difficulties of motherhood caused by excessive childbearing and CHILD REARING. As more adults seek higher education and delay marriage and childbearing, people of various cultures support birth control as a way to allow them to fulfill career goals unfettered by child rearing. In addition, some cultural groups have traditional beliefs that are somewhat supportive of birth control, such as Ameri-

can Indian groups that support natural contraception methods including the use of herbs and roots as well as withdrawal, and Jewish groups that support birth control in situations where the health of the woman would be adversely affected by childbirth.

Cultural values that do not support birth control include the perception that a large family is necessary for security especially in cultures that have experienced widespread poverty or health problems, and the desire for sons, motivating families of numerous cultures to keep having children if they have produced only girls. Some specific cultural values that mitigate against birth control are the result of the traditions, history, and socioeconomic status of a racial or ethnic group. For example, some African Americans, concerned about past forced sterilization programs and the survival of their people, have expressed the fear that birth control could lead to black GENOCIDE; they place a high value on children and reject any effort that might reduce their proportion in society. Among Latinos, emphasis on the family, especially the value of a large family, is a barrier to contraception. Some Latino males oppose any form of birth control because they believe their masculinity is demonstrated by having many children, and because they fear losing authority over their wives or are generally reluctant to discuss sexual issues. Government attempts to perform sterilizations on American Indian women have made some Indians fear birth control in general, seeing it as the government's way to limit the native population. Among some Asian Americans and other groups, female modesty and concepts of family privacy reduce the opportunity for informal conversation or education about contraception, especially among new immigrants.

Religious beliefs may also have a powerful impact on family planning. Religions ranging from Catholicism to Mormonism to Orthodox Judaism often favor large families, citing the biblical obligation to procreate. The strong opposition of the Roman Catholic church to most birth control methods affects many cultures whose members are predominantly Catholic, although some Catholic individuals continue to protest and defy such policies.

The Future of Birth Control. Most available birth control methods, ranging from the birth control pill and intrauterine device (IUD) to the newer sponge, female condom, and hormonal implant, were designed for women to use. Despite efforts to have both parties be equally responsible for contraception, it appears

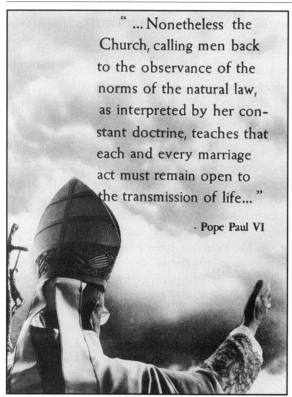

" ...Nonetheless the Church, calling men back to the observance of the norms of the natural law, as interpreted by her constant doctrine, teaches that each and every marriage act must remain open to the transmission of life... "

- Pope Paul VI

Pope Paul VI denounces contraception in a 1968 encyclical, continuing the Catholic church's position against birth control. (AP/Wide World Photos)

that the major burden falls upon the woman. Researchers claim that it is difficult to regulate male hormones (through, for example, a birth control pill) without reducing a man's sex drive. In the future, however, some believe that hormone injection and perhaps an implant system will be introduced for men. For women, items such as nonprescription diaphragms, skin patches that release hormones, and vaginal pills may be on the horizon. Sterilization methods for males and females may also improve as surgical techniques are refined.

A large majority of women across the United States appear to have accepted the position of "voluntary motherhood" that early women's rights activists advocated more than a century ago; that is, they believe a woman should have control over when she will become pregnant. Some ethnic and religious groups continue to oppose certain contraceptive methods for various reasons. In cultures that fear extermination or subordinate status because of their minority representation in the U.S. population, and in cultures that value large families or adhere to competing cultural and religious values, such beliefs may outweigh the perceived value of a woman's right to choose when to bear children.

SUGGESTED READINGS. For an overview of the history of birth control issues in the United States, see Linda Gordon's *Woman's Body, Woman's Right* (1976). *The New Our Bodies, Ourselves* (1984) by the Boston Women's Health Book Collective is useful for an overview of methods of birth control. On Margaret Sanger's life as it relates to the birth control movement, see *Birth Control in America: The Career of Margaret Sanger* (1970) by David Kennedy. To gain an overview of various cultures' views of birth control, *Population Policy and Ethics: The American Experience* (1977) by Robert Veatch is recommended.—*Mary C. Ware*

Bison and American Indians: Prior to their near extinction in the late 1870's, bison (a genus including buffalo) were critical to the subsistence, settlement, and economic patterns of Indians in the Great Plains. This area encompassed the grasslands stretching from present-day Alberta, Canada, south to the Mexican border, bounded on the west by the Rocky Mountains and on the east by the Missouri River. Groups inhabiting the region included, among others, the Blackfeet, CHEYENNES, COMANCHES, Kiowas, Crows, SIOUX, and Assiniboines.

Dependence upon bison had been characteristic of the inhabitants of the Great Plains since the Folsom Period ten thousand years ago. Until horses and guns became widely available during the eighteenth century, bison were hunted on foot with lances and bows and arrows. In order to approach the bison, hunters frequently camouflaged themselves in wolf skins or bison hides. Keeping downwind of the herd, the hunters would slowly move into shooting range. Other hunting techniques included the use of fire, cliff jumps, and impounds. The latter two methods generally involved the participation of an entire community. Women, children, and older people acted as beaters in order to compel the bison to move in a prearranged direction. Forcing bison over cliffs was a typical hunting technique in the northern Great Plains. Impounds involved the construction of a corral at the base of a cliff jump or at the apex of a *V*-shaped fence consisting of people and piles of stones. Dogs pulling a makeshift travois cart transported meat and other bison byproducts from the kill site back to the village.

The introduction of horses into the region revolutionized bison hunting. Herds became more accessible, and the transportation of bison products to the village became easier. Agile horses unafraid of approaching a bison herd closely became essential to Plains hunters. Frequently riders would surround a herd and then attack the bison in unison. Surrounds, cliff jumps, and impounds all required strict rules of organization. Religious and legal sanctions helped to ensure the proper behavior of each individual involved in the hunt. Frequently, a military society composed of successful male warriors policed the communal hunts.

Bison meat was a staple food in the Great Plains. The meat was cut into thin strips and hung to dry on racks. It was often pounded and mixed with marrow

horns were carved into spoons and ladles. Even bison dung was important; it was used for fuel.

SUGGESTED READINGS. An excellent overview of this subject can be found in *The Horse in Blackfoot Indian Culture* (1955) by John Ewers. Details concerning the hunting and uses of bison are included in *Bison Procurement and Utilization: A Symposium* (1978), edited by Leslie B. Davis and Michael Wilson. *The North American Buffalo* (1970) by Frank Roe and *Indians of the Plains* (1954, repr. 1982) by Robert Lowie provide essential information about the relationship between bison as a food resource and the richness of Plains Indian cultures.

Arapaho camp c. 1870 with buffalo meat drying, near Fort Dodge, Kans. (National Archives)

and dried berries to make pemmican, a delicacy that stayed edible for a number of years. Little of the bison was wasted. Hides were used for tipi covers, blankets, robes, parfleches, shields, and rope. They were also important trade items. The paunch and large intestine were used for storing and transporting water. Bison

Black. *Use* **African American**

Black Codes: Laws framed by southern legislatures in 1865 and 1866, designed to clarify the legal standing of newly freed slaves. Prior to the Civil War, "slave codes" had defined the legal status of most southern blacks; as slavery was abolished, state lawmakers wrote the black codes in order to specify blacks' legal rights and limitations on those rights. Among the rights clearly set out for the first time were blacks' right to make contracts, to own property, to sue, and to enter into legal marriages.

Southern lawmakers, however, devoted much more energy to limiting the rights of newly freed slaves. These limitations varied from state to state, but contained many of the same threads. Typically, black codes provided that blacks could not own guns, insult whites, congregate together at night, vote, hold office, or serve on juries. INTERMARRIAGE between whites and blacks was forbidden, and the penalty for certain crimes was made greater for freedmen than for other citizens. In South Carolina, blacks were barred from certain businesses and trades.

Two of the most ominous black codes dealt with testifying in court and with vagrancy. The testimony codes specified that while blacks had the right to testify in court, this right was limited to cases involving only other blacks. In practice, this meant that a black citizen who had been assaulted could not identify his white assailant in court. The vagrancy codes stated that blacks could be arrested for not having signed an annual labor contract; in lieu of incarceration, the prisoner's labor could be auctioned off to the highest bidder. Thus, the black codes allowed the return of a system of forced plantation labor.

Northern Republican congressmen were outraged at the black codes, taking them as evidence that little had changed in the southern states despite Confederate defeat in the war. Anger over the black codes led Congress to embark upon the ambitious program known as RECONSTRUCTION, destroying President Andrew Johnson's plans for an exceptionally lenient reconstruction.

Congress passed the Civil Rights Act of 1866 in order to nullify the black codes; the act stated that all citizens were to have equality before the law. Congress put this act on a stronger footing by inserting the same language into the FOURTEENTH AMENDMENT, ratified in 1868. Equality before the law would be safer before the courts and could be repealed only by passage of another constitutional amendment.

By the late nineteenth century, southern legislatures again began to write statues known as JIM CROW LAWS limiting the rights of blacks. These remained on the books until the 1960's, but they were never quite so limiting of the rights of African Americans as were the earlier black codes.

SUGGESTED READINGS. The basic history of the black codes is Theodore B. Wilson's *The Black Codes of the South* (1965). To understand the black codes in a larger context, see Eric Foner's *Reconstruction: America's Unfinished Revolution, 1863-1877* (1988).

Black English: Form of English spoken, to various degrees, by approximately 80 percent of African Americans. The language is also known as Ebonics, Black English Vernacular, African American Vernacular English, and Afrish. It is a much-debated speech phenomenon because of its uncertain origins and many variants. Some of its more common characteristics include the use of "been" to connote past activity, as in "She been had that baby"; the use of double negatives when starting a sentence, as in "Don't nobody know nothing about that"; and the dropping of *s* in third-person singular, present tense constructions, as in "he come."

There is very little documentation of the speech of the first African Americans. Many of the early views on Black English were based on attitudes toward the people who spoke it rather than evidence from factually based research. As a result of such ignorance, many people believed that Black English was merely an error-ridden dialect spoken by poor, uneducated individuals who had not had a proper introduction to Standard English. In 1966 these opinions seemed to be confirmed by the so-called deficiency theory. This theory claimed that African Americans were incapable of acquiring the English language correctly as a result of biological insufficiencies; thus, intervention was necessary in order to help them become academically successful and socially functional enough to survive outside their own culture.

The deficiency theory has since been disproved by many prominent linguists such as Lorenzo Dow Turner, the first African American scholar to study Black English. His research, presented in *Africanisms in the Gullah Dialect* (1949), provided concrete evidence linking GULLAH (a CREOLE language spoken by African Americans off the coast of South Carolina and Georgia) to the vocabulary and syntax of African languages such as Ibo (also written "Igbo"), Mandingo, Vai, Twi, Yoruba, and Wolof. Turner's data forced the linguistic community to acknowledge African American speech as a legitimate research area. According to Turner, Black English is a semi-Creole language that resulted from Gullah's contact with Standard English among former slaves who went North during the GREAT MIGRATION. Other linguistic researchers of Black English include William Labov, known as the father of sociolinguistics, who did numerous studies to prove that speakers of Black English were as cognitively effective as speakers of Standard English. Despite linguistic research, many Americans still consider Black English a faulty dialect of Standard English whose origins may be rooted in southern English or even Old English.

One of the problems with researching Black English is that it is not a contained unit of speech patterns that can be studied neatly. There are many patterns, which differ among neighborhoods, cities, states, countries, and even continents. Consequently, it is very difficult to pinpoint unique properties that apply to all variations. For example, linguist Joey Lee Dillard believes that some types of Black English are Creolized forms of an African pidgin English that was spoken by Africans and Europeans during trade activities.

Black English is extremely important to African Americans as a strong link to their multifaceted past. A better understanding of the language could benefit educators of all American ethnic groups, many of whom still harbor deficiency theory attitudes that affect the way Black English speakers are viewed and evaluated.

SUGGESTED READINGS. For more information refer to *Talkin' and Testifyin'* (1977) by Geneva Smitherman Donaldson as well as *The Study of Non-standard English Negro and Puerto Rican Speakers in New York City* (1968) by William Labov; *Black English: Its History and Usage in the United States* (1972) by Joey Lee Dillard; *Africanisms in the Gullah Dialect* by Lorenzo Dow Turner (1949); *The Cambridge Encyclopedia of Language* (1987), edited by David Crystal; and *The Ethnography of Communication* (1964), edited by John J. Gumperz and Dell Hymes.

Black Entertainment Television (BET): Cable television network. Black Entertainment Television was a part of the USA cable network from 1977 until 1980 and offered programming only a few hours per week. After becoming a separate cable network in 1980, it adopted the motto "Giving You a Voice." Its scheduling includes sport, educational, news, and music shows of particular interest to African Americans. The network provides coverage of football and basketball at historically black colleges and was the first to have a music show devoted to rap. In 1984, BET began broadcasting twenty-four hours a day.

Black Hand conspiracy: When the police chief of New Orleans, Louisiana, David C. Hennessey, was murdered in 1890, city leaders suspected that it was the work of a group of Italian American criminals known as the Mafia or Black Hand. Hennessey had doggedly tried to suppress the group's activities. Nineteen Italian Americans were indicted, and nine were originally tried for Hennessey's murder. Although the prosecution made a very strong case, none was found guilty. Outraged citizens, believing that the Black Hand had illegally influenced the outcome of the trial, took justice into their own hands on March 14, 1891, when a vigilante mob murdered eleven of the accused men. The incident interrupted relations between Italy and the United States in 1891 and 1892 until U.S. President Benjamin Harrison publicly expressed his regrets and paid a small indemnity to the victims' families.

Black History Month: Black History Month is an extension of Negro History Week, which was established to be observed during the second week of February (to incorporate both Frederick DOUGLASS' and Abraham

Black History Month serves to educate people about the substantial achievements of great African Americans, such as Martin Luther King, Jr. (left), and Malcolm X (right). (AP/Wide World Photos)

Lincoln's birthdays) in 1926 by the Association for the Study of Afro-American Life and History. The society's founder and president, Carter Godwin WOODSON, led the effort to establish this observance. In 1972, the celebration was renamed Black History Week, and during the 1976 bicentennial, the celebration was expanded to encompass the entire month of February. The purpose of Black History Month is to highlight and commemorate the history, achievements, and cultural contributions of African Americans.

Black immigration to Canada. *See* **Canada—black immigration**

Black Kettle [Motavato] (c. 1803-1868): Chief of the Southern CHEYENNES in Colorado well known for his attempts to make peace and for his ability to influence his warriors to refrain from battle. He and his people were the victims of an unprovoked attack by the Colorado Volunteers at what is now known as the SAND CREEK MASSACRE (1864). Black Kettle escaped and made continuing efforts for peace (Treaty of Little Arkansas, 1865; and Medicine Lodge Treaty, 1867), but he was killed when his village on the Washita River (in present-day Oklahoma) was attacked by troops under George Armstrong CUSTER.

Black Leadership Forum: Group that meets periodically in closed sessions to discuss matters of concern to African Americans. The Black Leadership Forum, composed of leaders of fourteen nationally recognized African American groups, was organized in 1977 by Vernon E. Jordan, Jr. Among the groups involved are the A. PHILIP RANDOLPH INSTITUTE; Congressional Black Caucus; Joint Center for Political Studies; Martin Luther King, Jr., Center for Social Change; NATIONAL ASSOCIATION FOR THE ADVANCEMENT OF COLORED PEOPLE (NAACP); NAACP Legal Defense and Education Fund; National Black Caucus of Local Elected Officials; National Business League; NATIONAL COUNCIL OF NEGRO WOMEN; National Urban Coalition; National Urban League; OPERATION PUSH; and Opportunities Industrialization Centers.

Black Muslims. *See* **Nation of Islam**

Black nationalism: In Africa, nationalism developed in response to the long nightmare of European COLONIALISM that plundered the continent's resources and enslaved thousands of Africans. The essence of African nationalism rested upon a resolute rejection of foreign domination and the demand for self-determination. Black nationalism in the Americas arose among Africans who were brought to the New World by the slave trade in the largest forced migration in world history. The immense black diaspora spawned a diverse set of nationalist ideologies that have proliferated since the latter half of the 1900's.

Black Nationalism in the Americas. Much of early black nationalism in the Western Hemisphere advocated the return to Africa as a resolution to the diaspora. These emigrationist currents emphasized the contributions that returning blacks could make to Africa's progress, liberating the continent from its Euro-

W. E. B. Du Bois, pictured here in 1909, founded the black nationalist Niagara movement. (Library of Congress)

pean oppressors and aiding the construction of a united African nation. As memories of Africa became increasingly distant among African Americans, black nationalism gradually turned toward the idea of black nation-building in the New World.

Forging the black nation in North America meant

the construction of independent black political institutions that could wield political control over diaspora communities. Some took a PAN-AFRICAN approach, calling for all Africans in the New World to unite with African nations to oppose colonialist and imperialist domination. Still other black nationalists pursued liberation and nation building through cultural expression, creating a vibrant African presence in community institutions that nurtured black arts and intellectual development.

Just as in Latin America and the Caribbean, the political aspirations of blacks in the United States experienced periodic shifts in accordance with the changing social conditions of racist oppression. When the U.S. government capitulated to southern slave owners and ratified the FUGITIVE SLAVE ACT of 1850, many African Americans abandoned hope for eventual equality. The result was an upsurge of black nationalism. Martin DELANY, one of the first African American physicians, declared in 1852 that blacks constituted an oppressed nation within the borders of the United States and needed to consider a mass resettlement in the Caribbean or Africa itself. Delany later became involved in the post-Civil War cause of creating Liberia, an independent African homeland built by and for black emigrationists.

In the decades following the collapse of progressive reforms implemented during RECONSTRUCTION (1865-1877), nonemigrationist currents of black nationalism were also developed such as the Niagara movement founded in 1905 by W. E. B. DU BOIS. His movement fiercely opposed the more conservative, accommodationist politics of black leaders such as Booker T. WASHINGTON. Du Bois asserted that pan-African solidarity among blacks throughout the diaspora, combined with a struggle for economic self-determination in their own communities, constituted a viable nationalist formula for black liberation. Although the NIAGARA MOVEMENT was short-lived, some of its most prominent members founded the NATIONAL ASSOCIATION FOR THE ADVANCEMENT OF COLORED PEOPLE (NAACP) in 1909, choosing to collaborate with white progressives in the struggle for racial equality. Du Bois eventually resigned from the NAACP in 1934, viewing its politics as too conservative.

In the post-World War I period, some black nationalist organizations were influenced by socialist ideology. Cyril V. Briggs formed a militant, prosocialist organization during the early 1920's known as the African Blood Brotherhood (ABB), which advocated armed self-defense of African Americans. By decade's end, Briggs drifted from his nationalist position, convinced that the only hope for genuine racial equality rested in a united front of black and white workers committed to socialist revolution.

Messianic Nationalism. Another important trend in black nationalism emerged under the leadership of Marcus GARVEY. This Jamaican-born leader founded the UNIVERSAL NEGRO IMPROVEMENT ASSOCIATION (UNIA) in 1914, a Caribbean-based movement that relentlessly denounced the evils of white society and championed the inherent goodness of African culture. As a highly charismatic leader, Garvey preached that Jesus Christ was an African man from Ethiopia and that evil Europeans had stolen and distorted Christianity just as they had stolen Africa itself.

Garvey's movement redefined Christian deliverance to signify the need for an independent black Africa that would raise the status of blacks everywhere. When Garvey arrived in the United States, his base of support grew quickly among African Americans of the most humble means, many of whom proved receptive to his messianic ideology. Although Garvey frequently declared that all African Americans must struggle for the return to Africa, he exhorted black communities to independently develop their economic base so as to finance large-scale projects that would strengthen black ties to the motherland.

Many rival black leaders despised Garvey for his propensity to label as traitors all blacks who collaborated with white-controlled institutions. Garvey proved to be shrewd in his ability to discredit his African American political opponents, using tactics such as red-baiting to denounce black socialists and asserting that lighter-skinned blacks could not be fully trusted.

By the 1920's, Garvey's UNIA was the largest black organization in the United States, building an economic empire designed to help link together Africans throughout the world. A key economic enterprise established by UNIA was the Black Star Line, a steamship company designed to handle trade and travel between the diaspora and the African continent. UNIA's economic activities proved to be Garvey's undoing, with financial scandals related to the failed steamship line eventually forcing him to leave the United States in 1927 to avoid imprisonment for federal tax evasion. With Garvey's charismatic presence absent and political opponents denouncing his financial conduct as hypocrisy, the UNIA rapidly crumbled.

Black Muslims in the United States. One important legacy of Garveyism was its influence upon the Black Muslim movement that arose in the early 1930's. The NATION OF ISLAM, formed in Detroit, echoed Garveyism in its denunciation of white-controlled Christianity. Elijah MUHAMMAD emerged as the influential leader of this black separatist sect, which promoted its own version of Islamic teachings and advocated economic self-reliance based on black-owned business ventures. Upon gaining control of their own communities, the Nation of Islam envisioned that African Americans could eventually establish a separate black nation.

The distinctive quality of the Nation of Islam rested in its rejection of white culture and Christian beliefs. It preached the need for strict abstention from "white vices" such as alcohol, tobacco, and drugs, and endeavored to create an alternative black media in support of black-nation building. The sect strongly opposed black participation in any political affairs outside of its community, including service in the U.S. armed forces. The refusal of Black Muslims to submit to the draft led to the incarceration of many of its leaders during World War II, including Elijah Muhammad himself.

After the war, the movement's leadership was released and the Nation of Islam grew once more. Networks of black-owned businesses were developed, the profits of which were channeled into community programs such as drug rehabilitation and rescue clinics for black prostitutes. Self-reliance and service to their community were extolled as the highest virtues by Black Muslims, who railed at black dependency on welfare. As a consequence of their earlier imprisonment, the movement's leadership became dedicated to prison outreach programs, which later proved to be fertile ground for recruitment.

One individual, Malcolm Little, was converted while serving a seven-year prison sentence for robbery. Following his release, he joined the Nation of Islam and took the name of MALCOLM X. Many Black Muslims changed their last name to X symbolize the historic loss of African surnames under slavery and to demonstrate their rejection of slave names issued by white slave owners.

Malcolm X quickly rose through the ranks of the Nation of Islam to become one of its most effective ministers in Harlem's black community. By the early 1960's, he was preaching a militant nationalist message that sharply criticized the politicized Christian ideology advocated by Martin Luther KING, Jr., and other civil rights leaders. Denouncing the call to "love your enemy," Malcolm's nationalist alternative advocated the formation of rifle clubs within black communities to provide self-defense against racists. This militancy, reinforced by his fiery oratory skills, proved attractive to many younger black activists impatient with the pace of gains being won by the nonviolent CIVIL RIGHTS MOVEMENT.

By early 1964, internal controversy shook the Nation of Islam as Malcolm X began to have personal differences with Elijah Muhammad. When Malcolm refused to abide by Muhammad's ban on outside political involvement, he was ordered to suspend his preaching, causing him to resign from the Nation of Islam. Shortly afterward, he founded an activist organization named the Muslim Mosque, Inc., that openly advocated militant involvement of Black Muslims in the civil rights struggle.

Malcolm's political radicalism became increasingly popular in the larger black community, and in 1964,

In his early speeches, Malcolm X strongly supported black nationalism through his affiliation with the Nation of Islam. (AP/Wide World Photos)

he created the Organization of Afro-American Unity (OAAU). This nonsectarian organization advocated both reformist and revolutionary strategies, including registration of black voters in support of independent black candidates; the formation of educational, cultural, and tenants' rights organizations; and the expansion of self-defense institutions. Malcolm's politics became increasingly anticapitalist, thus extending his popularity with black college students and black socialists. His revolutionary nationalist legacy flourished in the wake of his assassination in early 1965. The precise details concerning Malcolm X's murder never became clear; evidence strongly suggests police complicity despite the conviction of several Black Muslims for the crime.

Black Power Politics. The militant nationalist legacy of Malcolm X greatly influenced the Black Power movement of the late 1960's. Perhaps the most famous expression of this influence was the Oakland-based Black Panther Party (BPP), founded in 1966 by Huey P. Newton and Bobby Seale. The BPP organized popular community services such as food kitchens, day care, and educational and cultural programs but became embroiled in controversy over its formation of armed self-defense patrols of the black community. A series of widely publicized confrontations with the police soon catapulted the BPP into a national symbol of armed black militancy.

The Black Panthers became known for their black leather jacket and black beret uniforms, and their open espousal of armed revolutionary struggle. Their militancy dovetailed with the growth of radical white student organizations, many of which supported the BPP. Some Panther leaders advocated a revolutionary alliance with radical whites to achieve the goal of a socialist revolution. Almost from the onset, however, tensions developed within the BPP leadership as many black nationalists rejected collaboration with whites as an inherently unreliable strategy. When serious rifts developed within the BPP as well as between the BPP and other black organizations, the Federal Bureau of Investigation (FBI) succeeded in infiltrating and disrupting the Panthers as part of a large-scale police campaign known as COINTELPRO.

By the mid-1970's, much of the Panther leadership was either dead, imprisoned, or in exile. As the BPP began to collapse, some former members went underground and formed clandestine revolutionary organizations such as the Black Liberation Army (BLA). Others turned to create openly black nationalist orga-

nizations such as the Republic of New Africa (RNA) and the New Afrikan People's Organization (NAPO), both of which claim inspiration from Malcolm X in advocating the creation of an independent, black socialist republic ruled by and for black majority populations in the southern United States.

Conclusion. Black nationalism has consistently resurfaced as part of the continuing African American struggle for freedom. Depending upon the prevailing social conditions, African Americans have shifted their loyalties between nationalist and integrationist politics as a means for achieving economic, political, and cultural liberation. White intransigence in the face of organized black demands for full equality invariably tends to generate new expressions of militant black nationalism.

Suggested Readings. For an eloquent overview of black nationalism, see Wilson Jeremiah Moses' *The Golden Age of Black Nationalism: 1850-1925* (1978). Manning Marable's *W.E.B. DuBois: Black Radical Democrat* (1986) critically evaluates the Du Bois legacy while a concise introduction to both Marcus Garvey and Malcolm X is found in John White's *Black Leadership in America* (1990). Adib Rashad's *The History of Islam and Black Nationalism in the Americas* (1991) chronicles the Muslim influence within black nationalist politics while Imari Abubakari Obadele's *Free the Land!: The True Story of the Trials of the RNA-11 in Mississippi and the Continuing Struggle to Establish an Independent Black Nation in Five States in the Deep South* (1984) presents a black nationalist manifesto for African America.—*Richard A. Dello Buono*

Black Panther Party: Black nationalist group organized in Oakland, California, in the fall of 1966. The organization began in response to charges of racism in local government and brutality within the predominantly white police department.

The Black Panther Party was cofounded by Huey P. Newton, a twenty-four-year-old community activist and law student, and Bobby Seale, a twenty-nine-year-old entertainer and laborer. Initially called the Black Panther Party for Self-Defense, the group saw as its primary responsibility the self-preservation of the black community. Dressed in black berets, black leather coats, and black trousers, members patrolled their communities with firearms, carried openly, and legal manuals to protect residents from harassment and civil rights violations by the police.

Newton and Seale drafted a "Ten-Point Platform of the Black Panther Party" calling for: 1) the power to determine the destiny of the African American community; 2) full employment for African Americans; 3) suitable housing for African Americans; 4) the exemption of African Americans from military service; 5) the inclusion of a culturally relevant curriculum in the school system; 6) an end to price-gouging by white businesses; 7) the immediate end to police brutality and murder of African Americans; 8) the release of

Party members were subject to various rules, including prohibitions against stealing from other oppressed peoples or using illegal or harmful substances while fulfilling organizational responsibilities.

The Black Panther Party mainly attracted blacks who were disillusioned by the failed quest for the American dream. The most notable was Eldridge CLEAVER, who gave the party international notoriety with his best-selling book, *Soul On Ice* (1968), a collection of essays on the African American experience

Demonstrators in Los Angeles, Calif., 1970, show support for seventeen jailed Panther leaders. (AP/Wide World Photos)

all African American prisoners because they lacked access to equal justice; 9) the inclusion of African Americans on juries; and 10) a genuine application of the principles of the Declaration of Independence to all African Americans. The Panthers revised the platform in the spring of 1972 to reflect the broader focus of civil and human rights for oppressed people everywhere.

The party was headed by a Central Committee, chaired by Newton and Bobby Seale, his second-in-command. The cabinet, much like that of a government, included a field marshal, minister of education, minister of foreign affairs, minister of justice, minister of culture, and minister of defense, among others.

in white America. In 1971, Newton publicly expelled Cleaver during a highly publicized internal power struggle. A short-lived 1968 merger with the STUDENT NONVIOLENT COORDINATING COMMITTEE (SNCC) brought H. Rap BROWN, Stokely CARMICHAEL, and James Foreman into the party.

Party activities broadened in 1967, at which time "Self-Defense" was dropped from the name. The party began an intense program of community activism which included protesting tenant evictions, advocacy for welfare recipients, and demanding the installation of traffic lights at school crossings. The Black Panthers published a newspaper and taught black history to youth.

The Black Panthers' increasing notoriety led to

increased harassment by the police and the Federal Bureau of Investigation (FBI). FBI chief J. Edgar Hoover called the Panthers "the greatest threat to internal security in the United States." The FBI's Counterintelligence Program, COINTELPRO, sought to infiltrate and discredit the group. Many Black Panthers were killed under dubious circumstances. The most notable case was the murder of Fred Hampton, a Chicago Panther leader, and four others, who were killed in their sleep in an early-morning raid in 1968.

In 1967, Newton was charged with the murder of a police officer during a traffic stop. Convicted of voluntary manslaughter by a mostly white jury, Newton was retried three times over the next four years, with the first conviction being reversed and the last two juries deadlocking. The charges were eventually dismissed, and Newton was released after three years in

The now classic raised-fist gesture of black power created a great controversy when used by track stars Tommie Smith (center) and John Carlos (right) during an awards ceremony at the 1968 Olympic Games in Mexico City. (AP/Wide World Photos)

jail. By the end of 1969, most of the party's leaders had been killed, jailed, or forced into exile.

SUGGESTED READINGS. Additional information on the Panthers can be obtained in *Voices of Freedom: An Oral History of the Civil Rights Movement from the 1950's Through the 1980's* (1990) by Henry Hampton and Steve Fayer, *The Black Panthers* (1969) by Gene Marine, *Racial Matters: The FBI's Secret File on Black America, 1960-1972* (1991) by Kenneth O'Reilly, and *Red, Black and Green: Black Nationalism in the United States* (1976) by Alphonso Pinkney. See also *The Black Panthers* (1969) by Gene Marine.

Black Power movement: Militant movement born of frustration in the mid-1960's to push for the empowerment of African Americans in the political, economic, and social spheres. The slogan "black power" was popularized by Stokely CARMICHAEL as a challenge to the nonviolent, integrationist philosophy of the CIVIL RIGHTS MOVEMENT. Black power advocates were influenced by BLACK NATIONALISM to favor a more separatist approach to self-determination for African Americans. Groups that espoused black power after the mid-1960's included the CONGRESS OF RACIAL EQUALITY (CORE), the STUDENT NONVIOLENT COORDINATING COMMITTEE (SNCC), and the BLACK PANTHER PARTY. Their emphasis on the study of African history and pride in African and African American culture left an important legacy in the Black Arts movement and the establishment of AFRICAN AMERICAN STUDIES PROGRAMS.

Black studies programs. *See* **African American studies programs**

Black United Front: The name of two civil rights organizations. The first group, founded in 1968, was formed by individuals who were dissatisfied with the progress made by such established civil rights organizations as the NATIONAL ASSOCIATION FOR THE ADVANCEMENT OF COLORED PEOPLE (NAACP), the SOUTHERN CHRISTIAN LEADERSHIP CONFERENCE (SCLC), and the NATIONAL URBAN LEAGUE. Composed of a mixture of militant and moderate members from the Washington, D.C., area, the Black United Front called for community control over police and increased representation of blacks on the police force as a means of eliminating police violence against African Americans. After the first organization became defunct, a new national organization was established in July, 1980, by Herbert Daughtry, a black Pentecostal minister from

Brooklyn, New York. Daughtry invited delegates from thirty-four states to meet in his Brooklyn church to build a grass-roots movement that would address the problems of unemployment and other social problems affecting the African American community. Black social activists such as playwright/poet Amiri BARAKA, Ashiel Ben Israel of the Hebrew Israelites, Skip Robinson of the United League of Mississippi, and Imari Obadele of the Republic of New Afrika joined the organization. At the same time that the group lobbied policymakers on issues ranging from quality education and employment opportunities to improved housing and police relations, it also addressed international issues of racism and human rights abuses, particularly in Africa and the Caribbean.

Blackwell, Elizabeth (Feb. 3, 1821, Counterslip, near Bristol, England—May 31, 1910, Hastings, England): Physician and advocate for women in medicine. Blackwell was the first American woman to receive a medical degree. In 1849 she was graduated from Geneva Medical College in New York. After a period in Paris as a midwife—the only capacity in which she could work—Blackwell returned to the United States in 1851. She tried to set up practice in New York without much success; in fact, she received hate letters. Despite harassment, in 1857 she opened the New York Infirmary for Women and Children and in 1868 founded the adjoining Women's Medical College.

The multitalented Rubén Blades in 1988. (AP/Wide World Photos)

Blades, Rubén (b. July 16, 1948, Panama City, Panama): Panamanian American musician, actor, and attorney. After establishing himself as a successful attorney of the Banco Nacional in Panama, Blades came to the United States in 1974. He was legal adviser to and recording artist with Fania Records, where he earned six gold records. In 1984, he moved to the Elektra label to record SALSA MUSIC on such albums as *Buscando America* (1984) and *Escenas* (1985). As a composer and singer, Blades has earned four Grammy Awards. As an actor, he has appeared in several films, including *Crossover Dreams* (1985) and *The Milagro Beanfield War* (1988), and was the first Latino to be nominated for Best Actor at the ACE national cable awards (for the 1988 *Dead Men Out*). Politically active, Blades has spoken out on a variety of issues affecting Latinos and helped found the Papa Egoro political party in Panama in 1991.

Blasphemy laws: Statutes that impose penalties for statements or behaviors that show contempt or irreverence for God. In spite of many European settlers' history of having fled religious persecution themselves, blasphemy laws in colonial America were often harsh. For example, in 1658, Jacob Lumbrozo, a Jewish doctor, was charged under a Maryland blasphemy law; had he been convicted, the penalty would have been death. Clearly, definitions of blasphemy differed according to the party in power; thus, blasphemy laws could be a way of asserting the religious values of the dominant culture and oppressing religious minorities.

Blaxploitation films: Motion pictures made in the early 1970's featuring African American actors portraying bigger-than-life heroes known for their sexual exploits. Although these action-oriented films attempted to satisfy a need for African American heroes, these characters were too unrealistic to do so. Civil rights leaders and psychologists criticized the films because they perpetuated STEREOTYPES of African Americans as violent and criminal. African American performers created the Coalition Against Blaxploitation to encourage the film industry to feature African Americans in films with more substance. By the end of the 1970's, blaxploitation films were box office failures, and producers stopped making them. *Shaft* (1971), starring Richard Roundtree, and *Super Fly* (1972), starring Ron O'Neal, exemplify the Blaxploitation genre. Parodies of the genre can be seen in Robert Townsend's *Hollywood Shuffle* (1987) and Keenan Ivory Wayans' *I'm Gonna Git You Sucka* (1988).

"Blowout": Mexican American high school student strike in Los Angeles in 1968. The students walked out of their classes to protest the Anglo-dominated system that left them feeling excluded and virtually invisible. They wanted to lend support to the growing CHICANO MOVEMENT in the Southwest by demonstrating against what they felt to be rampant racism and discrimination from almost all sectors of society. Through the media, millions of Americans immediately became aware of the plight of Chicanos and their struggle to be heard.

Blue laws: State or local laws written to prohibit labor, business, or commercial activities on Sunday. They are also called "Sunday laws" or "Sunday closing laws." Exceptions were sometimes made for activities involving food, medicine, and recreation. In the United States, such regulations, based on the biblical rule against working on the Sabbath, date back to colonial times. Blue laws have been opposed and challenged on the grounds that they violate the U.S. Constitution's guarantee of separation of CHURCH AND STATE. In two cases in 1961, the Supreme Court upheld Sunday closing laws. Nevertheless, blue laws have gradually faded from importance as many communities have eliminated them or made them less restrictive. Frequently they are left on the books but simply ignored.

Blues music: Twentieth century African American secular FOLK MUSIC that had its origins in the leader and chorus (call and response) work songs of slaves in the pre-Civil War South. After the war, work songs began to take the form of solo calls or "hollers." Hollers were relatively free in form and probably gave rise to the blues vocal style. Early blues instrumentation relied heavily on stringed instruments such as the banjo, since the playing of drums by slaves was forbidden.

By the 1890's, the traditional British ballad form used in such songs as "John Henry" and "Po' Lazarus" became combined with the freer style of the "hollers." The first authentic country blues emerged from such combinations. Its unique lyric form had three rhyming lines, the second of which was most often a repetition or near-repetition of the first. The lyric was sung over a twelve-bar harmonic progression. Many southern blues singers traveled and worked as entertainers in patent medicine shows in the early 1900's, thus spreading the blues to towns and cities throughout the South.

The first blues song to become immensely popular was "St. Louis Blues," composed by W. C. HANDY (often called the "father of the blues") in 1914. Gradually blues singers began to express more personal themes in their songs. The subjects ranged from unrequited love to the oppressive social conditions of the day. By the 1920's the first blues recordings were being produced. The songs of Ma Rainey, the legendary Bessie Smith, and country blues singers such as Curley Weaver and Blind Willie McTell became available to audiences outside the South.

The legendary blues singer Bessie Smith. (AP/Wide World Photos)

The urban blues of the 1930's originated in Chicago. This aggressive style was played by bands that included piano and saxophone or trumpet as well as guitar. Among the notable performers of urban blues were Tampa Red and Big Bill Broonzy. Meanwhile, outstanding blues singers such as Robert Johnson from Mississippi created memorable songs with simple guitar and harmonica accompaniment, firmly rooted in the earlier tradition.

Following World War II, small African American-owned record companies started producing blues artists. The sales of blues records increased and included many types of blues-related music, such as rhythm and blues, which became popular with white audiences. Recordings by Muddy Waters, Howlin' Wolf, Robert Johnson, and others profoundly influenced British pop and rock music in the 1960's. Groups such as the Rolling Stones, the Animals, and the Yardbirds recorded versions of blues songs, while individual rock musicians such as Keith Richards and Eric Clapton devoted time and resources to the recording and promotion of forgotten black blues artists. Blues also influenced the development of American JAZZ. In the 1970's, widespread interest in the blues waned, and by the 1980's only a few blues singers such as B. B. King and Robert Cray had steady careers.

SUGGESTED READINGS. To learn more about the meaning of vocal blues as well as the historical development of blues forms, see *Blues Fell This Morning* (1990) by Paul Oliver. *The Blues Makers* (1991) by Samuel Charters offers insights into the personal, social, and musical background of the early blues musicians. William Barlow's *Looking up at Down* (1989) discusses the emergence of blues culture. *Black Pearls* (1988) by Daphne Duval Harrison is a thorough study of women blues singers of the 1920's.

B'nai B'rith, Independent Order of: Largest Jewish service organization in the world. Hebrew for "sons of the covenant," B'nai B'rith was founded in New York in 1843 with the mission of mutual aid, social service, and philanthropy. Its women's auxiliary was founded in 1897 and its youth group in 1924. Local lodges offer adult education programs, veterans' services, and support for Israel as well as social programs. The organization's Hillel Foundation sponsors groups on college campuses nationwide that encourage Jewish religious, cultural, and social activities. B'nai B'rith was also the original sponsor of the ANTI-DEFAMATION LEAGUE.

Boat people: Vietnamese REFUGEES who fled their country by boat after the VIETNAM WAR, especially in the late 1970's and early 1980's. After the fall of Saigon to the Communists on April 30, 1975, the last American troops and personnel and some 175,000 Vietnamese were evacuated to the United States. For years afterward, a constant flow of ethnic Chinese and native Vietnamese left Indochina in small boats. They fled to escape harsh "re-education camps," barren "new economic zones," and restrictions on the Chinese minority. The total exodus from Vietnam by sea and over land grew to about 1.5 million people between 1975 and 1991.

As early as 1975 the victorious Communist Vietnamese government began to nationalize the economy. Shops owned by ethnic Chinese, essentially Vietnam's business class, were ordered closed or confiscated, as were Chinese schools. South Vietnamese dissidents were also persecuted. Most who fled by boat were ethnic Chinese. They typically paid gold for the passage, paying both for tickets and for bribes to government officials. Their vessels were frail, overcrowded junks or fishing boats. They sailed north for Hong Kong or south for Thailand, Malaysia, and other points. No accurate records exist on how many boat people perished on the treacherous voyage in the South China Sea. Estimates run as high as 30 percent, or 250,000 people dead of hunger, thirst, exposure, drowning, military attack, or murder at the hands of Thai pirates.

Some boat people became passengers in the "Big Boat Trade," a highly organized profit-making operation set up by senior members of the Hanoi government and Mafia-like syndicates to ferry desperate refugees for huge profits. Conditions aboard the huge dilapidated and overcrowded ferries were miserable. Often these ships were turned away at port, prolonging the distress and need of thousands on board.

Those lucky enough to reach shore lived in sprawling, crowded refugee camps in Hong Kong, Thailand, the Philippines, Macao, Indonesia, and Malaysia. Their reception in "first asylum" Asian countries was often indifferent or even hostile. Refugees waited months, even years to be granted permanent residence in a third country. The largest number moved to the United States. France, Great Britain, Germany, Australia, and China received most of the others, after a 1979 Geneva conference on the refugee problem. As Vietnam's relations with China worsened, so, too, did its treatment of ethnic Chinese within its borders. By 1980, 300,000 boat people already waited in refugee camps, and refugee departures from Vietnam had reached 70,000 per month.

In 1989, Britain said Hong Kong would not accept boat people who were "economic migrants" fleeing impoverished Vietnam rather than political refugees fleeing persecution. In March, 1989, Hong Kong forcibly repatriated seventy-five boat people to Vietnam amid international controversy. Six more Asian nations announced the same month that they were also unable to assist so-called economic immigrants.

The traumatic pasts of Vietnamese boat people have sometimes made their resettlement in the United States difficult. Nevertheless, many studies have focused on their success in adapting to American life as owners of small businesses and their children's remarkable educational performance.

Haitian refugees have also been called boat people. They began arriving clandestinely in southern Florida in the 1970's in groups of a few boats carrying twenty or thirty people. Migration peaked in 1980, when Haitians arrived in droves to escape poor social conditions and oppressive poverty in Haiti. After a military coup in September, 1991, that deposed President Jean Bertrand Aristide, record numbers (more than 14,000 by February, 1992) fled by sea to the United States. A decision by President George Bush's administration to repatriate Haitian refugees forcibly who were considered "economic migrants"—not politically endangered—was highly controversial.

SUGGESTED READINGS. Bruce Grant's *The Boat People* (1979) raised international consciousness about the Vietnamese tragedy. *Voices from Southeast Asia* (1991) by John Tenhula collects first-hand accounts of escape from Indochina and resettlement. *Exodus Indochina* (1983) by Keith St. Cartmail provides passionate accounts of the voyages and camp life in "first asylum" countries. *The Boat People and Achievement in America* (1989) by Nathan Caplan et al. profiles their successes in the United States. Rose-Marie Chierici's *Demele: "Making It," Migration and Adaptation Among Haitian Boat People in the United States* (1991) investigates the Haitian refugee crisis.

Bond, [Horace] Julian (b. Jan. 14, 1940, Nashville, Tenn.): African American civil rights leader and politician. Born into a family of educators, Bond began his activist career protesting segregation at SIT-INS in Atlanta, Georgia, in 1960. He was a founder and officer of the STUDENT NONVIOLENT COORDINATING COMMITTEE (SNCC), an activist group that fought for civil rights in the South. At the age of twenty-five, he was elected to the Georgia state assembly. Denied a seat because of his anti-Vietnam War statements, Bond was reelected (1966) and seated by a favorable U.S. Supreme Court ruling. In 1968, he led a push for black representation at the Democratic Convention. Later he became an author and political analyst.

Border culture: A local culture unique to a border region that incorporates elements of the cultures on both sides. The term is most often applied to the border between the United States and Mexico. The concept stresses interchange across the border and notes that the political border actually has little effect on the way of life of people living along the border. Border culture demonstrates that political borders are artificial, not natural, boundaries. As observed in American cities such as El Paso and Mexican cities such as Monterrey and Ciudad Juarez, border culture is neither wholly American nor wholly Mexican but instead is a distinct hybrid.

The border is a dynamic element in the complex relationship between the United States and Mexico. Policy decisions made in Washington, D.C., and Mexico City are felt at the border, a place where, as one scholar has noted, "one of the superpowers comes into direct contact with a developing nation." The U.S. BORDER PATROL and IMMIGRATION AND NATURALIZATION SERVICE, legal and illegal immigrants, legitimate businesspeople, smugglers, and tourists all leave distinctive marks on border culture. Yet there are also many long-time residents, and for them this region of the Americas is a homeland in every sense of the word.

The border is a collection of towns cities which act as magnets or "way stations" for migration. It has been called a boundary "between two economies and two ways of life." On the Mexican side, in particular, one sees social traits and behaviors, lifestyles, and worldviews which distinguish border culture from Mexican national culture. The border is dynamic and undergoes constant transformations as a result of economic, cultural, and social forces from both sides.

Since the Spanish explorations of the sixteenth century, the northern frontier of Mexico existed in relative isolation from communication and resources at the center of the country. The result was an emerging lifestyle that was only tenuously integrated into the national culture. Instead, the Mexican side of the border became economically dependent on the American side. The Mexican people absorbed a cost in cultural terms from its encounter with the worldview and dreams of North American culture.

Among Mexican border cities, Monterrey is an industrial center, Ciudad Juarez is well-known for its maquiladoras (foreign-owned factories employing Mexican workers at lower cost), and Tijuana is a tourist mecca. American border cities from El Paso, Texas, to San Diego, California, also show great variety in

Scenes such as this one near Tijuana, Mexico, are common in border towns, where Mexican citizens may linger for days or weeks waiting for an opportunity to cross into the United States. (AP/Wide World Photos)

their manifestations of border culture, and have a flavor distinct from other American towns.

SUGGESTED READINGS. See Oscar Martinez's *Troublesome Border* (1988) for a historical account of conflict on the U.S.-Mexican border. For insights on literary developments consult *The Line: Essays on Mexican-American Border Literature* (1988), edited by Harry Polkinhorn et al., and Gloria Anzaldua's *Borderlands* (1987). An excellent general history of the Southwest is John Chavez's *The Lost Land: The Chicano Image of the Southwest* (1984).

Border Patrol, U.S.: Federal agency created as an enforcement arm of the IMMIGRATION AND NATURALIZATION SERVICE (INS) in 1924 to oversee and control the flow of undocumented immigrants into the United States at U.S. land borders, in Florida, and in the Gulf of Mexico. The immediate stimulus for the creation of the agency was the unprecedented migration of 700,000 Mexicans across the border between 1910 and 1930 after the Mexican Revolution. The work and public image of the patrol has shifted over the years with changes in legislation to control ILLEGAL IMMIGRATION along the

2,000-mile U.S.-Mexico border. During the 1980's, for example, the patrol came under attack by lawyers and human rights groups for reportedly unfair, often violent treatment of Central American REFUGEES attempting to cross the border. It has also been frequently criticized by Mexican American organizations for its alleged violation of their civil rights.

Bourke-White, Margaret (June 14, 1904, New York, N.Y.—Aug. 27, 1971, Stamford, Conn.): Photojournalist. Margaret was fascinated with machinery, the proof of industrialism and technology, and later combined this theme with a concern for human suffering. In 1936 her photograph from a documentary on the construction of a Montana dam and the people of the surrounding frontier land made the cover of the first issue of *Life* magazine. She was the first woman photographer for the Army Air Force and traveled with Patton's Third Army at the closing of World War II. Her photo documentaries include *You Have Seen Their Faces* (1937), on sharecroppers in the South, *The Drought* (1934), on conditions in the Dust Bowl, and *The Living Dead of Buchenwald* (1945).

Boy Scouts of America: Founded in 1910, the organization had a membership of more than five million boys and young adults and a staff of nearly four thousand adults in 1992. It maintains educational programs geared toward the character development, citizenship training, and mental and physical fitness of its members. The organization also studies the problems and needs of American youth, especially boys. There have been increased efforts to diversify Boy Scouts membership, staff, and programs to reach out to a multicultural population.

Mexico, the program facilitated the entrance of about 300,000 Mexican workers into the United States during the first three years of its operation. Both Mexican and U.S. government agencies were organized to administer the entrance of contracted laborers. The U.S. Department of Labor fingerprinted and verified the health conditions of incoming immigrants, and invited agents from prospective employers to interview them at federal contracting centers. The administrative machinery that was set up during wartime to address a critical labor shortage in the United States survived

Two young Boy Scouts at a United Nations Children's Summit candlelight vigil, 1990. (Frances M. Roberts)

Bracero program: Initiated to fill a labor shortage during World War II, the *bracero* program was introduced in August, 1942, as the "Mexican Contract-Labor Program." It consisted of a short-term agreement designed to allow for the temporary admission of laborers from Mexico, although migrants from Barbados, Jamaica, and Belize (formerly British Honduras) were eventually included.

Negotiated through a series of bilateral accords with

the war for almost two decades. During the 1942-1946 period, laborers primarily worked on the railroad and in agriculture.

Mexico's willingness to negotiate accords for emigration of its citizens, in spite of the opposition from Mexican businessmen, was governed by a desire to improve relations with the United States. The relative shortage of labor in Mexico itself meant that emigration of its laborers tended to drive up the price of wages. Yet Mexico, which had previously nationalized U.S.-owned oil holdings, was now accruing a growing financial debt with its northern neighbor and thus felt compelled to assist the Allied war effort. Mexico nevertheless retained a strong bargaining position given the labor shortage in the United States. This strength is evidenced by Mexico's enactment of a ban on labor contracts with the state of Texas because of charges that many Mexican laborers had been previously abused by employers. This ban remained in effect throughout the entire war, despite the intensive attempts of Texas to persuade the Mexicans to lift it, and was only lifted in 1947.

Following the war, the *bracero* program was suspended for several years but later was reinstated during the Korean War and remained in effect until 1964. The program brought a total of more than 4.5 million contract workers into the United States, primarily for work in the agricultural sector. During the final decade of its operation, it provided for the annual entrance of more than 300,000 *braceros*.

SUGGESTED READINGS. Kitty Calavita's *Inside the State: The Bracero Program, Immigration, and the INS* (1992) provides an excellent analysis of the factors shaping U.S. policy toward *braceros*. Peter G. Brown and Henry Shue's *The Border that Joins: Mexican Migrants and U.S. Responsibility* (1983) and Wayne A. Cornelius and Ricardo Anzaldúa Montoya's *America's New Immigration Law: Origins, Rationales, and Potential Consequences* (1983) present anthologies concerning Mexican migration to the United States. Ernesto Galarza's *Merchants of Labor: The Mexican Bracero Story* (1964) and Richard B. Craig's *The Bracero Program: Interest Groups and Foreign Policy* (1971) provide additional background on the program.

Bradley, Tom (b. Dec. 29, 1917, Calvert, Tex.): African American politician. Bradley's career encompassed a series of firsts for an African American. He was the first black officer to rise above the rank of sergeant and was eventually promoted to lieutenant in the Los Angeles Police Department. Bradley was the first African American elected to the Los Angeles city council in 1963 and the first to be elected as head of a predominantly white major American city when he became mayor of Los Angeles in 1973. Bradley served for five consecutive terms before declining to run for reelection in 1993. He has been praised for his work in improving the city's mass transit systems, establishing the city's business ties

with Pacific Rim trading partners, and bringing the 1984 Olympic Games to the city. Factors that contributed to his declining popularity included allegations of financial improprieties (which were eventually refuted) and criticism of his failure to investigate reports of police brutality brought to his attention before the highly-publicized Rodney King incident in 1991.

Mayor Bradley announces that he will not run for a sixth term as mayor of Los Angeles. (AP/Wide World Photos)

Braille: System of written communication for blind people. Education of the blind was not attempted on a large scale in Europe until the eighteenth century, when it became generally acknowledged that, though they lacked eyesight, blind people did not lack intelligence. Schools for blind students were founded throughout the Continent. Yet there was no clear, readily understood system of reading and writing that could be taught to the students.

A blind Frenchman named Louis Braille (1809-1852), who taught at the National Institute for the Young Blind in Paris, understood the need for an alphabet that could be read by touch and easily taught. After speaking with a captain in the French army who described military "night writing," Braille realized he had the answer. What was needed was a code—symbols to represent letters and numerals—rather than actual letters and numerals. He devised a system with a six-holed slate and a stylus that could produce a cell, with one to six raised dots in a variety of combinations, to represent letters or numerals on paper. The domino-like cells could then be arranged into words or mathematics, which blind people could read through their fingertips.

Braille first published his findings in 1829, with a more detailed explanation in 1837. His system, however, was either ridiculed or ignored, and he died of tuberculosis alone and penniless. Ironically, in 1854, two years after his death, the school where he had taught officially adopted the Braille alphabet and began to publicize it. By the mid-1900's, Braille had been translated into nearly every language and was being widely taught to the blind.

American educators of blind students were initially very slow to adopt the standard English Braille alphabet, which was closely modeled on the French Braille, primarily because of two other competing systems: American Braille (based on assigning the number of dots to the frequency of letter occurrence) and New York Point (in which the cells are two dots high and one to four dots long). The two latter systems were needlessly complicated, however, and standard English Braille was officially adopted for educating the American blind in 1916. Sixteen years later, it was recognized as the universal system for educating English-speaking blind people throughout the world.

The invention of the true Braille typewriter and of interpoint printing (which allows Braille to be printed on both sides of a page) late in the nineteenth century and early in the twentieth century, respectively, allowed a large supply of books for the blind to be produced. For the first time in the United States, schools for the blind could use the same texts and curriculum as public schools. The American Printing House for the Blind was established in Louisville, Kentucky, in 1858; in 1879 Congress passed a permanent appropriation to ensure that free schoolbooks would always be available to blind children.

SUGGESTED READINGS. More information about contemporary Braille can be found in *World Braille Usage* (rev. ed., 1990), published by UNESCO. For biographies of Louis Braille, see *Journey into Light: The Story of Louis Braille* (1964) by Webb B. Garrison and *Triumph over Darkness: The Life of Louis Braille* (1988) by Lennard Bickel. A good overview of the history of efforts to educate blind people may be found in Ishbel Ross's *Journey into Light: The Story of the Education of the Blind* (1951).

Braun, Carol E. Moseley (b. Aug. 16, 1947, Chicago, Ill.): African American politician. On November 3, 1992, Braun became the first African American woman elected to the U.S. Senate. Her victory followed other significant achievements. After graduation from the University of Chicago Law School in 1972, she served as assistant U.S. attorney. She was elected to the Illinois State Legislature and was the first woman to be assistant majority leader there. Each year she served (1978 until 1988), she earned the Best Legislator Award given by the Independent Voters of Illinois-Independent Precinct Organization. When elected recorder of deeds for Cook County, she became Chicago's highest-ranked African American county official. Braun's Senate election was part of a string of victories achieved by women candidates who sought public office in the wake of the 1991 confirmation hearings of U.S. Supreme Court Justice Clarence THOMAS.

Brazilian Americans: Although estimates vary, it is believed that approximately 750,000 Brazilians live in the United States. They hail from a country "discovered" in 1500 by Pedro Alvares Cabral, a Portuguese explorer. In 1822 the country, the largest in South America, became independent from Portugal. The multiethnic Brazilian population is of Portuguese, Italian, German, Syrian, Lebanese, Indian, and African descent. Attracted by economic opportunities there, many Asians, primarily Japanese, arrived in Brazil in the 1930's. Although Portuguese is the official language of Brazil, some immigrant groups are bilingual (Brazil is the only South American country whose official language is not Spanish).

High inflation in Brazil has prompted Brazilian emigration to the United States. Although some Brazilian Americans emigrated from São Paulo, most came from the city of Governador Valadares in Minas Gerais, a region in the center of Brazil. Since the largest wave of immigration did not occur until the 1980's, it is difficult to find accurate information and statistical data on Brazilian immigrants.

The largest community of Brazilian Americans is in Miami, Florida. Others have settled in cities such as New York, Washington, D.C., Boston, Chicago, Los Angeles, and San Francisco. New York's 46th Street is known as Little Brazil. At restaurants there and in other Brazilian neighborhoods, one can enjoy *feijoada*, a delicacy made of beans, pork, and sausage and served with rice. On September 6, Brazilians in the United States celebrate Brazilian Independence

Day with street fairs, music, and food. Another big celebration is Carnaval (Mardi Gras), which takes place several days before Lent. Although most Brazilians are Roman Catholics, the influence of African culture is also reflected in their religious rituals. This

ily. With more women entering the work force, however, traditional male/female social roles have become less rigid. Brazilians are respectful of the extended family, which may include not only grandparents but also aunts and uncles. Many Brazilian immigrants are

BRAZIL

cultural diversity is also present in literature and the arts, especially in music and dance, such as the *samba*.

The cultural values of most Brazilian families stress the dominant role of the father as the head of the fam-

educated, middle-class individuals escaping economic problems in their home country.

Several Brazilian American institutions help with the acculturation process of immigrants. *The Brazil-*

ians in New York and *The Florida Review* in Miami are examples of Brazilian American newspapers, while radio and cable television broadcast Brazilian programs (including those of Xuxa, a Brazilian children's entertainer. Neighborhood bookstores sell Brazilian literature, such as the novels of Jorge Amado. Organizations such as Partners of the Americas sponsor cultural exchanges between the United States and Brazil.

Many Brazilian immigrants have made outstanding contributions to American culture. Sérgio Mendes, João Gilberto, António Carlos Jobim (who has since returned to Brazil), and Airto Moreira are jazz musicians, while Astrud Gilberto, Flora Purim, and Tania Maria are jazz singers. Prominent Brazilians living in New York include film actress Sonia Braga, journalist Paulo Francis, executive Celita Jackson, and restauranteur Ricardo Amaral. Many other Brazilians contribute to American culture as professors and students at various American universities.

SUGGESTED READINGS. Among the books that discuss immigration from South America are David M. Reimers' *Still the Golden Door* (1985), Thomas Weyr's *Hispanic U.S.A.: Assimilation or Separatism?* (1988), L. H. Gann and Peter J. Duignan's *The Hispanics in the United States: A History* (1986), and Christopher Mitchell's edited volume *Western Hemisphere Immigration and United States Foreign Policy* (1992). The *Harvard Encyclopedia of American Ethnic Groups* (1980), edited by Stephan Thernstrom, includes a section on South American immigration in the article "Central and South Americans."

Breckenridge, Mary (Feb. 17, 1881, Memphis, Tenn.—May 16, 1965, Wendover, Ky.): Midwife and crusader for midwifery. After the death of her two children, Breckenridge was determined to help other mothers keep their children alive and healthy. A registered nurse, she was a volunteer for the American Red Cross in France after the Armistice of World War I. In 1923

Mary Breckenridge (left) receives the Distinguished Service Award, in 1954, from the National Federation of Business and Professional Women's Clubs, Inc. (AP/Wide World Photos)

she became a certified MIDWIFE in England. In 1925 she chose Kentucky as the site for the pioneering Frontier Nursing Service (FNS), funding some of it herself. The FNS was successful in substantially lowering the death rate for women in childbirth in Kentucky and in establishing midwifery as an affordable alternative to doctors for poor families.

Brook Farm: One of several experiments in communal living in the nineteenth century United States. Its founder was George Ripley, who with his wife, Sophia, and sixteen other shareholders took up residence in April, 1841, in the farm buildings in West Roxbury, Massachusetts, that became formally known as the Brook Farm Institute of Agriculture and Education. The novelist Nathaniel Hawthorne was one of the original members, attracted to the group by its Transcendentalist ideals, but he left after the first year.

Brook Farm grew from its original farmhouse (named the Hive) on about 200 acres to include a school (the Nest) run by Sophia Ripley, a large house (the Eyrie), the so-called Margaret FULLER Cottage, a large multipurpose dwelling called the Pilgrim House, a workshop, and four small dormitories. In 1844 work began on a Phalanstery, the master building demanded by the tenets of Fourierism, to which the small group was apparently converted by Albert Brisbane. In 1846, however, the incomplete building burned down, and the Brook Farm experiment never really recovered from the setback.

Over the course of its six-year life span, Brook Farm probably had about 200 members, with no more than 120 at any one time. Its entrepreneurial activities varied. Most of its farm products were consumed on the premises; neither its nursery nor its flower garden flourished, and its carpenters, shoemakers, and sash and blind workers were only intermittently busy. Its printers were occupied with *The Harbinger*, a Fourierist journal.

The daily rounds of working and dining were generally plain and healthy, if not always well organized. There were more men than women, and thus the men often worked at household tasks such as laundering. Skating and dancing were favorite pastimes, and literary readings were common. Music was much prized, and several of the members were talented singers. A strain of eccentricity ran throughout the whole Brook Farm adventure and occasioned much mirth from such observers as Ralph Waldo Emerson, but the resort by some members to practices such as cold-water cures remained well within the bounds of conventional human behavior.

The school enrolled children under six, primary schoolers, and college preparatory students in separate units. George Ripley taught mathematics and philosophy, and Sophia Ripley taught history and modern languages. Several of the students, such as the Curtis brothers, George William, and James Burrill, distinguished themselves. James became a curate in Cambridge, England, and earned a master's degree from the university there, while George became a writer and editor of *Harper's Weekly*. One of the most interesting of the students was Isaac Thomas Hecker, who left Brook Farm for Bronson Alcott's colony at Fruitlands. He went on to the Catholic priesthood and after a row with Rome became the leader of the Paulists and founded two religious publications.

Philosophical idealism wedded to Yankee individualism could be expected to bear something original, if not long-lasting. Brook Farm was the most distinctive American contribution to the tradition of Utopian visions for humanity.

SUGGESTED READINGS. Lindsay Swift's *Brook Farm: Its Members, Scholars, and Visitors* (1961) is a brisk account of its subject. *A Season in Utopia: The Story of Brook Farm* (1961) by Edith Roelker Curtis is anecdotal and very readable. Nelson Truman wrote a novel called *The Passion by the Brook* (1953) based on the colony, but the indispensable fictionalized account is Nathaniel Hawthorne's *The Blithedale Romance* (1852).

Brooks, Gwendolyn (b. June 7, 1917, Topeka, Kans.): African American poet. After growing up and attending college in Chicago, Brooks wrote the award-winning book of poems *A Street in Bronzeville* (1945). With *Annie Allen* (1949), she became the first black woman to win the Pulitzer Prize (1950). Numerous works including autobiography and children's books and many awards followed. After 1967, Brooks's writings focused more on political subjects, and she actively supported younger black writers. She was named poet laureate of Illinois in 1968 and poetry consultant at the Library of Congress in 1985.

Brotherhood of Sleeping Car Porters: Established in 1925, the first African American union to receive an international charter from the AMERICAN FEDERATION OF LABOR (AFL). A. Philip RANDOLPH, a prominent black socialist and editor of the radical magazine *The*

Messenger, was asked to lend assistance in forming a union of African American porters who worked on the railway sleeping cars operated by the Pullman Company. The company employed porters to wait on, and make and change beds for, passengers of railroad sleeping cars that the company built and leased to long-haul passenger railroads. Porters were expected to supplement their wages with tips. Although the Pullman cars provided sumptuous and elegant accommodations for white railroad patrons, the wages and working conditions of the porters who worked on the sleeping cars were deplorably low and demeaning. Nevertheless, these jobs were often considered prestigious within the African American community because they offered steady employment and travel opportunities.

Initially hesitant to become directly involved in union organization, Randolph began to investigate the porters' allegations of poor working conditions and to publish a series of articles that convinced others to support unionizing efforts. White railroad employees had already formed unions and successfully bargained for wage increases and better working conditions. Like other American labor unions, these railroad brotherhoods barred African Americans from membership or chose to segregate them into all-black "federal unions" with little bargaining power or recognition. Although the Pullman Company had established a plan for fair employee representation in 1924, this plan was indirectly controlled by the company. Randolph soon recognized that serious negotiations to improve wages and working conditions for the porters could only be conducted by an independent union.

On August 25, 1925, the Brotherhood of Sleeping Car Porters held its first organizational meeting in New York and outlined its demands. First among these demands was the condition that the minimum wage for porters be increased from the rate of $60 per month established by the Federal Railway Administration in 1919 to a rate of $150 per month. Supported by a variety of liberal organizations that supplemented the union's modest treasury formed from members' dues, Randolph visited the major cities on the Pullman routes in order to recruit additional members. By early 1927, the brotherhood had approximately seven thousand members.

The Pullman Company refused to recognize the union and attempted to threaten, coerce, fire, or blacklist union members. The company also tried, with some success, to divide the African American community in its support for the new union. Faced with an organization that refused to respond to the union's demands, Randolph petitioned for intervention by the railroad mediation board, which had been established by the Railway Labor Act of 1926 to act as a mediator in labor disputes that threatened to interrupt railroad operations. Although not compelled by law to negotiate, the Pullman Company attended some of the board's preliminary meetings in order to denounce the union. Recognizing the failure of the negotiations, Randolph began to organize a strike. He soon realized, however, that the brotherhood lacked the organizational and financial strength to challenge the company's power effectively.

The onset of the Great Depression marked a period of decline for the union, but with the passage of the Emergency Railroad Transportation Act in 1933, its fortunes began to change. The act guaranteed railroad laborers the right to organize, to bargain collectively, and to select representatives independent of company approval. After some dispute as to whether the Pullman Company was an independent "hotel service" not covered by the act, collective bargaining negotiations began in earnest in June of 1935. On August 25, 1937, the union achieved the victory it had long sought: Pullman reluctantly agreed to the concessions on wages and working conditions that the union demanded. Ironically, this success coincided with a gradual decline in long-distance passenger rail travel. By the 1960's, few railroads had the need for sleeping cars or their porters; by the 1970's, the union was practically defunct. By virtue of establishing the first success for African Americans within the American labor movement, however, the Brotherhood of Sleeping Car Porters paved the way for future advancements of blacks within white-dominated labor unions and established cooperative relationships that helped support the CIVIL RIGHTS MOVEMENT of the 1960's.

SUGGESTED READINGS. Sources of general historical interest include Julius Adams' *The Challenge: A Study in Negro Leadership* (1949) and Jervis Anderson's *A. Philip Randolph: A Biographical Portrait* (1972). Sally Hanley's biography, *A. Philip Randolph* (1989), provides a succinct overview of the Brotherhood of Sleeping Car Porters, and Paul Pfeffer's *A. Philip Randolph, Pioneer of the Civil Rights Movement* (1990) places Randolph's union work within the scope of his civil rights activism. For thorough detail, see William H. Harris' *Keeping the Faith: A. Philip Randolph, Milton P. Webster, and the Brotherhood of Sleeping Car Porters, 1925-1937* (1977). Oral histories of the porters' experiences may be found in Jack Santino's *Miles of Smiles, Years of Struggle: Stories of Black Pullman Porters* (1989).—*Richard Keenan*

Brown, H. Rap [Hubert Geroid] (Jamil Abdullah al-Amin; b. Oct. 4, 1943, Baton Rouge, La.): African American activist. While a student at Southern University (1960-1964), Brown worked in the antisegregation movement. By 1964 he was director of the Nonviolent Action Group (NAG), and in 1967 he became the national director of the STUDENT NONVIOLENT COORDINATING COMMITTEE (SNCC). In the late 1960's, he was an officer in the radical BLACK PANTHER PARTY. His advocacy of militant "black power" alienated white liberals and moderate blacks. While serving time for robbery in New York's Attica prison in the 1970's, Brown converted to Islam and changed his name. Later he opened a grocery story in Atlanta.

Brown, Helen Gurley (b. Feb. 18, 1922, Green Forest, Ark.): Magazine editor and creator of the "Cosmo girl"

Cosmopolitan *editor Helen Gurley Brown, in 1982.* (AP/ Wide World Photos)

image. Brown is best known as the editor of COSMOPOLITAN (beginning in 1965), and she was responsible for placing the magazine in the top five best-selling magazines in the United States. She has published numerous books, including the international best-seller *Sex and the Single Girl* (1962). Her other books include *Sex and the Office* (1964), *Outrageous Opinions* (1966), and *Sex and the New Single Girl* (1970). Brown is herself an example of women's independence in the working world.

Brown Berets: Militant Mexican American organization founded in Los Angeles in 1967 by David Sanchez, Carlos Montez, and Ralph Ramirez. The group's members were mostly young. It was one of the few Mexican American organizations that advocated the use of force to defend the Chicano community. The group's philosophy, rhetoric, and use of military-style uniforms instilled fear and suspicion in Anglo Americans. The Brown Berets received widespread negative publicity for demonstrations and protests centering on education in 1968 and for seizing Santa Catalina Island and renaming it "Aztlán Libre" in 1972. Later that year, cofounder David Sanchez announced the group's disbanding.

Brown Power movement: Organized effort to bring about a change in society that would benefit Chicanos and Latinos. The Brown Power movement began in the 1960's in California and other parts of the Southwest. Mexican Americans were encouraged by the national attention that the BLACK POWER and Red Power (INDIAN RIGHTS) movements were receiving. The Brown Power movement encompassed the CHICANO MOVEMENT, as well as demonstrations and the formation of new ethnic organizations that helped to unite and energize Mexican Americans and other Latinos. A central goal of the movement was to gain control of the economic, political, and social institutions in Latino communities.

Brown v. Board of Education (1954): Culmination of a series of court cases backed by the NATIONAL ASSOCIATION FOR THE ADVANCEMENT OF COLORED PEOPLE (NAACP) that invalidated state-enforced SEGREGATION by race in public education. The U.S. Supreme Court ruled on May 17, 1954, that separate education facilities for blacks and whites "are inherently unequal." The most famous case in the history of the CIVIL RIGHTS MOVEMENT, this landmark decision overturned the long-standing "separate but equal" precedent established by the 1896 *PLESSY V. FERGUSON* case, which had constitutionally sanctioned segregation-based discrimination for more than half a century.

When Oliver Brown's daughter, Linda, was denied admission to her elementary school because she was African American, Brown sued the Topeka, Kansas, Board of Education. En route to the Supreme Court, *Brown v. Board of Education* brought together five related cases from South Carolina, Delaware, Virginia, Kansas, and the District of Columbia. Led by NAACP lawyer and future Associate Court Justice Thurgood MARSHALL, the arguments heard by the Court challenged racial segregation as an unconstitutional violation of the equal protection clause guaranteed by the FOURTEENTH AMENDMENT. In making its ruling, the Court focused heavily on the intentionality of the framers and ratifiers of the amendment.

The Court voted unanimously in favor of overruling *PLESSY V. FERGUSON,* and Chief Justice Earl Warren delivered the Court's brief opinion: "We conclude that in the field of public education the doctrine of 'separate but equal' has no place. Separate education facilities are inherently unequal." The justices noted that equal protection under the law was impossible to maintain under segregation as long as it "generates a feeling of inferiority" in black schoolchildren that they carry with them into adulthood.

The Supreme Court's work was not over with this ruling. It still faced the difficult task of determining how to implement a decision that put an end to one of the most well-established social customs of the South. In the spring of 1955, the Court met to decide how to enforce compliance. Rather than risking the possibility of violent reprisal by ordering all segregation ended at once, the Court decided to empower district courts to work with local authorities to devise individual plans for DESEGREGATION. This moderate approach recognized the practical difficulties of upending the custom. The pace with which segregation was to be ended was the responsibility of individual school districts as long as it proceeded, in the words of the Court, "with all deliberate speed."

Brown v. Board of Education had immediate effects on the United States' segregated school systems. It also set a constitutional precedent that led to later cases ending legal segregation in other kinds of public facilities such as beaches in Maryland, recreation facilities in Memphis, and golf courses in Atlanta.

SUGGESTED READINGS. For further information, consult Richard Kluger's *Simple Justice: The History of Brown v. Board of Education and Black America's Struggle for Equality* (1975), and *Predjudice and Pride: The Brown Decision After Twenty-five Years* (1979) by Stephen Kemp Bailey.

Brownsville incident (August 13, 1906): One of many RACE RIOTS of the early twentieth century provoked by white racism. LYNCHINGS and vicious riots seem to have reached epidemic proportions around the turn of the century. For example, in 1898 in Wilmington, North Carolina, eight African Americans were killed; in 1904 at Statesboro, Georgia, local white residents virtually went to war against the town's black community.

Several detachments of African American soldiers were stationed at Fort Brown in Brownsville, Texas, near the Mexican border. Race relations in Brownsville had been strained for some time because many of the local whites objected to the presence of the soldiers in the town and often heaped insults and abuse on them. On a hot day in August, three companies of the African American Twenty-Fifth Regiment decided they had had enough racial slurs. They fought with a group of whites and ultimately shot up the town, killing one man, wounding others, and injuring the local chief of police. Although many local whites wanted to retaliate, the commander at Fort Brown stood firmly for order and kept the soldiers in their barracks while an inspector investigated the affair.

After studying the inspector's report, President Theodore Roosevelt dismissed the African American troops who had participated in the riot, giving all of them dishonorable discharges. African Americans across the nation were outraged when they learned of Roosevelt's action. Many believed that "their" boys had not been treated fairly; indeed, some evidence disclosed wrongdoing on the part of whites. Blacks believed that Roosevelt's handling of the affair showed that their president had little interest in or sympathy for their community. Further, many Anglos across the country protested what Senator Ben Tillman derisively called an "executive lynching."

John Milholland of the Constitution League began an unrelenting campaign on behalf of the soldiers. When Congress convened in December of 1906, Ohio Senator Joseph B. Foraker protested the president's action and launched a general investigation of the incident. Despite his strong position, Foraker—after months of study—lost his battle; a majority of the Senate upheld Roosevelt's actions. Still, Foraker wrote a minority report that repudiated the findings of the majority, and he refused to give up his cause. In 1909 he forced through Congress an act that established a court of inquiry which eventually returned some of the Brownsville troops to active duty.

Further investigations eventually cleared all the soldiers' names because evidence was finally produced showing that local whites had started the fray. Nevertheless, it was not until 1972 that Congress formally rescinded the dishonorable discharges and restored the black members—most already deceased—of the regiment to good standing in the army.

SUGGESTED READINGS. See Ann J. Lane's *The Brownsville Affair: National Crisis and Black Reaction* (1971) and John D. Weaver's *The Brownsville Raid* (1970). A brief summary of the incident may be found in John Hope Franklin and Alfred A. Moss, Jr.'s *From Slavery to Freedom* (1988). For a study of President Roosevelt's view of the African American community, see Thomas G. Dyer's *Theodore Roosevelt and the Idea of Race* (1980).

Bryn Mawr College (Bryn Mawr, Pa.): Independent liberal arts college for women. Bryn Mawr was founded in 1885 by Joseph Taylor, a QUAKER physician, and was at first associated with the Society of Friends. Since 1893, it has been nonsectarian. It is one of the Seven Sisters, a group first organized in 1915 consisting of seven COLLEGES that are considered pioneers in higher education for women. The college sponsored a Summer School for Women Workers in Industry from 1921 to 1938 and has invited leaders from a variety of fields to participate in lectures and seminars on campus. Admissions are highly selective and enrollment is limited in order to ensure superior academic standards. Graduate studies are also open to men.

Buddhists: Followers of the religion taught by the Buddha, or "enlightened one," who lived in India between 600 and 500 B.C.E. The most basic teachings of Buddhism are the Four Noble Truths. These state that suffering is the chief characteristic of existence; that this suffering is a result of desire; that suffering can be ended by ending this attachment to life; and that the attachment to life can be ended by doing good deeds and by meditating, so that the believer may reach Nirvana (the state of complete peace and selflessness that accompanies enlighten-

Buddhist monks, such as these, can now be found throughout North America. (Hazel Hankin)

ment). Buddhists generally believe in reincarnation, the rebirth of every individual into a series of lives. Reaching Nirvana is said to free the enlightened person from this continual chain of rebirth.

There are two main groups of Buddhists. Mahayana Buddhism, known as the "Northern School," is the major type of Buddhism in China, Japan, Tibet, Korea, and Vietnam. Theravada Buddhism, known as the "Southern School," is found throughout South and Southeast Asia. Followers of the Theravada school emphasize the necessity of becoming a monk and reaching Nirvana through one's own efforts. Mahayanists believe that lay people, as well as monks, can achieve Nirvana and that there are enlightened beings, *bodhisattvas*, who choose not to pass over into Nirvana in order to help others achieve liberation.

Although Buddhist thinking influenced many nineteenth century American writers and philosophers, including Walt Whitman, Ralph Waldo Emerson, and Henry David Thoreau, Buddhism did not become widespread among non-Asian Americans until the 1960's. The first Buddhists in the United States were the Chinese who came to California, drawn by the GOLD RUSH of 1849 and by railroad work in the 1860's. As the Chinese American population grew, Buddhists founded temples in the new country, many dedicated to the popular Chinese bodhisattva of compassion, Kuan Yin.

The Chinese, and the Japanese who arrived after them, usually did not try to spread their religion among European Americans. In the years before World War II, however, American intellectuals became increasingly interested in Buddhism, particularly in Zen, a form of Buddhism that places special emphasis on the practice of meditation. After the war, this interest became especially intense among "Beat" writers such as Gary Snyder, Allen Ginsberg, and Jack Kerouac. With the rise of the American counterculture, the Buddhism of artists and intellectuals began to appeal to larger numbers of non-Asian Americans, and temples and meditation centers were founded throughout the country.

The Vietnam War played an important part in spreading Buddhism in the United States. The nonviolence of Buddhism attracted many people opposed to the war, and the country's involvement with Southeast Asia brought it into close contact with Buddhist countries. Following the war, almost a million Southeast Asian refugees, many of them practicing Buddhists and prominent Buddhist leaders, arrived in the United States. Their temples, along with earlier ones set up by Chinese and Japanese Americans, have become important centers of community and cultural life as well as religion. For example, at the Wat Thai Temple near Los Angeles, resident monks in saffron robes chant and the faithful bring offerings or meditate individually, while outside, young people study Thai classical dance and food vendors sell an array of Thai specialties.

SUGGESTED READINGS. Rick Fields's *How the Swans Came to the Lake: A Narrative History of Buddhism in America* (1981) is a highly readable account of American Buddhism. Emma McCloy Layman's *Buddhism in America* (1976) offers a psychologist's approach to the subject. Bhikshu Sangharakshita's *A Survey of Buddhism* (6th ed., 1987) provides the general reader with an overview of the Buddhist religion. Dwight Goddard's *A Buddhist Bible* (rev. ed., 1932) remains the essential collection of classic Buddhist scriptures for Western readers.

Buffalo and American Indians. *See* **Bison and American Indians**

Buffalo soldiers: Name given to African American army regulars by American Indians, who thought that their hair looked like buffalo fur. Responsible for protecting frontier settlements in the western territories, these men served as volunteers in the all-black Ninth and Tenth Cavalry Regiments and Thirty-eighth, Thirty-ninth, Fortieth, and Forty-first Infantry Regiments established by Congress after the Civil War. Although the troops were all African Americans, their officers were white. The buffalo soldiers participated in campaigns against the APACHES, SIOUX, Kiowas, CHEYENNES, and other Indian tribes. Members of the Ninth and Tenth Cavalry later served in the SPANISH-AMERICAN WAR. Although their distinguished service has not received the attention it deserves, the buffalo soldiers were commemorated in an engraving by the noted western artist Frederic Remington, and fourteen soldiers were awarded the Medal of Honor.

Bujones, Fernando (b. Mar. 9, 1955, Miami, Fla.): Cuban American ballet dancer. Bujones entered the New York School of American Ballet at age twelve, graduating in 1972. He became a soloist with the American Ballet Theater in 1973 and was a principal dancer from 1974 to 1985. Bujones has been a guest artist with ballet and opera companies all over the world, including La

Scala Milano, the Royal Swedish Ballet, and the Paris Opera. His choreographies include "Grand Pas Romantique" (1984) and "Raymondal" (1988). He received a Dance Magazine Award in 1982 and a New York Times Artistic Award in 1985, and was named a permanent international guest with the Boston Ballet in 1987. The governor of Massachusetts proclaimed May 4, 1990, "Bujones Day."

Bulgarian Americans: Present-day Bulgaria lies south of Romania and north of Greece. Its territory is small compared to what it was in the eighth century, when it first became an independent state and covered much of the Balkans.

The Turkish Ottoman Empire conquered Bulgaria in the late 1300's and ruled there for five hundred years. With the help of the Russians, the Bulgarians threw off Ottoman rule in 1878. In 1908, Bulgaria became a kingdom and in 1946, it became a republic under the domination of the Soviet Union. In 1989, Bulgaria loosened its Soviet ties and soon thereafter established democratic rule.

Bulgarians, both from "the kingdom" proper and from its lost territory of Macedonia, began coming to North America at the turn of the twentieth century. They were mainly peasants who intended to earn enough money to return home and set up a business or a farm. Most early Bulgarian immigrants headed for the Midwest, especially Michigan, where they worked in factories, or Pennsylvania, where they worked in the mines. Many were unhappy with their new life and returned to Bulgaria within a few years;

BULGARIA

others arranged for mail-order brides to be sent from their homeland.

U.S. immigration restrictions curtailed their numbers from 1924 to 1965. Still, during this time, many Bulgarian workers entered the country illegally, and some women and children came between the world wars to join their relatives. After 1946, Bulgarian immigrants tended to be educated people opposed to the Communist domination of their homeland. Many of them established right-wing political groups.

Most Bulgarian Americans belong to EASTERN ORTHODOX churches, which are the center of community activities and the maintenance of heritage, as in FOLK DANCE troupes and traditional FOODS AND COOKING. The worldwide success in the late 1980's of the Bulgarian State Radio and Television Female Vocal Choir through concerts and recordings bolstered Bulgarian American pride in their native culture.

Bulosan, Carlos (Nov. 24, 1913 or 1914, Binalonan, Luzon, Philippines—Sept. 11, 1956, Seattle, Wash.): Filipino American writer. Bulosan came to the United States at the age of sixteen. He arrived in Seattle and spent the Great Depression working various menial and agricultural jobs from Alaska to southern California and

Best-selling author Bulosan. (AP/Wide World Photos)

Montana. He witnessed the prejudice and abuse heaped on Filipino MIGRANT WORKERS and resolved to address their plight through writing. Bulosan began writing poetry, stories, and articles in the late 1930's. Early works such as *Letter from America* (1942), *Chorus for America* (1942), and *The Voice from Bataan* (1943) established his Whitmanesque vision of a pluralistic society, and his volume of autobiographical social protest, *America Is in the Heart: A Personal History*, became a national best-seller in 1946.

Bunche, Ralph Johnson (Aug. 7, 1904, Detroit, Mich.—Dec. 9, 1971, New York, N.Y.): African American scholar, government official, and diplomat. Bunche's career in government service and world diplomacy began in academia. He earned degrees from the University of California, Los Angeles, and Harvard University. A distinguished social scientist specializing in race issues, he taught at Howard University. He was an adviser at the San Francisco conference that set up the United Nations (UN) and was the first African American to head a division in the Department of State (1945). He earned the Nobel Peace Prize in 1950 and was a longtime U.N. under secretary general for special political affairs (1958-1971).

Bureau of Colored Troops: Established by the War Department in May, 1863, to recruit and organize African American soldiers. The bureau was also expected to train black soldiers, provide economic aid, and to establish schools to educate liberated freedmen. Although the army provided them with employment, members of black regiments were paid at a lower rate because the army thought of them as laborers, not soldiers. After pressure from various groups, Congress passed the Army Appropriation Act of 1864, giving equal pay to men who took the so-called "Quaker Oath" that they had been free on April 19, 1861. In March, 1865, Congress passed the Enrollment Act, mandating that soldiers recruited before January 1, 1864, receive full pay from the date of their original enlistment. Despite these provisions, most black soldiers had to wait until the CIVIL WAR was over before they received the full pay that was owed to them.

Bureau of Indian Affairs (BIA): Federal government's chief agency in the development and administration of American Indian policy. The bureau operates under the direction of the Secretary of the Interior. For most of its history, the BIA has performed two primary functions. First, it has attempted to help Indians achieve self-sufficiency and live in mainstream American society. Second, it exercises trust responsibility for administering Indian land and resources as long as such administration is deemed necessary. Since the BIA's inception, both its goals and its actions have stirred controversy. Well into the twentieth century, for example, its policies were determined by white bureaucrats, often with little or no concern for what American Indians themselves truly wanted or needed. Its policy (pursued until the 1930's) of trying to force Indians to assimilate into the dominant American culture created severe disruptions in Indian life and culture.

Though the BIA was formally established in 1824, an Indian office existed in some form since the early days of the republic. Its roots lay in the superintendency system created by the Continental Congress on the eve of the American Revolution. Based on the British system that had centralized administration of Indian affairs after 1755, the superintendency system was integrated into the national government under the

A 1972 sit-in protest on the steps of the BIA. (Library of Congress)

Articles of Confederation. These gave the new government "sole and exclusive right and power of . . . regulating trade and managing all affairs with Indians." An ordinance adopted in 1786 placed the Indian office in the office of the Secretary of War and created a northern and southern superintendency. These superintendents had broad powers, especially under the various trade and intercourse laws enacted in the 1790's—laws intended to "civilize" Indians through the extension of education and agricultural training.

In 1806 Congress established the office of Superintendent of the Indian Trade. This became the focal point of Indian affairs until March of 1824, when Secretary of War John Calhoun created what he called the Bureau of Indian Affairs. He appointed Thomas L. McKenney as its first head. Statutory authority for an office of Indian affairs within the War Department was obtained in 1832, and a commissioner with power to direct and manage all Indian affairs was appointed. In 1849 the bureau was transferred to the Interior Department, where it remains today.

Throughout the nineteenth century, the bureau reflected the paternalism of the federal government's plan of INDIAN ASSIMILATION. Deeply involved in every facet of Indian administration, the bureau presided over a bevy of programs that ranged from education to allotments to suppression of the liquor trade. The goal was to produce an assimilated Indian citizenry that was as indistinguishable as possible from its white model, and thus to make the bureau an unnecessary agency. The BIA simply ignored the fact that many American Indians had no particular desire to be assimilated and that therefore such an approach was doomed to failure. In addition to Indian resistance, inefficiency and mismanagement plagued the bureau.

With the appointment of John Collier as commissioner in 1933, the bureau assumed a new direction. Intending to make the BIA an advisory rather than a supervisory agency, Collier's Indian New Deal of 1934 rejected forced assimilation and gave tribes greater autonomy and input into their administration. The direction of many programs was shared not only with the tribes but with other government bureaus and agencies as well. Since 1950, for example, the BIA has shared increasingly large portions of the budget with the Departments of Housing and Urban Development, Health and Human Services, Education, Labor, and the Treasury. Preferential hiring has produced a bureau dominated by Indians, and the BIA is now oriented toward transferring responsibilities to Indians themselves.

SUGGESTED READINGS. Laurence Schmeckebier's *The Office of Indian Affairs* (1927) remains a useful introduction to the history of the bureau through the early 1920's. Theodore Taylor's more recent *The Bureau of Indian Affairs* (1984) is a sound summary. Robert M. Krasnicka and Herman Viola's *The Commissioners of Indian Affairs: 1824-1977* (1979) is a good account of the men who directed the bureau, and Viola's *Thomas L. McKenney: Architect of America's Early Indian Policy, 1816-1830* (1974) is a useful discussion of the early years of the Indian office. Francis Paul Prucha's *The Great Father* (2 vols., 1984) is the best guide to the evolution of bureau policy. Prucha's *American Indian Policy in The Formative Years: The Indian Trade and Intercourse Acts, 1790-1834* (1962) is a brilliant introduction to the early republic's assessment of the Indian question.

Bureau of the Census. *See* **Census, Bureau of the**

Burlingame Treaty: Treaty passed in 1868 between China and the United States which stated that a citizen of either nation had the right to emigrate to the other. This treaty stood in the path of anti-Chinese activists, particularly in California, who wanted to pass laws prohibiting Chinese people from coming to the United States. For many years, attempts to pass exclusionary laws were blocked by higher court rulings that declared that the proposed laws violated this treaty. In 1889, the U.S. Supreme Court ruled unanimously that, on the contrary, the government could grant—or deny—the right to immigrate at any time.

Business and corporate enterprise: Since the 1890's, businesses and corporations have become the heart of the private American economy, providing the nation with a vital institutional network. Their response to MULTICULTURALISM, therefore, is considered critically important to American society.

Historical Overview. In the eighteenth and nineteenth centuries, agriculture and its dependent enterprises dominated economic life with the ideals of a white, agrarian society and the family farm in ascendance. A financial-industrial transformation distinguished economic development between 1865 and the 1950's, succeeded by the post-industrial economy of the late twentieth century. Some challenges of the postindustrial phase were inherited from an earlier phase, particularly issues of inclusion of women, racial minorities, and new immigrants.

During the long agrarian phase, the social values of WHITE ANGLO-SAXON PROTESTANT (WASP) males gave direction to society-at-large and to governments. The latter were small in size and restricted in their authority. Although governments had expanded by 1914, they remained WASP male domains, like the business world. The NEW DEAL and the aftermath of World War II, however, altered government's peacetime functions and responsibilities. The federal government in particular rapidly became the nation's major vehicle of social reform. Simultaneously, it became a principal source of the country's investment capital, its biggest lender and spender, and its hungriest consumer, with budgets rising from tens of billions of dollars into the trillions. Accordingly, its power to regulate or pressure businesses determined its relationships with the nation's 16 million enterprises. By 1986, these included 12.4 million nonfarm proprietorships and 3.4 million corporations.

The nature and scope of government-business relationships changed, too. By 1975, one-fourth of the total American work force was publicly employed. Like state and local governments, the federal government—with mixed degrees of success—attempted to reconcile the conflicting values and opinions of its own employees with the demands of a factious multicultural society. The forces of change since the 1960's that have affected government and, in turn, business, include legal reinterpretations of civil rights; radical views of women's roles; assertions of Chicano and Asian American identities and issues; reevaluations of American Indian history and modern realities; and adjustments to fresh waves of East and Southeast Asian, Latino, and other new immigration.

While businesses occasionally took the initiative in adjusting to the imperatives of these changes, most took a reactive stance instead. They fell under complaints of DISCRIMINATION and were soon constrained by governmental persuasion and legal mandates to alter their practices. Meanwhile, the country had also been drawn into the pressures of an interdependent global economy, as seen in the oil crisis of the mid-1970's. The U.S. economy became more dependent on foreign resources, international trade, and the cosmopolitan influences of world competition.

Business and Women. Although small businesses—3.2 million of which were corporations in 1986—provide the most employment and generate most of the jobs in the economy, about five hundred very large corporations occupy what might be called its commanding heights. About one hundred of these deal with assets, sales, earnings, losses, and profits in billions of dollars. Because they are intimately involved with governments by virtue of holding government contracts and more open to scrutiny by the public and by the media, these corporations often have been taken as bellwethers in their responses to societal change.

Corporate performance in regard to women's employment, status, pay, promotion, and special needs can be compared to women's inherited place in the economy. Historically, more than 90 percent of American jobs were long segregated by gender, with non-paying jobs (housewives), low-paying, repetitive, or generally low-status jobs (launderers, garment workers, typists, maids, receptionists, nurses, and teachers among them) constituting "the female job ghetto." In 1900, fewer than 2 percent of all American women were classifiable as executives or managers; by 1950, the census figures recorded for women in businesses and corporations had risen to only 7 percent.

President Franklin D. Roosevelt's appointment of the first female cabinet officer, Frances PERKINS, in 1933, set a precedent that was not really pursued until thirty years later. By 1988, women filled 48.2 percent of low, to mid-level federal jobs, after which their numbers, higher than earlier, declined notably.

Corporations and many other businesses may have kept pace with, or exceeded, government, for in 1988, 39.3 percent of their executives, managers, and administrators, as estimated by census classifications, were women. In some fields, this figure was higher: 42 percent for financial managers, 49 percent for personnel and labor relations managers, and 44.5 percent for managerial "officials and administrators."

Literature on women managers, however, continued to record problems into the 1990's. Two authorities, Douglas Basil and Edna Traver, began their 1972 study by noting that women were the country's greatest untapped source of managerial, professional, and technical talent. Women executives and experts on women in management also detected tokenism in their promotions to managerial-executive posts. Others complained of a "GLASS CEILING" that excluded them from rising to high level executive-managerial responsibilities, and some decried the necessity of having to change their behavior and warp their personalities to accommodate successfully to male-dominated organizations.

Women executives are a small but growing part of the labor force. (Jean Higgins, Unicorn Stock Photo)

Women accounted for slightly less than one-half of the civilian labor force, or 56.6 million in a total work force of 121.7 million, in 1988. They also made up slightly more than one-half of the nation's population of 245.8 million. Significantly more of them held high status managerial-executive jobs in 1990 than they had in 1900, 1950, or 1980. Nevertheless, in spite of the nation's growing shortage of high level skills, its world renown for managerial prowess, and the fact that women far outnumbered men in many fields (TEACHERS, counselors, SOCIAL WORKERS, health care

enterprises. African Americans established flourishing businesses in the generation after the Civil War. Famous black entrepreneurs sprang from the ranks of the growing middle classes, even in the South.

In 1990, 30.3 million African Americans composed 12.3 percent of the nation's population, its largest minority group. Through much of the 1960's and 1970's, the value of federal Small Business Administration loans to minority businesses, most of them African American, exceeded the black proportion of the population. By 1988, these had dropped to 13 percent of

Women- and Minority-Owned Firms: 1987

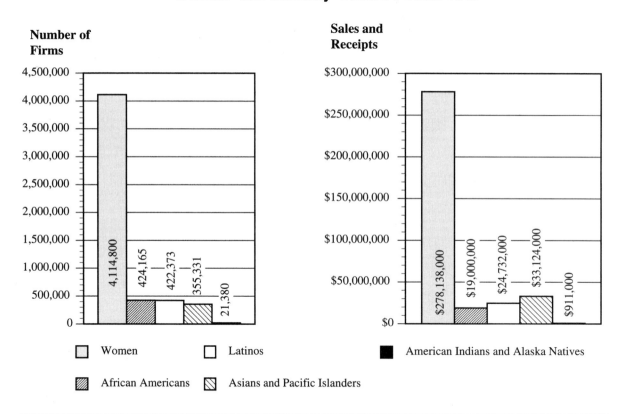

Source: Data are from *Statistical Abstract of the United States, 1992.* Tables 840 and 843. Washington, D.C.: U.S. Government Printing Office, 1992.

workers), women were underrepresented in high positions and were generally less well-paid than men. On the other hand, without pay equality, women occupied more white-collar jobs than men and fewer blue-collar jobs than they had in 1970 and 1980.

Business and Minorities. All American minority communities have lengthy histories of successful business endeavors, but they have generally been small

all such loans, the total value of which was 10 percent of all loans. Thus African American enterprises were gaining access to their fair share of public moneys.

In regard to managerial and executive positions in business, however, African Americans were underrepresented. This was true despite the stimuli of manpower programs, CIVIL RIGHTS LEGISLATION, and the operations of AFFIRMATIVE ACTION, as well as university and private business-government programs designed to train African American managers. This situation troubled many observers because the number of African American college graduates, including those with advanced degrees, doubled between 1970 and 1988. Other experts contended that better representation for blacks in top positions was only a matter of time. Meanwhile, in large corporations where African American managers were employed, many had the same complaints as did women managers about the GLASS CEILING, in this case traced to continuing institutional RACISM.

Underrepresentation in business and corporate seats of power likewise characterized the situations of Latinos and other minorities. Slightly more than 6 percent of managerial-executive posts were held by African Americans, and slightly under 4 percent by Latinos, although Latinos in 1990 were projected to become the nation's largest minority.

Nevertheless, minority-owned businesses and minority participation in the business world increased between the 1960's and 1990, revitalizing many American cities and reversing their decline. Some observers suggest that newer ethnic minorities often brought advantages with them since their ranks have been heavily composed of the highly motivated business and professional elites of their native countries. Middle-to upper-class immigrants from Cuba, South Korea, Taiwan, India, Hong Kong, and Vietnam, for example, have often fared well in developing small businesses as well as more ambitious corporate ventures.

Scholars and journalists have commented extensively on the restoration of the Southern California suburbs of Garden Grove and Westminster by Vietnamese Americans; on Monterey Park's emergence as the "Chinese Beverly Hills"; on the appearance of vigorous KOREATOWNS, "Little Saigons," and "LITTLE HAVANAS," along with the revivals of failed West Coast neighborhoods by Chicanos. The same phenomenon, spurred by hardworking new immigrants, occurred between 1970 and 1990 in cities such as Seattle, in New York's Flushing and Queens, in Brooklyn's Sunset Park, in Houston, and in Miami. Similarly, American Indians, many living in cities by 1990, have invested in a number of enterprises on Indian lands and have engaged in others, often unnoticed, among the general population.

SUGGESTED READINGS. Progress for women and minorities in business is confirmed by a growing literature and by increased public and media attention to their problems and opportunities in the business and corporate world. Two excellent overviews of women and minorities in business and society are Richard Polenberg's *One Nation Divisible: Class, Race, and Ethnicity in the United States Since 1938* (1980) and Reed M. Powell's *Race, Religion, and the Promotion of the American Executive* (1969).

Women in Management (1972), by Douglas C. Basil with Edna Traver, should be supplemented by Caroline Bird's The Two-Paycheck Marriage (1979), a broad survey of alternatives in women's lifestyles, employment, and business-professional careers, which notes business responses to women's problems. Juliet B. Schor's *The Overworked American: The Unexpected Decline of Leisure* (1992) and Susan Faludi's *Backlash: The Undeclared War Against American Women* (1991) both discuss the impact of affirmative action on the hiring of women. Edward Franklin Frazier's *Black Bourgeoisie* (1957, repr. 1965) is a classic account of the experiences of African Americans who succeeded in business and professional life despite racism. Shelley Green and Paul Pryde's *Black Entrepreneurship in America* (1990) reviews the economic successes of black entrepreneurs, while Floyd and Jacqueline Dickens have produced a lively, informative report on *The Black Manager* (1982).—*Clifton K. Yearley*

Business and employment discrimination. *See* **Discrimination—business and employment**